# The Songs of the Spheres: Lewis, Tolkien and the Overlapping Realms of their Imaginations

# The Songs of the Spheres: Lewis, Tolkien and the Overlapping Realms of their Imaginations

edited by Łukasz Neubauer and Guglielmo Spirito

2024

Cormarë Series No. 48

Series Editors:
Peter Buchs • Thomas Honegger • Andrew Moglestue • Johanna Schön • Doreen Triebel

Series Editors responsible for this volume: Thomas Honegger & Doreen Triebel

Library of Congress Cataloguing-in-Publication Data

Łukasz Neubauer and Guglielmo Spirito (eds.):
The Songs of the Spheres
Lewis, Tolkien and the Overlapping Realms of their Imaginations
ISBN 978-3-905703-48-1

Subject headings:
Tolkien, J.R.R. (John Ronald Reuel), 1892-1973
Lewis, C.S. (Clive Staples), 1898-1963
Fantasy
Interdisciplinary Perspectives
Middle-earth
Narnia
*The Lord of the Rings*
*The Hobbit*
*The Silmarillion*
*Narnia Chronicles*
*The Fall of Arthur*
*The Story of Kullervo*

Cormarë Series No. 48

First published 2024



Set in Adobe Garamond Pro and Shannon by Walking Tree Publishers

Cover picture by Łukasz Neubauer, cover design by Stefan Honegger

# Contents

Tolkien and Lewis. Tollers and Jack. Although the two men – scholars, colleagues, writers, and, above all, close friends – did not always enjoy the same level of affection for one another, over the years their names have become almost inseparable. So much so that it is hard today to consider one of them without, at least for a while, pondering upon the other. Ever since their earliest recorded encounter, on 11 May 1926, at a Merton College English Faculty meeting, for at least two decades, until their friendship gradually began to wane in the second half of the 1940s, Tolkien and Lewis were able to share their deep-seated fascination with medieval literature and thought, mythopoeic world-building and all kinds of faerie narratives, the 'Northernness' and the 'northern heroic spirit,' eucatastrophe and 'joy,' the development of languages and linguistic aesthetic, as well as, no less significantly, Christian theology and the application of faith in various aspects of life.

However, to say that their views upon these and other matters were even for the most part unanimous would be a sweeping exaggeration, not to say a complete fabrication. Whereas Tolkien would remain strongly devoted to the Catholic faith, Lewis, who was brought up as an Ulster Protestant, appears to have been unable to shake off some of his entrenched prejudices and, following his return to God (in the Anglican tradition) in the early 1930s, remained somewhat sceptical (to say the least) of such rudiments of Catholicism as the devotion to the Virgin Mary or the infallibility of the pope. Tolkien, on the other hand, frequently did not approve of Lewis's works and his quick rise to fame as a popular theologian, being chiefly of the opinion that the job of writing explicitly about God had better be left to those with sufficient expertise in religious studies. Also, when it comes to purely literary matters, Tollers and Jack sometimes differed to a notable degree, most famously perhaps with regard to their attitudes to the use of fantasy as an allegory, the narrative style which Tolkien claimed to dislike with great intensity (despite making good use of it in his academic papers and the short story *Leaf by Niggle*) and Lewis chose to employ as one of his foremost literary devices (even though he sometimes cleverly disguised it under the name of a more flexible 'supposal').

Notwithstanding all these differences, it ought to be stressed that, had it not been for their friendship, the stories of Middle-earth and Narnia would likely never have reached print. Although it is true that some of Tolkien's early narratives would perhaps have been preserved amongst his numerous papers, without the relentless encouragement from Lewis, the world would probably never have even heard of *The Lord of the Rings*, and it is not in the least certain whether its prequel, *The Hobbit*, would finally have taken the form it had at the time of its publication in 1937. Just as likely, it seems, is the scenario in which a vast majority of Lewis's fiction as well as his works in the apologetic genre never come to be written, its *sine qua non* being, of course, Jack's conversion, a long-term process in which no small part was played by his fellow Inkling.

All this (and more) may be said to lie behind our idea for the present volume, a rich tapestry of themes and motifs, or, perhaps, symphonies with their movements, repeatedly, sometimes even concurrently, explored by Tolkien and Lewis. Several of them deal with the two writers' commitment to the Christian faith, its values and ethics. Some touch upon such theoretically-grounded notions as modernity, justice, (sub-)creation, and time. Others look into the more mundane, though by no means less exciting and thought-provoking, aspects of everyday life, things like friendship or food and drink. All these numerous components are not, however, to paraphrase what Tolkien is believed to have once said of Lewis's *Narniad*, 'a jumble of unrelated matters.' Indeed, they are small pieces of a bigger picture, thematically overlapping 'Songs of the Spheres' (hence the title of this book), which, put together, make up, as in Johannes Kepler's sixteenth-century revision of the Pythagorean model of the universe, the kind of music which cannot quite be heard by the ear, but which is, first and foremost, perfectly 'audible' to the soul.

In the opening chapter, Justin Keena argues that no idea is more simultaneously Lewisian and Tolkienian than that of the 'true myth.' What Lewis found so compelling, following his famous late-night conversa-tion with Dyson and Tolkien, was at least one aspect of it, namely the notion that a story could be factual, historical, or otherwise real, and, at the same time, maintain its imaginative value as a story. This idea he was then able to apply to the story of Christ, which not only happens to be "a true myth," but is also "suggestive of meanings beyond [one's] grasp" (*CL I* 977), adapting some of Plato's (as well as Tolkien's) intuitions: the metaphysics of resemblance or likeness, solar imagery, levels of reality or truth, and sub-creation.

In the next chapter, Piotr Anicet Gruszczyński contends that both Tolkien and Lewis present an outlook which is often at odds with modernity and postmodernity, in fact, seeing modern thinking as a growing menace to mankind. In the traditional cultures of Antiquity and the Middle Ages, man often saw the need for some kind of unifying principle, the λόγος, thanks to which the world could be perceived and understood in a more complete manner. This worldview was later replaced by the modern outlook, somewhat more mechanistic, less holistic, more 'metallic' and less 'human.' To some extent, the two writers seem to have wished to go back in time in order to catch a glimpse of that fading past, the time when everything, both in heaven and on earth, seemed to be much closer to man. Their wish was to revive the old tales and write new ones, in this way endeavouring to make the contemporary man see that everything in this changeable world has a meaning in the λόγος.

Taking into consideration Tolkien's and Lewis's shared interest in the Apostle of the Gentiles, Giovanni Carmine Costabile, seeks, in the third chapter, to explore the possibility of reading the former writer's story of 'Finwë and Míriel' in the spirit of Saint Paul and whether it could be reconciled with the more overtly Pauline notion of justice in *The Lion, the Witch and the Wardrobe*, or what Lewis there refers to as "deep magic from the dawn of time" (42). However, as remarked by Tolkien's Manwë, one must not "forget that in Arda Marred *Justice* is not *Healing*" (*MR* 239, emphasis original), meaning that the actual remedy could only be found in the Divine Grace and Mercy.

The next chapter sees Chiara Bertoglio demonstrate that at the root of Lewis's and of Tolkien's fictional worlds there are two creation myths, vividly narrated, respectively, in *The Magician's Nephew* and in the *Ainulindalë*. Each of the two writers describes the act of creation in musical terms, gradually 'evolving' from what seems to be a primarily aural dimension (symbolised by the divine music) into a more concrete world. The whole process (or, rather, processes) can therefore be studied and analysed in connection with such indispensable components of a musical performance as notation and interpretation, denoting that the Creation and sub-creation are, to a certain extent, dynamically interwoven processes. So much so that Saint Bonaventure, following in the footsteps of Saint Augustine, likened the universe to a "most beautiful canticle", which develops "according to the best consonances" (*Commentaria* book I, distinction 44, article 1, question 3) in a harmonic sequence of parts.

In his chapter, Łukasz Neubauer holds the view that the cosmogonic dramas which unfold in Tolkien's Arda and Lewis's Narnia easily rank amongst the most ingenious mythopoeic narratives of the twentieth century. A vital component in their rich cosmogonic mosaics is the Christian doctrine of *creatio ex nihilo*, the notion that, by the Lord's command, the world came into being out of nothing. Its fundamental tenets may not always be so easily detectible, though. From Genesis Tolkien must have got the idea of the Timeless Void and Lewis derived his vision of the unnamed primeval darkness. Some light upon this matter could also, it seems, be shed by Plato's theory of 'forms,' obviously well-known to both writers, and Tolkien's own concept of sub-creation. Having, like all of us, but a faint notion of what the elusive pre-creative *nihil* could actually entail, Tolkien and Lewis turned to the boundless deposits of their unrestrained imagination, the effect of which is some of the most intriguing passages in the whole of their fiction.

Joanna Łękawska seeks to examine, in the following chapter, the interpenetration of the past, present and future in *The Chronicles of Narnia* and *The Lord of the Rings* as an interesting backdrop for the development of the plot in each of these works. Of the two writers, Lewis makes this interpenetration more explicit, with the shifts of setting from the primary world of late-nineteenth- and early-twentieth-century England to the secondary world of Narnia. The temporal interpenetration in Tolkien's work is, perhaps, just as considerable, but in a less explicit way, though there is a historical depth in it that is significant to the plot at every stage. No less significantly, in both works there is also a tangible, though hidden, extratemporal Providence behind the events that unfold.

Chapter Seven sees Gabriel Schenk explore the widely held view that Middle-earth is a far more coherent and consistent world than Narnia; a world which

Tolkien is said to have disparagingly characterised as "a jumble of unrelated mythologies" (Sayer 1988: 189). He argues that, although this view has some factual foundations, the contrast is not as stark as it is often thought to be. If done well, the art of turning imagination into a sub-created work should result in what Tolkien calls "the inner consistency of reality" (*TOFS* 59ff.). Lewis, like Tolkien, uses temporally and culturally misplaced items for a purpose, albeit, in a slightly different fashion creating the sense of familiarity or otherness. In effect, neither Narnia nor Middle-earth turns out to be a perfectly cohesive and internally consistent world.

The core of Hamish Williams's argument in the following chapter rests upon the assumption that, in *Prince Caspian*, Lewis chose to depict the Dionysiac forces of nature in the manner which subtly exposes their Christian (or 'Aslanine') foundations. On the other hand, the Apolline attempts of the Telmarines to establish some kind of order based on human will alone, along with their scornful attitudes towards the divine law and aesthetic beauty, constitute factors which ultimately lead to their destruction. When it comes to Tolkien, his viewpoint concerning the Dionysiac-Apolline dichotomy seems best reflected in the enigmatic character of Tom Bombadil, a kind of 'nature spirit,' who resists the Dionysiac chaos of the Old Forest taking on a shepherding, Orphic form of ordering through singing. In this, however, he does not try to assert the Apolline will to exert his power over others (the Nietzschean will of Sauron's One Ring has no effect upon Tom). Finally, one should also be able to see that, through Tolkien's and Lewis's eucatastrophic moments of ultimate joy, Dionysiac and Apolline illusions could be dispelled.

In the ninth chapter Andrzej Wicher analyses what might be referred to as the ontological status of Tolkien's non-human species, particularly when it comes to liminality. It is worth noting that Lewis provides us with a few medieval conceptions of fairies, some of whom appear to have a liminal character, especially when they are thought of as "a third rational species distinct from angels and men" (*DI* 134), or as "demoted" (135) angels. It could therefore be reasoned that Tolkien's Elves are 'liminal,' primarily because their mode of existence represents an intermediate stage between mortality and immortality. The same, perhaps, could be said of his Ents, inhabiting the conceptual space between human beings and trees. Characteristically enough, Tolkien defines the Faërie in a liminal fashion, as neither this nor that, at the same time making a good use of the late medieval ballad of *Thomas the Rhymer*.

Franz Georg Àrpàd Klug argues, in the penultimate chapter, that the foremost villains in the works of Tolkien and Lewis, such as, most notably, Melkor/ Morgoth and the White Witch Jadis, may be viewed as truly satanic figures, in varying degrees inspired by the Christian impressions of the devil. In doing so, he highlights some of the differences and similarities between their respective archvillains, demonstrating that at least some of the views that Tolkien and Lewis had on evil were for the most part analogous. Clearly modelled upon the viewpoints of Saint Augustine and Boethius, evil is to them nothing more than a parasite, a corruption of spiritual and natural good. Likewise, Lewis and Tolkien share the belief that evil represents a rejection of God and the joy and beauty that originate in Him.

Last but not least, with a sense of taste which only a real master chef could accomplish, Kris Swank, explains that meals in Narnia and Middle-earth are truly abundant in local, simple, natural fare. Both Tolkien and Lewis are known to have specified their preferences for eating in just such a fashion – "good plain food" (*Letters* 288, #213), as Tolkien calls it. Several authors of 'The Golden Age' of British children's literature (including the two fellow Inklings) claim to have experienced a poignant feeling of the loss of childhood innocence, having hitherto spent some of it in idyllic rural retreats. Their use of nostalgically simple and natural food fulfils a similar longing, not necessarily for their actual childhoods, but for an imagined time and space, an Edenic Britain as it may have been.

The authors and editors have done their part. Now it is up to the reader to venture into Narnia and Middle-earth, the two realms of Tolkien's and Lewis's vivid imaginations, and measure up themselves with the marvels of their sub-creative works. How the adventure will unfold, we are not given to know. One thing may be taken for granted, though. As a reader, you are invited on a quest, sometimes perilous and sometimes less so, in the company of Tollers and Jack. And *this* is certainly an encouraging thought.

*Łukasz Neubauer and Guglielmo Spirito, Koszalin and Assisi, July 2023*

## Bibliography

BONAVENTURE of Bagnoregio. 1934. 'Commentaria in IV libros Sententiarum.' *S. Bonaventurae Opera theologica selecta* Vol. 1. Quaracchi: Collegio San Bonaventura.

LEWIS, Clive Staples. 2004. *The Collected Letters of C.S. Lewis. Vol. I. Family Letters 1905- 1931.* Ed. Walter Hooper. London: Harper San Francisco.

2012. *The Discarded Image. An Introduction to Medieval and Renaissance Literature.* Cambridge: Cambridge University Press.

2014. *The Lion, the Witch and the Wardrobe.* London: HarperCollins.

TOLKIEN, John Ronald Reuel. 1981. *The Letters of J.R.R. Tolkien.* Ed. Humphrey Carpenter with the assistance of Christopher Tolkien. London, Boston and Sydney: George Allen and Unwin.

1995. *Morgoth's Ring. The History of Middle-earth 10.* Ed. Christopher Tolkien. London: HarperCollins.

2008. *Tolkien On Fairy-stories.* Expanded Edition with Commentary and Notes. Eds. Verlyn Flieger and Douglas A. Anderson. London: HarperCollins.

Justin Keena



# C.S. Lewis and J.R.R. Tolkien: Friendship, True Myth, and Platonism[1]

**Abstract**

Of the two major senses of 'true myth' used by C.S. Lewis and J.R.R. Tolkien, the first was a foundational principle in their respective approaches to fantasy writing, while the second was based on Classical Platonic metaphysics. The first part of this chapter describes and analyzes the three most significant appearances of true myth in their friendship. The second part distinguishes its two major senses, showing that the first meaning of true myth was a foundational principle in their respective approaches to fantasy writing. The third section explains the second meaning and identifies its metaphysical basis as Classical Platonism. The final section establishes four specific ways in which Lewis and Tolkien's idea of true myth in its second sense depends upon Platonic metaphysics.

## True Myth in Lewis and Tolkien's Friendship

No idea is more simultaneously Lewisian and Tolkienian than that of 'true myth.' It appears at the center of the most pivotal moment in their friendship, and indeed in Lewis's entire life, on the night of September 19, 1931. Describing his conversation that night with Tolkien and Hugo Dyson in a letter to Arthur Greeves on September 22, 1931, Lewis wrote: "I have just passed on from believing in God to definitely believing in Christ – in Christianity. I will try to explain this another time. My long night talk with Dyson and Tolkien had a good deal to do with it" (*CL I* 974). As Lewis would later put it even more concisely in a letter to Dom Bede Griffiths: "Dyson and Tolkien were the immediate human causes of my own conversion" (*CL II* 501). But if they were the immediate human causes of his conversion, what were its immediate intellectual causes? What idea or ideas made such an impact on Lewis's mind, compelling him to convert to Christianity?

1 An earlier version of this chapter was first published on Brenton Dickieson's blog *A Pilgrim in Narnia*, 2 June 2020, https://apilgriminnarnia.com/2020/06/02/cls-jrrt-keena/. It appears here, revised and updated, with Dr. Dickieson's kind permission.

What Lewis found so compelling was at least one aspect of the idea of true myth: namely, the notion that a story can be *both* factual, historical, or otherwise real *and* maintain its imaginative value as a story. This idea he was now able to apply to Christianity, as he explained to Greeves on October 18, 1931: "the story of Christ is simply a true myth," both factual (as true) and "suggestive of meanings beyond [one's] grasp" (as a myth) (*CL I* 977). As Tolkien would later say in 'On Fairy-stories' with regard to the Incarnation and Resurrection: "Art has been verified. God is the Lord, of angels, and of men – and of elves. Legend and history" – one might say, myth and historical truth – "have met and fused" (78). Lewis fully absorbed Tolkien and Dyson's proposal that Christianity unified myth and truth. In 1944 he published an essay entitled 'Myth Became Fact,' in which he maintained that

> The heart of Christianity is a myth which is also a fact. The old myth of the Dying God, *without ceasing to be myth*, comes down from the heaven of legend and imagination to the earth of history. It *happens* – at a particular date, in a particular place, followed by definable historical consequences. We pass from a Balder or an Osiris, dying nobody knows when or where, to a historical Person crucified (it is all in order) *under Pontius Pilate*. By becoming fact it does not cease to be myth: that is the miracle. ...To be truly Christian we must both assent to the historical fact and also receive the myth (fact though it has become) with the same imaginative embrace which we accord to all myths. The one is hardly more necessary than the other. ('Myth Became Fact' 42; emphasis original)[2]

Ultimately, Lewis developed Tolkien's fusion of myth and truth farther than Tolkien (or Dyson, for that matter) ever did. But Lewis's innovations, such as his explanation of how myths give rise to allegories by concretizing abstractions but without being tied to full particularity (in 'Myth Became Fact'); or why, if the Christian story is a myth, it is not as beautiful in the telling as certain pagan myths (*Miracles* 218); or what, more precisely, qualifies a story or event as being of mythical value (*EC* 40-49), are beyond the scope of this chapter.

2 See also *Surprised by Joy*: "I was by now too experienced in literary criticism to regard the Gospels as myths. They had not the mythical taste. And yet the very matter which they set down in their artless, historical fashion – those narrow, unattractive Jews, too blind to the mythical wealth of the Pagan world around them – was precisely the matter of the great myths. If ever a myth had become fact, had been incarnated, it would be just like this. And nothing else in all literature was just like this. Myths were like it in one way. Histories were like it in another. But nothing was simply like it" (222).

We should appreciate the complete about-face that Tolkien and Dyson convinced Lewis to make. At some point, likely on the night of September 19, 1931, Lewis had claimed that myths, though beautiful and demanding, as he would later put it in *An Experiment in Criticism*, "the lasting allegiance of the imagination" (47), were untrue and hence, in some sense, less valuable or serious than the realities of the actual world. In his own words (at least, as quoted by Tolkien), mythmaking was "Breathing a lie through Silver" (*TOFS* 65). Myth and truth were totally divorced. Indeed, at one time in his life – namely, when he had been an atheist and a materialist – Lewis's whole mind had been divided precisely along that fault line:

> Such, then, was the state of my imaginative life; over against it stood the life of my intellect. The two hemispheres of my mind were in the sharpest contrast. On the one side a many-islanded sea of poetry and myth; on the other a glib and shallow 'rationalism'. Nearly all that I loved I believed to be imaginary; nearly all that I believed to be real I thought grim and meaningless. (*SJ* 161)

Though he had ceased to be an atheist and a materialist by the time his friendship with Tolkien began, these two halves of his mind were not fully reconciled until September 1931.[3] But then, finally, his imaginative life, "a many-islanded sea of poetry and myth," could be integrated with what he "believed to be real" (*SJ* 161) by means of Tolkien and Dyson's idea of true myth. We may thank them for unifying Lewis's intellectual and philosophical powers with his imaginative life and thus, indirectly, for all the writings which were the fruit of that unification. For what would C.S. Lewis have become, if his intellectual life had never been fully reconciled with his imagination? Where would *The Pilgrim's Regress*, the Ransom trilogy, *The Great Divorce*, *The Screwtape Letters*, *The Chronicles of Narnia*, or *Till We Have Faces* be without that integration?

Despite the unique significance of true myth for Lewis in his conversion to Christianity, September 1931 was not the first time that this idea had appeared in his friendship with Tolkien. Sometime towards the end of 1929, Tolkien

3 Even as an idealist – that is, after his materialist period but before his conversions either to theism in 1930 or to Christianity in 1931 – Lewis denied that myths could be factually true. See 'Clivi Hamiltonis Summae Metaphysices Contra Anthroposophos Libri II': "It should be noticed, however, that if such beings [as fairies] were shown to exist, the *first*, though not necessarily the final, result would be to destroy their symbolical value. [...] If all mythology were proved as fact, the poets would throw it away and invent a new one, warranted untrue" (100-01; emphasis original). Lewis's *Summa* was completed in November 1928.

showed Lewis about 3,000 lines of a poem called 'The Geste of Beren and Lúthien.'[4] By admitting Lewis to the private world of his imagination, Tolkien was recognizing him as a kindred spirit and a much closer friend. Likewise, Lewis began to recognize his affinity for Tolkien in a letter to Greeves on January 30, 1930, having recently read the 'Geste':

> Tolkien is the man I spoke of when we were last together – the author of the voluminous unpublished metrical romances and of the maps, companions to them, showing the mountains of Dread and Nargothrond the city of the Orcs. In fact he *is*, in one part of him, what we were. (*CL I* 880; emphasis original)

"[H]e *is*, in one part of him, what we were" (880; emphasis original). With this remark, Lewis was beginning to recognize the elements in Tolkien that had formed the basis of his own deep and lasting friendship with Greeves. But what did Lewis have to say about Tolkien's "voluminous unpublished metrical romances" (880)? His comments, written in December of 1929, are worth dwelling on:

> I sat up late last night and have read the *Geste* as far as to where Beren and his gnomish allies defeat the patrol of orcs above the sources of the Narog and disguise themselves in the *reaf* [Old English: 'garments, weapons, taken from the slain']. I can quite honestly say that it is ages since I have had an evening of such delight: and the personal interest of reading a friend's work had very little to do with it. I should have enjoyed it just as much as if I'd picked it up in a bookshop, by an unknown author. The two things that come out clearly are the sense of reality in the background and the mythical value: the essence of a myth being that it should have no taint of allegory to the maker and yet should suggest incipient allegories to the reader. (qtd. in *LB* 184)

Of particular interest in this passage, other than Lewis's evident enjoyment of Tolkien's work, is his identification of two particularly outstanding elements in the poem: first, the sense of verisimilitude, the feeling that one has entered into a fully realized secondary world, and second, its mythical value. That mythical value consists simultaneously in a lack of direct allegory intended by the author alongside a more flexibly suggestive power for the reader. It is as if Lewis were paraphrasing in advance, what he did not live to see, Tolkien's comments in his Foreword to the Second Edition of *The Lord of the Rings*: "I cordially dislike allegory in all its manifestations. [...] I much prefer history, true or feigned, with its varied applicability to the thought and experience of readers" (*FR* xxii). Both

4 The poem was first published in *The Lays of Beleriand* (184-85).

Lewis and Tolkien were attracted by the combination of mythical significance with a sense of reality, of history, of fact, whether "true or feigned" (xxii), and the potent effects of that combination in literary experience.

The story of Lewis's reaction to the 'Geste' is complemented, long after Lewis's conversion to Christianity, by Tolkien's similar reaction to *Out of the Silent Planet*. Tolkien was thoroughly drawn in by that work, which he had read by the time he wrote to Stanley Unwin on March 4, 1938:

> I read the story in the original MS. and was so enthralled that I could do nothing else until I had finished it. My first criticism was simply that it was too short. I still think that criticism holds, for both practical and artistic reasons. [...] But I should have said that the story had for the more intelligent reader a great number of philosophical and mythical implications that enormously enhanced without detracting from the surface 'adventure'. I found the blend of *vera historia* with *mythos* irresistible. (*Letters* 32-33, #26)

We may note once again the importance for the reader's literary experience of combining myth with *vera historia* 'true history'. The mythical and philosophical value of Lewis's story, it would seem, gained in potency by being presented as something historically true. Myth and (supposedly) historical truth were not at odds in Lewis's story, but mutually supportive, which Tolkien appreciated – just as we would expect, given their conversation of September 19-20, 1931.

In what way did *Out of the Silent Planet* unify myth and historical truth? One possibility is as follows: given that the underlying myth of *Out of the Silent Planet* is the Fall of the angels and the Fall of man – events which Lewis and Tolkien regarded as real, historical facts – it is more than likely that they both would have considered the "philosophical and mythical implications" (*Letters* 33, #26) of Lewis's story as, in some sense, factually or historically true. Not, of course, that they believed in the actual existence of *hrossa* or *sorns* on Mars, or the existence of the angelic *eldila* just as Lewis describes them; but that Lewis's story reveals something about how the doctrines of Christianity might operate in a cosmic, and not simply terrestrial, setting; that contrasting the *hrossa* or *sorns* or *pfifltriggi* with humans reveals what it means to be a fallen (or 'bent,' as Lewis puts it) creature; and that the ruling *eldil* of Mars might reveal something of the angelic nature and its relation to the physical universe.

Tolkien's enthusiasm for *Out of the Silent Planet* helped it to reach the press in 1938 (Carpenter 2000: 173). But what is perhaps even more significant for our purposes is that Tolkien was involved in its genesis as well. Lewis's story was originally intended to work side by side with a thematically related one by Tolkien. According to Tolkien's letter to Stanley Unwin on February 18, 1938:

> We originally meant each to write an excursionary 'Thriller': a Space-journey and a Time-journey (mine) each discovering Myth. But the Space-journey has been finished, and the Time-journey remains owing to my slowness and uncertainty only a fragment, as you know. (*Letters* 29, #24)

Tolkien recounted the conversation that sparked the joint project, which must have occurred in the mid-1930s, as follows:

> L. said to me one day: 'Tollers, there is too little of what we really like in stories. I am afraid we shall have to try and write some ourselves.' We agreed that he should try 'space-travel', and I should try 'time-travel'. His result is well known. My effort, after a few promising chapters, ran dry: it was too long a way round to what I really wanted to make, a new version of the Atlantis legend. The final scene survives as *The Downfall of Númenor*. (*Letters* 378, #294)[5]

The "effort" that "ran dry" to which Tolkien refers is his unfinished story *The Lost Road*, in which pairs of fathers and sons with names meaning 'Bliss-friend' and 'Elf-friend' throughout human history (Edwin and Elwin, Eädwine and Ælfwine, Audoin and Alboin) are traced back to and ultimately explained by the original Númenorean father-son pair, Amandil and Elendil (*Letters* 347, #257; Carpenter 2000: 174). Actual historical realities (that is, the recurrence of names like Elwin, Ælfwine, and so on) are explained with reference to a mythological, but supposedly real, invention (or, re-invention) of Tolkien's: the ancient speech of the Elves and the downfall of Númenor. A mythical past is here introduced to explain historical names. Once again, myth merges with history.

## True Myth: Disambiguation and Principle of Fantasy

We have seen the notion of true myth in three places so far: first, Lewis's acceptance, due to Tolkien and Dyson, of the unity of truth and myth in

5 See also his letters to Dora Marshall (209, #159); Michael Tolkien (342, #252); and Christopher Bretherton (347, #257).

Christianity; second, Lewis's appreciation of the fusion of mythical value and the strong sense of reality in 'The Geste of Beren and Lúthien;' and third, in "the blend of *vera historia* with *mythos*" (*Letters* 33, #26) in Tolkien and Lewis's space- and time-travel stories.

There is no question, then, that the notion of true myth was a major factor in their personal lives and friendship; its role in converting Lewis to Christianity alone would secure its place among their major common ideas. What remains to be shown is threefold: first, that this idea has two major senses; second, that the first sense is foundational for Lewis's and Tolkien's fantasy writings; and finally, that the second sense of true myth has a metaphysical background informed by, and in some ways deliberately based upon, Classical Platonism.

The distinction between the two senses of 'true myth' depends on what is meant by 'true.' The first sense has to do with a myth that is true in the sense of being historically or factually true in the way that 'Caesar crossed the Rubicon in 49 BC' is historically true. According to Lewis and Tolkien, the story of Christ is a myth which is also historically, literally true. Likewise, according to Tolkien, Lewis's *Out of the Silent Planet* blended *vera historia* (albeit feigned) with *mythos*. This sense of true myth will be referred to as 'historically true myth.' The second sense has to do with a myth that may be called true insofar as it resembles some reality, usually divine or eschatological. For example, Tolkien held that the eucatastrophe of fairy stories – "the sudden joyous 'turn'" (*TOFS* 75) of events, or happy ending – "may be a far-off gleam or echo of *evangelium* in the real world" (77). In the same way the pagan myths of the dying and resurrecting god – Balder, Osiris, Dionysus – might be said to be true insofar as they resemble or foreshadow the resurrection of Christ. As Lewis put it in *Reflections on the Psalms*: "The resemblance between these myths and the Christian truth is no more accidental than the resemblance between the sun and the sun's reflection in a pond" (107). They are, at least in some attenuated sense, true likenesses or anticipations (or better yet, transpositions) of "the Christian truth." This second sense of true myth will be referred to as 'non-historically true myth.' This is the sense whose metaphysical background is largely based on Plato, as argued in the next section and illustrated in the last. But the first sense, historically true myth, is the sense that we will now proceed to demonstrate was a ubiquitous and indeed foundational principle of Tolkien's and Lewis's fantasy writings.

Lewis's fantasies, by which are primarily meant the Ransom trilogy, *The Chronicles of Narnia*, and *Till We Have Faces*, will be considered first, and then Tolkien's. Perhaps the most direct expression of historically true myth comes in *Perelandra*. At one point the main protagonist, Ransom, seeing a dragon coiling around a tree loaded with golden fruit, thinks of the Hesperides with wonder. Then he

> remembered how in the very different world called Malacandra – that cold, archaic world, as it now seemed to him – he had met the original of the Cyclops, a giant in a cave and a shepherd. Were all the things which appeared as mythology on earth scattered through other worlds as realities? (46)

In other words, were mythological beings actually real entities, and hence did the myths about them have some basis in historical or factual truth? Later, Ransom answers the question definitively in the affirmative, once again comparing his Malacandrian and Perelandrian experience:

> Long since on Mars, and more strongly since he came to Perelandra, Ransom had been perceiving that the triple distinction of truth from myth and of both from fact was purely terrestrial – was part and parcel of that unhappy division between soul and body which resulted from the Fall. [...] In Perelandra it would have no meaning at all. Whatever happened there would be of such a nature that earth-men would call it mythological. All this he had thought before. Now he knew it. (*Perelandra* 163-64)[6]

Anything that really occurred on Perelandra, Ransom concludes, would also be mythological: historical truth, fact, and myth have been united. And indeed that same unification motivates the whole Ransom trilogy. What we on earth might think of as speculative theology – namely, the Fall of the angels and its ramifications for the rest of the rational universe – Lewis relies upon as historical background in *Out of the Silent Planet*. What we on earth regard as a mythical part of human history, the story of the temptation of our first parents, Lewis shows us as *vera historia* in its parallel occurrence in *Perelandra*. What we regard as a fanciful imaginative construction of the Greeks and Romans – namely, their elaborate pantheon – we see incarnated in the vision of Mars and Venus in

6 See also See also *Out of the Silent Planet*, chapter 21: "It even occurred to him that the distinction between history and mythology might be itself meaningless outside the Earth" (237), and *The Pilgrim's Regress*, book 8, chapter 8 and book 9, chapter 5..

*Perelandra*, the role of Mars in *Out of the Silent Planet*, and in the descent of all the planetary gods upon the N.I.C.E. and St. Anne's in *That Hideous Strength*. In the final book of the trilogy, the Arthurian legend, too, turns out to be historically accurate with the introduction of Merlin as a character. There are even references to Tolkien's mythology being real and historical: we hear of the existence of "the true West" and "Numinor" – a name which Lewis misspells (with an 'i' instead of an 'e'), since at the time he had only heard the story read aloud to him (*Letters* 361, #276). Not only *Out of the Silent Planet*, then, but each installment in the Ransom trilogy is a book "discovering Myth," as Tolkien had put it (*Letters* 29, #24) – that is, among other things, discovering that certain myths were historically true. To remove the idea of the historically true myth from the Ransom trilogy would be to alter its fundamental nature.

The same idea motivates the *Narniad* to some extent as well. All kinds of mythological beasts, people, objects, and situations appear, woven into the very fabric of the stories as fairy tales. In *The Chronicles of Narnia*, Lewis answers Ransom's question ("Were all the things which appeared as mythology on earth scattered through other worlds as realities?;" *Perelandra* 46) with a definitive 'Yes.' Centaurs and fauns appear in *The Lion, the Witch, and the Wardrobe*; Bacchus and Maenads in *Prince Caspian*; giants in *The Silver Chair*. For, as *The Magician's Nephew* discloses, there are many other worlds: ours, Narnia, and Charn, are only three among countless others. Much of what we consider to be mythological in our world is completely historical and factual in Narnia, and vice versa: remember the title of one of the books on Mr. Tumnus' shelf, *Is Man a Myth?* in *The Lion, the Witch, and the Wardrobe* (23) or the delight of Prince Caspian upon finding out that our world is round, unlike Narnia, in *The Voyage of the Dawn Treader* (238). Lewis thus collapses the distinction between historical truth and myth, or myth and fact, not only in the Ransom trilogy but also in the *Narniad*.

Finally, we will briefly examine *Till We Have Faces*, Lewis's last and arguably greatest work of fantasy. Consider just these two points: first, that it is set in pre-Christian times, in which pagan polytheism, Greek or otherwise, was in fact the dominant religious force; and second, that the book is subtitled 'A Myth Retold.' Thus we have a myth – specifically, the myth of Cupid and Psyche – being presented as an historical account. Indeed, a great part of the meaning of the work depends on its being set in actual pre-Christian times. The dramatic shift in the number of addressees to whom Orual is speaking at the very end, for example, would not have the impact that it does if Orual had not come from the perspective of polytheism. Likewise, the novel's structure, written as Orual's complaint against the gods, *ipso facto* depends on the framework of historical pagan polytheism.

Several of Lewis's fantasies, then, are founded upon the notion of the historically true myth.[7] This idea also finds remarkable expressions in some of his theological works,[8] but we must leave them aside to focus now on Tolkien's fantasy. For Tolkien, too, was fascinated by Ransom's question: "Were all the things which appeared as mythology on earth scattered through other worlds as realities?" (*Perelandra* 46). But he answered it in a different way. 'No,' Tolkien would have said, 'not in *other* worlds; but Yes, in *our* world.' For Middle-earth, as he insisted, is *our* earth: dragons, Dwarves, Ents, and Elves existed in *our* past.[9] It is only distance of time that separates us from them. Their historical presence in our dimly remembered past explains the appearance in our ancient documents of mythological beings and other spiritual forces, just as Eärendil's historical voyage beyond the walls of the world with the Silmaril shining on his brow explains why an Anglo-Saxon poet would address him as the morning

7 His short story 'Forms of Things Unknown' could also be included here. His other fictional works (*The Pilgrim's Regress*, *The Screwtape Letters*, *The Great Divorce*, and the rest of his short fiction) do not fit so neatly into that group. In other words, they are not stories that present or reinterpret a certain myth or legend as *vera historia*.

8 For example, see *The Problem of Pain*: "If it offends less, you may say that the 'life-force' is corrupted where I say that living creatures were corrupted by an evil angelic being. We mean the same thing: but I find it easier to believe in a myth of gods and demons than in one of hypostatised abstract nouns. And after all, our mythology may be much nearer to literal truth than we suppose. Let us not forget that Our Lord, on one occasion, attributes human disease not to God's wrath, but quite explicitly to Satan" (123-24). See also 'The Weight of Glory': "For if we take the imagery of Scripture seriously, if we believe that God will one day *give* us the Morning Star and cause us to *put on* the splendour of the sun, then we may surmise that both the ancient myths and the modern poetry, so false as history, may be very near the truth as prophecy" (43; emphasis original).

9 See Tolkien's letter to W.H. Auden: "I am historically minded. Middle-earth is not an imaginary world. The name is the modern form (appearing in the 13th century and still in use) of *midden-erd* > *middle-erd*, an ancient name for the *oikoumene*, the abiding place of Men, the objectively real world, in use specifically opposed to imaginary worlds (as Fairyland) or unseen worlds (as Heaven or Hell). The theatre of my tale is this earth, the one in which we now live, but the historical period is imaginary" (*Letters* 238, #183).

star.[10] Or again, consider the following passage from the *Valaquenta* describing the ruling powers of the world, the Valar: "The Great among these spirits the Elves name the Valar, the Powers of Arda, and Men have often called them gods" (*Sil* 13). The reason why we hear about cloud-gathering Zeus, ruler of Mount Olympus, in Greek mythology is ultimately because of Manwë, who rules the Valar from Mount Taniquetil and whose special province is the winds and airs (13). Tolkien's whole mythology, from the cosmogony of the *Ainulindalë* all the way to the fading of the Elves and the rise of Men at the close of the Third Age, was meant to be a history of our world, a window into a lost time. It was not arbitrary that Tolkien and Lewis decided amongst themselves that Tolkien was to write a time-travel story and Lewis a space-travel story. For Tolkien's mythology was an attempt to recreate the long-forgotten mythological, but historical past of earth; whereas many of Lewis's mythological figures and stories occur on other planets, such as in the first two books of the Ransom trilogy (thus dividing us from them by space), or in other universes, entirely other Spaces altogether (such as in the *Narniad*). But in any case, for both Lewis and Tolkien, the notion of the historically true myth was an essential principle in their respective approaches to fantasy writing.

## The Nature and Metaphysics of Non-Historically True Myth

Having shown, if only in outline, the importance of historically true myth for Lewis and Tolkien, we turn now to the nature and metaphysical background of non-historically true myth. The *locus classicus*, so to speak, of the notion of non-historically true myth comes in Tolkien's 1931 poem 'Mythopoeia,' written after and because of his Addison's Walk conversation on September 19-20 with Lewis and Dyson. In the poem, Tolkien attempts to respond to Lewis's *dictum* that mythmaking is "Breathing a lie through Silver" (*TOFS* 65). Thus, he addressed the poem "Philomythus to Misomythus" (*TL* 85) – that is, from Tolkien (a "Myth-lover") to Lewis (a "Myth-hater," given his assessment of myths as "lies"). Now notice what Tolkien's response to Lewis in this poem

10 Lines 104-05 in *Crist I* read as follows: *éala éarendel engla beorhtast ofer middangeard monnum sended*: 'Hail Earendel, brightest of angels / above the Middle-earth sent unto men' (qtd. in Carpenter 2000: 72). As Carpenter notes, Tolkien's poem is called 'The voyage of Earendel the Evening Star' (79). See also Tolkien's letter to 'Mr Rang' (*Letters* 385, #297).

must entail. Lewis had accused myths of being lies, that is, of being falsehoods. By rejecting Lewis's position, Tolkien was arguing that myths were not false, but true. But, it must be immediately noted, 'Mythopoeia' does not argue in defense of *historically* true myth – a story with mythical or imaginative value that also really happened. Keep in mind, too, that Lewis seems to have already been convinced, or at least nearly convinced, by their Addison's Walk conversation that Christianity was to be approached as an historically true myth. In 'Mythopoeia,' therefore, Tolkien was maintaining that myths are also true in some non-historical way. Having gained ground with Lewis on one point, he sought to gain ground on another. How, then, can myths be true in a non-historical sense? To begin formulating our answer to this question, consider the following lines from the poem:

> The heart of Man is not compound of lies,
> but draws some wisdom from the only Wise,
> and still recalls him. Though now long estranged,
> Man is not wholly lost nor wholly changed.
> Dis-graced he may be, yet is not dethroned,
> and keeps the rags of lordship once he owned,
> his world-dominion by creative act:
> not his to worship the great Artefact,
> man, Sub-creator, the refracted light
> through whom is splintered from a single White
> to many hues, and endlessly combined
> in living shapes that move from mind to mind.
> Though all the crannies of the world we filled
> with elves and goblins, though we dared to build
> gods and their houses out of dark and light,
> and sowed the seed of dragons, 'twas our right
> (used or misused). The right has not decayed.
> We make still by the law in which we're made.
> (*TL* 87)

There are two important points to notice in this passage. First, the human impulse to make stories and myths, to sub-create, is raised to the dignity of an imitation of divine creation. God made us, and we make other things: "We make still by the law in which we're made" (87). As Tolkien put it in 'On Fairy-stories': "Fantasy remains a human right: we make in our measure and in our derivative mode, because we are made: and not only made, but made in the image and likeness of a Maker" (*TOFS* 66). Or as Aulë, the god of crafting and earth and artistry in *The Silmarillion*, said to Eru after he had made the

Dwarves: "As a child to his father, I offer to thee these things, the work of the hands which thou hast made" (31). God is an artist, and an artisan; therefore, so is Aulë; therefore, so are the Dwarves; therefore, so are we. Sub-creation, including mythmaking, is an imitation of divine creation.

The second point is to identify more precisely what sort of relation our sub-creations have to the Creator. Notice the imagery with which Tolkien describes how the mythmaker imitates divine creativity, and the sort of relation it implies between human art and God: "man, Sub-creator, the refracted light / through whom is splintered from a single White / to many hues, and endlessly combined / in living shapes that move from mind to mind" (*TL* 87). The "single White," that is the Light of God, is refracted through human mythmaking into the many colors of the "living shapes" in our minds: that is, Elves, Goblins, Ents, Dwarves, and all other invented creatures (87). Something contained pre-eminently in God, who is the Light itself, is filtered through the human mind into the colors of human mythmaking. Myths thus convey something that is contained pre-eminently in God, just as colors and their hues are contained pre-eminently in white light. Later in the poem Tolkien extends the metaphor of light to make a substantially similar point: "In Paradise perchance the eye may stray / from gazing upon everlasting Day / to see the day-illumined, and renew / from mirrored truth the likeness of the True" (90). That is to say, the blessed in heaven may look upon creation to "renew" their understanding of God by seeing His likeness in what He has made. The "everlasting Day" (90), or the Sun, just like the "single White" (87), is God; both are pre-eminent sources of light. And just as the "single White" is refracted into the many colors of human sub-creation, so the "everlasting Day" is mirrored in creation and, we may add, in our sub-creations. God is "the True" (90) with a capital T; but the heavenly landscape of Paradise is "mirrored truth" and "the likeness of the True" (90). Creation resembles its Creator by a relation of likeness, albeit an attenuated likeness. God is the Archetype; His creatures are made in His image and likeness; therefore, some glimpse of Him can be discerned by looking at His creation. But the same could be said of human sub-creations, as Tolkien himself suggests. For elsewhere in 'Mythopoeia' he writes of mythmakers as weaving story-threads "gilded by the far-off day" (80) – that is, catching gleams, no doubt, of the "everlasting Day" (90) and thus faintly resembling the Creator.

Or again, they make an "image blurred of distant king" (89), catching the likeness of the King of creation in some capacity.

We have learned already that the act of sub-creation itself is an imitation or likeness of divine creation. But now we can see that the way in which the *results* of sub-creation (particularly, myths) are related to the Creator is also by a relation of imitation or resemblance or likeness: something that God contains pre-eminently or archetypically is conveyed in the glimmers or gleams of "mirrored truth" (90) in human myths. They, like objects in the created world, also qualify in some measure as being "likeness[es] of the True" (90) – that is, of God. As Tolkien put it in 'On Fairy-stories': "in the 'eucatastrophe' we see in a brief vision that the answer may be greater – it may be a far-off gleam or echo of *evangelium* in the real world" (*TOFS* 77). Or, as Lewis put it in *Reflections on the Psalms*, "The resemblance between these myths [of dying and rising gods like Balder and Adonis] and the Christian truth is no more accidental than the resemblance between the sun and the sun's reflection in a pond" (107). Blurred or faint or refracted as they may be, the hues and colors of certain human myths are still related to God (or heavenly life more generally) by a relation of imitation, likeness, or resemblance.

We have now identified the metaphysical core of non-historically true myths: they have the nature of imitations, likenesses, or resemblances, being related to their divine Source as to an archetype, or as refracted light to the pure light of the Sun. But before connecting these (and other) ideas to ancient Greek metaphysics in the final section, it will be well to first analyze some examples of such myths in Lewis and Tolkien themselves. We will focus on two particularly revealing eschatological myths, for it is these that we would naturally expect to catch glimmers of heavenly life and act as likenesses of God. Tolkien's *Leaf by Niggle* will be examined first, and then the end of Lewis's *The Last Battle*, as the two clearest expressions of non-historically true myth in their writings. By the end of this section the impact of the particular ancient Greek metaphysician that Lewis and Tolkien were drawing from will become unmistakably clear.

First, then, let us turn to *Leaf by Niggle*. Niggle is a painter who paints trees: this is his vocation. All his life, he tries, and mostly fails, often due to unwelcome interruptions, to put onto his canvas his vision of an elaborate tree – a project which consumes all his artistic endeavors. It is his life's work, but he is unable to complete it. Before he can finish, the time comes for him to go on a journey, leaving his life behind. But it is only then, after he has embarked and endured a long, purgatorial experience, that he discovers the real Tree, whose existence he had never suspected but which had inspired all his earthly art, the Tree whose outlines he had tried with all his might and artistry to capture, but had largely failed to reproduce:

> Before him stood the Tree, his Tree, finished. If you could say that of a Tree that was alive, its leaves opening, its branches growing and bending in the wind that Niggle had so often felt or guessed, and had so often failed to catch. All the leaves he had ever laboured at were there, and as he had imagined them rather than as he had made them; and there were others that had only budded in his mind, and many that might have budded, if only he had had time. (*TL* 109-10)

All Niggle's earthly painting, therefore, had caught some glimpse, had been some imperfect likeness or resemblance or imitation, of this heavenly Tree, which surpassed all his artistic efforts in beauty and detail. Thus the results of sub-creation, despite any flaws they may have, whether due to the artist or simply due to the fact of being sub-creations, can still foreshadow something of heaven.

The eschatological vision of Narnia and England at the end of Lewis's *The Last Battle*, to turn to the second example of non-historically true myth, also foreshadows heavenly experience. The Pevensie children and their companions discover the real Narnia and the real England, not as they had known them in their lives but as they were meant to be. Like Niggle at the sight of his Tree, they felt that all that was good and beautiful in their earthly vision had been preserved, yet, even more so than Niggle, that its beauty had been realized beyond all hope. It was familiar and yet beyond their imagining. As Jewel the Unicorn put it upon seeing the real Narnia:

> I have come home at last! This is my real country! I belong here. This is the land I have been looking for all my life, though I never knew it till now. The reason why we loved the old Narnia is that it sometimes looked a little like this. (*LB* 207)

The old Narnia, then, had only resembled the true Narnia – had only "looked a little like" (207) it. For as Professor Kirke had said:

> When Aslan said that you could never go back to Narnia, he meant the Narnia you were thinking of. But that was not the real Narnia. That had a beginning and an end. It was only a shadow or copy of the real Narnia, which has always been here and always will be here: just as our own world, England and all, is only a shadow or copy of something in Aslan's real world. You need not mourn over Narnia, Lucy. All of the old Narnia that mattered, all the dear creatures, have been drawn into the real Narnia through the Door. And of course it is different; as different as a real thing is from a shadow or as waking life is from a dream. (*LB* 205-06)

At this point the ancient Greek metaphysical background to these ideas can be put off no longer. All the pieces of the puzzle are now in place: imitation and resemblance of God as an Archetype, illumination by the divine Sun, shadows or copies of eternal and more fully real things, and sub-creation. Students of ancient Greek philosophy will not be surprised at how this passage continues immediately: "His voice stirred everyone like a trumpet as he spoke these words: but when he added under his breath 'It's all in Plato, all in Plato: bless me, what *do* they teach them at these schools!' the older ones laughed" (*LB* 206). For the metaphysical background of the second sense of true myth was established by Plato in dialogues such as the *Symposium*, *Phaedrus*, *Phaedo*, *Republic*, and *Timaeus*.

But given the ubiquity of Professor Kirke's *dictum* "It's all in Plato" in Lewis-Plato scholarship,[11] and the variety of interpretations surrounding it, the assertion that it refers primarily (and, in all probability, merely) to the 'two worlds' metaphysics of Classical Platonism as expressed in the middle and late dialogues requires some defense. The central issue in understanding what Kirke's remark means is the precise extent of what is included in the phrase "all in Plato." Both the terms 'all' and 'Plato' can be approached in a more or less restrictive way. On the most restrictive interpretation, the extent of 'all' would be limited just to the immediate context of Kirke's explanation of the metaphysics of 'shadows and copies' and the more fully real objects that they resemble, instead of the broader context of all the heavenly experiences contained in chapters 15 and 16 of *The Last Battle*, or of the plot and themes of the whole book, or of the entire *Narniad*. Likewise, on the most restrictive view, the extent of 'Plato' would be limited to a particular passage in a particular Platonic dialogue, instead of to

11 Almost every single piece in this sub-field, most of which are listed in note 14 below, makes some use of it.

recurrent ideas across several dialogues, or to those ideas as developed in one or more of the several intertwining post-Classical strands of Platonism, notably ancient Neoplatonism, sixteenth-century Renaissance Platonism, seventeenth-century Cambridge Platonism, and varieties of Christian Platonism from the early Church to Lewis's own time. Let us first consider what Kirke meant by 'Plato,' and then what he meant by 'all,' in constructing the safest and most accurate interpretation of this passage possible.

The most restrictive approach to the term 'Plato' advanced in the literature so far, as proposed by Mark Edwards (2010: 66; later endorsed by Bryson 2021: 23), takes it as an allusion to a specific passage in the *Phaedo* (namely, 110b-c). While Edwards nowhere says that Kirke was only or exclusively referring to Phaedo 110b-c, and to that extent may not be taking the most restrictive approach possible, he nevertheless creates too restrictive an interpretation even by singling out the *Phaedo* as a primary allusion. It is true that Lewis *may* have had this text uppermost in mind when composing this passage. But that is as far as we can safely go. There is not enough similarity in imagery, phrasing, or conceptual arrangement between Kirke's dialogue in *The Last Battle* and Plato's language in *Phaedo* 110b-c to secure such an allusion with certainty. What we do know is that Kirke brings up Plato by name in the context of having just explained in a condensed, yet evocative fashion the dualistic metaphysics of copies and originals, half-real likenesses and fully real things, partially valuable imitations and robustly valuable archetypes. We also know that this is a doctrine repeatedly expounded in the middle and late Platonic dialogues, not just in the *Phaedo*. And we know, finally, that when Lewis himself brings up Plato (or Platonism) by name in his own academic books without explicitly mentioning a particular dialogue, he, like Kirke, limits himself to tersely but effectively recapitulating the essence of Plato's 'two worlds' metaphysics. Consider the following chronologically arranged examples, which both predate and postdate the publication of *The Last Battle* in 1956:

> *The Allegory of Love* (1936): Symbolism comes to us from Greece. It makes its first effective appearance in European thought with the dialogues of Plato.

> The Sun is the copy of the Good. Time is the moving image of eternity. All visible things exist just in so far as they succeed in imitating the Forms. (45-6)[12]
>
> *Arthurian Torso* (1948): For [Charles] Williams, as for Plato, the phenomenal world – the world studied by the sciences – is primarily a reflection or copy or adaptation of something else. (101)
>
> *English Literature in the Sixteenth Century* (1954): Nature, the phenomenal world, is in Plato's dualism a copy of the real and supersensuous world. (319)
>
> *English Literature in the Sixteenth Century* (1954): Spenser inherited the Platonic and Christian dualism: heaven was set over against earth, being against becoming, eternity against time. He knew from the outset that the lower, half-unreal world must always fail to copy its archetype exactly. (392)
>
> *Studies in Words* (1960): In Platonism, as everyone knows, the whole perceptible universe in space and time is an imitation, and product, of something different: the imperceptible, timeless, archetypal forms. (38)
>
> *The Discarded Image* (1964): If, as Platonism taught – nor would [Thomas] Browne himself have dissented – the visible world is made after an invisible pattern... (152)

Though Professor Kirke is by no means a purely autobiographical character, we can recognize that he is making the same point about Plato's 'two worlds' metaphysics at the close of *The Last Battle* as Professor Lewis is in all of the foregoing quotations. By referring to Plato (or Platonism, or Platonic dualism, as the case may be) both academics are at least, and probably also at most, identifying him as the primary expositor of a dualistic metaphysics in which the world of our everyday experience imperfectly imitates, copies, or resembles another, more fully real world. Plato's name is being used as shorthand for this broad metaphysical vision, and not just for one aspect of the ascent to the true earth in the *Phaedo*. Nothing less than the 'two worlds' metaphysics of the middle and late dialogues in general, so memorably expressed in the mythopoeic prose at the end of the *Phaedo* (especially 108c-111c) as well as the Allegory of the Cave in the *Republic* (514a-518a), the ladder of love and the ascent to Beauty Itself in the *Symposium* (210a-212b), the soul-chariot's journey beyond the spatiotemporal realm in the *Phaedrus* (246a-247e), and the divinely-directed cosmogony of the *Timaeus* (27c-52d), is required.

---

12 Of all the quotations in this sequence, this is the only one which contains (implicit) references to particular dialogues. The sentence "The Sun is the copy of the Good" (45) refers to *Republic* 508b, and "Time is the moving image of eternity" (45) to *Timaeus* 37d.

But if an over-restrictive interpretation of 'Plato' in "It's all in Plato" (*LB* 206) is possible, so also is an over-expansive one. The immediate context of Kirke's comment only requires, as we have seen, that the connotation of 'Plato' be dualistically metaphysical (and perhaps, in addition, mythopoeically expressed). But whether that connotation also includes other aspects of Plato's metaphysics, or aspects of Plato's philosophy other than metaphysics, or Platonic philosophies other than Plato's, is much less probable. This can be shown by introducing the term 'all.' By taking it too expansively, scholars are forced to take 'Plato' too expansively as well. Those who take 'all' to mean something more than Kirke's speech on 'shadows and copies' are quick to point out – and rightly so – that many elements of the ending of *The Last Battle* and in Narnia as a whole are better described, not as "pure Platonism, but an Augustinian and medieval sacramental metaphysics" (Muth 2008: 238), or again that "What Digory blithely refers to as 'Plato' might much more accurately be described as "Plato as his doctrines are filtered through St. Paul, Augustine, the Florentine Neo-Platonists, and the Christian Humanists" (Johnson and Houtman 1986: 76-77). On such a reading Kirke (or Lewis) is either oversimplifying the relationship between Platonism and Christianity (or at least, Narnian eschatology) or somewhat disingenuously disguising his own selective and idiosyncratic approach to what constitutes Platonism. Scholars who take 'all' expansively have also pointed out that Kirke must be speaking hyperbolically when he says that "It's all in Plato" (*LB* 206) since "At numerous points in his essays and letters Lewis takes care to distinguish his Christian faith from Platonic and Neoplatonic ideas" (Tiffany 2014: 357). Not everything Narnian or Lewisian or Christian can be in Plato, since some of what is in Plato conflicts with what is Christian, Lewisian, or Narnian. That is true, so far as it goes, and the studies such observations have generated are insightful and worth reading. But as a guide to interpreting what "It's all in Plato" (*LB* 206) means in its literary context, they are not so helpful.

For notice what has happened. The more you expand the connotation of 'all' in Kirke's saying beyond its immediate context, widening it to include Narnian eschatology as a whole, or the Narnian series as a whole, or even Lewis's thought as a whole, the more you must also expand the connotation of 'Plato.' To keep the interpretative problem (what does "It's all in Plato" mean, exactly?) worth exploring, you must now include in your analysis "medieval sacramental metaphysics" (Muth 2008: 238), now Pauline and Augustinian theology, now Florentine Neoplatonism, now Christian Humanism, now all varieties of Platonism, and eventually all the factors and movements that shaped these systems, too. Taking "It's all in Plato" as a summative epigraph for the ending of *The Last Battle*, or for the Narnian 'philosophy' in general, or even for Lewis's thought in its entirety, would be too obviously false and therefore untenable if 'all' meant something that wide while 'Plato' meant something as narrow as 'the best known middle and late Platonic dialogues.' All of *that*, in just these works of Plato? Of course not. To keep the scholarly problem meaningful, the critical arguments worth making, and the interpretations of Lewis charitable, the connotation of 'all' must increase proportionately with the connotation of 'Plato.' But such rapidly widening horizons of interpretation, which could if unchecked expand so far as to include the entirety of Christianity, its doctrines and history, all kinds of post-Classical Platonisms and Lewis's attitudes to them in all his essays, books, letters, and other fiction, would require nothing less than a full-scale study of centuries of religious and philosophical thought, far beyond the scope of any focused, well-planned monograph or dissertation and the powers of any but the most gifted of polymaths. Surely such an apparatus, even when scaled down considerably, is disproportionate to an adequate interpretation of this one passage in chapter 15 of *The Last Battle*? Its interest and value should be neither under- nor over-estimated. The critical apparatus we use should be proportionate to the literary evidence. And that evidence, by Occam's razor, only requires 'all' to mean the 'two worlds' metaphysics of 'shadows and copies' explained by Kirke, and 'Plato' to mean 'that doctrine as found in any or all of the following dialogues: the *Phaedo*, *Phaedrus*, *Symposium*, *Republic*, and *Timaeus*.'[13] When these restrictions are in place, the concerns over Kirke's, and by extension Lewis's, inaccuracy or hyperbole or disingenuousness, simply vanish. All of that dualistic metaphysics really is in Plato. Kirke was simply telling the pedantic truth. And that pedantic, philosophical, propositional, Platonic truth, concretized and mythologized in Lewis's story, gives us a glimpse of heavenly experience, a reflection of heavenly truth.

---

13 Walter Hooper goes even farther by applying the same reading to one of Kirke's similar antecedent sayings in *The Lion, the Witch, and the Wardrobe*: "I wonder what they *do* teach them at these schools" (57). According to Hooper, "He was referring to the absence of the teaching of metaphysical thought in the new schools – especially as found in the Platonic Dialogues" (1996: 427).

## The Platonism of Non-Historically True Myth

In this final section, four connections will be drawn between Lewis and Tolkien's idea of non-historically true myth and Plato's metaphysics. Cataloguing just these four in succession – there are certainly others[14] – will establish Classical Platonism as a main source of inspiration for this aspect of their joint theory of myth.

(1) We have seen that, according to Lewis and Tolkien, certain myths can act as imitations or resemblances of otherworldly, divine realities, whether God or heaven or both. Now this metaphysical relationship of an earthly imitation to a divine paradigm, of an empirical resemblance to a non-sensible Form or archetype, is of course a main feature of Plato's metaphysics. In the *Timaeus*, Plato has Timaeus straightforwardly state that the things that come to be in time and space are τῶν ὄντων ἀεὶ μιμήματα (50c) "imitations of those things that always are" – namely, the eternal, immutable, paradigmatic, divine Forms – and as such are τυπωθέντα ἀπ᾽ αὐτῶν (50c) "imprinted after their likeness" in a marvelous but mysterious way (transl. Donald Zeyl). He reiterates the same thought later on, writing of space as τῷ τὰ τῶν νοητῶν ἀεί τε ὄντων κατὰ πᾶν ἑαυτοῦ πολλάκις ἀφομοιώματα καλῶς μέλλοντι δέχεσθαι (51a) "the thing that is to receive repeatedly throughout its whole self the likenesses of the intel-

14 The number of connections would increase dramatically if we were to include other aspects of Plato's philosophy besides metaphysics, or other aspects of Lewis and Tolkien's use, approach to, and theory of myth besides non-historically true myth, or Platonisms other than Classical. Some of these connections have been drawn already, but as yet there is no monograph on Plato in Tolkien or the Inklings as a whole, and apparently just one extended work on Plato in Lewis (Moate 2017). The following five lists are arranged chronologically. (1) The most prominent thread of Plato-Tolkien scholarship connects the Ring of Gyges episode in *Republic* 2 with the One Ring. See Morse 1980, Herbert 1985, de Armas 1994, Katz 2003, Korpua 2015, and Neubauer 2021. (2) A sampling of the rest of Plato-Tolkien scholarship includes Cox 1984, Flieger 1986, Nagy 2004, Weinreich 2008, Korpua 2015 (who covers the *Timaeus* and Tolkien's cosmogony on 47-52), and Kleu 2021. (3) The most prominent thread of Plato-Lewis scholarship focuses on the connections between the dialogues and the *Chronicles of Narnia*. See Johnson and Houtman 1986, Simmons and Simmons 1991, Riga 1992, Joeckel 1997, Ford 2005 (entry on 'Plato'), Starr 2009, Fisher 2010, and Chapa 2016. (4) For studies on Lewis, Plato, and other Platonisms without a primary focus on Narnia, see Walker 2002, Barkman 2009 (especially 53-65 on 'Neoplatonic Christianity,' 68-71 on 'Platonic Eros,' and 132-53 on 'Myth during the Neoplatonic Christian phase'), Dickerson and O'Hara 2009 (especially 31-35 on 'Lewis as Platonist (but Not a Gnostic)'), Brazier 2009, Sellars 2011 (especially ch. 4, 'Desire and Longing in Lewis, Plato, and Augustine'), Duriez 2013 (entry on 'Plato'), Tiffany 2014, Hermann 2015, Baker 2016, Wendling 2016, Clarke 2017, Williams 2021 (especially 124-33 on 'A Brief Comparison & Contrast with Plato'), and Bryson 2021. (5) For Plato and the Inklings, see Rose 1982.

ligible objects, the things which always are."[15] In the *Phaedo*, Socrates argues that at least certain spatiotemporal objects can serve as reminders of the Forms due to their likeness to them: "We must then possess knowledge of the Equal before that time when we first saw the equal objects and realized that all these objects strive to be like the Equal [ὀρέγεται εἶναι οἷον τὸ ἴσον] but are deficient in this" (74e-75a, transl. G.M.A. Grube).[16] The same idea appears in the *Phaedrus*, where Socrates contrasts the earthly ὁμοιώμασιν "images" (250b) and εἰκόνας "likenesses" (250b) of Justice and Temperance, in which the nature of the Form being imitated can be discerned, but only with difficulty (transl. Alexander Nehamas and Paul Woodruff), with the Form of Beauty, whose images in the sensible world are all the more powerfully inspiring because they are discerned with ease (250d-e).

The best-known illustration of the metaphysical relationship of participants to Forms comes from the seventh book of the *Republic*. There, Plato imaginatively – or better, mythopoeically – describes the levels of reality from images of sensible objects all the way up to Forms, maintaining some degree of resemblance or imitation between these different levels. The shadows on the wall of the Cave resemble the statues and artifacts that cast them, lit from behind by the fire in the Cave; these subterranean statues and artifacts in turn resemble the shadows of the real creatures and natural objects above the Cave (that is, in the intelligible world); and finally, there are the real creatures, natural objects, and celestial bodies themselves, lit by the most supreme being of all, the Sun (514a-516b). Thus the lowest level of reality – the shadows cast upon the wall of the Cave – does ultimately resemble and convey something of the nature of the real objects above the Cave, though imperfectly, having been, so to speak, filtered (or, shall we say, refracted) through many intermediary steps. Likewise, Lewis and Tolkien's non-historically true myths imperfectly convey

15 Zeyl accepts one of the variant readings of Burnet's text that inserts the word νοητῶν "intelligible."
16 See also 75b. However, Plato does grant that one can be reminded of something (including a Form) by *un*likeness as well.

something of otherworldly, divine realities by way of likeness or resemblance.[17] "The reason why we loved the old Narnia is that it sometimes looked a little like this" (*LB* 207).

(2) In describing the Allegory of the Cave, we have already raised another connection between Platonic metaphysics and Tolkien and Lewis's notion of non-historically true myth: namely, their use of the Sun as the most apt symbol of the divine source of meaning. For Tolkien and Lewis this divine, sunlike source, whether conceived as God or as the truth of Christianity, is what makes non-historically true myths possible. It illuminates them with imaginative meaning, conveying in a lesser or veiled or reflected fashion some of its own reality or truth, just as in Plato the sunlike Form of the Good makes the physical world possible by illuminating it with a lesser kind of existence and intelligibility. We will consider Tolkien first, and then Lewis.

You will remember that Tolkien's two metaphors of light in 'Mythopoeia' both focused on a pure source of divine Light and its filtration by, or illumination of, other beings. The nature of these metaphors highlights the absolute dependence of human sub-creations upon the divine Reality. Without the "single White" (*TL* 87) which is refracted in the colors of human imagination or the "everlasting Day" (90) and its implied Sun which illumines the rest of creation, there would either be no sub-creations at all (for without a source of light, there would be no refracted colors) or, even if they did exist, they would be unintelligible (for without a source of light, nothing would be illumined or visible). But these two functions of the divine Light – namely, to be the cause of existence and the cause of intelligibility – are the two functions that Plato attributes to the Form of the Good, of which the Sun is a symbol in *Republic*

17 There are, however, two major differences between Plato and Lewis and Tolkien. First, Lewis and Tolkien seem to think that their (non-historically true) myths directly imitate divine realities, whereas for Plato they would first be imitations of the sensible world, and *then* (thus, indirectly) imitations of the intelligible, divine world. Second, there would seem to be another significant difference between Lewis and Tolkien on the one hand and Plato on the other concerning the epistemological, and perhaps also ethical, value of sub-creations or imitations. In *Republic* 10 (597d-602b), Plato criticizes artistic objects, paintings and poetry among them, which he describes as being imitations of imitations (that is, imitations of earthly things, which are themselves imitations of the Forms), for, *inter alia*, being so metaphysically inferior to what they indirectly imitate (the Forms) that they cannot allow us to adequately grasp or know the truth about the Forms. Indeed, Plato seems to think, though perhaps he is speaking hyperbolically, that sub-creations and art objects allow *no* grasp of the truth of the Forms (600e-601b). Consequently, he concludes that imitative poetry is not a serious endeavor (599a, 602b). Tolkien and Lewis, it seems, would strongly disagree.

6-7. Just as the visible Sun both causes the growth and nourishment (that is, the existence) of visible things on earth and also illumines them (that is, grants them visibility), so does the intelligible Sun, the Good, grant existence and intelligibility to the Forms and, through them, to the objects of the visible world (*Republic* 509b). Thus, Tolkien not only used light-based and solar imagery in a Platonic context, illustrating the metaphysical relationship between imitations and divine realities, but he even did so, consciously or not, in a Platonic way: that is, his two metaphors of divine Light parallel the two functions of Plato's Sun. For Tolkien, the Sun represents the divine Reality that makes the attenuated reality or truth of certain mythopoeic sub-creations possible, just as for Plato it represents the divine Reality that makes the lesser reality of the empirical world possible.

Lewis also used light-based and solar imagery to describe the metaphysics of mythopoeia, explaining in prose what Tolkien had expressed in poetry. His most concise statement comes from *Reflections on the Psalms*: "The resemblance between these myths [of dying and rising gods like Balder and Adonis] and the Christian truth is no more accidental than the resemblance between the sun and the sun's reflection in a pond" (107).[18] But not only do non-historically true myths resemble "the Christian truth" in a non-accidental, and therefore significant way, as all genuine images or likenesses or reflections must significantly resemble their originals. The relation, at least for Lewis, is far closer than that. Some quality or feature of the higher object is truly, though in a lesser fashion, conveyed by some quality or feature of the lower object. The sun's light is actually present, though not in its completeness or full intensity, in its reflection in the pond. Likewise, as Lewis claims in *Miracles*, a non-historically true myth is,

---

18 Here, "the Christian truth" is the sun, as in his closing *dictum* from 'Is Theology Poetry?': "I believe in Christianity as I believe that the Sun has risen, not only because I see it but because by it, I see everything else" (165). In other places Lewis makes God the sun: see, for example, *The Problem of Pain*, "A blessed spirit is a mould ever more and more patient of the bright metal poured into it, a body ever more completely uncovered to the blaze of the spiritual sun" (139). In *Mere Christianity*, God as the Sun confers goodness (like light) upon us, just as Plato's Good makes its participants good: the Christian "does not think God will love us because we are good, but that God will make us good because He loves us; just as the roof of a greenhouse does not attract the sun because it is bright, but becomes bright because the sun shines on it" (50). Or, again, in *Letters to Malcolm: Chiefly on Prayer*, "Adoration says, 'What must be the quality of that Being whose far-off and momentary coruscations are like this!' One's mind runs back up the sunbeam to the sun" (118). To date there are three major studies of Lewis's light-based and solar imagery: Ward 2008, ch. 5 on 'Sol;' Starr 2012 (especially 100-02 on 'The Weight of Plato'), and McGrath 2014 (especially 93 on Plato).

"at its best, a real though unfocussed gleam of divine truth falling on human imagination" (161). The light of God, the spiritual Sun, is somehow present to our minds in appreciating these pagan myths. To use one of Lewis's technical terms, the infinite meaning of divine truth has been *transposed*, in however humble a fashion, into meaning(s) graspable by the human imagination. What he says of pictorial and artistic sub-creations in 'Transposition' would also, it seems, apply to mythopoeic sub-creations:

> The suns and lamps in pictures seem to shine only because real suns or lamps shine on them; that is, they seem to shine a great deal because they really shine a little in reflecting their archetypes. The sunlight in a picture is therefore not related to real sunlight simply as written words are to spoken. It is a sign, but also something more than a sign, and not only a sign because it is also more than a sign, because in it the thing signified is really in a certain mode present. (102)[19]

Unlike Tolkien's language in 'Mythopoeia,' which may or may not have been consciously influenced by his knowledge of Plato, Lewis's language about sunlight and reflected archetypes in 'Transposition' is deliberately Platonic. Or at least, if it was not in 1944 when the sermon was originally preached, it became so when he revised it in 1961 (Hooper 2001: 19). For the heart of the passage that he added is a philosophical fable modeled after, though by no

19 See also *Surprised by Joy*: "The comparison is of course between something of infinite moment and something very small; like comparison between the Sun and the Sun's reflection in a dewdrop. Indeed, in my view, very like it, for I do not think the resemblance between the Christian and the merely imaginative experience is accidental. I think that all things, in their way, reflect heavenly truth, the imagination not least. 'Reflect' is the important word. This lower life of the imagination is not a beginning of, nor a step towards, the higher life of the spirit, merely an image. In me, at any rate, it contained no element either of belief or of ethics; however far pursued, it would never have made me either wiser or better. But it still had, at however many removes, the shape of the reality it reflected" (159).

means a simple retelling of, the Allegory of the Cave.[20] A mother gives birth to her son in a dungeon. Like the prisoners in Plato's Cave, chained to the floor in such a way that they can only see the shadows cast on the wall in front of them (514a), the boy "grows up seeing nothing but the dungeon walls," though unlike them he can also see "the straw on the floor, and a little patch of the sky seen through the grating, which is too high up to show anything except sky" ('Transposition' 109). His mother, a skilled draughtswoman, tries, for the most part unsuccessfully, to convince him through her drawings "that the outer world is far more interesting and glorious than anything in the dungeon" (110). Likewise, Plato's escaped prisoner, having returned to the Cave to rescue the others, unsuccessfully tries to explain to them that the shadows they see pale in comparison to the real things above ground (517a). And Lewis's fable ends where the escape of Plato's prisoner had culminated (516b), with a vision of "the blaze of the risen sun" ('Transposition' 111). For both Lewis and Tolkien, then, the relation between objects illuminated by the sun and the sun itself captures the metaphysical relation between non-historically true myths and their dependence on, and even their participation in, a divine source of meaning.

(3) The Allegory of the Cave also raises yet another aspect of Platonic metaphysics that Tolkien and Lewis accepted and made use of in their notion of non-historically true myth: namely, the idea of levels or hierarchical kinds of reality. We have already observed Plato's distinction between different levels or kinds of reality in the Cave: each step upwards, from the shadows on the wall to the natural and celestial bodies that represent the Forms, brings with it an increase in being or reality. Whatever it means, philosophically, to say

20 There are significant differences in detail and overall purpose between Lewis and Plato's fables. On the whole Plato's takes a more negative view of the empirical world by emphasizing how shadowy and unreal things underground are. Lewis, in addition to acknowledging this approach, also offers a more positive take on the empirical world by showing how the realities outside the dungeon are validly conveyed by their pictorial representations. The mother's two-dimensional pencil drawings are *transpositions*, and not merely counterfeit copies, of three-dimensional qualities. Lewis's story also owes something to Edwin A. Abbott's *Flatland* (1884). But the primary connection between this passage and Plato's Allegory of the Cave, which deserves further development, seems to be hardly acknowledged in the scholarship. Rare instances of such an acknowledgement include Clarke, who calls the fable in 'Transposition' "an obvious adaptation" of the Cave (2017: 49) and Lisa Moate (2015: 158-59). Andrew Walker also points out that the notion of transposition itself is Platonic, but draws no comparison to the Allegory of the Cave specifically (2002: 29, 31). Far more frequently noted is Lewis's use of the Cave in *The Silver Chair*, ch. 12: see Bryson (2021: 8-10), Chapa (2016: 64-68), Duriez (2013: 246), Fisher (2010: 5-6); Joeckel (1997) 8-11, Johnson and Houtman (1986: 80), Matthews (2005: 173), McGrath (2013: 301-02); Moate (2015: 114-24), Simmons and Simmons (1991: 12-15), Starr (2009: 13-14), and Tiffany (2014: 364-65).

that one thing has 'more reality' or '*is* more' than another, or that one thing is 'more true' than another, this is the language Plato uses in *Republic* 7. In one passage he describes what the experience of the newly released prisoner of the Cave would be like. At first, when he is brought above ground, he would mistakenly believe that the underground things he had turned from were ἀληθέστερα (515d) "*more true than* the ones he was now being shown" (transl. G.M.A. Grube, rev. C.D.C. Reeve; emphasis added) in the sunlit world above ground. But in fact, his upward journey has brought him "closer to the things that are" and turn him πρὸς μᾶλλον ὄντα (515d) "towards the things that are more." For the Forms "are more," have more reality, are "more true" than the things which merely resemble them in the Cave.

The phrases ἀληθέστερα "more true" and μᾶλλον ὄντα (515d) "are more" are synonymous here, allowing us to use phrases like 'levels or kinds of reality' and 'levels or kinds of truth' synonymously. For by 'true' Plato does not mean propositional truth as opposed to propositional falsehood, but what is real and original as opposed to what is only by imitation or resemblance or likeness. To use the example from book 10 of the *Republic*, the painting of a bed is not *really* a bed (or, not a 'true' bed) though we may call it such. But, according to Plato, even a bed made by a carpenter (and not a mere pictorial representation by a painter) is not *really* a bed in comparison with the Form of Bed. For, as he says, only the Form of Bed is κλίνης [...] ὄντως οὔσης (*Republic* 597d), the "truly real bed." The real Bed, the true Bed, is the Form. Thus for Plato the highest level, or primary kind, of 'reality' or 'truth' is the reality or truth of the Forms. The reality of the physical world, where things such as beds made by carpenters exist, insofar as it imitates or strives to be like the Forms, is secondary to them. There is primary reality and secondary reality. And the reality of artistic representation, such as the painting of the bed, insofar as it imitates or strives to be like the secondary reality of the physical world, occupies a tertiary level of reality. The closer one approaches to the primary reality of the Forms, the more real or true things become.

We find similar language and concepts in both Lewis and Tolkien. In 'On Fairy-stories,' Tolkien contrasts "the real (primary) world," the created world of time and space, with the mythmaker's sub-created "Secondary World" (52). Likewise, there is the truth of the primary world and the truth of the secondary world, to which we accord Primary and Secondary or literary Belief, respectively (52). In Tolkien's essay, however, these levels of reality or truth are not always arranged simply on the basis of the principle of resemblance or likeness, as in Plato. But in 'Mythopoeia,' they are. Recall the line in which he writes of the blessed in heaven receiving "from mirrored truth the likeness of the True" (90). "[M]irrored truth" is clearly subordinate to 'the True' with a capital T; the former is secondary, the latter primary, just as a reflection in a mirror is subordinate to its original. But not only are there levels of truth or reality; they are related by virtue of likeness, just as a reflection in a mirror is a likeness of its original. For the blessed receive "from mirrored truth the *likeness* of the True" (90), just as Plato would say that the likeness of the Forms can be discerned even in the spatiotemporal world.

Lewis, too, relied on these aspects of Platonic (or at least, idealistic) metaphysics in a passage we have already discussed: namely, his letter of October 18, 1931 to Arthur Greeves. To discern the presence of such concepts in this letter, it will help to realize that Lewis here makes use of both senses of true myth, though he does not himself draw the distinction between them. For we find that he not only wrote of "the story of Christ" as "a true myth" insofar as "*it really happened*" (*CL I* 977; emphasis original) – that is, in the sense of its being an historically true myth – but also that he treated the story of Christ, in another respect, as a non-historically true myth. Just as we saw in Plato's Allegory of the Cave, we find in Lewis's letter different levels or kinds of reality, and thus of truth as well. Lewis gives us a threefold hierarchy: (1) God, (2) the created world and its historical events, and (3) doctrines about those events. And just as the Forms anchored Plato's kinds of reality theory according to how directly the lower levels echoed or resembled or imitated them, so Lewis arranges these levels of reality according to how directly they reveal God's nature. God directly expresses Himself through the actual events of the Christian story in history, or, as Lewis puts it, "Christianity is God expressing Himself through what we call 'real things'" (*CL I* 977); and the actual events of the Christian story in history are in turn expressed in our doctrines about them, thus indirectly revealing God's nature. These doctrines are certainly true; but they are, as Lewis says, "of course *less* true" than the events which they are about: "they are translations into our *concepts* and *ideas* of that wh. God has already expressed in a language more adequate, namely the actual incarnation, crucifixion, and resurrection" (977; emphasis original). Therefore these "actual" events are *more true* – remember Plato's language in *Republic* 7 – than their doctrinal counterparts. But by the same reasoning, these events are themselves less true than the highest level of reality, namely the being of God Himself. As we ascend levels of reality, we also ascend levels of truth, just as we would expect in a Platonic metaphysical context.

Understanding this letter in a Platonic metaphysical context, which supplies us with its own peculiar meaning of the term 'true,' also avoids a philosophical problem. For Lewis's key phrase "*less* true" (977) is inexplicable if we take 'true' to mean 'historically true.' For historical claims are true if and only if they correspond to some actual event; if they do not, they are not true. Strictly speaking, there are no comparative levels of historical truth: that is to say, historical claims, or indeed, any claims of any sort, cannot be more or less true. When they correspond to reality, they are true; when they do not, no matter how small the deviation may be, they are false. 'Caesar crossed the Rubicon in 49 BC' is true; but if we substitute any other year for 49, even if it is increased or decreased by only one or two years, the claim would still be equally false. Thus, Lewis's use of the comparative "*less* true" reveals, on a charitable interpretation, that he cannot be thinking of something historically or propositionally true at that point in the letter. Therefore, when he says that "The 'doctrines' we get *out* of the true myth are of course *less* true" (*CL I* 977), he must mean 'true myth' in a non-historical, non-propositional sense. Given the context of levels of reality, that sense takes on a decidedly Platonic, or at least idealistic,[21] metaphysical flavor.

(4) Finally, the Tolkienian act of sub-creation itself is, at least in part, based on the Platonic concept of sub-creation. We have already observed Tolkien's idea in 'Mythopoeia' that the sub-creator imitates God the Creator precisely by sub-creating. To demonstrate the Platonic roots of this idea, we must turn to the

21 Lewis held a similar position even as a non-Christian idealist. See his 'Replies to Objections in Detail' in the 'Great War' papers: "The doctrine of levels or degrees of reality may be stated thus. For every soul there is something objective and something subjective: but when what is objective to A [e.g., Hamlet] is subjective to B [e.g., Shakespeare], when that in which A exists itself exists in B, then B is said to be on a higher level of reality than A" (128). This was written sometime between November 1928 and June 1930.

*Timaeus*, which is, *inter alia*, Plato's account of cosmology and cosmogony.[22] It is his cosmogony that interests us here, and particularly the ways in which it parallels Tolkien's cosmogony in the *Ainulindalë*. Plato describes a divine Craftsman (δημιουργός or 'Demiurge' in Greek; *Timaeus* 28a6) who (a) initially begins and also (b) helps to shape the universe after its beginning. These two functions of Plato's Demiurge are split by Tolkien into the one uncreated God, Eru, or Ilúvatar, who creates the universe and all other rational beings, on the one hand, and the created gods, or Valar, who help to shape the universe after its creation, on the other. We will consider first how Plato's Demiurge parallels Tolkien's Ilúvatar, and then how the Demiurge parallels Tolkien's Valar.

First, then, in the *Timaeus*, the Demiurge directly addresses the gods whom he has created about their future task of shaping the world. He begins with an assertion of his ultimate authority over their actions: "O gods, works divine whose maker and father I am, whatever has come to be by my hands cannot be undone but by my consent" (*Timaeus* 41b, transl. Donald Zeyl). Likewise in the *Ainulindalë*, Ilúvatar creates the gods and then speaks to them directly. In one of his speeches, he conveys to them the same notion of final authority over their actions: "no theme may be played that hath not its uttermost source in me, nor can any alter the music in my despite" (*Sil* 6). Second, both Plato and Tolkien are anxious to define the relationship between the supreme rational being (the Demiurge, Ilúvatar), the gods, and lower rational creatures, especially human beings. Tolkien makes it clear that Ilúvatar alone creates other rational beings, including human beings. On the other hand, the Demiurge delegates the creation of human beings to the gods. And though this is a significant difference between Plato's supreme being and Tolkien's (it may, in fact, have been a conscious reaction on Tolkien's part to the *Timaeus* in obedience to the Christian account of human creation), the way in which Plato's Demiurge entrusts this task to the gods is significant: for he does so in terms of sub-creation as imitating himself, a divine being. Speaking of human beings, the Demiurge says to the gods:

22 It is also the source of the Atlantis myth, which partially inspired the creation of Tolkien's Númenor. For the fullest treatment of this connection to date see Kleu 2021. For additional insightful parallels between the *Timaeus* and Tolkien's cosmogony, see Korpua (2015: 47-52).

> But if these creatures came to be and came to share in life by my hand, they would rival the gods. It is you, then, who must turn yourselves to the task of fashioning these living things, as your nature allows. This will assure their mortality, and this whole universe will really be a completed whole. *Imitate the power I used in causing you to be* [μιμούμενοι τὴν ἐμὴν δύναμιν περὶ τὴν ὑμετέραν γένεσιν]. [...] I shall begin by sowing that seed, and then hand it over to you. The rest of the task is yours. (*Timaeus* 41c-d; emphasis added)

Not only is the Demiurge assigning a task of sub-creation to lower rational beings (the gods), as Tolkien's Ilúvatar does (*Sil* 4); he explicitly points out the way in which sub-creation imitates his own divine creativity. Sub-creation imitates divine creation in both Plato and Tolkien.

So far we have only compared the Demiurge with Ilúvatar, or God. Now we will observe another significant parallel between the Demiurge and Tolkien's gods, or the Valar. The parallel is simply this: they all continue to shape the universe, using their creative, or rather, sub-creative talents to order it and bring it from chaos to greater stages of organization. Plato writes of the chaotic initial stages of the universe:

> The god wanted everything to be good and nothing to be bad so far as that was possible, and so he took over all that was visible – not at rest but in discordant and disorderly motion – and brought it from a state of disorder to one of order, because he believed that order was in every way better than disorder. (*Timaeus* 30a)

Likewise, the task Tolkien assigned to the Valar in his cosmogony was for them to bring the universe from disorder to order:

> But when the Valar entered into Eä they were at first astounded and at a loss, for it was as if naught was yet made which they had seen in vision, and all was but on point to begin and yet unshaped, and it was dark. For the Great Music had been but the growth and flowering of thought in the Timeless Halls, and the Vision only a foreshowing; but now they had entered in at the beginning of Time, and the Valar perceived that the World had been but foreshadowed and foresung, and they must achieve it. So began their great labours in wastes unmeasured and unexplored, and in ages uncounted and forgotten, until in the Deeps of Time and in the midst of the vast halls of Eä there came to be that hour and that place where was made the habitation of the Children of Ilúvatar. (*Sil* 8)

Tolkien's Valar were, in this respect, in his cosmogony what the Demiurge was in Plato's. We should not be surprised, then, to find, as Verlyn Flieger has pointed out, that "The adjective Tolkien used to describe the labors of the Valar in making the world is *demiurgic*" (2002: 55; emphasis original).[23] Sub-creation, then, and its connection to divine powers was, at least for Tolkien, a thoroughly and consciously Platonic idea.

Only some of the connections between Plato's metaphysics and Tolkien and Lewis's second sense of true myth have been identified here: the metaphysics of resemblance or likeness, solar imagery, levels of reality or truth, and sub-creation. Other strong links exist between Plato's philosophy and their theory of true myth more broadly: for example, their collective concern with, and response to, the charge of escapism, which would criticize their keen interest in other worlds for being out of touch with truth and reality; the parallel between Platonic *eros* as the motive force for reaching the heavenly intelligible world and Tolkien's longing for the True West and Lewis's Joy or romantic longing as motive forces for reaching towards heaven;[24] and, perhaps most importantly, the fact that Plato himself philosophized in a mythopoeic fashion, constructing various kinds of myths and images for purposes similar, or at least comparable, to those of Tolkien and Lewis. The persistent trend in Inklings scholarship of identifying their philosophy as some form of 'Christian Platonism' or 'Christian Neoplatonism' is a valid, accurate, and insightful one.[25]

## About the Author

Justin Keena received his Master of Studies in Ancient Philosophy from Oxford University in 2012. He has since taught Classics at Franciscan University of Steubenville and rhetoric and writing at the Catholic University of America, where he also earned an MA in English. He currently resides in New Hampshire with his family, working as a web developer and teaching Ancient Greek philosophy at Nashua Community College. He maintains a website collecting all the rare and obscure works of C.S. Lewis (https://jwkeena.github.io/csl-opera-obscura/).

23 However, Flieger does not provide a reference to any particular instance of this word. For one of them, see *Morgoth's Ring*. There, Tolkien describes the Valar as having "been for nameless ages engaged in a demiurgic labour completing to the design of Eru the structure of the Universe" (330). For additional instances applied to the Valar, see also *Morgoth's Ring* 330, 370, and 395, as well as Fimi (2019), for Tolkien's use of the word in some of his voice recordings.

24 For Lewis's Joy and Platonic *eros*, see Baker (2016: *passim*), Barkman (2009: 68-71 and 81-85), Johnson and Houtman (1986: 81-82), and Sellars (2011: 80-87).

25 See, for example, Barkman (2009: 5), Clarke (2017: 29), Cox (1984: 53), Rose (1982: 203 *et passim*), Johnson and Houtman (1986: 76), Moate (2015: 47-70), and Tyson (2014: 23).

## Bibliography

BAKER, Samuel. 2017. 'Platonic *Eros* and 'Soul-Leading' in C.S. Lewis.' *Brill's Companion to the Reception of Classics in International Modernism and the Avant-Garde*. Eds. Adam J. Goldwyn and James Nikopoulos. Leiden: Brill, 199-219.

BARKMAN, Adam. 2009. *C.S. Lewis & Philosophy as a Way of Life: A Comprehensive Historical Examination of his Philosophical Thoughts*. Allentown, PA: Zossima.

BRAZIER, P.H. 2009. 'C.S. Lewis: A Doctrine of Transposition.' *The Heythrop Journal* 50.4, 669-88.

BRYSON, James. 2021. "It's all in Plato': Platonism, Cambridge Platonism, and C.S. Lewis.' *The Journal of Inklings Studies* 11.1, 1-34.

CARPENTER, Humphrey. 2000. *Tolkien: A Biography*. New York: Houghton Mifflin.

CHAPA, Joseph. 2016. 'Puddleglum, Pascal, and Plato.' *VII: An Anglo-American Literary Review* 33, 62-72.

CLARKE, Richard L.W. 2017. 'The Neo-Platonic Christianity of C.S. Lewis.' *Sehnsucht: The C.S. Lewis Journal* 11, 29-62.

COX, John. 1984. 'Tolkien's Platonic Fantasy.' *VII: An Anglo-American Literary Review* 5, 53-67.

DE ARMAS, Frederick A. 1994. "'Gyges' Ring: Invisibility in Plato, Tolkien, and Lope de Vega." *Journal of the Fantastic* 3.4, 120-38.

DICKERSON, Matthew and David O'HARA. 2009. *Narnia and the Fields of Arbol: The Environmental Vision of C.S. Lewis*. Lexington, KY: University of Kentucky Press.

DURIEZ, Colin. 2013. *The A-Z of C.S. Lewis: An Encyclopaedia of His Life, Thought, and Writings*. Oxford: Lion Books.

EDWARDS, Mark. 2010. 'Classicist.' *The Cambridge Companion to C.S. Lewis*. Eds. Robert MacSwain and Michael Ward. Cambridge: Cambridge University Press, 58-74.

FIMI, Dimitra. 5 May 2019. 'Demiurgic Beings: A Platonic Word in Tolkien', http://dimitrafimi.com/2019/05/05/demiurgic-beings-a-platonic-word-in-tolkien. Accessed 23 June 2021.

FISHER, H. Dennis. 2010. 'C.S. Lewis, Platonism, and Aslan's Country: Symbols of Heaven in the Chronicles of Narnia.' *Inklings Forever* 7, Article 5.

FLIEGER, Verlyn. 1986. 'Naming the Unnameable: The Neoplatonic 'One' in Tolkien's *Silmarillion*.' *Diakonia: Studies in Honor of Robert T. Meyer*. Eds. Thomas Halton and Joseph P. Williman. Washington, DC: The Catholic University of America Press, 127-32.

2002. *Splintered Light: Logos and Language in Tolkien's World*. Kent, OH: Kent State University Press.

FORD, Paul F. 2005. *Companion to Narnia: A Complete Guide to the Magical World of C.S. Lewis's* The Chronicles of Narnia. New York: HarperSanFrancisco.

HERBERT, Gary B. 1985. 'Tolkien's Tom Bombadil and the Platonic Ring of Gyges.' *Extrapolation* 26.2, 152-59.

HERMANN, Frank. 2015. 'The Disordered Soul: Platonic Injustice and the Law of Nature in the Writings of C.S. Lewis.' *Duchovná cesta a jej podoby v literature*. Ed. Magda Kučerková. Nitra: Univerzita Konštantína Filozofa, 158-66.

HOOPER, Walter. 1996. *C.S. Lewis: A Companion & Guide*. New York: HarperSanFrancisco.

2001. 'Introduction.' *C.S. Lewis. The Weight of Glory and Other Addresses*. New York: HarperCollins, 1-21.

JOECKEL, Samuel T. 1997. 'In Search of Narnia on a Platonic Map of Progressive Cognition.' *Mythlore* 22.1, 8-11.

JOHNSON, William G. and Marcia K. HOUTMAN. 1986. 'Platonic Shadows in C.S. Lewis's Narnia Chronicles.' *Modern Fiction Studies* 32.1, 75-87.

KATZ, Eric. 2003. 'The Rings of Tolkien and Plato: Lessons in Power, Choice, and Morality.' *The Lord of the Rings and Philosophy*. Eds. Gregory Bassham and Eric Bronson. Chicago, IL: Open Court, 5-20.

KLEU, Michael. 2021. 'Plato's Atlantis and the Post-Platonic Tradition in Tolkien's Downfall of Númenor.' *Tolkien and the Classical World*. Ed. Hamish Williams. Zurich and Jena: Walking Tree Publishers, 193-215.

KORPUA, Jyrki. 2015. *Constructive Mythopoetics in J.R.R. Tolkien's Legendarium*. Tampere: Juvenes Print.

LEWIS, Clive Staples. 1936. *The Allegory of Love*. Oxford: Oxford University Press.

2015. 'Clivi Hamiltonis Summae Metaphysices Contra Anthroposophos Libri II.' *The 'Great War' of Owen Barfield and C.S. Lewis: Philosophical Writings, 1927-1930*. Eds. Norbert Feinendegen and Arend Smilde. *Inklings Studies Supplements* 1, 58-102.

2004. *The Collected Letters of C.S. Lewis. Vol. I: Family Letters 1905-1931*. Ed. Walter Hooper. San Francisco: HarperSanFrancisco.

2004. *The Collected Letters of C.S. Lewis. Vol. II: Books, Broadcasts, and the War 1931-1949*. Ed. Walter Hooper. San Francisco: HarperSanFrancisco.

1964. *The Discarded Image: An Introduction to Medieval and Renaissance Literature*. Cambridge: Cambridge University Press.

1954. *English Literature in the Sixteenth Century Excluding Drama*. Oxford: Oxford University Press.

2012. *An Experiment in Criticism*. Cambridge: Cambridge University Press.

1962. 'Is Theology Poetry?' *They Asked for a Paper*. London: Geoffrey Bles, 150-65.

2014. *The Last Battle*. London: HarperCollins.

1964. *Letters to Malcolm: Chiefly on Prayer*. London: Geoffrey Bles.

2014. *The Lion, the Witch and the Wardrobe*. London: HarperCollins.

1947. *Miracles*. London: Geoffrey Bles.

1971. 'Myth Became Fact.' *Undeceptions*. London: Geoffrey Bles, 39-43.

1938. *Out of the Silent Planet*. London: The Bodley Head.

1943. *Perelandra*. London: The Bodley Head.

1943. *The Pilgrim's Regress*. London: Geoffrey Bles.

1940. *The Problem of Pain*. London: Geoffrey Bles.

1958. *Reflections on the Psalms*. London: Geoffrey Bles.

2015. 'Replies to Objections in Detail.' *The 'Great War' of Owen Barfield and C.S. Lewis: Philosophical Writings, 1927-1930*. Eds. Norbert Feinendegen and Arend Smilde. *Inklings Studies Supplements* 1, 124-30.

1960. *Studies in Words*. Cambridge: Cambridge University Press.

1955. *Surprised by Joy*. London: Geoffrey Bles.

2001. 'Transposition.' *The Weight of Glory and Other Addresses*. New York: HarperCollins, 91-115.

2014. *The Voyage of the Dawn Treader*. London: HarperCollins.

1948. 'Williams and the Arthuriad.' *Arthurian Torso: Containing the Posthumous Fragment of the Figure of Arthur*. London: Oxford University Press, 91-200.

2001. 'The Weight of Glory.' *The Weight of Glory and Other Addresses*. New York: HarperCollins, 25-46.

McGrath, Alister. 2014. 'The Privileging of Vision: Lewis's Metaphors of Light, Sun, and Sight.' *The Intellectual World of C.S. Lewis*. Oxford: Wiley-Blackwell, 83-104.

Moate, Lisa. 2015. *Through the Shadowlands: Platonism in the Works of C.S. Lewis*, https://researchrepository.murdoch.edu.au/id/eprint/28350/. Accessed 23 June 2021.

Morse, Robert E. 1980. 'Rings of Power in Plato and Tolkien.' *Mythlore* 7.3, 38.

Muth, Michael. 2008. 'Beastly Metaphysics: The Beasts of Narnia and Lewis' Reclamation of Medieval Sacramental Metaphysics.' *C.S. Lewis as Philosopher: Truth, Goodness, and Beauty*. Eds. David Baggett, Gary R. Habermas and Jerry L. Walls. Downer's Grove, IL: InterVarsity Press Academic, 228-44.

Nagy, Gergely. 2004. 'Saving the Myths: The Re-creation of Mythology in Plato and Tolkien.' *Tolkien and the Invention of Myth: A Reader*. Ed. Jane Chance. Lexington, KY: University Press of Kentucky, 81-100.

Neubauer, Łukasz. 2021. 'Less Consciously at First but More Consciously in the Revision: Plato's Ring of Gyges as a Putative Source of Inspiration for Tolkien's Ring of Power.' *Tolkien and the Classical World*. Ed. Hamish Williams. Zurich and Jena: Walking Tree Publishers, 217-46.

Plato. 1997. *Complete Works*. Ed. John M. Cooper. Indianapolis/Cambridge: Hackett.

*Platonis Opera*. 5 vols. Ed. John Burnet. Oxford: Clarendon Press, 1900-07.

*Phaedo*. Transl. G.M.A. Grube, 49-100.

*Phaedrus*. Transl. Alexander Nehamas and Paul Woodruff, 506-56.

*Republic*. Transl. G.M.A. Grube, rev. C.D.C. Reeve, 971-1223.

*Symposium*. Transl. Alexander Nehamas and Paul Woodruff, 457-505.

*Timaeus*. Transl. Donald Zeyl, 1224-91.

Riga, Frank. 1992. 'The platonic imagery of George MacDonald and C.S. Lewis: The allegory of the cave transfigured.' *For the Childlike: George MacDonald's Fantasies for Children*. Ed. Roderick McGillis. Methuen, NJ & London: Scarecrow, 111-32.

Rose, Mary Carman. 1982. 'The Christian Platonism of C.S. Lewis, J.R.R. Tolkien, and Charles Williams.' *Neoplatonism and Christian Thought*. Ed. Dominic O'Meara. Albany, NY: State University of New York Press, 203-12.

Sellars, Jeff T. 2011. *Reasoning Beyond Reason: Imagination as a Theological Source in C.S. Lewis*. Eugene, OR: Pickwick Publications.

Simmons, Courtney Lynn and Joe Simmons. 1991. 'The Silver Chair and Plato's Allegory of the Cave: Archetypes of Spiritual Liberation.' *Mythlore* 17.4, 12-15.

Starr, Charlie W. 2009. 'The Silver Chair and the Silver Screen: C.S. Lewis on Myth, Fairy Tale, and Film.' *Revisiting Narnia: Fantasy, Myth and Religion in C.S. Lewis's Chronicles*. Ed. Shanna Caughey. Dallas, TX: BenBella Books, 3-23.

2012. *Light: C.S. Lewis's First and Final Short Story*. Hamden, CT: Winged Lion Press.

Tiffany, Grace. 2014. 'C.S. Lewis: The Anti-Platonic Platonist.' *Christianity and Literature* 63.3, 357-71.

Tolkien, John Ronald Reuel. 2008. *Tolkien On Fairy-stories*. Expanded edition, with commentary and notes. Eds. Verlyn Flieger and Douglas A. Anderson. London: HarperCollins.

1994. 'The Geste of Beren and Lúthien.' *The Lays of Beleriand*. The History of Middle-earth 3. Ed. Christopher Tolkien. New York: Ballantine, 184-85.

2001. 'Leaf by Niggle.' *Tree and Leaf including the poem Mythopoeia. The Homecoming of Beorhtnoth*. London: HarperCollins, 91-118.

1981. *The Letters of J.R.R. Tolkien*. Ed. Humphrey Carpenter with the assistance of Christopher Tolkien. London: George Allen & Unwin.

2005. *The Lord of the Rings. Part 1. The Fellowship of the Ring*. London: HarperCollins.

1993. *Morgoth's Ring: The Later Silmarillion*. The History of Middle-earth 10. Ed. Christopher Tolkien. Boston: Houghton Mifflin Company.

2001. 'Mythopoeia.' *Tree and Leaf including the poem Mythopoeia. The Homecoming of Beorhtnoth*. London: HarperCollins, 83-90.

2006. *The Silmarillion*. Ed. Christopher Tolkien. London: HarperCollins.

Tyson, Paul. 2014. *Returning to Reality: Christian Platonism for Our Times*. Portland, OR: Cascade.

Ward, Michael. 2008. *Planet Narnia: The Seven Heavens in the Imagination of C.S. Lewis*. Oxford: Oxford University Press.

Wendling, Susan. 2016. 'Henry More and C.S. Lewis: Cambridge Platonism and its Influence on Lewis's Life and Thought.' *Inklings Forever: Published Colloquium Proceedings 1997-2016*, 10, 102-13.

Williams, Brian M. 2021. *C.S. Lewis: Pre-Evangelism for a Post-Christian World: Why Narnia Might be More Real Than We Think*. Cambridge, OH: Christian Publishing House.

Walker, Andrew. 2002. 'Scripture, Revelation and Platonism in C.S. Lewis.' *Scottish Journal of Theology* 55/1, 19-35.

Weinreich, Frank. 2008. 'Metaphysics of Myth: The Platonic Ontology of 'Mythopoeia'.' *Tolkien's Shorter Works. Essays of the Jena Conference 2007.* Eds. Margaret Hiley and Frank Weinreich. Zurich and Jena: Walking Tree Publishers, 325-47.

Piotr Anicet Gruszczyński


# "What *do* they teach them at these schools?": A Critique of Modern and Postmodern Outlook in the Writings of Lewis and Tolkien

**Abstract**

C.S. Lewis and J.R.R. Tolkien are indisputably among the most popular contemporary writers of fiction. Paradoxically, though, they never had great expectations of publishing success; nor are they really 'contemporary' in the sense that their books do not suit our times. In their works, both writers present an outlook that seems more characteristic of Antiquity and the Middle Ages. Hence, it is often at odds with modernity and postmodernity, seeing modern thinking as a growing menace to mankind. The aim of the chapter is to demonstrate how this outlook manifests itself in the works that flowed from their pens, in the reality that Lewis refers to in *The Discarded Image* as 'the Model.' While dealing with the thought of Tolkien, it draws chiefly on his Legendarium and correspondence. When it comes to the ideas of his fellow Inkling, however, its main focus is on the two cycles of novels – *The Chronicles of Narnia* and *The Space Trilogy* – as well as his theological and scholarly books, which often provide a context for Lewis's fiction. The first part deals with Lewis's views on opinions concerning three worldviews, namely: natural, modern and so-called 'moral nihilism.' The second one looks at the works of Tolkien, focusing on the struggle between the malevolent 'Machine' and the old-fashioned communities of the Shire, Rohan and Gondor. The last part reveals the two writers' intentions to use literature as a link between modernity and tradition in order to help mankind see the beauty of the world and find in it the meaning of life.

"Bless me, what *do* they teach them at these schools?" (*LWW* 197; emphasis original) wonders Professor Kirke at the end of the first book of *The Chronicles of Narnia*,[1] after the four Pevensie children have given him an account of the startling adventures they had in the land beyond the doors of an old wardrobe. Contrary to their expectations, the professor is not really surprised, and he does not find their words incredible. In fact, he seems to believe their story even more than they do. As he advises the Pevensies not to spread a word about it, they decide to keep it solely in their hearts, at the same time, willingly

1 *The Lion, the Witch and the Wardrobe* is the first book in the order of publication, not the chronology of events.

or not, accepting the fact that there is a great abyss between our world and the one beyond the wardrobe. The old professor rejects this division when, echoing the words of Aslan (189-90), he utters the famous words: "Once a King in Narnia, always a King in Narnia" (196), in this way placing the responsibility for the disjunction in their perceptionof the schooling system, which, in his opinion, lacks something important.

Let us therefore take a closer look at the subject of schools as presented by C.S. Lewis in *The Chronicles of Narnia*, first focusing on the Experiment House that Eustace Scrubb and Jill Pole attend in *The Silver Chair*. Although there is no further information about it in the Narniad, it seems clear from the context that this school constitutes only one piece within a larger system aimed at perverting young minds. One of these minds belongs to Eustace, the character who appears in the last three books of the cycle. From the opening pages of *The Voyage of the Dawn Treader*, where Eustace makes his first appearance, one may be intrigued by the fact that there are also some 'modern rules' in his family home: his parents are called by their first names (rather than 'Father' and 'Mother'), a special kind of underclothes is worn, whereas meat, alcohol and tobacco are practically forbidden (*VDT* 13). His school is not a place where Eustace could gain real wisdom and experience, but one where he is only fed with information (13). It is no place for fairytales, so when Eustace eventually enters one, it causes him a lot of suffering, in that he becomes disconnected from the only reality he knows. The gentle rocking of Caspian's ship is interpreted by him as a storm, as Eustace sees the vessel being hit by huge waves, while "all the others pretend to take no notice of this" (40). He loses even the sense of time. Not only is Eustace unable to experience the fairyland with which he is presented, but he has, in fact, lost the ability of logical thinking. He even presents Caspian with a theory that high perspiration during rowing can lower the temperature of the body, and therefore diminish the need for consumption of water, the supplies of which are running out onboard the ship (81). Eustace's own 'logic' then allows him to 'rationally' explain his attempt at stealing water. Fortunately, this changes radically as a result of his meeting with Aslan, although the character of this transformation is actually not seen by some as being good at all. For his progressive parents, for instance, he seems to have become "very commonplace and tiresome" (256).

This sense of his losing touch with reality – whether in Narnia, or in the primary world – could only be compared with the situation in which a group of Dwarfs find themselves in chapter 13 of *The Last Battle* ('How the Dwarfs Refused to be Taken In'), although it appears that the latter is actually far worse. The Dwarfs cannot even smell the scent of wild violets, instead sensing the stink of "filthy Stable-litter" (*LB* 177). Likewise, they take the delicious dishes presented to them for "hay[,] a bit of an old turnip and [...] a raw cabbage leaf" (180). Nothing, it seems, can make them experience the world of reality in the way it actually is. Instead, they shut themselves away in their own world of illusions, and even Aslan cannot release them from this mental prison.

Let us now take one more look at the Experiment House that Eustace and Jill are said to attend in *The Silver Chair*. This co-educational, or "mixed," school (*SC* 13), Lewis comments, is "not nearly so mixed as the minds of the people who ran it" (13). The teachers are not really interested in the improvement of the children, because, for them, difficult pupils can make interesting psychological cases. Indeed, the actual effect of the stress-free education they provide there is that stronger boys and girls bully the weak ones. We also learn that swearing on the Bible is not encouraged at the Experiment House (17). Even the intervention of Aslan does not improve this situation. The Head is fired, but she manages to find another and more responsible job as an Inspector, and later becomes a member of the Parliament "where she lived happily ever after" (253).

All this seems to imply that C.S. Lewis considered schools as a potential threat, but in saying so one would only be scratching the surface of this complex issue. The last reference to the ills of modern schooling, so explicitly echoing the first one – "It's all in Plato, all in Plato: bless me, what *do* they teach them at these schools!" (*LB* 206; emphasis original) – makes it quite clear that the root of the problem lies not in the process of education itself, but in what is taught and learned: the modern outlook, which means that, among other things, children are not meant to be open to the ideas conveyed by non-mimetic narratives like fairy tales and legends. Therefore, the aim of this chapter is not to provide a critique of school as an institution, but to explore the way in which reality is perceived. This will be examined in three stages. The first part looks at some of the major points concerning this issue in Lewis's thought. The second is devoted to Tolkien and his critique of the malevolent 'Machine.' The last part discusses the way in which, according to both authors, the mythical can help to regain the natural worldview.

## The Three Worldviews

A suitable introduction to some of the concepts that will be discussed below, may be found in Lewis's novel *That Hideous Strength*. In it, 'the Belbury people,' affiliated with the National Institute of Coordinated Experiments (N.I.C.E.), seek full control over the globe, and in doing so they plan to exploit the power of the wizard Merlin, whom they bring back to life. What they, however, fail to realise, is that the way in which Merlin perceives the world is radically unlike their own worldview and the goals of their Institute:

> Merlin is the reverse of Belbury. He's at the opposite extreme. He is the last vestige of an old order in which matter and spirit were, from our modern point of view, confused. For him every operation on Nature is a kind of personal contact, like coaxing a child or stroking one's horse. After him came the modern man to whom Nature is something dead — a machine to be worked, and taken to bits if it won't work the way he pleases. Finally, come the Belbury people, who take over that view from the modern man unaltered and simply want to increase their power by tacking onto it the aid of spirits — extra-natural, anti-natural spirits. (*THS* 621)

On the basis of the above quotation, one can distinguish between three distinct worldviews.[2] The first one is the 'natural worldview,' expressing itself in the unity of the spirit and the body, of the divine and the human, so common in many cultures of Antiquity and the Middle Ages, one that ceased to be dominant in Europe with the dawn of the Renaissance. The second one is the 'modern' worldview, characterised by the precedence of science and power over spirituality. As for the third worldview, while Lewis does not provide his readers with any specific term, in *The Abolition of Man* he writes about the so-called 'Conditioners' and their plans of transforming the civilisation. In *The Cosmic Trilogy*, he makes a clear distinction between that kind of view and other outlooks. In contrast to the 'modern' one, the worldview of the 'Conditioners' is open to the supernatural, but reflects a desire to use it in order to achieve their own goals. The repudiation of all values (except for those construed by the

2 For an in-depth treatment of this issue, see Gruszczyński (2019).

'Conditioners') distinguishes them from the first, natural worldview. For this, I will use Marek Oziewicz's term "moral nihilism" (2005: 320).

## 1. The Natural Outlook

For a more in-depth look into Lewis's ideas, let us now consider Professor Kirke's exclamation "it's all in Plato" (*LB* 206) and broaden the scope of our enquiry by first examining the ancient philosophical thought concerning the order of the world. Looking at the heavens and the earth, human society and into themselves, some of the early Greek thinkers noticed that everything seems to be arranged in rational patterns. The proper word to describe this is the κόσμος (Maryniarczyk et al. 2004: 891-95), literally meaning 'a beautiful world,' a semantically broad term that covers a wide range of areas, including political and social. A *cosmos* is thus a reality which is well-arranged, ordered, and, at least in theory, beautiful. This is how Plato describes it in the *Gorgias*:

> And philosophers tell us, Callicles, that communion and friendship and orderliness and temperance and justice bind together heaven and earth and gods and men, and that this universe is therefore called Cosmos or order, not disorder or misrule, my friend. (507d-508a)

Why should the world be seen as a well-arranged reality? The roots of Greek philosophy are to be found in the attempt to identify the so-called ἀρχή, the principle on which the existence of the world is based. Not a physical or chemical element, but a metaphysical one. Perhaps the first man ever to identify ἀρχή as λόγος, the principle standing behind the unity and harmony of all beings, was Heraclitus. Despite the fact that, in his opinion, everything in the world is changeable (πάντα ῥεῖ), the world itself remains quite static. The principle of its self-identity is therefore not to be found inside but outside of it, in the dynamic divine thought, likened by Heraclitus to fire (Leszczyński 2003: 59-69). A similar idea of a uniting principle can be found in many philosophical schools of Ancient Greece and Rome. Anaxagoras called it νοῦς 'the mind,' the Pythagoreans saw it in numbers, and Plato in the idea of 'the Good,' also called 'the One.' Aristotle had a slightly different view on the matter, inspired by Democritus, the precursor of materialism and determinism, claiming that the world is nothing but the effect of an accidental collisions of atoms. In his doctrine of the four causes, he also speaks of the final cause, the very reason for the existence of all being. Hence, it might be said that, just like the other philosophers, Aristotle also sees the uniting principle of the world in the ἀρχή, although his understanding of it seems to be more intrinsic. Finally, the Stoics also used the term coined by Heraclitus, however giving it a wider meaning. For them, the *logos* constitutes not only the ontic principle, the design of the world, but it is also to be identified with logic, the area of human thought and ethic principles (Reale 1994 (1): 109, 185-86; 1994 (2): 113-16, 155, 401-02;1994 (3): 331-33).

The idea of a unifying principle of the world is, however, neither exclusively Greek, nor is it, in fact, a purely philosophical one. The history of religion tracks this concept back to various early cultures and polytheistic beliefs. The Hindus, for instance, named it *tad ekam*, 'this One' (Eliade 1988: 159; Leszczyński 2003: 20-5). Over the centuries, the beliefs of many peoples evolved from polytheism to henotheism, and ultimately to monotheism. It can therefore be quite safely assumed that the thoughts which led the religious founders and reformers to this path towards monotheism arose from their reflections on morality. After all, the very existence of an idea of morality and stability of its rules inevitably raises the question of its foundations, something that is 'beyond.' As Lewis points out in *The Abolition of Man* and *Mere Christianity*, there must be a single principle behind the unity of the ethical rules of all ancient cultures, the foundation of all moral systems; to name it he uses the Chinese term *tao* (*AM* 15-16).

The advent of Christianity did not make this worldview in any way obsolete. Indeed, it rather gave it a special framework. Meditating on Christ, who, through His Resurrection, revealed Himself as the Lord of the heavenly and earthly reality, Christians began to apply to Him the term λόγος. Jesus Christ is God's Thought, the eternal Plan by which the world was created, and the Providence whose paths lead to the ultimate fulfilment. In this view, Christian theology is, in some sense, a rightful heir to Ancient Greek thought (Świeżawski 2000: 255; Leszczyński 2003: 12). This can be seen with even more clarity through the legacy of Boethius, the man who stands not only between philosophy and theology, but also between Antiquity and the Middle Ages. It is this sixth-century scholar who may be credited with the construction of what, in *The Discarded Image*, Lewis calls 'the Model' (11), a coherent combination of the Christian faith and everything that preceded it. By continuously referring to the ancient philosophical thought and mythology, Boethius builds an intricate, if not always dogmatically consistent, portrait of the Christian God, aptly demonstrating the uniformity of providence, order of fate, unpredictability of chance, divine knowledge, predestination, and free will (*De consolatione philosophiae* book IV, chapter 6).[3]

What does 'the Model' stand for in the mind of C.S. Lewis? The Middle Ages was by no means a 'dark' period. In fact, in some areas of philosophical inquiry, medieval scholars drew abundantly from the work of their predecessors: Greeks and Romans as well as the inheritors of Classical Greco-Roman culture. No doubt, this organizing factor can be found in Christianity. Indeed, it is inherent in its nature, and thus perfectly capable of incorporating the rich legacy of the past centuries. However, all the many pieces of this medieval puzzle could not be so easily pieced together. This is how Lewis puts it:

> All the apparent contradictions must be harmonised. A Model must be built which will get everything in without a clash; and it can do this only by becoming intricate, by mediating its unity through a great, and finely ordered, multiplicity. This task, I believe, the Medievals would in any case have undertaken. But they had a further inducement in the fact that it had already been begun, and indeed carried a fair way. In the last age of antiquity many writers [...] were, perhaps half-consciously, gathering together and harmonising views of very different origin: building a syncretistic Model not only out of Platonic, Aristotelian, and Stoical, but out of Pagan and Christian elements. This Model the Middle Ages adopted and perfected. (*DI* 11-12)

Such eclectic aspirations were, according to Lewis, particularly well expressed in two medieval works of thought and art: the *Summa Theologica* and the *Divine Comedy*. Saint Thomas Aquinas, the author of the former, set for himself the goal of adapting Aristotle's metaphysics to Christian theology. Although he carefully distinguished between faith and reason, giving them different roles in the process of cognition, Aquinas also clearly stated that both faith and reason ultimately recognise the same truth: "everything that is true, regardless of who says it, comes from the Holy Spirit" (*Expositio in evangelium Ioannis* 1, 4b, lect. III, fn. 103). In the light of this, a pagan philosopher can also be a guide for a

3 This treatise was an important source for both Lewis and Tolkien. As far as the latter is concerned, the issue is widely discussed by Bratford Eden (2003: 183-93), Kathleen Dubs (2004: 133-42), Helen Lasseter (2006), and Olli-Pekka Vainio (2020). C.S. Lewis very often refers to Boethius in his works, in fact even calling *De Consolatione* the most important book of the Middle Ages (*DI* 75).

believer on the path to salvation, as may be seen in the *Divine Comedy*, a kind of a poetic encyclopaedia of the Middle Ages which seamlessly chains together Christian and pagan thought. What makes it possible is the existence of the unifying principle, λόγος, thanks to which the world can be seen in a more holistic manner.

## 2. The Modern Outlook

The above-outlined natural worldview was replaced by the modern outlook. Lewis himself places this breakthrough in the 1800s, although its effects are not clearly visible until the following century, the age of machines, the theory of evolution, and the "myth of progress" ('*De Descriptione Temporum*' 10-11). In fact, this paradigm shift may have begun a few centuries earlier, with the dawn of nominalism in the fourteenth century. Denying a clear connection between the name and the object resulted in a gradual decay of the holistic view of the world. As a result, around the time of the Renaissance, science began to develop so rapidly that humanity would understand the world more in detail, but less as a whole. In consequence, the question of the ἀρχή became marginalised, first in metaphysics, then in ethics (with individualism and subjectivity rapidly growing in importance over the centuries). Eventually, man's perception of the world (and of man himself) became fragmentary, uncertain and contingent. Zygmunt Bauman calls it 'fluidity,' thus recalling the Heraclitan concept of constant flux (πάντα ῥεῖ), although it needs to be stressed that, while for Heraclitus the world constituted a unity thanks to λόγος, in the modern era this perspective has been seriously undermined (Urbaniak 2014: 6).

How does this fragmentation of reality manifest itself in the eyes of Lewis? The world (as well as mankind itself) has ceased to be an object of man's admiration, and thus become the object of extensive exploitation. That is why, in Lewis's own words, "Cutting trees and cutting them into boards, we see neither dryads nor beautiful natural phenomena in them. [...] The stars lost their divinity with the development of astronomy, and in the era of fertilizers there is no place for a Dying God" (*AM* 42).[4] This does not mean, of course, that scientific and techni-

4 The idea of "a Dying God" is an allusion to the deities of vegetation, dying for the winter only to be resurrected in the spring.

cal development processes are in themselves negative. Indeed, scientists are often the ones who are still able to be amazed by the world of reality, thus upholding the Buberian 'I-Thou' relationship with it (*AM* 42, 46). Lewis is also aware of the fact that man's power over Nature is really the power of one man over another, thus ultimately (and paradoxically) giving it the power over humanity, as man begins to be less and less distinguishable from it. This situation bears striking resemblance to the Faustian bargain, the one in which man gives his soul to the devil in order to gain power and knowledge, only to find out in the end that this power and knowledge belong to him no longer (*AM* 34-35, 42-43). In the poem 'Pan's Purge,' Lewis puts it in a very comprehensive way: the 'victory' over nature, as symbolised by Pan's funeral, has proved to be futile:

> And now, descending, ravening, loud and large, the avalanche,
> And after it the earthquake, was loosed upon Man.
> Towering and cloven-hoofed, the power of Pan came over us,
> Stamped, bit, tore, broke. It was the end of Man. (l. 5)

Lewis's prose abounds in the examples of such a utilitarian approach to reality. One of them is provided in *The Magician's Nephew* by Uncle Andrew, a self-taught wizard whose main concern is the lack of 'specimens' to experiment on (34). In *Out of the Silent Planet*, Devine and Weston treat their houseboy Harry in a similar manner – that is to say, not as a human being but a "preparation" (17) – although their reasons are rather different. Devine's only goal is profit (27), as is also the case with Gumpas, the Governor of the Lonely Islands, whose justification of slave trade lies in what he sees as the need for modernisation and development (*VDT* 67). Weston's goal is a more sophisticated one: the ultimate triumph of the human race. Achieving this goal is worth sacrificing the weak and unproductive units of his own race, not to mention other intelligent races and Nature itself:

> Life is greater than any system of morality; her claims are absolute. It is not by tribal taboos and copy-book maxims that she has pursued her relentless march from the amoeba to man and from man to civilisation. [...] It is in her right, the right, or, if you will, the might of Life herself, that I am prepared without flinching to plant the flag of man on the soil of Malacandra: to march on, step by step, superseding, where necessary, the lower forms of life that we find, claiming planet after planet, system after system, till our posterity – whatever strange form and yet unguessed mentality they have assumed – dwell in the universe wherever the universe is habitable. (*OSP* 123-24)

### 3. Moral Nihilism

It is rather difficult to draw a clear line distinguishing between the modern worldview and moral nihilism. As has been noted, the latter is characterised by the use of natural and supernatural powers. The application of magic is, however, in many ways not much different from the utilitarian approach to reality exemplified by modern science and technology. According to Lewis, "For the wise men of old the cardinal problem had been how to conform the soul to reality, and the solution had been knowledge, self-discipline, and virtue. For magic and applied science alike the problem is how to subdue reality to the wishes of man: the solution is a technique" (*AM* 45).

In order to provide a good illustration of what constitutes moral nihilism, two other notions need to be mentioned. First of all, by subjecting nature to man, man effectively subjects one person to another, or, more precisely, to the elite group that Lewis calls "the Conditioners" (*AM* 34-38). Secondly, these 'Conditioners' regularly put themselves above all values. It does not, however, mean the end of values as such. Along with education (or, rather, propaganda) and eugenics, the system of values they hold is useful as a tool of power, their content depends entirely on the whims of the planners of a new humanity. Paradoxically, people at the bottom of this hierarchical pyramid are much happier, being even endowed with some sort of substitute of conscience. Following Boethius (*De consolatione* book IV, chapter 3 and song 3), Lewis sees these 'Conditioners,' as those who have completely lost their sense of humanity (*AM* 38-39).

The very term 'Conditioners' (in the sense of those who place themselves above good and evil), may sound rather enigmatic, almost as if Lewis were a proponent of some conspiracy theory. However, this concept perfectly reflects the relationship that exists between *The Abolition of Man* and *That Hideous Strength*, indeed, a perfect illustration of the theses laid out in the present chapter (*THS* 345). In the novel, the 'Conditioners' are the people of Belbury, with N.I.C.E. always working in the background. One of them is the deputy headmaster Wither, who, in many ways, reflects the above-outlined history of philosophy:

> He had long ceased to believe in knowledge itself. What had been in his far-off youth a merely aesthetic repugnance to realities that were crude or vulgar, had deepened and darkened, year after year, into a fixed refusal of everything

> that was in any degree other than himself. He had passed from Hegel into Hume, thence through Pragmatism, and thence through Logical Positivism, and out at last into complete void. The indicative mood now corresponded to no thought that his mind could entertain. He had willed with his whole heart that there should be no reality and no truth. (*THS* 688)

Belbury provides a vivid illustration of how the 'Conditioners' may strive to change the world. The first stage of the process is the remodelling of human thinking by means of creative journalism. Mark Studdock, advised by Devine, is wondering how the 'proper' use of words can modify people's attitude to a given issue (*THS* 380).[5] Devine also has far-reaching plans for an extensive interference in human life through, among others, birth control and mass sterilisation, which is, in fact, a eugenics programme, aimed at 'prenatal education' based on psychological, biological and neurological stimulation. The outcome of this process is a new type of human being, one totally subordinated to the 'Conditioners' (379). Compared to this, Filostrato's plans of clearing the entire planet of trees and the elimination of its fauna seem to be a child's play. Moreover, the joy and fertility of human sexuality also appear to be a threat. The new civilisation will therefore have to manage thoroughly without the organic matter. What constitutes the human mind will be transferred to a machine (408-09). In other words, the aim of the 'Conditioners' is

> To bring out of that cocoon of organic life which sheltered the babyhood of mind the New Man, the man who will not die, the artificial man, free from Nature. Nature is the ladder we have climbed up by, now we kick her away. (*THS* 513)

The aim of the Institute is only seemingly mundane. In fact, it subjects the world to a supernatural, though not divine, reality. Michael Ward notes some striking similarities between the works of, on the one hand, Lewis, and, on the other, George Orwell, who, in his *Nineteen Eighty-Four*, also warns against totalitarianism. However, whereas for Orwell this danger has its roots in bad philosophy, not perceiving the place of a man as God's beloved creature, Lewis sees the threat as "coming through bureaucrats, planners and philosophers alike, from a far deeper and darker source" (Ward 2008: 149). The head of N.I.C.E. is not simply a resurrected head of Alcasan, but the epiphany and incarnation

5 Although the topic of education is generally absent in the novel, the term "experimental school" in the above-quoted passage clearly has a close connection with the school that Eustace attends.

of the Lord of Sulva, the fallen archon of the Earth, Satan, in the same way in which he mastered the body of Weston in *Perelandra*. Alcasan's Head is worshiped as a god and is offered human sacrifices (*THS* 689-91). The activity of N.I.C.E is, in fact, an action directed against God, a parody of the Kingdom of Heaven and the resurrection of Christ. Therefore, the necessary initiation for its adepts is trampling on the Cross (415-17, 670-02). The basic anthropological truth that man is God's creation, is reversed: here, as Straik declares, God is created by man (515). That is why God will claim his rights. Although He is far on the horizon of the events in *The Cosmic Trilogy*, He acts through His servants, the archons of the planets, who give their powers to Merlin, whose words – "They that have despised the word of God, from them shall the word of man also be taken away" (*THS* 686) – demonstrate that this war is taking place in the name of God.

## The Tolkienian 'Machine'

Unlike his friend and fellow Inkling, Tolkien does not devote any special place in his works to describing the intricacies of the history of worldviews and ideas. This does not, however, mean that he did not undertake this type of reflection at all. As his letters clearly demonstrate, in constructing his Legendarium, he focused on something else, a meticulous description of the world of the past which could then be made more accessible to the modern reader. A brilliant illustration of this attitude is his Elves, who, as Andrzej Szyjewski puts it, constitute the memory of Arda (2004: 22-23). Indeed, their songs provide a vivid insight into the history of Tolkien's world, one that can be read in the way one reads a book (22-23).

This spirit of the past is also present in the communities of men. During their quest, two of the Hobbits, Merry and Pippin, reach Gondor, the kingdom whose rebuilding and reuniting with Arnor is compared by Tolkien to the re-establishment of the Holy Roman Empire (*Letters* 376, #294). The Rohirrim, on the other hand, often evoke associations with the Anglo-Saxons,[6] particularly with regard to their language, elegiac songs, and desperate courage in the face

6 However, as Tom Shippey states, they "are not to be equated with the Anglo-Saxons of history, but with those of poetry, or legend" (1992:112)

of danger and death. The Hobbits themselves are also 'English' in their own way, but belonging to a different era: the simple inhabitants of Warwickshire villages of the period of Queen Victoria's Diamond Jubilee (*Letters* 230, #178). The world described in *The Lord of the Rings* is thus a world of the past, with Tolkien consciously alluding to several layers of history, the contrast between them being one of the sources of his success as a writer of fiction.

However, despite being markedly different from one another in a great number of aspects, all of the above-described communities – the Gondorians, the Rohirrim, and the Hobbits – evidently share the same goal: to survive the invasion of the malevolent 'Machine.'[7] The Kingdom of Gondor is, in fact, born of its people's confrontation with Sauron. For many centuries, its history has been that of endless wars with Mordor and its allies. The image of the two towers, Minas Tirith and Minas Ithil, looking at each other from across the Anduin, as well as the ruins of Osgiliath, may give the impression of some kind of equality between the two opponents and their powers. A closer analysis of their conflict in *The Lord of the Rings* reveals, however, that the forces of Gondor and Mordor are entirely different from one another. Sauron's realm could definitely be seen as the more 'industrialised' of the two. In the words of Tolkien,

> Neither he [Sam] nor Frodo knew anything of the great slave-worked fields away south in this wide realm, beyond the fumes of the Mountain by the dark sad waters of Lake Núrnen; nor of the great roads that ran away east and south to tributary lands, from which the soldiers of the Tower brought long wagon-trains of goods and booty and fresh slaves. Here in the northward regions were the mines and forges, and the musterings of long-planned war; and here the Dark Power, moving it armies like pieces on the board, was gathering them together. (*RK* 923)

The most important 'forge' of Mordor is, of course, Mount Doom, where the most powerful weapon of Sauron is forged, namely the One Ring. The organisation of Mordor's troops is also remarkable. Soldiers are typically referred to by their numbers, and ruled with a hard hand, living in constant fear of the Nazgûl (*RK* 925). The Gondorian troops are presented in a completely different way, being subordinate to their leaders not by means of power and fear, but through their loyalty and love. In a similar way, the Grey Company follows Aragorn to the Paths of the Dead motivated solely by the love for their leader (*RK* 781). There

7 For a more in-depth examination of this topic, see Gruszczyński (2018: 152-60).

is no room for any slavish devotion there. In effect, the foremost objective of Sauron (and his servants) is power, while those of the Captains of the West are best expressed in the following words of Faramir:

> For myself, I would see the White Tree in flower again in the courts of the kings, and the Silver Crown return, and Minas Tirith in peace: Minas Anor again as of old, full of light, high and fair, beautiful as a queen among other queens: not a mistress of many slaves, nay, not even a kind mistress of willing slaves. War must be, while we defend our lives against a destroyer who would devour all; but I do not love the bright sword for its sharpness, nor the arrow for its swiftness, nor the warrior for his glory. I love only that which they defend: the city of the Men of Númenor; and I would have her loved for her memory, her ancientry, her beauty, and her present wisdom. Not feared, save as men may fear the dignity of a man, old and wise. (*TT* 671-72)

A similar opposition can be seen in the conflict between Isengard and the Kingdom of Rohan. The Rohirrim are a simple folk whose culture is largely based on oral tradition and songs, and whose history is resplendent with the accounts of their struggles against the shadows of evil (*UT* 373-98). Their opponent, Saruman, is, on the other hand, a glaring illustration of how knowledge could be used in order to gain power. In Shippey's words, he is therefore "a technologist" (2000: 170-01), a man who, in the eyes of Treebeard, "has a mind of metal and wheels" (*TT* 472). Without any regret, Saruman turns the beautiful, green circle of Isengard into a smoking factory where weapons are produced. Likewise, the neighbouring woodland area is cleared, and the timber is used as fuel. Finally, and no less shockingly, Isengard is also some sort of centre for 'genetic engineering,' a place where humans and orcs are crossbred, producing a host of menacing Uruk-hai.

The third invasion concerns the Shire, a peaceful country of, literally and figuratively, little people. Like Gondorians, Hobbits are an 'ancient folk,' far from lusting for power, desiring "peace and quiet, and good, tilled earth" (*FR* 1). They are also characterised by their aversion to advanced technology, with "forge-bellows, a water-mill or a hand-loom" being just enough for their needs (1). Their language and culture are in some sense similar to those of the Rohirrim, and, in the end, they have to face the very same threat. Saruman's invasion in the Shire is a two-step process. In the first phase, using Lotho Sackville-Baggins as his puppet ruler, he revolutionises the whole structure of the Hobbit economy, thus transforming it from an agricultural country to an industrial one, crushing the free market and private property in order to supplant it with central planning. The destruction seems nearly complete, with the ever-present smoke, stench, and pollution of water. Perhaps the best symbol of these changes is Ted Sandyman's mill, purchased from the miller by Lotho Sackville-Baggins (Pimple). In the words of Farmer Cotton,

> He'd funny ideas, had Pimple. Seems he wanted to own everything himself, and then order other folk about. [...] he was always grabbing more [...] mills and malt-houses and inns, and farms, and leaf-plantations. He'd already bought Sandyman's mill [...]. Pimple knocked it down almost as soon as he came to Bag End. Then he brought in a log o' dirty-looking Men to build a bigger one and fill in full o' wheels and outlandish contraptions. Only that fool Ted was pleased by that, and he works there cleaning wheels for the Men, where his dad was the Miller and his own master. (*RK* 1012-13)

The second stage of the invasion is the introduction of martial law, with the plundering activity of Sharkey's ruffians causing constant shortages of basic commodities. Civil authority is also abolished, and the only thing that is not lacking is the growing host of the police forces: the so-called "gatherers" and "sharers," who actually do "more gathering than sharing" (*RK* 999).[8]

The governmental techniques of Sauron and Saruman are thus perfect examples of what, in his letter to Milton Waldman, Tolkien calls "the Machine" (*Letters* 145, #131). Next to the Fall and Mortality, it is also one of the main themes of *The Lord of the Rings.* Tolkien refers to it as

> [the] use of external plans or devices (apparatus) instead of development of the inherent inner powers or talents – or even the use of these talents with the corrupted motive of dominating: bulldozing the real world, or coercing other wills. (145-46, #131)

Not surprisingly, his description agrees with what, in *The Abolition of Man*, Lewis writes about magic and technology, namely that the 'Machine' has a "more obvious modern form though more closely related to Magic than is usually recognized" (*Letters* 146, #131). In Tolkien's works, however, the word

---

8 The situation may be reminiscent to those who lived in the Polish People's Republic at the time of Martial Law (1981-1983): long queues in front of shops, where there was hardly anything to buy, ration cards, censorship, arrests and internments. The system eventually collapsed due to the loss of its social mandate and the 'Solidarity' grassroots movement. One could say, perhaps, that, in a way, Tolkien turned out to be a prophet.

'magic' is quite ambiguous.[9] When Sam wants to see some Elf-magic, Galadriel leads him to distinguish between "the deceits of the Enemy" and "the magic of Galadriel" (*FR* 362).[10] The former, whose focus is on "domination and tyrannous re-forming of Creation" (*Letters* 146, #131), is one of the forms of 'the Machine.' The latter offers an extension of sub-creation and its object is "Art, delivered from many of its human limitations" (146, #131). Indeed, Sam even feels the "Elf-magic" spring from the connection of the land and its inhabitants (*FR* 362).

If there is anything magical in Gondor, Rohan and the Shire, it is some form of enchantment. The healing powers of Aragorn are firmly grounded in his royal dignity and elvish ancestry as well as the virtues of *athelas*, the Kingsfoil. When it comes to Hobbits, their only 'magic' is the ability to move noiselessly, which, in fact, has nothing to do with magic, and is only perceived as such by the Big Folk (*FR* 1). These communities evidently oppose the crushing steamroller of magic and technology with the powers that are of a wholly different kind: the solidarity of their citizens, courage and sacrifice, and an emotional attachment to their respective lands, all of which give them the motivation to fight. To these, one should also add the powers of nature: the aid that comes unexpectedly from the Ents, the landform of Helm's Deep, the speed of their horses, and, no less importantly, the support of the Forest People, Drúedain, the most primitive of all the peoples of Arda.

Like Lewis, Tolkien notes that the 'Machine' is not just an aberration of human dreams of world domination, but a tool in the hands of a primordial force. Saruman and Sauron come from outside Middle-earth and they are representatives of someone greater, the Lord of Darkness beyond the Walls of the World – the first unconsciously so, by falling into pride and lust for power, the second openly desiring Morgoth's return and being in opposition to "Eru, a phantom devised in the folly of [the Valar's] hearts" (*Sil* 147). Gandalf describes Sauron as "but a servant or emissary" (*RK* 879), but in the Third Age, Sauron

9 The theme of magic in Tolkien's works is a matter of great complexity. Here only one distinction, between *goeteia* and the enchantment, is made, but it very difficult to draw a line between good and evil magic. For further reading, see Hutton (2016).

10 "For this is what your folk would call magic, I believe; though I do not understand clearly what they mean; and they seem to use the same word of the deceits of the Enemy. But this, if you will, is the magic of Galadriel" (*FR* 362).

officially claims to be "Morgoth retuned," demanding from his servants a well-nigh divine worship (*Letters* 154, #131; 243, #183).

This is in many ways similar to what Lewis argues for in *That Hideous Strength*. Since, in Tolkien's work, the evil 'Machine' has an anti-divine origin, fighting it cannot be a purely human matter. Indeed, it is not in the power of the free peoples of Middle-earth to defeat Sauron and Saruman. They have to remain on guard, and, when the opportunity arises, step up to fulfil their mission, making good use of, as Gandalf says, "the time given to [them]" (*FR* 51), the victory really coming from beyond the boundaries of the world by way of 'fate,' one of Tolkien's 'names' for Eru (*NME* 228). Indeed, this comes through divine providence, working first in Bilbo and then in Frodo in their role as the Ringbearers. The destruction of the Ring of Power eventually becomes possible not through the efforts of the Fellowship of the Ring, but as a result of the mercy shown to Gollum (*FR* 59-60; *Letters* 234-35, #181). God, "that one ever-present Person who is never-absent and never-named" (*Letters* 253, #192), fights against the forces of Evil because only He, and no one else, to use the words from 'Myths Transformed,' the final part of *Morgoth's Ring*, can rewrite the story of Arda (392). This is confirmed by the symbolism behind the day of Sauron's fall, 25 March. Shippey sees it as a reminiscence of the date of Christ's death (2000: 208-09), while Alison Milbank links it with the memory of the Incarnation (2008: 101). This multiple symbolism includes both the announcement of future salvific events – Middle-earth is, after all, not a Christian world but a pre-Christian one – and the fruits of Redemption already present in the history of Tolkien's world.

## The Living Past

The questions that should now be asked are: (1) what did these two writers really want to achieve?, and (2) did they not know the impossibility of turning the clock back? As for the second question, they certainly knew this. Although their works of fiction are immersed in the natural, pre-modern worldview, they knew very well that a time machine of the type described by Wells does not exist. Is it then the case that their literary works were intended to be no more than a nostalgic commemoration of the past and a manifesto against the contemporary fallen world? Well, it could be argued that both Lewis and Tolkien were firmly convinced that it is indeed possible to construct a time machine, although of an entirely different kind.

One major source of their inspiration was certainly Owen Barfield's concept of the original unity of words and their meanings, although Barfield himself is rarely quoted directly in Lewis's writings (but often enough to make us aware of his influence, for instance in *Perelandra* (172) and *That Hideous Strength* (596)). This theory, Verlyn Flieger argues, had a significant impact on Tolkien's "holistic outlook" (2002: 35). Barfield's theory concerns the evolution of language, progressively differentiating the meaning of the words and separating them from the reality they describe. Hence, going back in time until the moment in which myths were born, one can see how they once again could be brought into semantic unity. Words and expressions in the 'primeval language' were not in any way ambiguous; each had a single, undivided meaning. Back then, people could not even think of the separation of the spiritual and the bodily, of the human and the divine. In our times, the separated meanings of words can only meet in a poetic metaphor, whose kiss can bring life back to the reality locked in the Castle of Logic (Barfield 2010: 80, 109).[11] One may therefore say, with only some exaggeration, that literature is indeed a time machine.

In the mid-1930s, both writers decided to write "books [they themselves] want[ed] to read", that is to say on time- (Tolkien) and space-travel (Lewis), each narrative culminating in the discovery of Myth (*Letters* 29, #24; 209, #159). Lewis's novel, *Out of the Silent Planet*, not planned at the time to be the first part of *The Space Trilogy*, was written without any delay. Tolkien's story, *The Lost Road*, however, got stuck after a few chapters and was never completed. In fact, however, neither Lewis's success nor Tolkien's failure to write their respective stories meant the end of their plans. Lewis subsequently wrote a number of mythopoetic novels, including two other volumes of *The Space Trilogy*, The *Chronicles of Narnia*, and *Till We Have Faces*, while Tolkien transferred some of the ideas from *The Lost Road* to his opus magnum, namely *The Lord of the Rings*. The assignation of the topics that the two writers agreed on would also

11 In the light of this theory one may better comprehend Lewis's claim that the Middle Ages were an epoch of people who "could think of two things at the same time" (*AL* 173).

be blurred. Lewis's books, such as the unfinished novel *The Dark Tower*, deal with both time- and space-travel, thus opening the perspective of renewing original harmony between the planets of the Field of Arbol and their inhabitants, taking us to the age of the dawn of myth (*Narnia*), and showing the process of myth formation (*Till We Have Faces*). In Tolkien's stories, on the other hand, the principal narrative axis is the motif of the quest. In his wanderings and adventures, Tolkien's hero comes in contact with new lands and people, an experience that often has a formative effect on his character.

The poetic effect of this may be demonstrated on two examples. The first of these is the conversation between Professor Kirke and the four Pevensies. When the children are convinced that the chapter of their life titled 'Narnia' is irretrievably closed, the old professor adopts an entirely different view, famously exclaiming: "Once a King in Narnia, always a King in Narnia" (*LWW* 196). In this way, he makes them realise that the Narnian experience, an experience he also had himself as a young boy in *The Magician's Nephew*, will allow them to see further into the world in which they now live. This would then be the fruit of the "real metaphor" that Barfield argues for in his book: it gives one not only pleasure but also knowledge, deepens consciousness, and allows one to see the world as something more than mere sensual perception could allow for (2010: 44-48).

Some characters in *The Lord of the Ring* also go through a similar experience. Éomer, for instance, approaches the wanderers that he encountered in the steppes of Rohan with the following question:

> 'Do we walk in legends or in the green earth in the daylight?'

To which Aragorn replies:

> 'A man may do both'[...]. 'For not we but those who come after will make the legends of our time. The green earth, say you? That is a mighty matter of legend, though you tread it under the light of day!' (*TT* 434)

What constitutes the 'matter of legend' for Éomer – the Hobbits and the Ents – in less than a month will become reality, bringing salvation from the threat of 'the Machine.'

It is a much better machine than the time machine of H.G. Wells. It allows one to connect both worlds, enjoy their benefits simultaneously, without having to choose only one of them. But this distant, 'secondary' world cannot be experienced in the same way as the 'primary' one. In one of the afore-cited passages, Faramir shows this difference by saying: "I would have her loved for her memory, her ancientry, her beauty, and her present wisdom" (*TT* 672). He is well aware of the fact that clinging to the past is a trap his countrymen have often fallen into, holding "old names in the rolls of their descent dearer than the names of sons" (678). Hoarding memories and the desire to stop the flow of time is also the bait with which Sauron lures the Elves, offering them the Rings of Power. Even the Hobbits are not entirely free from this kind of danger: too fond of reciting the genealogies of their families to the ninth generation and carefully commemorating their name days and anniversaries, they are, at the same time, not able to notice the incoming danger. It is impossible to go back to the world of the past. This would be a false escapism, against which both Tolkien and Lewis explicitly warned (*TOFS* 69-70; 'On Three Ways of Writing for Children' 64-65). It is, however, possible to love it for its "beauty" and "ancientry," and draw "present wisdom" from it.

The entire series of *The Chronicles of Narnia* can be viewed as this type of a 'time machine.' Michael Ward, using Lewis's other writings, especially *The Discarded Image*, *The Space Trilogy*, and some poetic works, interprets the cycle as an attempt to recreate a special atmosphere in the spirit of what he calls Lewis's own mythology (2008: 24-25), the ancient image of the universe as planetary spheres surrounding the earth. The technique used by Lewis links the elements of the plot, numerous lexical details and the way in which Aslan is described with the features intuitively associated by the author with celestial bodies, thus creating a special atmosphere for each of the books (42, 74-75). *The Lion, the Witch and the Wardrobe* is thus clothed in the robe of Jupiter, the royal planet, whose joyful ('jovial') spirit is revealed even through such incompatible elements as the figure of Father Christmas, the hearty, jovial, old man who gives special presents to Peter, Susan and Lucy. *Prince Caspian* is immersed in the atmosphere of Mars, the patron god of war as well as forests and game (hence the forest itself comes ready to fight under the command of Aslan). *The Voyage of the Dawn Treader* describes the journey to the land of the Sun and the fight against darkness, vividly symbolised by the dragon that Eustace turns into. *The Silver Chair* is lined up with the concept of the Silver Globe as a border between the sublunary world and the spheres of the heavens that evil cannot reach. There, the wanderings of Eustace and Jill become not just a horizontal journey, but, in fact, a vertical one, from (1) the Land of Aslan, through (2) Narnia and (3) Underland, to (4) the mysterious land of Bism. As they go deeper, the protagonists, can see how easy it is to lose the clarity of one's thought, to forget even about the existence of the higher realm. Mercury, the lord of language, trade and athletics, and the messenger of the gods, overseees the fifth part, *The Horse and His Boy*, where the two children and 'their' horses spare no effort to save Narnia and Archenland. *The Magician's Nephew*, the story of the birth of Narnia, takes place under the auspices of Venus, the goddess of love and fertility. Finally, *The Last Battle* evokes the image of gloomy Saturn, the planet of death and destruction, in whose sphere Dante places the contemplatives (this is probably the reason why Aslan does not reveal himself until the very end of the story, remaining, so to say, 'undercover'). In this interpretation, *The Chronicles of Narnia* is about God the Creator and Saviour, about the created world, and about our place in it. As in the final volume of *The Space Trilogy*, the story thus helps to regain the natural outlook, to see that the "matter and spirit [...] are confused" (*THS* 621).

## Conclusion

To some extent, both writers evidently wished to go back in time in order to catch a glimpse of the past, the time when everything in heaven and earth seemed to be much closer to man. Drawn into the Land of Faëry, the reader should be able to perceive this with ease. By loving that world for its "memory, ancientry and beauty," he or she is granted a "present wisdom" (*TT* 672), so much needed in our modern world. In a sense, he or she becomes an inhabitant of both worlds.

But could this secondary world be interpreted as a world of faith? Should we allow for such a narrow reading, the works of the Inklings would be seen mainly as allegories of Christianity. Of course, in these mysterious realms, extending far beyond the confines of the Old Wardrobe and borders of the Shire, the divine presence may be felt to the degree that is often impossible to be experienced in this world. However, it is also a world of fairy tales, the Land of Faëry, quite different – as the Queen of Elfland explains to Thomas the Rhymer in an old Scottish tale – from heaven and hell. Still, the more this world of faith is mediated by the world of fairy tales, the closer it comes to the sacred. Undoubtedly, in the case of Tolkien and Lewis, this proximity is very near, but it should be neither absolutised nor extended to pertain to all fantasy literature. As the way in which this mediation is carried out is a topic for further discussion, here I will only allow myself to point out two solutions. The first one is based on Ward's idea that the planetary atmosphere of each Narnian story always somehow refers to the Creator of the celestial music of the spheres (2008: 223-24), as in *The Space Trilogy*, where Oyarses are only servants of Maleldil.

Just because God does not show His face does not mean that He is absent and does not act. In *The Chronicles of Narnia*, Lewis reveals to us seven icons of the face of Christ: "King, Leader, Light, Son, Word, Life [and] Mystery" (Ward 2008: 238). However, this is a mediated face, present not only in the transcendence of the coming figure of Aslan, but also in many other, seemingly insignificant, elements of the Narnian novels. Similarly, in the works of Tolkien, although God is always present, though never named (*Letters* 253, #192), thanks to the atmosphere of the world, in which the sacred and the profane are intertwined, this presence can really affect the reader. As can be seen in the strong Christian receptions of both writers, it works very effectively.

The second way of mediation is in the propaedeutics of faith as offered by fairy tales. This is perfectly described by Tolkien in one of the letters to his son Christopher, in which he describes a certain thought present at the gatherings of the Inklings:

> Lewis recently wrote a most interesting essay [...] showing of what great value the 'story-value' was, as mental nourishment – of the whole Chr. story (NT especially). It was a defence of that kind of attitude which we tend to sneer at: the fainthearted that loses faith, but clings as least to the beauty of 'the story' as having some permanent value. His point was that they do still in that way get some nourishment and are not cut off wholly from the sap of life: for the beauty of the story while not necessarily a guarantee if its truth is a concomitant of it, and a fidelis is meant to draw nourishment from the beauty as well as the truth (*Letters* 109, #96).

Towards the end of *The Voyage of the Dawn Treader*, the children are sad because they will not be able to meet Aslan again, to which he replies that he is, in fact, also present in England, although there he is known under a different name: "You must learn to know me by that name. This was the very reason why you were brought to Narnia, that by knowing me here for a little, you may know me better there" (*VDT* 255). Thanks to the beauty of the story, the 'fainthearted' should be able to find a hidden sense in the profession of faith, and see its truth, a truth which, according to Johann Baptist Metz, is by itself incomprehensible in the post-modern world, burnt out like an outdated secret (2008: 72). However, fantasy can revive it and give it a meaning again, thus turning into a sort of *præparatio fidei* for the modern man.

By understanding the relationship between faith and the world of fairy tales in such a way, the distinction which was once proposed by Marek Oziewicz, distinguishing between 'Lewis's religion' (Christianity) and 'religion in Lewis' (Oziewicz calls it 'magic'), appears to be superficial, and thus unnecessary (2005: 208-09). Rather, it could be argued that, in the works of Lewis (and in those of Tolkien), one can see the world of faith through a sort of medieval lens, quite specific of the time when people "could think of two things at the same time" (*AL* 173).

The modern (or post-modern) world, focusing on meticulous analyses of things, and, at the same time, overlooking the need to teach one the ability to see them in a more holistic way, results in the creation of "men without chests" (*AM* 19), men who are not prepared to live by the values. In other words, as Lewis notes in 'Mediation in a Toolshed,' modernity teaches man how to look at a beam of light, but not along with the ray (233). Both authors stress the importance of using the wisdom of the ages past. Although is impossible to eliminate fully the negative aspects of the modernity, to revive old metaphors and tales may help to revive the contemporary man, more and more fragmentary, uncertain and contingent, to see that everything in this changeable world has the meaning in λόγος (cf. Flieger 2002: 39). To put this in figurative terms, while the apple tree from the land of myth, planted in the primary world, may not bear health-restoring fruit, as is the case with Digory's mother, it does nevertheless bring "apples more beautiful than any others in England, [which] will be extremely good for you, though not fully magical" (*MN* 207). Likewise, in the view of Tolkien, the love of Faëry "is essential to the full and proper human development" (*SWM* 131), and so the things forged by Smith Smithson are not only "good and lasting" but also "shapely in their kinds, good to handle and to look at" (17). And this is what fairy tales can give to us.

## About the Author

Piotr Anicet Gruszczyński OFM is a Franciscan friar, vice-rector of the Theological Seminary in Kalwaria Zebrzydowska, and lecturer in fundamental theology and history of religion. He holds a PhD in theology from the John Paul II Catholic University of Lublin. His thesis, *Problematyka zła w twórczości J.R.R. Tolkiena. Ocena w świetle teologii katolickiej* ('The Question of Evil in the Works of J.R.R. Tolkien: A Study in the Light of Catholic Theology' (2017), was published in 2018. He is also the editor of two volumes of essays: *Chrześcijaństwo w epoce smartfonów* ('Christianity in the Era of the Smartphone,' 2014) and *Legendy uświęcone. Twórczość J.R.R. Tolkiena a chrześcijaństwo* ('The Hallowed Legends: The Works of J.R.R. Tolkien and Christianity,' 2016).

## Bibliography

Barfield, Owen. 2010. *Poetic Diction. A Study in Meaning.* Oxford: Barfield Press.

Dubs, Kathleen. 2004. E. 'Providence, Fate, and Chance: Boethian Philosophy in *The Lord of the Rings.*' *Tolkien and the Invention of Myth. A Reader.* Ed. Jane Chance. Lexington, KT: The University Press of Kentucky, 133-42.

Eden, Bradford L. 2003. 'The "Music of the Spheres": Relationships between Tolkien's *The Silmarillion* and Medieval Cosmological and Religious Theory.' *Tolkien the Medievalist.* Ed. Jane Chance. New York and London: Routledge, 183-93.

Eliade, Mircea. 1988. *Historia wierzeń i idei religijnych. Vol. 1: Od epoki kamiennej do misteriów eleuzyńskich.* Transl. Stanisław Tokarski. Warszawa: Instytut Wydawniczy PAX.

Flieger, Verlyn. 2002. *Splintered Light: Logos and Language in Tolkien's World.* Kent, OH and London: The Kent State University Press.

Gruszczyński, Piotr Anicet. 2018. *Problematyka zła w twórczości J.R.R. Tolkiena. Ocena w świetle teologii katolickiej.* Lublin: Wydawnictwo KUL.

2019. 'Koniec człowieczeństwa. J.R.R. Tolkien i C.S. Lewis o kondycji współczesnego człowieka.' *Teologia fundamentalna wobec wyzwań współczesnych nauk o człowieku.* Ed. Przemysław Artemiuk. Płock: Płocki Instytut Wydawniczy, 177-201.

Hutton, Ronald. 2016. 'Tolkien's Magic'. *The Year's Work in Medievalism* 31, 144-53.

Lasseter, Helen T. 2006. *Fate, Providence, and Free Will: Clashing Perspectives of World Order in J.R.R. Tolkien's Middle-earth* (unpublished PhD thesis). <https://baylor-ir.tdl.org/baylor-ir/bitstream/handle/2104/4845/Helen_Lasseter_phd.pdf>.Accessed 20 March 2018.

Leszczyński, Rafał. 2003. *Starożytna koncepcja logosu i jej wpływ na myśl wczesnego chrześcijaństwa*. Warszawa: Wydawnictwo Naukowe Semper.

Lewis, Clive Staples. 2010. *The Abolition of Man*. Las Vegas, NV: Lits.

1958. *The Allegory of Love: A Study in Medieval Tradition*, Oxford: Oxford University Press.

1969. 'De Descriptione Temporum.' *Selected Literary Essays*, Ed. Walter Hooper. Cambridge: Cambridge University Press, 1-14.

2012. *The Discarded Image*. Cambridge: Cambridge University Press.

2014. *The Last Battle*. London: HarperCollins.

2014. *The Lion, the Witch and the Wardrobe*. London: HarperCollins.

2014. *The Magician's Nephew*. London: HarperCollins.

2014. 'Meditation in a Toolshed.' *God in the Dock. Essays on Theology and Ethics*. Ed. Walter Hooper. Grand Rapids, MI and Cambridge: William B. Eerdmans Publishing Company, 230-4.

1982. 'On Three Ways of Writing for Children.' *Of This and Other Worlds*. Ed. Walter Hooper. London: Collins, 56-70.

2013. 'Out of the Silent Planet.' *The Space Trilogy*. London: HarperCollins, 1-146.

1992. 'Pan's Purge.' *Poems*. Ed. By Walter Hooper. San Diego, CA, New York and London: Harcourt Inc., 5-6.

2013. 'Perelandra.' *The Space Trilogy*. London: HarperCollins, 147-341.

2014. *The Silver Chair*. London: HarperCollins.

2013. 'That Hideous Strength.' *The Space Trilogy*. London: HarperCollins, 343-718.

2014. *The Voyage of the Dawn Treader*. London: HarperCollins.

Maryniarczyk, Andrzej et al. (eds.). 2004. *Powszechna encyklopedia filozofii. Vol. 5*. Lublin: Polskie Towarzystwo Tomasza z Akwinu.

Metz, Johann Baptist. 2008. *Teologia wobec cierpienia*. Transl. Juliusz Zychowicz. Kraków: WAM.

Milbank, Alison. 2008. *Chesterton and Tolkien as Theologians. The Fantasy of the Real*. London and New York: T&T Clark.

Oziewicz, Marek. 2005. *Magiczny urok Narnii. Poetyka i filozofia „Opowieści z Narnii" C.S. Lewisa*. Kraków: Universitas.

Reale, Giovanni. 1994. *Historia filozofii starożytnej. Vol. 1-3*. Transl. Edward Iwo Zieliński. Lublin: Wydawnictwo KUL.

Shippey, Tom. 1992. *The Road to Middle-earth*. London: Grafton.

2000. *J.R.R. Tolkien: Author of the Century*. London: HarperCollins.

Świeżawski, Stefan. 2000. *Dzieje europejskiej filozofii klasycznej*. Warszawa and Wrocław: Wydawnictwo Naukowe PWN.

Szyjewski, Andrzej. 2004. 'Prawda i mit. Klucz do Tolkienowskiego świata.' *Znak* 9, 19-34.

Tolkien, John Ronald Reuel. 1994. *Morgoth's Ring. The History of Middle-earth. Vol. 10*. Ed. Christopher Tolkien. London: HarperCollins.

1981. *The Letters of J.R.R. Tolkien*. Ed. Humphrey Carpenter with the assistance of Christopher Tolkien. London: George Allen & Unwin.

2005. *The Lord of the Rings. Part 1. The Fellowship of the Ring*. London: HarperCollins.

2005. *The Lord of the Rings. Part 2. The Two Towers*. London: HarperCollins.

2005. *The Lord of the Rings. Part 3. The Return of the King*. London: HarperCollins.

2021. *The Nature of the Middle-earth*. Ed. Carl F. Hostetter. London: HarperCollins.

2006. *The Silmarillion*. Ed. Christopher Tolkien. London: HarperCollins.

2005. *Smith of Wootton Major*. Ed. Verlyn Flieger. London: HarperCollins.

2008. *Tolkien On Fairy-stories*. Expanded edition, with commentary and notes. Eds. Verlyn Flieger and Douglas A. Anderson. London: HarperCollins.

2006. *Unfinished Tales of Númenor and Middle-earth*. Ed. Christopher Tolkien. London: HarperCollins.

Urbaniak, Marcin. 2014. 'Gorzki posmak płynnej nowoczesności. Wybrane zagadnienia z filozofii społecznej Zygmunta Baumana.' *Kwartalnik Naukowy Uczelni Vistula* 4, 5-27.

VAINIO, Olli-Pekka. 2020. 'How Boethius Influenced C.S. Lewis.' *Journal of the Evangelical Theological Society* 63, 161-72.

WARD, Michael. 2008. *Planet Narnia: The Seven Heavens in the Imagination of C.S. Lewis*. Oxford: Oxford University Press.

Giovanni Carmine Costabile 

# Deep Magic from the Dawn of Time is not Healing: Pauline Law in C.S. Lewis and J.R.R. Tolkien

**Abstract**

All cultures enforce justice by means of law. Law is seen everywhere as the impartial judge determinining what is right and what is wrong. It is also common knowledge that society might never find its balance, peace and harmony unless given a set of laws. And yet, according to Saint Paul of Tarsus, even Divine Law, given by the Lord to Moses on Mount Sinai through the Torah, is a cause of sin, injustice, and death, meaning that only in Christ one may find liberation. In one of his letters, Tolkien praises his fellow Inkling's ability to deliver Christian sermons in wartime as a reparation undertaken "in a Pauline spirit," as "an imitation of St. Paul." Taking into consideration their shared interest in the Apostle, this chapter seeks to explore the possibility of a Pauline reading of Tolkien's 'Finwë and Míriel' and whether it may be reconciled with the more explicitly Pauline notion of justice as "deep magic from the dawn of time" in *The Lion, the Witch and the Wardrobe* by C.S. Lewis.

In a time which is normally reported to have fallen between 33 and 37 AD, the pharisee called Saul of Tarsus had a vision as he was riding with his retinue toward Damascus. He was a persecutor of Christians, and his task there was to take them captive and bring them back to Jerusalem, in order to be executed. Saul was determined in his convictions. As a strict adherent of Judaism, a devoted believer in the God of Abraham, Isaac, and Jacob, he believed it was his duty to prevent the new cult, as it was seen back then, from spreading the absurd 'fake news' according to which the longed-for Messiah had already come, only to be crucified like a common villain, and subsequently reported to be back from the dead on the third day.

The vision he saw was an epiphany of light, within which he could hear a voice asking: "Saul, Saul, why persecutest thou me?" (Acts 9:4).[1] As soon as Saul asked the unknown speaker to identify himself, the voice spoke: "I am Jesus whom thou persecutest" (9:5). Saul, whose Latin name was Paul (13:9), after years of

1 Unless otherwise specified, all quotes from the Bible are taken from King James Version.

being a sworn enemy of the creed, became a zealous Apostle of Jesus, bringing the Gospel to the Gentiles, and praising the Grace of Christ the Lord.

About nineteen hundred years later, on Saturday 19 September 1931, the scholar and hitherto misomyth Clive Staples Lewis went to bed late. In fact, he had spent many hours at night discussing the idea of Myth and its relation to Truth in the company of Professor John Ronald Reuel Tolkien and their shared friend Hugo Dyson (Carpenter 2006: 42-45). As a result of this conversation, Lewis, who had already grown into a theist, after years of being away from God, became a philomyth and embraced Christianity. While I do not dare to claim that, in their causative effect, the words of Tolkien as he spoke to Lewis could even roughly be compared to those of God Himself, as in the case with Paul, I would still like to demonstrate how the zeal of the two converts in their newly-acquired faith after their respective 'epiphanies' is comparable, and in fact was compared, by none other than Tolkien himself.

In the present chapter, therefore, I shall endeavor to trace Saint Paul's influence over the literary works of both Lewis and Tolkien, as rooted in their personal life and faith, as well as in the friendship they shared. More specifically, I shall survey their notion of Divine Law as rooted in that of Saint Paul, who put Divine Love and Mercy before it. Since both Tolkien and Lewis reflected on such theological notions, as consistently shown in their private correspondence, I shall proceed to highlight further reflections of this found throughout their fiction.

## Pauline Law

In an unpublished letter by Tolkien, quoted by C.S. Lewis's biographer A.N. Wilson, the author of *The Lord of the Rings* praises his fellow Inkling's resolve to deliver Christian sermons at a time of war as a reparation undertaken "in a Pauline spirit," or as "an imitation of St. Paul."[2] Tolkien writes:

---

2 That Lewis experienced his conversion under Saint Paul's patronage is also evident from his October 1931 letter to Arthur Greeves, where he writes: "I have just finished *The Epistle to the Romans*, the first Pauline epistle I have ever seriously read through" (*CL I* 975). The key term is 'seriously,' since he was already quite acquainted with Saint Paul's Epistles even many years before his conversion, as later shown.

> He took it [the task] up in a Pauline spirit, as a reparation; now the least of Christians (by special grace) but once an infidel, and even if [Lewis] had not persecuted the faithful, he would do what he could to convert men or stop them from straying away. The acceptance of the RAF mission, with its hardship of travel to distant and nasty places and audiences of anything but the kind he was humanly fitted to deal with, lonely, cheerless, embarrassed journeys leaving little behind but doubt whether any seed had fallen on good soil; all this was in its way an imitation of St. Paul. (qtd. in Wilson 1990: 179)

But it was not only Saint Paul's attitude that was influenced by his personal experience. His theology may also be seen as a reflection of his own life. In fact, as Walenty Prokulski wrote, prior to his conversion, Paul was

> a Pharisee and an ardent upholder of the Law and of the tradition of his fathers. He was more attached to Judaism than the majority of his contemporaries. As a Pharisee he lived in accordance with strictest rules of his religion and was perfect in the observance of the Law (Acts 26:5; Galatians 1:14; Philippians 3:6). Thus, if the Law revealed by God was to every Jew God's supreme grace, the perfect manifestation of Wisdom and of His love for Israel, the pride and glory of the nation, it was even more so to a zealous Pharisee. In the eyes of a Jew it had the inexorable authority of God and pointed out the only sure way to salvation. Truly, much self denial, effort and constancy were required if the Law was to be faithfully observed; but the rewards of observance were peace, light and life. (1957: 458)

After his conversion, having realized how the Law he observed had made him play the role of an enemy of Christ, a bringer of havoc and death to those who now became his fellow Christians, Paul reconsidered his views concerning the Jewish Law. According to him, now, where "the law entered, [...] sin abounded" (Rom 5:20), and "the motions of sin [...] were by the law" (7:5). Hence, the Law "worketh wrath: for where no law is, there is no transgression" (4:15). Subsequently, in the same Epistle to Romans, Paul explains:

> But sin, taking occasion by the commandment, wrought in me all manner of concupiscence. For without the law sin was dead. For I was alive without the law once: but when the commandment came, sin revived, and I died. And the commandment, which was ordained to life, I found to be unto death. (Rom 7:8-10)

Notwithstanding his conversion, Paul still obeys the Law, and claims in front of other Jews to be still an observant Jew (Acts 21:39, 22:3), even a Pharisee (23:6, 26:5). The reason for this ostensible inconsistency lies in his keeping faith to the promise made by God to Abraham, the Old Testament patriarch to whom the Lord revealed that, despite his age and the fact that his wife Sarah was considered barren, He "will make [his] seed to multiply as the stars of heaven, and will give unto [his] seed all these countries; and in [his] seed shall all the nations of the earth be blessed" (Gen 26:4). In the Epistle to the Galatians, Paul asks his followers:

> Have you suffered so many things in vain? If it be yet in vain. He therefore that ministereth to you the Spirit, and worketh miracles among you, doeth he it by the works of the law, or by the hearing of faith? Even as Abraham believed God, and it was accounted to him for righteousness. Know ye therefore that they which are of faith, the same are the children of Abraham. [...] Christ hath redeemed us from the curse of the law, being made a curse for us: for it is written, Cursed is every one that hangeth on a tree: That the blessing of Abraham might come on the Gentiles through Jesus Christ; that we might receive the promise of the Spirit through faith. Brethren, I speak after the manner of men. Though it be but a man's covenant, yet if it be confirmed, no man disannulleth, or added thereto. Now to Abraham and his seed were the promises made. He saith not, And to seeds, as of many; but as of one, And to thy seed, which is Christ. And this I say, that the covenant, that was confirmed before of God in Christ, the law, which was four hundred and thirty years after, cannot disannul, that it should make the promise of none effect. For if the inheritance be of the law, it is no more of promise: but God gave it to Abraham by promise. (3:4-7, 13-18).

In other words, Paul here claims that the Promise God made to Abraham has precedence over the Law, since chronologically the former came before the latter, and so, logically, the Law could be given to the Jews so that they may learn how to be worthy of the Promise (Gal 3:19-26), thus entailing that without the Promise there would be no Law (4:21-31). Now, since the Promise, "thy seed [will] multiply as the stars of heaven," is given by God to reward Abraham's faith (3:6; see also Rom 4:13,16), and since the seed is identified by Paul as being synonymous with Jesus Christ (Gal 3:16), the obvious consequence is that true lawfulness means having faith in Jesus, more than in the letter of the commandments (Rom 4:11).[3] In short, according to Paul, by becoming a Christian he is not only a Jew observant, but he is actually all the more so.

---

3 The role of faith as complementary to law is not always a specifically Christian concept: for example, twentieth century Rabbi Abraham Joshua Heschel developed the so-called 'deep theology model,' which Potgieter defined as "a theology of the act of believing" (2014: 1). According to David Hartman, as reported by Raymond Potgieter in the article also citing C.S. Lewis (2014: 4), Heschel "did not want to lose sight of God by obscuring deity with a normative *halakhah* [Jewish law as way of life] expressing commitment to behaviour. Whilst Heschel does represent a Chasidic tradition, his faith represents both rational and mystic expressions" (Hartman 1997: 2, qtd. in Potgieter 2014: 2).

It then follows that what has been termed the Pauline concept of the Law is defined as the idea that the Law as a (rational) code of conduct, or a set of rules, even those decided by God, is negative for men, whereas the only true Law is the (rationally undefinable) criterion of Mercy, Love, and Faith.

## C.S. Lewis and Pauline Law: Epistles and Letters

Although C.S. Lewis is generally considered to be a strictly rationalist thinker, and therefore, after his conversion, a strictly rational theologian, it is still possible to observe how he agreed with the above-defined notion by Saint Paul. In fact, in *The Abolition of Man*, Lewis writes:

> It is the well-nurtured man, the *cuor gentil*, and he alone, who can recognize Reason when it comes. It is Paul, the Pharisee, the man 'perfect as touching the Law' who learns where and how that Law was deficient. (80)

Indeed, Lewis was very well acquainted with Saint Paul's Epistles, and even attempted some critical remarks on the character of their author, particularly as regards the alleged imperfection of his rational theology, as in his 1958 book *Reflections on the Psalms*:

> I cannot be the only reader who has wondered why God, having given him [Saint Paul] so many gifts, withheld from him (what would seem necessary for the first Christian theologian) that of lucidity and orderly exposition. (401)

Lewis's comments are explained in the immediately preceding passage, where he also analyzes Jesus's speech, in which Christ "preaches but does not lecture" (400), and whose teachings are given in the form of "paradox, proverb, exaggeration, parable, irony" (400), so that even the Lord sometimes seems to lack a systematic theology. In the following passage, after the above-quoted remarks on Saint Paul, Lewis clarifies his target:

> Thus on three levels, in appropriate degrees, we meet the same refusal of what we might have thought best for us – in the Word Himself, in the Apostle of the Gentiles, in Scripture as a whole. Since this is what God has done, this, we must conclude, was best. It may be that what we should have liked would have been fatal to us if granted. It may be indispensable that Our Lord's teaching, by that elusiveness (to our systematising intellect), should demand a response from the whole man, should make it so clear that there is no question of learning a subject but of steeping ourselves in a Personality, acquiring a new outlook

> and temper, breathing a new atmosphere, suffering Him, in His own way, to rebuild in us the defaced image of Himself. So in St. Paul. (401)

In Lewis's terms, then, human reason is unable to define the Law of God, or even God in general. It is the Lord Himself that, having created human reason, acts in accordance with His own criterion, variably called the Reason, or the Law. It is the human inability to formulate, express, and maintain God's Law, that accounts for the erroneous interpretation of the Law by the Pharisees, absurdly accusing Christ of not complying with God's Law, thus, in fact, demonstrating their own limited understanding of it.

Such an observation suggests that it is possible for Paul, as a converted Pharisee, not only to hold God's Law as sacred and inviolable (in itself), but also, in a sense, to see it as a cause of sin, wrath, and death (in its improper understanding and application, for example by the Pharisees). The intrinsic limitedness of human reason, as related to Paul's idea of Law, is something that Lewis clearly has in mind, as in a letter to his brother Warren (8 April 1932), when he refers to 1 Cor 1:26:

> Of course one sees, from all history and from ones own circle, that the people who already have a high intellectual and moral tradition of their own, are, of all people, the least likely to embrace Christianity. Fancy converting a man like J.S. Mill! Or, again, the really good Stoic emperors of Rome were the most anti-Christian. Even in the Gospels – does one suppose that the Pharisees, the 'High Church Party' of Judaism, did not contain most of the refined, educated, enlightened population of Palestine – people, by ordinary standards very much nicer than the women of the town and little tax-farmers (that is modern English for 'publicans and sinners') who seem to have made up the background of Our Lord's circle. Still, we would reply that *some* Pharisees (e.g. Joseph of Arimathea and Nicodemus) did come in: and, on the other hand, none of the riff-raff came in for money, because there 'was *no* money in the thing.' (*CL II* 70)[4]

Lewis's habit of referring to Saint Paul, or even directly quoting from his Epistles, in fact predates his conversion. Already in 1917, in a letter to Arthur Greeves (3 June), he makes a reference to the very same work, 1 Cor 13:11 (*CL I* 312). Eight months later, on 22 February 1918, writing to his own father, he compares the German Front to the residence of Satan calling it "spiritual wickedness in high places" (Eph 6:12). On 26 January of the following year, in another letter

4 John Stuart Mill (1806-1873) was a moral philosopher and propounder of Utilitarianism.

to Arthur Greeves, he implicitly (and ironically) compares his stay at the pious landlord Mrs. Moore's place to Paul's remark about "two whole years in his own hired house" (Acts 28:30; *CL I* 425). Finally, less than two months later, on 15 March, Lewis's 'Papy' receives a letter, coming, as in 1 Cor 15:8, "after its due time" (*CL I* 444).

Even funnier than these random quotes, though, especially in the light of his subsequent conversion, is Lewis's explicit parody of 1 Cor 13:7, Saint Paul's famous praise of Charity that "beareth all things, believeth all things, hopeth all things, endureth all things," which can be found in the letter to his brother begun on 2 August 1928: a "Pigiebotie [...] eateth all things, neglecteth all things, moveth not himself, is not waked up" (*CL I* 776). As Walter Hooper explains in a note to a much earlier (8 January 1917) letter to Warnie (nickname for his brother Warren, who, in his turn, called C.S. Lewis by the name of Jack):

> Jack sometimes addressed Warnie as 'APB' and, in turn, Warnie addressed his brother as 'SPB.' When Warnie and Jack were very young their nurse, Lizzie Endicott, when drying them after a bath, threatened to smack their 'pigieboties' or 'piggiebottoms.' In time the brothers decided that Warnie was the 'Archpiggiebotham' and Jack the 'Smallpiggiebotham' or 'APB' and 'SPB.' Thereafter they used these terms of one another, particularly in their correspondence. (*CL I* 265, fn 1)

The difference between the context of all these citations and what Lewis comes to write following his conversion could hardly be more astonishing. A factual leap of faith indeed separates the former from the latter,[5] and Lewis seems immediately aware of it, as he writes to Arthur Greeves on 18 October 1931, less than a month after the memorable late night conversation with Tolkien and Dyson:

> Right in the centre of Christianity, in the Gospels and St Paul, you keep on getting something quite different and very mysterious expressed in those phrases I have so often ridiculed ('propitiation' – 'sacrifice' – 'the blood of the Lamb') – expressions wh. I cd. only interpret in senses that seemed to me either silly or shocking. (*CL I* 976)

And, in the spirit of this awareness, he also immediately realizes the distinction between God and (human) reason:

5 In fact, the next time Lewis cites the same passage from 1 Eph, he does so in a devout fashion, in his 10 August 1948 letter to Don Giovanni Calabria, a letter written in Latin! (*CL II* 868).

> Now what Dyson and Tolkien showed me was this: that if I met the idea of sacrifice in a Pagan story I didn't mind at all [...]. The reason was that in Pagan stories I was prepared to feel the myth as profound and suggestive of meanings beyond my grasp even tho' I could not say in cold prose 'what it meant.'
>
> Now the story of Christ is simply a true myth: a myth working on us in the same way as the others, but with this tremendous difference that it *really happened* [...]. Therefore it is *true*, not in the sense of being a 'description' of God (that no finite mind could take in) but in the sense of being the way in which God chooses to (or can) appear to our faculties. The 'doctrines' we get *out* of the true myth are of course *less* true: they are translations into our *concepts* and *ideas* of wh. God has already expressed in a language more adequate, namely the actual incarnation, crucifixion, and resurrection. (976-77)

Lewis's understanding of 'doctrines' as 'translations' of God's language "into our *concepts* and *ideas*," the understanding he seems to have derived from Tolkien, says a lot about the previously discussed role of human reason, but does not only apply to the 'true myth' of "the actual incarnation, crucifixion, and resurrection" of Christ. Instead, it also has much to bear on the question of God's Law, as given in the Torah to Moses on Mount Sinai. To paraphrase Lewis in a way we might think he would probably approve of, the doctrines we get out of God's Law, namely the actual Ten Commandments, are, of course, less binding, for they are translations into our codes and laws of what God has already expressed in a language more adequate: 'love thy neighbour.'

'Thou shalt not kill,' by way of example, is apparently quite straightforward, but only so as long as one takes it as an absolute: 'nobody can kill anybody.' Yet, that was not the way the commandment was understood, neither by rabbis, nor by pharisees, and the very angels did not specify otherwise except by the other codes and laws of which Leviticus and Deuteronomy are full. Thus, when one finds a killer, the killer can be killed, or, rather, must be killed, for that is what the Law foresees. Also a woman found guilty of adultery must be killed, even though she did not kill anybody. The whole corpus of tractates and commentaries to the Law composed by rabbis on the foundations of the Torah, read through the lenses of the oral rabbinic tradition, or Mishnah, is called the Talmud. The goal of the huge mishnaic and talmudic tradition is to foresee and cover any real circumstance in Jewish life to offer the right behaviour that a Jew must display so to please the Lord. Thus one finds a clearer context for both Jesus's opposite tendency to reduce the whole of the Law to

'Love thy neighbour,' and Saint Paul's complaint against the oppression of the Law in the first century AD. In fact, Talmudic writings were entirely rabbinic speculation and deduction ('our codes and laws'), while Mishnaic tradition claimed its angelic origin ('doctrines we get out of God's Law').

And yet, we have to wonder, are things actually so? Saint Paul wrote that the Law "was ordained by angels in the hand of a mediator" (Gal 3:19). In fact, in Exodus, we read that on Mount Horeb "the angel of the Lord came unto him [Moses] in a flame of fire out of the midst of a bush: and he looked, and, behold, the bush burned with fire, and the bush was not consumed" (3:2). In consequence, the laws of the Ten Commandments arrive via a string of mediators, i.e. Moses, who received them from 'angels,' and angels who received them from God. So, even those laws are actually not only twice, but *thrice* removed from God. If we compare such a distance to the immediateness of Christ as God Himself made flesh in order to speak to all men and women, it should become evident that, according to both Saint Paul and Lewis, it is not just our codes and laws, but also the Ten Commandments themselves, that actually represent mere 'translations' of God's Law, and the only true Divine Law is Christ Himself, or, to quote from the Epistle to the Galatians, "the Law of Christ"(6:2).[6]

Interestingly, as we will see more at length in the following, Lewis's expertise on the role of the angels as mediators between God and men also transpires from his fiction, as in *That Hideous Strength*, where he has the character named Ransom say:

> [W]hile it may be true at the end of the world to describe every eldil either as an angel or a devil, and may even be true now, it was much less true in Merlin's time. There used to be things on this earth pursuing their own business, so to speak. They weren't ministering angels sent to help fallen humanity, but neither were they enemies preying upon us. Even in St. Paul one gets glimpses of a population that won't exactly fit into our two columns of angels and devils. And if you go back further... all the gods, elves, dwarfs, water-people,

---

6 By the 'Law of Christ,' I suppose Saint Paul means the following: "Thou shalt love the Lord thy God with all thy heart, and with all thy soul, and with all thy mind. This is the first and great commandment. And the second is like unto it, Thou shalt love thy neighbour as thyself. On these two commandments hang all the law and the prophets" (Mt 22:37-40). Interestingly, the second commandment (also 'new commandment' in John 13:34-35) is also to be found as a rule in Lev 18:18.

> *fata, longaevi.* [...] I think there was room for them then, but the universe has come more to a point. (351)

Judging from his deep knowledge of Pauline Epistles, as well as from other points in his works, it should be evident how Lewis was aware not any less than the Apostle of the fact that the inevitable ambiguities and uncertainties in the application of the Law are the favoured terrain of the battle between good and evil angels, so much so that, as has been mentioned, God's Law may be distorted so as to condemn God. In fact, the angelic mediation in the communication of the Law entails both the role of God's angels and the fallen angels, and, as mentioned above, Lewis's letter to his father on 22 February 1918 shows that he was aware of the Pauline concept of Satan's rule over the material world, since he quotes from Epistle to the Ephesians:

> For we wrestle not against flesh and blood, but against principalities, against powers, against the rulers of the darkness of this world, against spiritual wickedness in high places. (6:12)

Eighteen years later, on 23 May 1936, Lewis writes a compelling reply to Dom Bede Griffiths, a former student of his at Magdalen College in Oxford who has recently had an experience of reconversion to Catholicism. Griffiths would later become a priest, a Prior, as well as a zealous advocate of ecumenism and founder of the Shantivanam Ashram centre of interreligious dialogue in India. Griffiths reportedly wrote to Lewis that the Lord "is essentially a poet and not at all a philosopher" (*CL II* 193). His former tutor's response could never be more telling:

> Again, if you are suggesting that the Hebrew consciousness was just right and the Greek just wrong, this seems to me to be quite foreign to the tenor of St. Paul's teaching. He seems to hold quite definitely (a) That Our Lord has 'broken down the middle wall of partition and made one Man' [Eph 2:14-15], wh. is quite different from simply bringing errant Hellenism back to Hebraic rectitude (b) That the 'reasonings' of the Pagan (see Rom) are related to the new Faith much as the Jewish Law is [Rom 2]. In Galatians he even seems to equate the Pagan bondage to the στοιχεια with Jewish bondage to the Law [Gal 4:3]. (*CL II* 193)

The Pauline reference to the στοιχεια (*stoicheia*, Ancient Greek for 'elements'), also used in Col 3:20, is of great importance, since it is used by the Apostle to signify both the angels through whom the Law is given to Moses, as we read in

Gal 3:19, *and* the "principalities and powers" of evil against whom, as we have seen, "we wrestle," in Eph 6:12, Christ being triumphant above both categories (Eph 1:21, 3:10; Col 1:16; also Heb 1:6; 1 Peter 3:22).

Saint Paul's allusion to the 'lawmaking' angels and the corrupted ones is probably less striking if we consider that the Greek term στοιχεια in late ancient thought could represent the letters of the alphabet, the principles of musical harmony, and the rudiments of a teaching, the natural elements and the powers that rule over them. It is also a term denoting magical items, charms, idols, or zodiacal signs (Tóth 2019: 410, 414, 421-27), sometimes in a context of Judaeo-Pagan syncretism (Delling 1971; Schweizer 1988), and perhaps even with Gnostic connotations (Grant 1966; Pagels 1975; Perkins 1993; Pearson 2001).[7] It is interesting, therefore, to observe that Lewis must have been perfectly aware of the semantic complexity of this word, since, immediately after the above-quoted passage, in the same letter to Griffiths he writes:

> I know they dispute what στοιχεια means, whether elemental powers (gods, angels) or 'rudiments' in the educational sense: but surely it is clear that it means both, that St. Paul is using a *double entendre*. For the 'rudiments' meaning is demanded by [Eph] III 25 [20?], [Gal] IV 1-3: and the other by [Gal] IV 3 (τοῦ κοσμου) and 8. In fact the whole relation between Paganism and Judaism wh. I hinted [at] in my *Regress* is quite Pauline – more so than I really knew at the time. (*CL I* 193-94)

Walter Hooper comments:

> *The Pilgrim's Regress* (1933; Fount, 1998), book 8, ch. 8, pp. 191-92. 'The Pagans couldn't read ... but they had pictures ... And then the Pagans made mistakes. They would keep on trying to get the same picture again: and if it didn't come, they would make copies of it for themselves ... They went on making up more and more stories for themselves about the pictures, and then pretending the stories were true ... The Shepherds could read: that is the thing to remember about them. And because they could read, they had from the Landlord, not pictures but Rules.' (*CL II* 194, fn 47)

Here we get whole new evidencece of Lewis's appreciation of Saint Paul: not only did Lewis enjoy reading the words of the Apostle, and thus meditate on the Word of God for spiritual growth, but he was also interested in a critical debate concerning the exegesis and theological interpretation of the Pauline

7 Obviously, the Coming of Christ did not supersede the ban imposed on magical practices in Exodus 22:18 and Leviticus 20:27. Any magician's power comes from Satan (2 Cor 11:13-15).

Epistles. I think it is also crucial to point out how Lewis here suggests further developments of his life-changing conversation of September 1931. Pagans had pictures to depict their myths, but the only true Myth was Christ. Jews had the Law, but the only true Law was Christ's. Thus Lewis's comments on his work, *The Pilgrim's Regress*, can be read as the natural continuation of his above-quoted fresh comments from his letter to Arthur Greeves (18 October 1931).

It is evident then that, when it comes to the angelic role of mediators in the presentation of the Law to Moses, Lewis is in perfect agreement with Saint Paul. In the conclusion of the letter to Griffiths, he also appears to have reflected upon the same matter of the Pauline Law which is under discussion here,[8] when he comments,

> I wholly agree with what you say about escaping from the circle of morality into the love of God: in fact you have written an excellent commentary on St. Paul's view of the 'Law.' (*CL II* 194)

Lewis's understanding and agreement with "St. Paul's view of the 'Law'" is also something which would later surface in his fiction.

## Lewis and Tolkien on Pauline Law: Fictions and Factions

To begin with, Lewis's reference to the Pauline struggle with 'principalities and powers' is also explicitly referred to in the second chapter of *Perelandra*, the second novel of his *Space Trilogy*. After the protagonist of the first novel, Elwin Ransom, comes back to Thulcandra (Earth) from his trip to Malacandra (Mars), he tells everything to Lewis himself, whom we see at the very beginning of the book on his way to Ransom's place in order to meet his friend after his space-travelling experience. When the latter explains that the reason for his going to Perelandra (Venus) was to help in the fight against the Bent One, the evil eldil (angel) of Thulcandra, he voices the author's doubts in Lewis's stead:

8 Also in later years, Lewis repeatedly returned to the same subject. He once again writes to Griffiths (9 April 1950) commenting on "the Pauline sense of *liberation* from the Law" (*CL III* 24; emphasis original); to Mary Van Deusen (15 May 1955), focusing on Saint Paul's notion "of Love being the real fulfilment of the Law" (Rom 13:10; *CL III* 610); and, finally, pointing out, once again to Mary Van Deusen, in the letter dated 16 December 1955, the Apostle's claim that "when love fulfils the Law, Law (as such) flies out of the window" (685).

> "You are feeling the absurdity of it. Dr. Elwin Ransom setting out single-handed to combat powers and principalities. You may even be wondering if I've got megalomania."
>
> "I didn't mean that quite," said I.
>
> "Oh, but I think you did. At any rate that is what I have been feeling myself ever since the thing was sprung on me. But when you come to think of it, is it odder than what all of us have to do every day? When the Bible used that very expression about fighting with principalities and powers and depraved hypersomatic beings at great heights (our translation is very misleading at that point, by the way) it meant that quite ordinary people were to do the fighting." (*Perelandra* 21)

*Perelandra* was published in 1943, and so it is curious to observe how, at the same time, Lewis's close friend Tolkien was writing *The Lord of the Rings*, in which one can see Elrond justify the decision to send the Hobbits on a quest to destroy the One Ring in the cracks of Mount Doom in the following words:

> The road must be trod, but it will be very hard. And neither strength nor wisdom will carry us far upon it. This quest may be attempted by the weak with as much hope as the strong. Yet such is oft the course of deeds that move the wheels of the world: small hands do them because they must, while the eyes of the great are elsewhere. (*FR* 269)

It is worthwhile to stress the difference between Lewis and Tolkien in these two passages, the general meaning of which is roughly the same: great deeds may be performed by small people. First of all, Lewis keeps closer to our own present reality, always maintaining some sort of reference to it. And indeed, it is in the initial chapters of the second volume that we find the protagonist having the above-quoted talk in our own world with the very author of the book. Such a case entails the second point, namely that the Biblical references are explicit, since the Bible is even quoted in the text.

Conversely, the fictional connection of *The Lord of the Rings* with our world is clarified in the Prologue and the Appendices, as Tolkien feigns the whole work to be a translation of his into English from a copy of the presumed original book written by its Hobbit protagonists, but it is way feebler a connection. Furthermore, throughout the novel there is no direct reference whatsoever to our present times, and even when a passage echoes the Bible, the echo is set so as to make us wonder whether it was intended by the author or not.

Nonetheless, it is obvious that Tolkien shared the same preoccupation for our times that Lewis evidently demonstrates, and at the same time the former was learned in theology and biblical exegesis as well as the latter, so much so that often the aforementioned echoes were indeed to be understood as a fruit of his conscious mind, or, in case they were not, the religious formation and piety of the author of *The Lord of the Rings* would account for a spontaneous rephrasing.

In the case of the above-quoted passages, for example, it is tempting, considering the link in Lewis's mind, as well as the friendship between them, to read the same reasons as underlying Tolkien's letter of 28 October 1966 to his grandson Michael George, who had just graduated at Oxford. In fact, the very same quote from Saint Paul is quite clearly a confirmation of the association of the theme of the greatness of the humble, in the Professor's mind and throughout his writings, both with a concern for our times and with its biblical, religious, Pauline sense:

> I am interested to hear what you say about your work, and your growing view of 'research' as applied to modern literature. I am myself and always have been sceptical about 'research' of any kind as part of the occupation or training of younger people in the language-literature schools. There is such a lot to learn first. It is often forced on students after schools because of the desire to climb on to the great band-waggon of Science (or at least onto a little trailer in tow) and so capture a little of the prestige and money which 'The Sovereignties and Powers and the rulers of this world' shower upon the Sacred Cow (as one writer, a scientist, has named it) and its acolytes. But many of those devoted to the Arts privately desire nothing more than a chance to read more. (*Letters* 370, #290)

'Sovereignties' is simply the Jerusalem Bible translation of the same Greek term ἀρχάι which the King James Version, usually preferred by both Catholic Tolkien and Anglican Lewis, referred to as 'principalities.'[9] In most of the Christian tradition these terms are interpreted as peculiar graecized references to Hebraic angelic hierarchies, in the same way as the above-quoted στοιχεια, originally meaning 'element,' has been noted to have come to mean, in Modern Greek, 'angel,' 'spirit,' or 'ghost' (Burton 1928: 510-13; Delling 1971: 670-83; Esser 1976: 451-52).

---

9 As a child, however, Tolkien read the Challoner Bible, a revised version of the Douay-Rheims Bible. (I owe this piece of information to Jessica Yates from the Tolkien Society).

To see these names and concepts thus applied, although perhaps under a veil of irony, to hypocrisy and corruption in the domains of science, politics, and economics, cannot but recall the N.I.C.E. institute in *That Hideous Strength*. The institute exploits the advancement of science and research for their own purposes, which are eventually revealed to consist in a satanic cult.

It is hard to suppose that Lewis might have influenced Tolkien in this respect, since, as we have seen, it was the latter comparing the former in his newly-converted state to the Apostle. But it is equally difficult to suppose that the other way around was the case as far as Saint Paul is concerned, since Lewis knew his writings well from the start. The most convincing solution is to assume that Tolkien did not influence Lewis in the sense of convincing him to read and study the New Testament, which, again, he already had. Nonetheless, certainly the former helped the development in the latter, who was his natural match in temperament and taste, of a mental disposition and a way of *reading* the New Testament, towards which that very same nature tended. Features which, as we have seen, Tolkien himself called 'Pauline' (Wilson 1990: 179).

Their differences, instead, are rooted in their respective creeds: broadly speaking, the acceptance, even only by way of quote, of the identification of the evil powers as 'sovereignties' (as in the Jerusalem Bible) seems to entail a political character of the evil powers, confirmed by the pretence of the Dark Lord in Tolkien's narrative, which instead of 'principalities' (as in the King James Version) would rather classify as chiefly educational, specifically in the sense of religious education, which seems to be exemplified by the satanic N.I.C.E. in Lewis's novel.

In other words, as in many other instances of comparison between the Catholics and the Anglicans, it all comes down to allegiance to the Pope or the King/ Queen. Indeed, in one of his letters Tolkien writes how:

> hatred of our church [i.e. Roman Catholic, my note] is after all the real only final foundation of the C[hurch, my note] of E[ngland, my note] – so deep laid that it remains even when all the superstructure seems removed (C.S.L. for instance reveres the Blessed Sacrament, and admires nuns!). Yet if a Lutheran is put in jail he is up in arms; but if Catholic priests are slaughtered – he disbelieves it (and I daresay really thinks they asked for it). (*Letters* 95, #83)

Such statements by Tolkien are particularly relevant when put in the context of another letter, where he explicitly puts side by side Frodo's eventual failure to resist the power of the Ring at Mount Doom with 1 Cor 10: 12-13: "Wherefore let him that thinketh he standeth take heed lest he fall. There hath no temptation taken you but such as is common to man: but God is faithful, who will not suffer you to be tempted above that ye are able; but will with the temptation also make a way to escape, that ye may be able to bear it" (*Letters* 252, #191).

On the other side, in his 8 May 1945 letter to H. Lyman Stebbing, Lewis commented in detail on the differences between Roman Catholicism and Anglicanism:

> What is most certain is the vast mass of doctrine wh. I find agreed on by Scripture, the Fathers, the Middle Ages, modern R.C.'s, modern Protestants. That is true 'catholic' doctrine. Mere 'modernism' I reject at once. The Roman Church where it differs from this universal tradition and specially from apostolic Xtianity I reject. Thus their theology about the B.V.M. I reject because it seems utterly foreign to the New Testament: where indeed the words 'Blessed is the womb that bore thee' receive a rejoinder pointing in exactly the opposite direction. Their papalism seems equally foreign to the attitude of St Paul towards St Peter in the Epistles. The doctrine of Transubstantiation insists in defining in a way wh. the N.T. seems to me not to countenance. In a word, the whole set-up of modern Romanism seems to me to be as much a provincial or local variation from the central, ancient tradition as any particular Protestant sect is. I must therefore reject their claim: tho' this does not mean rejecting particular things they say.
>
> I'm afraid I haven't read any modern books of Roman-Anglican controversy. Hooker (Laws of Ecclesiastical Polity) is to me the great formulation of Anglicanism. But the great point is that in one sense there's no such thing as Anglicanism. What we are committed to believing is whatever can be proved from Scripture. On that subject there is room for endless progress. (*CL II* 646-47)

Therefore, while both authors may be advocating Saint Paul as their witness, it is still evident how their respective creed is reflected in their conduct and writing. Thus we have the Anglican actively preaching in order to teach people the exact doctrine of the Christian message and ethos, so to oppose the educational perversion of moral means (the way a King should act by Law), whereas the Catholic only tells stories imbued with implicit Christianity in their plot and symbolism (*Letters* 172, #142), so to release society from the political corruption of devotional ends (what a Pope should do by Grace). The two approaches do not necessarily contraddict each other, hence the writers' mutual friendship;

nonetheless, they seem to have never actually found a full agreement, hence their occasional parting of ways.

To better explain their diverging views, one needs only to refer to the authors themselves. Tolkien, as we saw earlier, was also critical towards institutions, labelling University "the Sacred Cow" (*Letters* 370, #290), but he thought the key issue to be elsewhere. On the other side, we have Lewis, stating how "we have lived to see the second death of ancient learning. In our time something which was once the possession of all educated men has shrunk to being the technical accomplishment of a few specialists," so far so that "if one were looking for a man who could not read Virgil though his father could, he might be found more easily in the twentieth century than in the fifth" (*SLE* 4). Such a 'death' of learning also takes place because "our rulers have become like schoolmasters and are always demanding 'keenness'," and the whole phenomenon is due to the fiendish schemes of the devils, as in *Screwtape Proposes a Toast*, where the devil called Screwtape says

> [T]he spirit of *I'm as good as you* has already begun something more than a generally social influence. It begins to work itself into their educational system. [...] The basic principle of the new education is to be that dunces and idlers must not be made to feel inferior to intelligent and industrious pupils. That would be "undemocratic." These differences between pupils – for they are obviously and nakedly individual differences – must be disguised. This can be done at various levels. At universities, examinations must be framed so that nearly all the students get good marks. Entrance examinations must be framed so that all, or nearly all, citizens can go to universities, whether they have any power (or wish) to profit by higher education or not. At schools, the children who are too stupid or lazy to learn languages and mathematics and elementary science can be set to doing things that children used to do in their spare time. Let them, for example, make mud pies and call it modelling. But all the time there must be no faintest hint that they are inferior to the children who are at work. Whatever nonsense they are engaged in must have – I believe the English already use the phrase – "parity of esteem." An even more drastic scheme is not possible. Children who are fit to proceed to a higher class may be artificially kept back, because the others would get a trauma – Beelzebub, what a useful word! – by being left behind. The bright pupil thus remains democratically fettered to his own age group throughout his school career, and a boy who would be capable of tackling Æschylus or Dante sits listening to his coeval's attempts to spell out A CAT SAT ON A MAT. (125-26)

Lewis's Screwtape then sums up his analysis in a single straightforward programme declaration:

> In a word, we may reasonably hope for the virtual abolition of education when *I'm as good as you* has fully had its way. All incentives to learn and all penalties for not learning will vanish. The few who might want to learn will be prevented; who are they to overtop their fellows? And anyway the teachers – or should I say, nurses? – will be far too busy reassuring the dunces and patting them on the back to waste any time on real teaching. We shall no longer have to plan and toil to spread imperturbable conceit and incurable ignorance among men. The little vermin themselves will do it for us. (*SPT* 126)

To assume that such 'democratic' changes in the education system are imputable to devils is obviously, at least in part, meant to be taken as satire. Nonetheless, it is entirely consistent with what Lewis, in a fully serious fashion, also declares concerning Christian religion and education. For Lewis, also better qualifying his above-quoted contempt at the decline of the educational system, the very importance of education has in fact a religious, Christian relevance. Of course, he admits that there are indeed forms of learning that are not Christian at all, but they should be taken as a child's first attempt to reconstruct the way things actually work, therefore calling for a deep concern and careful avoidance of bad influences (he cites the 'enemies' who want to keep people ignorant on all subjects, and specifically concerning Christian views):

> If all the world were Christian, it might not matter if all the world were uneducated. But, as it is, a cultural life will exist outside the Church whether it exists inside or not. To be ignorant and simple now – not to be able to meet the enemies on their own ground – would be to throw down our weapons, and to betray our uneducated brethren who have, under God, no defense but us against the intellectual attacks of the heathen. Good philosophy must exist, if for no other reason, because bad philosophy needs to be answered. The cool intellect must work not only against cool intellect on the other side, but against the muddy heathen mysticisms which deny intellect altogether. Most of all, perhaps we need intimate knowledge of the past. Not that the past has any magic about it, but because we cannot study the future, and yet need something to set against the present, to remind us that periods and that much which seems certain to the uneducated is merely temporary fashion. A man who has lived in many place is not likely to be deceived by the local errors of his native village: the scholar has lived in many times and is therefore in some degree immune from the great cataract of nonsense that pours from the press and the microphone of his own age. ('Learning in War-Time' 374-75)

Summing up, it can be deduced that, in Lewis's views, the corruption ascribed to Modern Age is chiefly depending on the abuse and misuse of education and learning which misapplies and perverts its proper application and means so much as to seriously hinder and even prevent further development of its spread and practice, while, at the same time, adopting a twisted parody thereof as a form of political language. Obviously, the remedy to such a crisis can only be the furthering of studies and the active testimony and preaching of the Christian Truth, which he in fact himself did throughout his life since conversion, because what people fundamentally needed, in Lewis's mind, was the right understanding.

On the other side, Tolkien appears to be seeing the matter quite differently, as we can infer from his own writing. In his opinion, it was, in fact, Lewis's own philosophy which, if misapplied and perverted, constituted precisely what he saw as Evil. According to Tolkien, Lewis had grown into a "hatred of our church" (*Letters* 95, #83). This means that Tolkien, by probably overstating the case, could even see Lewis as one of the Pharisees Jesus reproaches, or, despite his own awareness of such a peril, inadvertently is prone to the same error as the ancient Gnostics, who misunderstood the whole Christian faith by reducing it to Manichaeism. In fact, even after Lewis's death, in a letter dated 22 November 1966, Tolkien addressed Walter Hooper, the editor of Lewis's works, claiming that

> I noticed, for the first time consciously, how dualistic Lewis' mind and imagination [were], though as a philosopher his reason entirely rejected this. So the pun Hierarchy/Lowerarchy. And of course the 'Miserific Vision' is rationally nonsense, not to say theologically blasphemous. (*Letters* 371, #291)

As we can see, the issue here is consistent with Lewis's conception of the evil hierarchies which we previously discussed. The concept of 'Lowerarchy,' meaning the distribution of power in proportion inverse to merit, is expressed by Lewis in *The Screwtape Letters*. By looking at the very first conception of the work, related to his brother Warnie in a letter dated 20 July 1940, one can notice a few things. The letter begins by ironically observing how, by listening to one of Adolf Hitler's speeches, one might be convinced he were right by the mere assertiveness of his voice (*CL II* 425). Interestingly, Lewis absurdly remarks how he himself might similarly have to check who was the author of *Paradise Lost* as long as a student wrote it was Wordsworth in a very persuasive, unflinching handwriting (425).

Immediately thereafter, Lewis relates how he attended Mass (*CL II* 426), and, as the celebration unfolded, he came up with the idea of a book which he would then have titled *As one Devil to Another*, dealing with the correspondence of a retired devil to a young one doing his apprenticeship (426-27). After so relating, the letter reaches an end, but not before citing Lewis's appreciation of the Anglican priest and poet James Matthew Thompson's book of poetry titled *My Apologia* (427-28). Explaining such praise, Lewis cites Thompson's mention of the last days of King Louis XVI during the French Revolution, as well as the priest's lines concerning his own being, in his youth, a "soft creature" despite the "hard outside" (427), and then the impossibility for an Historian to learn the real causes of any event, the "whimsicality" of the shame of having been a layman (428), eventually to get to the changes introduced in Oxford University's "*acta* and *agenda*" by the "one successful cycle-mender," Lord Nuffield (428).[10]

It should be evident from such concurrent remarks how Lewis retained Evil to be fundamentally associated with, on the one hand, misunderstanding, unlearnedness, and ignorance, and, on the other, despisal and even purposeful repression of knowledge. In his spontaneous thread of associations, he puts into a single chain of mental links Adolf Hitler, the Fall of Adam and Eve, Satan and his devils, illiteracy, the end of Monarchy, juvenile fragility, the opposition between secular and sacred, and the innovations in University regulations. When putting the whole picture together, one gets a distinct idea, only as an hypothesis at a first reading, that Lewis is here subtly advocating the equation of Evil with ignorance, which constituted one of the chief arguments proposed by the ancient Greek philosophers Socrates and Aristotle.

By contrast, and although he too disparaged modern Academy and its trends, Tolkien would rather argue in support of the Augustinian views, according to which it is possible to commit evil actions in the full awareness of their evil nature, as the Church Father in his *Confessions* famously admitted he himself had done in his youth, as he stole pears from another man's tree. As I noted elsewhere (2017: 163), Tolkien's familiarity with the episode is proven by his abortive attempt at a sequel to *The Lord of the Rings*, tentatively titled *The New Shadow*, where the arrogant youth Saelon rebukes old Borlas for having harshly

10 Born William Richard Morris (1877-1963), taking the title Lord Nuffield from his native village in Oxfordshire, he was the industrialist and philantropist to whose memory Nuffield College of Social Sciences in Oxford came to be dedicated.

reproached him years earlier on account of his theft of unripe apples in a clearly Augustinian frame.

If it is possible to commit a sin in the awareness of the sinful nature of the act, though, it will only be evident, then, how the nature of Evil is not exhaustively defined as ignorance. In Tolkien's view, then, it is better to say that Evil consists in the forgetfulness of one's own createdness, in the vain attempt at impersonating the Creator, which is precisely the reason for Melkor's Fall in *The Silmarillion*, as well as Lucifer's in the Christian narrative tradition. In this case, perhaps, a better one-word definition would be 'insubordination,' precisely entailing the violation of hierarchies and rejection of legitimate authority, and which is therefore comparable to a sort of political sin, instead of an educational one. In the mind of Tolkien, himself a humble sub-creator of literary fantasies, who always remembered to apply the prefix 'sub-' to himself, as well as to any earthly creator of stories, what people mostly needed was, instead of humility, the virtue of his simple-minded, yet virtuous, Hobbits.

Tolkien's interest in Saint Paul's views on evil is, instead, made evident in the discovery I made while studying Tolkien's unpublished manuscripts. In fact, in Weston Library MS. Tolkien A13/2 (1), one finds a note by the Professor, citing a passage from the Epistles, more specifically from Philippians 3:18-19:

> For many walk, of whom I have told you often, and now tell you even weeping, that they are the enemies of the cross of Christ: Whose end is destruction, whose God is their belly, and whose glory is in their shame, who mind earthly things. (fol. 159r)

When it comes to what Lewis calls 'the Miserific Vision,' Tolkien appears to be referring to one of the letters in which Screwtape addresses his pupil Wormwood. The senior devil states that

> [God]'s a hedonist at heart. All those fasts and vigils and stakes and crosses are only a façade. Or only like foam on the sea shore. Out at sea, out in His sea, there is pleasure, and more pleasure. He makes no secret of it; at His right hand are "pleasures for evermore". Ugh! I don't think He has the least inkling of that high and austere mystery to which we rise in the Miserific Vision. He's vulgar, Wormwood. He has a bourgeois mind. He has filled His world full of pleasures. There are things for humans to do all day long without His minding in the least – sleeping, washing, eating, drinking, making love, playing, praying, working, Everything has to be twisted before it's any use to us. We fight under cruel disadvantages. Nothing is naturally on our side. (*SL* 83)

The supposed hellish 'Miserific Vision,' as an opposite of the heavenly 'Beatific Vision,' is something contradicting the teaching of the Catholic Church, therefore Tolkien warns the readers that, besides being 'rationally nonsense,' it may even be 'theologically blasphemous.' In fact, in the *Roman Catechism*, under the heading 'The Beatific Vision,' one reads that

> For the blessed always see God present and by this greatest and most exalted of gifts, being made partakers of the divine nature, they enjoy true and solid happiness. Our belief in this happiness should be joined with an assured hope that we too shall one day, through the divine goodness, attain it. This the Fathers declared in their Creed, which says: I expect the resurrection of the dead and the life of the world to come. (*The Catechism of the Council of Trent* I, xii)

Such a concept is even older than the Council of Trent, and yet even we today may find an answer in the younger *Catechism of the Catholic Church*, under the heading '533. What is the greatest human desire?':

> The greatest desire of the human person is to see God. "I want to see God" is the cry of our whole being. We realize our true and full happiness in the vision and beatitude of the One who created us out of love and draws us to himself with infinite love. (*CCC* III, iii-ii, 533. 2548-50; 2557)

And to this passage the following quote from Saint Gregory of Nyssa is appended: "Whoever sees God has obtained all the goods of which he can conceive" (*De beatitudinibus* 6: 44, 1265A). It is therefore clear how a theoretical opposite of the Beatific Vision would entail the realization of complete unhappiness, which at the same time would repel us with infinite hate and deprive us of all goods, which simply makes no sense at all, nor might anyone see how that might be desirable, or even possible. The notion is based on the idea that Evil had a substance of its own, the view which Saint Augustine disproved of, much as Saint Thomas Aquinas, another theologian that Tolkien admired, as Jonathan McIntosh has convincingly demonstrated (2017: 203-60). However, it would still be impossible to make any sense of the idea of a conscious mind attempting to be totally miserable and to lose all goods, and even less so, if at the same time, it would also be denied the fulfilment of such attempts. It is therefore clear that such a concept, however satyrically or fictitiously treated, could not, in Tolkien's opinion, be meaningfully used to refer to devils, let alone men.

However that may be, though, Lewis's chief reformulation of the concept of Pauline Law comes in *The Chronicles of Narnia*. In the first-published novel of the series, *The Lion, the Witch and the Wardrobe*, the youngest of the male Pevensies, Edmund, betrays his siblings by siding with the evil White Witch, whose plans are to achieve complete dominance over the Kingdom of Narnia. By way of 'reward,' the witch sentences Edmund to death, because, as she urges the Lion King Aslan to consider, "[y]ou have a traitor there". When the King replies: "Well, [...] [h]is offence was not against you," the witch remains insistent: "Have you forgotten about the Deep Magic?," to which Aslan evasively replies: "Let us say I have forgotten it[.] [...] Tell us of this Deep Magic" (*LWW* 149). The witch then rages,

> "Tell you?" said the Witch, her voice growing suddenly shriller. "Tell you what is written on the very Table of Stone which stands beside us? Tell you what is written in letters deep as a spear is long on the fire-stones on the Secret Hill? Tell you what is engraved on the sceptre of the Emperor-beyond-the-Sea? You at least know the Magic which the Emperor put into Narnia at the very beginning. You know that every traitor belongs to me as my lawful prey and that for every treachery I have a right to a kill."
>
> "Oh," said Mr Beaver. "So *that's* how you came to imagine yourself a Queen – because you were the Emperor's hangman. I see."
>
> "Peace, beaver," said Aslan, with a very low growl.
>
> "And so," continued the Witch, "that human creature is mine. His life is forfeit to me. His blood is my property." (*LWW* 149-50)

The precise nature and meaning of the Deep Magic is already indicated here by the expression '*lawful* prey,' [emphasis added] but the explicit identification of this Magic with the Law comes shortly thereafter, in the follow up to the dialogue between the Witch and Aslan. Meanwhile, it is also interesting to consider that, since the Witch herself in a way stands for the Law, the beaver's notion of her claiming to be 'Queen' because she is 'the Emperor's [i.e. God's] hangman' is very Pauline, entailing the same role for the Witch as the ones which belonged to the fallen angels and the corrupted Pharisees in the New Testament. The narrative then gradually unfolds towards the resolution:

> "Come and take it then," said the Bull with the man's head, in a great bellowing voice.
>
> "Fool," said the Witch with a savage smile that was almost a snarl, "do you really think your master can rob me of my rights by mere force? He knows the Deep Magic better than that. He knows that unless I have blood as the Law says, all Narnia will be overturned and perish in fire and water."
>
> "It is very true," said Aslan. "I do not deny it."

> "Oh, Aslan!" whispered Susan in the Lion's ear. "Can't we – I mean, you won't, will you? Can't we do something about the Deep Magic? Isn't there something you can work against it?"
>
> "Work against the Emperor's Magic?" said Aslan, turning to her with something like a frown on his face. And nobody ever made that suggestion to him again. (*LWW* 150-51)

Obviously the proposal of the Bull with a man's head cannot be accepted: 'mere force' cannot stand on the same level as 'my rights,' as the witch says, otherwise the Law would be unjust, nullifying its worth. This is, in fact, even stressed and greatly exaggerated by her saying that, if such were the case, "all Narnia w[ould] be overturned and perish in fire and water" (*LWW* 150), a very powerful symbol of chaos and destruction such as the anarchic suppression of laws would probably entail.

But that is not all. Even King Aslan himself (not to mention the man-headed Bull) cannot "work against the Emperor's Magic" (*LWW* 151). The solution must be different, and so Aslan leaves the company to confere with the witch in private. In this way, they settle for a compromise: Aslan will give his own life to save Edmund and the witch will have her blood. The Law will not be broken, and Edmund will stay alive. Everybody is going to be happy, except, as it turns out, Aslan.

However, when the Lion is dead and, the children are lamenting their loss, little mice come and gnaw at the ropes tying Aslan's body, and, as soon as they have finished, flocks of birds fly above the Stone Table. Then a "loud noise" is heard, like "a great cracking, deafening noise, as if a giant had broken a giant's plate" (*LWW* 169). When they turn around, the children see that "[t]he Stone Table [i]s broken into two pieces" (169), and so they wonder whether some unknown magic has done that.

> "Yes!" said a great voice behind their backs. "It is more magic." They looked round. There, shining in the sunrise, larger than they had seen him before, shaking his mane [...] stood Aslan himself. [...]
>
> "But what does it all mean?" asked Susan when they were somewhat calmer.
>
> "It means," said Aslan, "that though the Witch knew the Deep Magic, there is a magic deeper still which she did not know. Her knowledge goes back only to the dawn of time. But if she could have looked a little further, into the stillness and the darkness before Time dawned, she would have read there a different

> incantation. She would have known that when a willing victim who had committed no treachery was killed in a traitor's stead, the Table would crack and Death itself would start working backwards." (*LWW* 170-71)

The Deeper Magic from before the Dawn of Time is evidently another name for the Divine Love and Mercy,[11] which, according to both Saint Paul and Lewis, are incarnated in Jesus Christ. Probably the most detailed commentary to date on the Pauline echoes in the above-discussed episode in *The Lion, the Witch and the Wardrobe* is the account by David G. Clark in *C.S. Lewis: A Guide to his Theology*. In it, Clark writes:

> The mysterious stone table requires a separate note. Paul Ford describes it well in his *Companion to Narnia*: it's covered with strange carvings, seems to have been around forever, and its history is unknown. But what does it represent? Since the main point of the Deep Magic is that the Witch has a right to the life of every traitor, and since the stone table is the place where such are killed, one possible interpretation is that the place represents the Old Testament Law, which Paul describes by the words "the ministry of death, chiseled in letters on stone tablets" (2 Cor 3:7). That Law was unforgiving: every sin must be atoned for with blood. But when Christ died in our place, he paid that penalty with his own blood, "erasing the record that stood against us with its legal demands" (Col 2:13). Thus, when Aslan dies, the great stone table is broken in two, signifying that the power of what was written upon it is nullified, since its demands have been met. (Clark 2007: 62-63)

The religious meaning of the passage in *The Lion, the Witch and the Wardrobe* rarely escapes the readers' attention. Already in 1974 John Warwick Montgomery commented on the whole episode by remarking that 'Deep Magic' obviously meant "God's Justice" (1974: 110). To be fair, also in Tolkien's case there was an early reviewer who had stated that "[f]or a generation that can't make head or tail of St. Paul, Mr. Tolkien has got Isaiah and St. Paul back before readers' eyes" (Davenport 1965: 334).

Eventually, however, it is Lewis himself who, as it is argued by Marvin D. Hinten in the book *The Keys to the Chronicles: Unlocking the Symbols of C.S.*

---

11 *Genesis Rabbah*, a Talmud period *midrash*, comments on the creation act of heaven and earth by God in Genesis 1:1 by stating: "To what is this like? A king who had empty glasses. The king said: 'If I put hot water in them, then they will expand and break, and if I put cold water in them, they will contract and shatter.' What did the king do? He mixed hot water with the cold water and put them in the glasses. So too the Holy One of Blessing said: 'If I create the world with the attribute of compassion alone, no one would be concerned with the consequences of their actions. With the attribute of judgment alone, how could the world stand? Rather, behold I create it with both the attribute of judgment and the attribute of compassion, and hopefully it will stand'" (12, 15).

*Lewis's Narnia*, "asserted, in a 1960 letter, that the Stone Table represented (he said 'is') Moses' table" (*Letters to Children* 93, qtd. in Hinten 2005: 16). It is then clear that:

> This "table" is another word for the stone tablets upon which the Ten Commandments were inscribed, as described in Exodus 32:16: "And the tables were the work of God, and the writing was the writing of God, graven upon the tables." [...] [Therefore,] [w]hen the witch confronts Aslan, [and] she reminds him of the "Deep Magic", that "every traitor belongs to me as my lawful prey and that for every treachery I have a right to a kill." [...] [T] his seems an oblique reference to Romans 6:23a, "The wages of sin is death". The word *lawful* is appropriately chosen, as the magic is written on the Stone Table, which represents the requirements of the Old Testament law. (Hinten 2005: 16-17)

The said passage from the *Letters to Children* actually reads: "The stone table *is* meant to remind one of Moses' table" (93; emphasis original). It is therefore evident that the Pauline reading of the passage lies on a very firm ground.

## Tolkien and Pauline Law: Marring and Marrying

Although any analogous claims are somewhat less evident when applied to Tolkien, it does not mean that the reasons for such an interpretation of some key elements in his works are feeble. In fact, in the ninth issue of the journal of *Tolkien Studies*, Amelia A. Rutledge published an insightful article titled "'Justice is not Healing': J.R.R. Tolkien's Pauline Constructs in 'Finwë and Míriel'." There she argues that "Pauline teachings about the law's insufficiency in the economy of grace can serve as an heuristic that makes possible some clarification both of the Valar's debate and the judgments of Manwë and of Námo/Mandos, Manwë's voice in the judgments of Arda" (2012: 60).

Miriel's case, which is judged by the Valar in their debate, is crucial to the understanding of both Middle-earth theology and Tolkien's own view of things. Although being essentially immortal, Miriel, the elven wife of Finwë, wishes to die because her giving birth to Fëanor drained the whole of her vital forces. Her husband, also an Elf, desires to have more children, and so he wishes to remarry, thus coming into conflict with the natural monogamy of the Elves.

The discussion ensuing among the Valar demonstrates that, despite the fact that immortality and monogamy are unviolable principles of the elven natural law, the validity of that law in its conception by the Lawmaker is dependent upon the uncorrupted state of the very same nature in the original plan of the Creator Ilúvatar, a plan which was subsequently altered in the wake of Morgoth's rebellion, thus causing the Marring of Arda. This entails that the application of these principles as inviolable in the context of Arda Marred cannot be straightforward, but needs to be carefully reconsidered. Eventually, the King of the Valar, Manwë, overrules his decision, which shall prove to be ripe with consequences for the Elves' subsequent history: both requests, that of Miriel and that of Finwë, are granted.

In their debate, as Rutledge points out, it soon becomes evident how Manwë's speech resonates with the echoes of Pauline teachings:

> Regarding the insufficiency of the law, Manwë provides further exposition when he asserts that "Justice worketh only within the bonds of things as they are, accepting the marring of Arda..." (*Morgoth* 239), and further: "The liberty that it gave was a lower road that, if it led not still downwards, could not again ascend" (*Morgoth* 240). Compare "Wherefore then serveth the law? It was added because of transgressions, ...." (Galatians 3:19 ) or "Is the law then against the promises of God? God forbid: for if there had been a law given which could have given life, verily righteousness should have been by the law" (Galatians 3:21). (2012: 68)

Manwë's pronouncement is such that the Pauline overtones are immediately evident to anyone well-versed in the canon of the New Testament. Moreover, the praise of Healing is stressed in tones strikingly resembling Saint Paul's praise of Charity in 1 Cor 13:

> And Manwë spoke to the Valar, saying: 'In this matter ye must not forget that you deal with Arda Marred – out of which ye brought the Eldar. Neither must ye forget that in Arda Marred *Justice* is not *Healing*, Healing cometh only by suffering and patience, and maketh no demand, not even for Justice. Justice worketh only within the bonds of things as they are, accepting the marring of Arda, and therefore though Justice is itself good and desireth no further evil, it can but perpetuate the evil that was, and doth not prevent it from the bearing of fruit in sorrow.' (*MR* 239, emphasis original)

Rutledge then comments:

> In words similar to Paul's assertions, Manwë's rueful arguments ironically must limit the ultimate efficacy of law even as the Valar constitute a court of judgment. Justice can restore balance or equity, perhaps, but not heal; for Paul, the law may punish or exact compensation, but it does not conduce to salvation. (2012: 68)

In all the cases discussed in this chapter, both in Lewis and in Tolkien, the limitedness of Law depends on some prior misappropriation of the same Law.[12] In *Perelandra* and *That Hideous Strength*, it is the evil of the Bent One, who is also responsible for the misconduct of N.I.C.E., that has misappropriated both the role of Maleldil (Jesus) and true science. In Tolkien's letter to Michael George (28 October 1966), the "Sovereignties and Powers" (*Letters* 370, #290) are the evil politicians misappropriating science and research to their own ends. In *The Lion, the Witch and the Wardrobe*, the White Witch fancies herself a 'Queen' because she had been the 'Emperor's hangman.' In 'Finwë and Miriel,' Morgoth misappropriates the natural law in Arda by marring nature.

In the same way, we could add, in *The Lord of the Rings* Gollum claims the "Bagginses" to be thieves who "stole" his "precious" (*TT* 633), although the actual story is quite different. It is he who indeed stole the Ring from his friend Déagol, after having killed him. The Hobbits, instead, either found the Ring abandoned (Bilbo), or were given it (Frodo).

Likewise, the very claim to the Ring by Sauron himself, if taken on a legal basis, probably proves to have no foundation whatsoever. In the lack of precise information concerning the law codes of Middle-earth, we may still speculate how the case might be handled by stating that, although it was Sauron who forged the Ring, it was subsequently lost to Isildur, who won it by right of conquest. In consequence, only another conquest could once again legitimize Sauron's reclaim of his lost treasure. In a hypothetical lawsuit any person who finds it in the place where Isildur fell (Déagol), or where the previous owner lost it (Bilbo), or received it as a gift (Frodo), would probably be granted the right to keep it.

---

12 This should also demonstrate that, in agreeing with Saint Paul, neither Lewis nor Tolkien might be accused of any sort of antisemitism. In fact, the opposite seems to be the case, with Tolkien evidently inspired by a number of Jewish sources (Cramer 2006).

And so, without even taking into account the fact that the very creation of the Ring was a vile act of treachery, Sauron founds his claim to the Ring on the notion of an inviolable, absolute, and exclusive property of an item by its maker, which is a principle no code recognizes (nor probably could), and is not even valid when applied to Eru/God bestowing the gift of freedom upon his creatures. As Morgoth before him, Sauron thus wishes to misappropriate the Law.

Personally, I think that the evidence of the case concerning Tolkien and Pauline Law points toward something more than a simple "heuristic that makes possible some clarification" (Rutledge 2012: 60). To be straightforward, Tolkien proves not only to be acquainted with the Apostle, quoting from his Epistles[13] and comparing Lewis to him, but also to be endowed with a precise understanding of the Pauline concept of Law. On the other side, Lewis's usage of the aforesaid Pauline frame in his fiction is proven by a greater wealth of documents than in Tolkien's case. Therefore, the degree by which the two of them are recognizably inspired by Saint Paul is probably limited by the availability of biographical information, as we have three lenghty volumes of Lewis's correspondence edited by Walter Hooper and only a relatively short selection of Tolkien's letters, edited by Humphrey Carpenter.

Perhaps unsurprisingly, given my previous remarks on the confessional character of the two authors' creed, in the note to a letter to his son Michael (1 November 1963), Tolkien writes:

> Not that one should forget the wise words of Charles Williams, that it is our duty to tend the accredited and established altar, though the Holy Spirit may send the fire down somewhere else. God cannot be limited (even by his own Foundations) – of which St Paul is the first & prime example – and may use any channel for His grace. Even to love Our Lord, and certainly to call him Lord, and God, is a grace, and may bring more grace. Nonetheless, speaking

13 Tolkien cites Saint Paul also in another letter to his son Michael (undated). This time providing a negative example: "The 'protestant' search backwards for 'simplicity' and directness – which, of course, though it contains some good or at least intelligible motives, is mistaken and indeed vain. Because 'primitive Christianity' is now and in spite of all 'research' will ever remain largely unknown; because 'primitiveness' is no guarantee of value, and is and was in great part a reflection of ignorance. Grave abuses were as much an element in Christian 'liturgical' behaviour from the beginning as now. (St Paul's strictures on eucharistic behaviour are sufficient to show this!) Still more because 'my church' was not intended by Our Lord to be static or remain in perpetual childhood; but to be a living organism (likened to a plant), which develops and changes in externals by the interaction of its bequeathed divine life and history – the particular circumstances of the world into which it is set" (*Letters* 394, #306).

> institutionally and not of individual souls the channel must eventually run back into the ordained course, or run into the sands and perish. Besides the Sun there may be moonlight (even bright enough to read by); but if the Sun were removed there would be no Moon to see. What would Christianity now be if the Roman Church had in fact been destroyed? (*Letters* 339, #250)

In the letter in which the ecumenical openness to other churches does not question the primacy of Roman Catholicism, Tolkien significantly notes how Saint Paul is a witness to the impossibility for God to be limited, not even by 'his own Foundations,' the expression clearly signifying the ancient alliance between God and Israel, an alliance the terms of which were determined, specified and made possible by Moses' acceptance of the Law. To call for Saint Paul as witness to the limitedness of the Law is an evident indicator of Tolkien's awareness of the Pauline notion of Law. Therefore, I would suggest that the influence that this notion has on Tolkien's narrative, which Rutledge finds so implicit, should be considered almost explicit, though not as well documented as in C.S. Lewis.

## Conclusions

To admit that both authors were influenced by Saint Paul's concept of Law does not obviously entail that such an influence was developed in the same way by the two, as I hope to have clarified. What might be termed as the moral, if not always political or social, ethics of responsability towards others seems to be the basis upon which Tolkien conceived his understanding of evil as causing the inadequacy of the Law by selfish tyranny and usurpation. Conversely, Lewis declines the same Pauline concept on an educational and intellectual basis, classifying the evil that misappropriates the Law chiefly as obscurantism and ignorant teaching. As I hope to have demonstrated, the difference is also rooted in their respective Christian confessions, without diminishing the importance of their shared affinities to faith, knowledge, taste, and character, as well as their mutual friendship and the fact that they were both members of the Inklings.

The evil Witch in Narnia may still perhaps understand the error in her ways and be redeemed, her evil being chiefly blindness to the truth of God that Aslan personifies. Her evil thus, in a sense, stems from 'insufficient' education. Tolkien's Sauron – and to some extent Saruman – know perfectly well that what they are doing is both practically and morally wrong, and yet they do it, and would keep on doing it until their eventual annihilation. They are irredeemable, and their evil pertains to free will. At Mount Doom, Frodo knows perfectly well he will become a traitor by claiming the Ring, and yet such is his choice, although he is, at least partially, saved before it is too late. Edmund Pevensy, instead, appears to have little understanding of the consequences of his betrayal, as does Mark Studdock, working for the evil powers without fully realizing it, in *The Space Trilogy*. However, when they learn the actual truth, they both act in the right and proper way. Even the Witch's fault is explained as ignorance of the 'Deeper Magic.' It seems that, at the crucifiction of Jesus, the Witch's role would be rather that of the Pharisees, condemning the Lord as a false teacher, while Sauron would probably be the Romans, executing Him as a political rebel.

Accordingly, in a 1959 letter to Dan Tucker, Lewis wrote that the whole issue with politics was actually a matter of education:

> A hundred years ago we all thought that Democracy was it. Neither you nor I probably think so now. It neither allows the ordinary man to control legislation nor qualifies him to do so. The real questions are settled in secret and the newspaper keep us occupied with largely imaginary issues. And this is all the easier because democracy always in the end destroys education. (*CL III* 1105)

As Justin Buckley Dyer and Micah J. Watson report, "Six days before he died in November 1963, Lewis responded to a Mrs. Frank Jones, noting that 'Our papers at the moment are filled with nothing but politics, a subject in which I cannot take any interest'" (2016: 6). Some scholars claim that Lewis was probably overstating his dislike, yet the very fact he overstated it is quite significant, for it inevitably entails that politics is not the actual focus of his position, the focus which we have previously seen to be chiefly educational.

A lesser known letter by Tolkien in response to a fellow teacher Mrs. Mountfield, dated 17 January 1964, discloses more of his scepticism concerning the subject of education as a privileged means of religious salvation and any other long-standing formative effect (although, after years, he always seems to recall his pupils with affection):

> All teaching is exhausting, and depressing and one is seldom comforted by knowing when one has had some effect. I wish I could now tell some of mine

> (of long ago) how I remember them and things they said, though I was (only, as it appeared) looking out of the window or giggling at my neighbour. (qtd. in Flood 2014)

To conclude, by returning to the place where we started, while Tolkien always maintained that he, like every Christian, was after all a "converted heathen" ('English and Welsh' 162), Lewis looked at conversions in a more general sense, and no doubt, referring to his own, when he claimed that

> When the most important things in our life happen we quite often do not know, at the moment, what is going on. [...] You can see it even in simple matters. A man who starts anxiously watching to see whether he is going to sleep is very likely to remain wide awake. As well, the thing I am talking of now may not happen to every one in a sudden flash – as it did to St. Paul or Bunyan: it may be so gradual that no one could ever point to a particular hour or even a particular year. And what matters is the nature of the change itself, not how we feel while it is happening. (*MC* 146)

Also in *Mere Christianity*, shortly before the above-quoted passage, Lewis says something which could also be a perfect comment on Frodo's quest to Mount Doom: "we cannot [...] discover our failure to keep God's law except by trying our very hardest (and then failing)" (146).

To briefly sum up the whole account of Pauline Law as understood by Tolkien and Lewis, I would like to put side by side their formulations of Saint Paul's views on Law. As we have seen, in the words of Aslan, "though the Witch knew the Deep Magic, there is a magic deeper still which she did not know. Her knowledge goes back only to the dawn of time. But if she could have looked a little further, into the stillness and the darkness before Time dawned, she would have read there a different incantation" (*LWW* 170-71). The Deeper Magic from before the Dawn of Time, is, simply put, Grace and Mercy. In the same way, the Elder King Manwë remarks that "Neither must ye forget that in Arda Marred *Justice* is not *Healing*" (*MR* 239, emphasis original), meaning that it is, instead, Mercy that heals. In brief, somehow merging the Pauline views of Tolkien and Lewis, one gets what seems like a riddle, but actually is only an oblique way to praise God's Grace: Deep Magic from the Dawn of Time is not Healing.

## About the Author

Giovanni Carmine Costabile holds an MPhil in Philosophy from the Università della Calabria in Italy. An independent researcher, freelance translator, and private teacher, he has published on Tolkien and C.S. Lewis in several journals and periodicals, and presented papers at conferences and events in Leeds, San Marino, Oxford, and throughout Italy. In 2018, his authorized research in the Weston Library in Oxford resulted in the publication in Italy of a much-discussed monograph on Tolkien *Oltre le Mura del Mondo: Immanenza e Trascendenza nell'opera di JRR Tolkien*. In the following year, his contribution to Oronzo Cilli's praiseworthy volume *Tolkien's Library* was acknowledged by the author both in the book itself and, later, in a reply to Christina Scull and Wayne Hammond's review. In the same year, an essay of his was included in the Walking Tree Publishers volume *'Something has gone crack'd': New Perspectives on J.R.R. Tolkien in the Great War*. Giovanni Carmine Costabile also translates into and from Italian various works of fiction and non-fiction related to philosophy, theology, history, imagination and myth.

## Bibliography

Barnett, Paul. 2002. *Jesus and the Rise of Early Christianity: A History of New Testament Times*. Westmont, IL: Intervarsity.

Bromiley, Geoffrey W. (ed.). 1979. *The International Standard Bible Encyclopedia*. Grand Rapids, MI: William B. Eerdmans.

Burton, Ernest De Witt. 1928. *A Critical and Exegetical Commentary on the Epistle to the Galatians*. New York: Scribner's.

Carpenter, Humphrey. 2006. *The Inklings*. London: HarperCollins.

Clark, David G. 2007. *C.S. Lewis: A Guide to his Theology*. Oxford: Blackwell Publishing.

Costabile, Giovanni. 2017. 'Stolen Pears, Unripe Apples: The Misuse of Fruit as a Symbol of the Original Sin in Tolkien's 'The New Shadow' and Augustine of Hippo's 'Confessions'.' *Tolkien Studies* 14, 163-67.

Cramer, Zak. 2006. 'Jewish Influences in Middle-earth.' *Mallorn* 44, 9-16.

Davenport, Guy. 'The Persistence of Light.' *National Review*, April 1965, 334.

Delling, Gerhard. 1971. 'Stoicheion.' *Theological Dictionary of the New Testament. Vol. 7*. Ed. Gerhard Kittel. Grand Rapids, MI: William B. Eerdmans, 670-83.

Dyer, Justin Bucklet and Micah Joel Watson. 2016. *C.S. Lewis on Politics and the Natural Law*. Cambridge: Cambridge University Press.

Esser, Hans Helmut. 1976. 'Law, Custom, Elements.' *The New International Dictionary of New Testament Theology*. Ed. Colin Brown. Grand Rapids, MI: Zondervan, 436-56.

Flood, Alison. 'JRR Tolkien called teaching 'exhausting and depressing' in unseen letter.' *The Guardian*, 12 June 2014. <https://www.theguardian.com/books/2014/jun/12/jrr-tolkien-teaching-exhausting-depressing-unseen-letter-lord-rings>. Accessed 30 May 2021.

Grant, Robert McQueen. 1966. *Gnosticism and Early Christianity*. New York: Columbia University Press.

Guyot, Gilmore H. 1944. 'The Chronology of St. Paul.' *Catholic Biblical Quarterly* 6/1, 28-36.

Hartman, David. 1997. 'Foreword.' *Between God and Man: An Interpretation of Judaism*. Ed. Abraham J. Heschel. New York: Free Press Paperbacks, 1-3.

Hinten, Marvin D. 2005. *The Keys to the Chronicles: Unlocking the Symbols of C.S. Lewis's Narnia*. Nashville, TN: Broadman and Holman.

Hooper, Walter (Ed.). 2004. *The Collected Letters of C.S. Lewis: Family Letters (1905-1931). Vol. I.* New York: HarperSanFrancisco.

2004. *The Collected Letters of C.S. Lewis: Books, Broadcasts, and the War (1931-1949). Vol. II.* New York: HarperSanFrancisco.

2004. *The Collected Letters of C.S. Lewis: Narnia, Cambridge, and Joy (1950-1963). Vol. III.* New York: HarperSanFrancisco.

Horrell, David G. 2015. *An Introduction to the Study of Paul*. London: T&T Clark.

Lewis, Clive Staples. 2017. *The Abolition of Man*. Great Britain: TellerBooks.

1985. *Letters to Children*. Eds. Marjorie Lamp Mead and Lyle W. Dorsett. New York: Macmillan.

1998. 'Learning in War-Time.' *The Essential C.S. Lewis*. Ed. Lyle W. Dorsett. New York: Colliers/Macmillan.

2014. *The Lion, the Witch and the Wardrobe*. London: HarperCollins.

2001. *Mere Christianity*. London: HarperCollins.

1996. *Perelandra*. New York: Scribner.

1998. 'Reflections on the Psalms.' *The Essential C.S. Lewis*. Ed. Lyle W. Dorsett. New York: Colliers/Macmillan.

1996. *The Screwtape Letters. Also includes 'Screwtape Proposes a Toast'.* New York: Simon & Schuster.

1979. *Selected Literary Essays*. Ed. Walter Hooper. Cambridge: Cambridge University Press.

1945. *That Hideous Strength*. London: John Lane The Bodley Head.

McIntosh, Jonathan S. 2017. *The Flame Imperishable: Tolkien, St. Thomas and the Metaphysics of Faërie*. Kettering, OH: Angelico Press.

Montgomery, John Warwick (Ed.). 1974. *Myth, Allegory and Gospel*. Minneapolis: Bethany House.

Niswonger, Richard. 1993. *New Testament History*. Grand Rapids, MI: Zondervan.

Pagels, Elaine. 1975. *The Gnostic Paul: Gnostic Exegesis of the Pauline Letters*. Philadelphia, PA: Fortress Press.

Pearson, Birger. 2001. 'Early Christianity and Gnosticism in the History of Religion.' *Studia Theologica* 55, 81-106.

Perkins, Pheme. 1993. *Gnosticism in the New Testament*. Minneapolis, MA: Fortress Press.

Potgieter, Raymond. 2014. 'Rabbi Abraham Joshua Heschel's Religious Antecedents as Legitimising a Christian Faith Expression.' *In die Skriflig/In Luce Verbi* 48/1, 1-8.

Prokulski, Walenty. 1957. 'The Conversion of St. Paul.' *Catholic Biblical Quarterly* 19, 453-73.

Ramsay, William Mitchell. 1895. *St. Paul the Traveller and the Roman Citizen*. New York: Putnam & Sons.

Rutledge, Amelia A. 2012. ''Justice is not Healing': J.R.R. Tolkien's Pauline Constructs in 'Finwë and Míriel'.' *Tolkien Studies* 9, 59-73.

Schweizer, Eduard. 1988. 'Slaves of the Elements and Worshipers of Angels: Gal. 4:3, 9 and Col. 2:8, 18, 20.' *Journal of Biblical Literature* 107, 455-68.

Tolkien, John Ronald Reuel. 2006. 'English and Welsh.' *The Monsters and the Critics and Other Essays*. Ed. Christopher Tolkien. London: HarperCollins, 162-97.

1994. *Morgoth's Ring*. London: HarperCollins.

2005. *The Lord of the Rings. Part 1. The Fellowship of the Ring*. London: HarperCollins.

2005. *The Lord of the Rings. Part 2. The Two Towers*. London: HarperCollins.

1981. *The Letters of J.R.R. Tolkien*. Ed. Humphrey Carpenter with the assistance of Christopher Tolkien. London: George Allen & Unwin.

Tóth, Ann Judith. 2019. 'Telesma and Stoicheion: Magical Statues in Byzantium.' *The Magical and Sacred Medical World*. Ed. Éva Pócs. Newcastle upon Tyne: Cambridge Scholars Publishing, 405-34.

Votaw, Clyde Weber. 1909. 'The Conversion and Early Ministry of Paul.' *The Biblical World* 33/4, 272-78.

Wilson, Andrew Norman. 1990. *C.S. Lewis: A Biography*. New York: W.W. Norton & Company.

Chiara Bertoglio



# The Lion and the Pitch: Creation Myths and Music in Lewis and Tolkien

**Abstract**

At the root of Lewis's and of Tolkien's fictional worlds there are two creation myths, narrated respectively in *The Magician's Nephew* (the first volume of *The Chronicles of Narnia*) and in the *Ainulindalë*, the first part of Tolkien's *The Silmarillion*. These two myths have numerous points in common, intertwined with substantial differences. First of all, both myths are closely related to the Christian narrative and theology of creation, even though both do not aim at re-presenting it or at re-telling it faithfully. Secondly, both myths describe in musical terms the act of creation: Lewis's Lion Aslan and Eru Ilúvatar, the Godhead of Tolkien's myth, call the creatures to Being through musical activities. Thirdly, there is a fascinating connection among the aural world (as symbolized by the divine music), the visible world, and the real world; the processes evoked by both Lewis and Tolkien can therefore be studied and analyzed also in connection with musical phenomena such as notation and interpretation. These common elements may derive both from common sources, arising from the cultural, religious, philosophical and literary background shared by both authors, and from the two writers' personal interaction. On the other hand, there are also important differences, partially arising from their different approaches to allegory and to the role of the Christian dogma in the literary world of fantastic fiction, and partially from the two authors' personality and style.

It may be argued that every human being on earth is a 'poet' inasmuch as he or she is able to perceive the beauty and wonder of the created world and to feel its enchantment. The ability to translate this feeling of awe and amazement into words is poetry proper, and, at its zenith, it may reach such heights that the reader is led to contemplate the world with new eyes, perceiving the mysterious greatness of creation beyond the normal appearance of the things we are so used to. This is probably a common experience, for readers of both J.R.R. Tolkien's and C.S. Lewis's novels: along with the undeniable delight their plots give to the reader and with the chiselled quality of their language, the reader frequently enjoys this perception of a renewed and refreshed gaze on the natural world. After one has been introduced to Tolkien's Ents or to Lewis's Dryads, trees may start to look very different.

If this enchantment for the created world may be considered as the first manifestation of a religious feeling among the human beings, then it may be argued that, by awakening our consciousness of the miracle and beauty of Nature (and, therefore, by suggesting the hidden/revealed presence of the supernatural behind Nature itself), the novels by Tolkien and Lewis act as a 'pre-Gospel', as an *euangelion* in their own way (Bassham 2018: 11).

This may be comprehended, in fact, as a symbol for how these two authors actually saw their own literary mission within the framework of their Christian faith. Even though their works of fiction should not be considered as 'apologetic' works, neither their value as literary creations should be downplayed by seeing them as mere paraphrases of Christian teachings. However the debate concerning the role of the artist as a 'sub-creator' is at the heart of their understanding of the poet's calling.

Within this framework, which inspires and surrounds the whole of their literary activity (at least, in Lewis's case, since his conversion), the role of their interpretation of the biblical narrative of Creation as staged in their novels acquires a fundamental importance, being not 'only' the restatement of one of the basic truths professed by the Christian faithful, but also the source and inspiration of Tolkien's and Lewis's life's work.

In this Chapter, I will focus my attention principally on the two accounts of Creation found, respectively, in Tolkien's 'Ainulindalë' (in the version published as the opening pages of *The Silmarillion*) and in Lewis's *The Magician's Nephew*, constituting the first episode of the multi-volume opus collectively known as *The Chronicles of Narnia*. In particular, I will analyse the theological implications of their choice to narrate Creation in musical terms;[1] thus, I would like to emphatically affirm that my standpoint is not that of literary criticism (though I will make use of findings and techniques derived from this discipline), nor will I attempt to trace the historical connections and relationships between the

---

1 On this subject, see Larsen 2010.

two authors and their literary activity; rather, I will try and give a theological interpretation of their 'myths' in what they musically signify.

## Myth and Sub-creation

Myth had an important role in the relationship between Tolkien and Lewis.[2] As is common knowledge, in fact, Lewis's conversion to Christianity (which he had abandoned as a youth) happened by stages. In 1929, Lewis came (rather reluctantly) to accept the existence of God, thus actually dropping the 'a' from his identification as an 'atheist' and becoming a 'theist':

> You must picture me alone in that room at Magdalen, night after night, feeling, whenever my mind lifted even for a second from my work, the steady, unrelenting approach of Him whom I so earnestly desired not to meet. That which I greatly feared had at last come upon me. In the Trinity Term of 1929 I gave in, and admitted that God was God, and knelt and prayed: perhaps, that night, the most dejected and reluctant convert in all England. (*SJ* 266).

However, it would take him another two years for embracing the Christian faith in full. On 19 September 1931, Lewis, Tolkien and Hugo Dyson had a famous night stroll on Addison's Walk, in the grounds of Magdalen College; Lewis expressed his skepticism as regards some of the Christian dogmas because of their similarity with archetypal narratives and mythological 'tales' found in earlier cultures. In other words, Lewis's thesis seems to have been that if a biblical episode or story appears to have literary models in other religious traditions, then the Bible is a mere cultural product which preserves interesting and sometimes fanciful interpretations of the 'real' world rather than historical facts and 'truths.' Interestingly, this stance embodies the (typically modern) chasm between scientific truth, made of solid, mathematically logical and rationally demonstrable 'facts,' and the symbolic world of poetry, art and religion. This chasm was not only a matter of cultural or philosophical speculation, for Lewis, since it translated into a very intense, deep and sometimes painful experience:

> Such, then, was the state of my imaginative life; over against it stood the life of my intellect. The two hemispheres of my mind were in the sharpest contrast. On the one side a many-islanded sea of poetry and myth; on the other a glib and

2 For an in-depth discussion of the two writers' friendship and how they influenced one another in terms of their literary work, see the first chapter in the present volume written by Justin Keena.

> shallow 'rationalism'. Nearly all that I loved I believed to be imaginary; nearly all that I believed to be real I thought grim and meaningless. (*SJ* 197).

During that famous walk (and possibly on other occasions as well), Tolkien helped Lewis to see matters differently. If a narrative sounds like a myth, it does not perforce follow that it is a lie; there may be myths which cannot claim to represent 'hard facts' in the same fashion as a chronicle would, but which nevertheless do speak real truths about the meaning of life; and there may be other 'myths' which, so to speak, grow on the soil prepared by the first type of myths, but nonetheless *do* represent 'hard facts' which one can define as 'true' under whichever meaning of the word. Lewis would summarize thus the gist of the belief he had embraced following his debate with Tolkien and Dyson:

> The heart of Christianity is a myth which is also a fact. The old myth of the Dying God, *without ceasing to be myth*, comes down from the heaven of legend and imagination to the earth of history. It *happens* – at a particular date, in a particular place, followed by definable historical consequences. We pass from a Balder or an Osiris, dying nobody knows when or where, to a historical Person crucified (it is all in order) *under Pontius Pilate*. By becoming fact it does not cease to be myth: that is the miracle. [...] To be truly Christian we must both assent to the historical fact and also receive the myth (fact though it has become) with the same imaginative embrace which we accord to all myths. The one is hardly more necessary than the other. ('Myth Became Fact' 343)[3]

This is, of course, Lewis's personal interpretation and later reworking of what had been sown by Tolkien and Dyson during their promenade, and so we cannot assume that this represents Tolkien's view precisely. What we do know is what Tolkien himself wrote to Lewis shortly after that episode, in the form of the poem *Mythopoeia*, and what he systematized in a more philosophical fashion in his essay 'On Fairy-Stories.' I will later touch upon some passages of *Mythopoeia* which seem to encapsulate a few of the most memorable ideas found in 'Ainulindalë;' here, however, I would like to recall some lines which embody Tolkien's concept of the relationship between human creativity (or *poiesis*) and God's revelation. Countering Lewis's earlier conviction that "myths were lies and therefore worthless, even though 'breathed through silver'" (*Myth* 97), Tolkien affirms:

---

3 See also Lewis's letter to Arthur Greeves (22 September 1931), in which he expresses this viewpoint more succinctly but chronologically more closely to Lewis's conversion (*CL I* 970), and *Surprised by Joy* (222).

> The heart of man is not compound of lies,
> but draws some wisdom from the only Wise,
> and still recalls him. Though now long estranged,
> man is not wholly lost nor wholly changed.
> Disgraced he may be, yet is not dethroned,
> and keeps the rags of lordship once he owned,
> his world-dominion by creative act. (*Myth* 98)

Here Tolkien's poetry is reminiscent of some passages from the biblical Book of Genesis: firstly, when we learn that God created the human beings "in our image, according to our likeness" (1:26), we have only been taught that God is Creator. The other attributes of the Godhead (such as omniscience, goodness, love etc.) have not yet been revealed; and if God's omniscience will invite humans to pursue knowledge and particularly knowledge of Him, if God's goodness will prompt us to pursue charity etc., the first calling of the human being is precisely that of fulfilling the Creator's likeness by being 'creative' (or 'sub-creative', as Tolkien would have put it).[4] Moreover, and consequently (2:19-21), Adam's very first action is to "give names" to God's creatures, corresponding (in the Jewish tradition) to a form of lordship over God's creation.[5] This is what, in my opinion, Tolkien implies by mentioning the 'throne,' 'lordship' and 'dominion' granted by God to humans.

The poet's and author's vocation is instead explicitly evoked in other lines of the same poem: "Blessed are the legend-makers with their rhyme / Of things not found within record time [...]. / I would that I might with the minstrels sing / And stir the unseen with a throbbing string" (*Myth* 99). As Caldecott put it, Tolkien "believes that our capacity to create is part of our resemblance to God. In every act of creation – *poesis* – we echo the divine creation of the world itself. The creation of whole worlds in fantasy is, Tolkien believes, the highest form of human creativity" (2014: 68). Tolkien further explores these topics in his justly famous essay *On Fairy-Stories*, which may be considered almost as a manifesto of his aesthetics and of his spiritual view. There is no op-

4 In Tolkien's own words, "Fantasy remains a human right: we make in our measure and in our derivative mode, because we are made: and not only made, but made in the image and likeness of a Maker" (*TOFS* 50).

5 See also Caldecott (2014), where it is stated that "Made in the image of the Creator, Man cannot but create, and thus attempt to continue the Creator's work. Imagination is the garden or landscape of the soul, and the Creator's command to tend and cultivate the land applied just as much to this interior world as it did to Eden" (80).

position between the Story of Salvation and the tales narrated by human beings; rather, the pleasurable thrill we experience when a captivating tale manifests the providential design of God's love through the symbol of the *eucatastrophe* is a resonance of our predisposition to receive the Good News of the Gospel. In Tolkien's words, "in the 'eucatastrophe' we see in a brief vision that the answer may be greater – it may be a far-off gleam or echo of *evangelium* in the real world" (*TOFS* 77); moreover, "[t]he Evangelium has not abrogated legends; it has hallowed them, especially the 'happy ending'" (78). As we will later see, the same dynamics apply to the rules of music, of how it works on the human sensitivity, and may explain why both Lewis and Tolkien chose musical symbols in order to narrate the Creation of the world.

Here, however, what I wish to point out is that, for both Tolkien and Lewis, the (sub-)creation of mythical narratives (or 'fairy-stories'), far from being in competition with the Christian Revelation, was a privileged way of responding to God's primeval call to creativity, and to transmit the truth of the Gospel to the other human beings. As Lewis put it, "The resemblance between these myths [e.g., Balder or Adonis] and the Christian truth is no more accidental than the resemblance between the sun and the sun's reflection in a pond" (*RP* 124).

However, the human sub-creation is – in theological terms – an *analogue* of God's own creative activity; i.e. it is a creatural parallel to something which God possesses, is or does not just 'more' than what a human being can do, but on an utterly different ('Other') plane. Notwithstanding this, it remains possible, through analogy, to state meaningful truths about God by likening them to human experience, and, to a certain extent, vice-versa. Thus, God's creation is ex-nihilo, while human creativity is closer in kind to the 'composition' of music: i.e. an artistic combination of an (aural) material which is bestowed on us so that we may make something beautiful and meaningful out of it, with an activity which mirrors God's creativity as applied to our own creatural plane. This viewpoint was clearly Lewis's, as he explicitly affirmed:

> I won't admit without a struggle that when I speak of God 'uttering' or 'inventing' the creatures I am 'watering down the concept of creation'. I am trying to give it, by remote analogies, some sort of content. I know that to create is defined as 'to make out of nothing', *ex nihilo*... '*not* out of any pre-existing material'. It can't mean that God makes what God has not thought of or that He gives his creatures any powers or beauties which He Himself does not pos-

> sess. Why, we think that even human work comes nearest to creation when the maker has 'got it all out of his own head'. [...] This act [creation], as it is for God, must always remain totally inconceivable to man. For we – even our poets and musicians and inventors – never, in the ultimate sense make. We only build. We always have materials to build from. All we can know about the act of creation must be derived from what we can gather about the relation of the creatures to their Creator (*LM* 69).

Christian theology, by reading the biblical account of Genesis through the lens of the Prologue to St. John's Gospel, has interpreted God's 'utterances' by which the world was created as a manifestation of the divine *Logos*, the second Person of the Holy Trinity; it has also been argued that the Father's eternal generation of the Son within the Holy Trinity, but also the creation of the world by the Father through the Son in the Spirit are two aspects of a kenotic process which will culminate in Christ's Incarnation and in his Passion. In other words, the Father 'gives Himself' eternally and wholly to the Son, He gives life to the created world through the Son, and gives His divine life to humankind through the Incarnation and the ultimate Gift of Christ's Cross.

God's Word, his *Logos*, is therefore his Son; this Word is simultaneously a self-Revelation, a Gift, and a *kenosis*. It is within this framework that we should construe a Christian understanding of the process of Creation, and also of what human creativity may signify and imply. For a human being, to create is not to assert his or her individuality to the detriment of others, let alone exert a form of power or possession by means of the creative forces we have received; rather, it is a form of self-sacrifice, of oblation in which we give our innermost self in response to a divine calling.[6] This sacrificial dimension was perhaps glimpsed by Lewis when he stated that

> God, besides being the Great Creator, is the Tragic Redeemer. Perhaps the Tragic Creator too. For I am not sure that the great canyon of anguish which lies across our lives is *solely* due to some prehistoric catastrophe. Something tragic may... be inherent in the very act of creation (*LM* 91).

As we will see, this kenotic dimension is fully present (though frequently overlooked) in both Tolkien's and Lewis's creation narratives, and is very meaning-

6 For instance, this concept underlies Sofia Gubaidulina's composition of *Offertorium*, a violin concerto dedicated to Gidon Kremer. In the composer's words, this work embodies "the sacrificial offering of Christ's crucifixion... God's offering as He created the world... The offering of the artist, the performing violinist... The composer's offering" (qtd. in Bannister 2017: 70).

fully embodied by their choice to represent Creation as a musical act. Moreover, it also impacts on their very choice to write, and to give voice through their writings to the message of the incarnate *Logos*.

## Seeds of the Word

While some Christians will be surprised by the idea that myths may be an embryonic form of revelation, this concept is not alien from Christian history and theology; rather, its roots are found in the earliest Patristic era, and contributed to that extraordinary flowering of Christian theology which resulted from the encounter between the Jewish tradition of Biblical revelation and the Greek system of thought and practice which we call philosophy. The first trace of such an inclusive attitude (which does not imply either syncretism or relativism) is found in Paul's famous Discourse of the Areopagus (Acts 17), and its development is attributed to Justin Martyr's *Apologies* (Roberts et al, 1885), where the idea of the Seminal *Logos* (*Logos spermatikos*) is discussed. For Justin, "Whatever things were rightly said among all men, are the property of us Christians" (XIII); since God's *Logos* exists outside Time and therefore 'before' Time itself, "He was and is the Word who is in every man" (X). Thus, for Justin, "all the writers were able to see realities darkly through the sowing of the implanted word that was in them" (XIII). This beautifully resonates with Tolkien's idea that "Only by myth-making, only by becoming a 'sub-creator' and inventing stories can Man aspire to the state of perfection he knew before the Fall. Our myths may be misguided, but they steer however shakily towards the true harbour" (qtd. in Carpenter 1977: 147). This experience is explicitly narrated by Lewis in *The Last Battle*, where the experience of the righteous pagan is embodied by the character of Emeth, who has honestly and faithfully believed in the false god Tash while constantly searching Truth; after his death, Emeth meets Aslan, who states: "Child, all the service thou hast done to Tash, I account as service done to me" (199). At the same time, Aslan explicitly denies all possibility of syncretism or relativism: Aslan accepts Emeth's worship of Tash "Not because he and I are one, but because we are opposites; [...] for I and he are of such different kinds that no service which is vile can be done to me, and none which is not vile can be done to him" (199-200). Aslan eventually grants eternal bliss to Emeth by affirming: "Unless thy desire had been for me thou wouldst not have sought so long and so truly. For all find what they truly seek" (200).

Thus, for both Tolkien and Lewis, creation myths were not the naïve attempt of pre-scientific people to explain (or explain away) those natural phenomena for which they did not (yet) have a convincing rational account; rather, they were narratives "woven by us" and which, "though they contain error, will also reflect a splintered fragment of the true light, the eternal truth that is with God" (Carpenter 1977: 147). This expression mirrors the one found in *Mythopoeia*, where Tolkien contemplates sub-creation as the refraction of light "splintered from a single White / to many hues, and endlessly combined / in living shapes that move from mind to mind" (99). As a matter of fact, these many "hues" which refract the "single White" are beautifully paralleled by the idea of the Ainur adorning Ilúvatar's theme, each singing in his or her individual and personal style.

In this perspective, creation myths occupy a unique place in the history of humankind. In the biblical Book of Wisdom, it is argued that the enchanting beauty of the created world should have led the heathen to the Creator: "If through delight in the beauty of these things people assumed them to be gods, let them know how much better than these is their Lord, for the author of beauty created them" (13:3). This topic was later developed and constituted the root of the (especially Catholic) teaching about 'natural theology;' a topic which was brought once more to the fore in 1879, when Pope Leo XIII issued the Encyclical Letter *Aeterni Patris* on the relationship between philosophy and faith.[7]

Thus, the study of creation myths and narratives acquired, for Tolkien and Lewis, a dimension far exceeding that of the anthropological curiosity, and became a standpoint from which to contemplate a primeval form of revelation and from which to take inspiration for their own creation stories. As I have elsewhere argued,[8] there may be numerous sources which could have suggested to either or both of them the idea of a creation in music: among them, and without repeating myself, I would like to cite the pseudo-Anglo-Druidic

7 On how *Aeterni Patris* sees the dialogue of faith and reason, see Bertoglio (2017).
8 See Bertoglio 2021.

*Barddas*, where God, "alone in the universe [...] said His own name, and the voice was so beautiful that the universe burst into being with sound, light and form" (Leeming 2010: 274).[9] The "melodious sweetness" of God's voice makes "nonentity [...] rejoice into life" (Williams 2020: 259). Moreover, there are Irish myths (which may have been of particular interest to Lewis, if he happened to know them) whereby the universe is given order and ratio through music and *poiesis* (Leeming 2010: 152).

The idea, found in Tolkien's 'Ainulindalë,' that there is a "musical" relationship between the One Godhead and a class of superhuman beings, the Ainur, has, in turn, of course, a long and august history. In the West, it is particularly identified with the Pythagorean (and later Platonic) myth of the Sirens producing what came to be known as the harmony of the Spheres.[10] It is obviously impossible to trace the development of this myth here; moreover, I have treated elsewhere some of its declinations with reference to Tolkien's 'Ainulindalë' and to Dante's *Commedia*, which, it should be pointed out, was one of the many literary works which Tolkien and Lewis liked to discuss together.[11] Thus, it is unsurprising that also Lewis had a clear perspective on the topic of the harmony of the Spheres (Schakel 2002: 103-04), and that he made use of this topic almost as a case-study in order to discuss the mindset of a medieval person:

> A man of the Middle Ages [...] did not think that the spaces he looked up at were silent, or dark or empty. Far from being silent, they were perpetually filled with sweet, immeasurable sound. The vast hollow spheres, turning each at its proper interval inside its superior, gave out a blended harmony. [The music of the spheres] is the only sound which has never for one split second ceased in any part of the universe; with this positive we have no negative to contrast. Presumably if (*per impossibile*) it ever did stop, then with terror and dismay, with a dislocation of our whole auditory life, we should feel that the bottom had dropped out of our lives. But it never does. The music which is too familiar to be heard enfolds us day and night and in all ages (*SMRL* 52).

Medieval philosophy and theology were, of course, indebted to the figure and works of St. Augustine, whose writings embody the encounter between biblical Revelation and philosophical thought which St. Justin had both imagined

9 See, also, Williams (2020: 47, 250-53, 2590).
10 On this topic, see Godwin (1992), in which a large collection of sources regarding the Harmony of the Spheres is found.
11 See Bertoglio 2021. As regards Tolkien and the music of the Spheres, Eden 2003.

and practised in turn. As Houghton perceptively observed, it is possible that Augustine's appraisal of the universe as "a wonderful song of succeeding events" (Letter 166, §13) may have influenced Tolkien's and Lewis's musical myths (Houghton 1995: 7); the connection between Augustine's discussion of Time and musical imagery is found also in other important works such as book XI of his *Confessions*. Following in Augustine's footsteps, St. Bonaventure likened the universe to a "most beautiful canticle," which develops "according to the best consonances" in a harmonic sequence of parts (*Commentaria* book I, distinction 44, article 1, question 3). Augustine's model (in particular his *De Genesi ad litteram*) is discernible also behind the description of creation provided by Hugh of Saint-Victor (in Taylor 1991: 156). For both of them, and even though what we perceive as a sequence of events did actually happen simultaneously, a series of stages can be observed in God's creative process, consisting of the divine will to create, the transmission to the angels of some kind of knowledge of this divine will and what we would call 'creation proper.' To this, Augustine also adds the contemplation of the created world by the angels, and, as summarized by Houghton "God's eternal support of the Creation through the Holy Spirit" (1995: 6). In fact, just as God's creative process should not be seen as a string of consecutive actions, conversely the creative act is not exhausted in 'the making of' the world, but rather (in its temporal dimension) is to be conceived as a continuing process to which the universe owes its life and existence.[12] This benign and loving care which God bestows on the world and particularly on His children is therefore both an integral part of 'creation' itself, and what we tend to call 'Providence.' It may be said, therefore, that 'Providence' is the unfolding in time of the *eucatastrophe* par excellence which is the Story of Salvation: we will later see the musical overtones of such a concept.

Among the many other sources which may have influenced Lewis's and Tolkien's creation myths, other scholars[13] have noted the importance of Milton's *Paradise Lost* and of Raphael's account of creation:

12 On this topic, see Hebrews 1:3. Fascinatingly, the following lines of Hebrews discuss the subordination of the angels to the divine *Logos*.

13 Among them Sayer (1994: 51) and Hardy (2014: 113-14). Hardy's monograph takes a look at Milton and Spenser as sources for Lewis's *Chronicles of Narnia*, whereas Sayer's biography of Lewis discusses his interest in early English poetry.

> Nor passed uncelebrated, nor unsung
> By the celestial choirs, when orient light
> Exhaling first from darkness they beheld;
> Birthday of heav'n and earth; with joy and shout
> the hollow universal orb they filled,
> And touched their golden harps, and hymning praised
> God and his works. (book VII, ll. 253-59).

As in Augustine, the celestial beings contemplate the work of 'God's hands,' rejoicing for its beauty and expressing their amazement through music. Schakel (2002: 105) has also observed the similarity of some lines of Dryden's *Song for St. Cecilia's Day* (1687) with Lewis's creation myth:

> From Harmony, from heav'nly Harmony
> This universal Frame began. [...]
> The tuneful Voice was heard from high,
> Arise ye more than dead.
> Then cold, and hot, and moist, and dry,
> In order to their stations leap,
> And MUSICK's pow'r obey" (stanza 1, ll. 1-10).

Also fascinating is a comparison of the creation accounts under discussion with Samuel T. Coleridge's *The Eolian Harp*, where the poet mentions the "soft witchery of sound / As twilight Elfins make," before invoking

> the one Life within us and abroad,
> Which meets all motion and becomes its soul,
> A light in sound, a sound-like power in light,
> Rhythm in all thought, and joyance everywhere." (ll. 26-29)

In these lines, we can observe the Platonic theme of the World-Soul embodied by the image of the intertwining of light and sound, as well as the typically Lewisian theme of the supernatural joy. Coleridge then wonders whether "all of animated nature / be but organic Harps diversely framed / That tremble into thought" (ll. 44-46) when they are animated by the "one intellectual breeze" which is "at once the Soul of each, and God of all" (ll. 47-48). The idea that God creates also by breathing his life-giving Spirit on the world's matter is also one which Lewis (certainly) and Tolkien (possibly) would allude to in their creation myths. The pantheistic touch inherent in Coleridge's poetry, it should be noted, is countered by the poet himself who, in the subsequent lines, adopts an explicitly Christian terminology that includes a humble request for mercy.

These examples may be complemented with others discussed, for example, in Caldecott (2014); among those I cited in some of my earlier publications I think it necessary to briefly mention Young's *Night Thoughts*, where "The song of Angels, all the melodies / of choral gods" (Night IX, ll. 2366-67) are cited; these "gods" behold man who is "the glory of [...] God" (Night IV, l. 442), and whose redemption is the true highpoint of God's creative act:

> Could angels envy, they had envied here;
> And some did envy; and the rest, though gods,
> Yet still gods unredeem'd (their triumphs man,
> Tempted to weigh the dust against the skies),
> They less would feel, though more adorn, my theme.
> They sung creation (for in that they shared);
> How rose in melody, that child of love! (Night IV, ll. 443-49).

Thus, a circular path starts to appear: on the one hand, the contemplation of the created world leads human beings to search for the origins of that beauty, and therefore to awaken in them the first spark of a religious feeling; on the other, by re-telling the process of creation, and/or by revealing the magic (or rather the mystery) hidden in the created world, the sub-creator opens the readers' eyes to a new appraisal of creation, which ultimately translates into a prayerful praise.[14] While this process is undoubtedly true, it does not imply that the beauty of creation may have originated religion by itself: rather, it is an instrument used by God in order to reveal Himself to human beings, in a process which maintains an important dimension of mystery and unfathomability. This was clearly in Lewis's mind when he famously wrote that "all the great religions were first preached, and long practiced, in a world without chloroform" (*PP* 5). As I have argued elsewhere (2018), dissonance and discord are two meaningfully different terms, and Tolkien demonstrated his mastery of the musical language by describing the emergence of evil in 'Ainulindalë' as 'discord.' In our post-lapsarian world, reason alone may stumble on the scandal of pain and evil, as actually happened to Lewis himself for "many years" (*MC* 38). The enchantment and joy we feel when we contemplate nature and life might lead to pantheism or to some kind of Manichaeism, unless they are understood as a form of revelation of a God who gave Himself in the *kenosis* of Creation.

14 See, for instance, Bassham (2018: 18). This experience is also beautifully described in Chesterton (2017: 32ff), where the enchantment provided to the soul capable of wonder is intensely portrayed.

## Musical Creations

Within this conceptual and cultural perspective, we will now discuss the creation myths found in *The Silmarillion* and *The Magician's Nephew*, by pointing out their similarities and differences. Lewis's and Tolkien's choice to represent Creation as a 'musical' act may be largely justified through the authors' love for music. Already in 1916, Lewis defined music as "the highest of the arts" (*They Stand Together* 112); he employed musical imagery to describe literary phenomena (for example, he wrote that fantasy stories are closer to symphonies than to novels, or he likened Milton's use of silences to that of a composer with rests in music: 'Edmund Spenser' 96 and 'A Preface to *Paradise Lost*, chapter 7). Even more significantly, Lewis stated that, "for many people (not all) music is the thing known in the present life which most strongly suggests ecstasy and infinity" (*MC* 137), and he meaningfully compared the medieval universe "to a fugue – the orderly and varied reiteration of the same *subject*" (*SMRL* 57). This viewpoint fascinatingly resonates with the 'polyphonic' concept of creation and of the universe which Tolkien depicted in 'Ainulindalë,' and which is less immediately apparent in Lewis's own book *The Magician's Nephew*. Finally, we should mention a fundamental concept in Lewis's theological thought, i.e. that of 'joy,' as clearly distinct from happiness or pleasure; for him, 'joy' was akin to the untranslatable German word of *Sehnsucht*, a mixture of longing, nostalgia, desire which is at the same time utterly delightful and piercingly painful. This very special kind of 'joy' was one of the clearest revelations of the Transcendent for him; and, well before his official conversion, music was one of the means through which this ecstatic experience inhabited his life (Hess 2010: 11). As concerns the importance of music in Tolkien's thought and writings, it cannot be overestimated, and has been extensively studied by some of the most important Tolkien scholars.[15]

Both Tolkien and Lewis, therefore, knew music, its language and also some of its technical issues and terms to a much higher degree than most casual listeners do. Their use of music as a symbol in their writings is therefore careful, precise, powerful and meaningful. And it is particularly impressive precisely in their

15 Among the most important works in the field are Eden (2003), Flieger (2005), the essays collected in Eden (2010) and in Eilmann and Schneidewind (2019), as well as Carswell (2018) etc.

creation myths, with which we are now particularly concerned. As is commonly known, Tolkien's *Silmarillion* was left unfinished at the author's death and posthumously collected, edited and published by his son, the late Christopher Tolkien. However, a detailed description of 'The Music of the Ainur' is found in Tolkien's famous letter to Milton Waldman (*Letters* 146, #131), and, as we have seen (and more significantly) some of its main themes are already present in Tolkien's *Mythopoeia*, his gift to Lewis. Excerpts from *The Silmarillion* had been read by Tolkien at the Inklings' meetings, and (as Tolkien himself explicitly acknowledged) had left an important impression on Lewis and inspired some of his writings. As Tolkien recalled, "Lewis was, I think, impressed by 'the Silmarillion and all that', and certainly retained some vague memories of it and of its names in mind" (*Letters* 361, #276). In *Mythopoeia*, we read a meaningful rhyme where 'lyre' and 'legendary fire' are coupled (as well as many passages which may have inspired Lewis's *The Voyage of the Dawn Treader*), as well as a description of evil as lying "not in God's picture but in crooked eyes / not in the source but in the tuneless voice" (*Myth* 101), thus already equating the Fall with a musical 'discord.'

Just as 'Ainulindalë' was printed after Tolkien's death, even though it narrates the beginnings of Arda, likewise *The Magician's Nephew*, where the genesis (and the Genesis) of Narnia are told was neither the first of the Narnia books to be written, nor the first to be published. Interestingly, both Narnia's 'Genesis' and its 'Apocalypse,' i.e. *The Magician's Nephew* and *The Last Battle* were written comparatively late; in particular, *The Magician's Nephew* was completed in 1954 and published in 1955. The influence of (or borrowings from) Tolkien's *legendarium* found in *The Chronicles of Narnia* has been repeatedly discussed, among others by J.R. Christopher (1987 and 1988a-b). Indisputably, however, the similar perspective found in the two works is not accidental. At the same time, there are also very apparent differentiations, such as the difference in style between the two accounts of Creation (a high, archaic, epical and almost Scriptural style in Tolkien's case, whereas in Lewis there are humorous touches even during the comparatively solemn narrative of the Creation of Narnia), or the context ('Ainulindalë' begins very directly, just as the Book of Genesis or the Gospel of John, while the Creation of Narnia takes place after several chapters of an adventurous and sometimes funny narrative).

We will therefore proceed to some more detailed comparisons between the two stories. First of all, the Creator is portrayed differently by the two authors: in Tolkien's case, there is no description of Eru/Ilúvatar (we only infer that He may have traits which can be interpreted as anthropomorphic when we are told about his 'hands' and his 'countenance'); moreover, and even though the case has been made for recognizing Trinitarian traits in Tolkien's description (Caldecott 2014: 72), the point is at best implicit, and at worst doubtful. Perhaps most importantly (at least as concerns the present discussion), Ilúvatar does not appear directly as a 'providential' God in Tolkien's legendarium. Of course, the whole of Arda's history is condensed within, and originates from, Ilúvatar's 'themes,' but He does not intervene manifestly and openly in the development of Tolkien's narratives.

By way of contrast, the Creation of Narnia is the work of Aslan, a Christological figure who is portrayed in the shape of a majestic and oversized Lion; he is described as the son of the 'Emperor-Beyond-the-Sea,' who never appears in *The Chronicles of Narnia*, and his life-giving breath (who also gives intelligence to the Talking Beasts) may be likened to a symbol for the Holy Spirit. Thus, the framework is much more explicitly Trinitarian than in Tolkien's case.

Then there is the role of Tolkien's Ainur. Their role is described clearly by the author in his above-quoted letter to Milton Waldman,

> The cycles begin with a cosmogonical myth: the *Music of the Ainur*. God and the Valar (or powers: Englished as gods) are revealed. These latter are as we should say angelic powers, whose function is to exercise delegate authority in their spheres (of rule and government, not creation, making or re-making). They are 'divine', that is, were originally 'outside' and existed 'before' the making of the world. Their power and wisdom is derived from their Knowledge of the cosmogonical drama, which they perceived first as a drama (that is as in a fashion we perceive a story composed by someone else), and later as a 'reality'. On the side of mere narrative device, this is, of course, meant to provide beings of the same order of beauty, power, and majesty as the 'gods' of higher mythology, which can yet be accepted – well, shall we say baldly, by a mind that believes in the Blessed Trinity. (*Letters* 146, #131)

It is particularly tantalizing to note Tolkien's emphasis in specifying that the Ainur have no authority of 'creation, making or re-making,' since their role in the shaping of Arda may seem very close to that of 'creators.' If we are to use Tolkien's language, however, even the Ainur are sub-creators rather than

'Creators.' The fashioning of Arda is the embodiment of their adornment of those themes which have their only and ultimate origin in Ilúvatar. Melkor's 'original sin' is precisely that of wanting "to bring into Being things of his own" (*Sil* 4), and to him Ilúvatar clearly states, "no theme may be played that hath not its uttermost source in me" (5).

Another trait which may easily be overlooked is the kenotic aspect of 'Ainulindalë.' As Tolkien states in the above-quoted letter, the "power and wisdom" (146) of the Ainur comes from a Knowledge with a capital K. This mirrors what is found in the first lines of 'Ainulindalë,' where Eru/Ilúvatar 'speaks' to the Ainur, who are "the offspring of his thought" (*Sil* 3). At first, "each comprehended only that part of the mind of Ilúvatar from which he came," but later, by listening to their brethren, "they came to deeper understanding, and increased in unison and harmony" (3). As in the Christian theological tradition, by creating intelligent Beings, God commits Himself to entering a relationship with them, and, since this relationship cannot by definition be one among peers, it will unavoidably take the shape of a Gift of Grace. Finally, Tolkien's mention of Creation as of a "cosmogonical drama, which [the Ainur] perceived first as a drama," i.e. as "we perceive a story composed by someone else" is also worth noting; the idea of drama[16] refers to such concepts as 'plot' (with its narrative overtones as concerns the presence of a dynamics of tension/distension), 'struggle,' 'relationship' – and also, of course, artistry and beauty.

The role of the Ainur, therefore, is first and foremost to receive Ilúvatar's theme (as 'a story composed by someone else'), and to engage (sub-)creatively with it, by adorning it in an activity which, far from being passive, involves their personality in full, thus linking their self-realization with their acceptance of Ilúvatar's Gift. The Ainur are later involved in the 'fashioning' of Arda, and intervene (more or less directly) in many events recounted in *The Silmarillion* (occasionally committing blunders which may have unforeseen and sometimes tragic consequences).

---

16 This definition enticingly anticipates Balthasar's monumental work Theo-Drama, one of the pillars of twentieth-century Catholic thought (in the second volume of *Theo-Drama*, interestingly, Lewis's definition of God as the 'Tragic Creator' is cited). There is also more than an echo of Tolkien's 'music of the Ainur' in Balthasar's view of the Truth as 'symphonic.' On Tolkien's possible influence on Balthasar, see Coutras (2016: 14), and the works cited there.

Among the Ainur, the character of Melkor stands out, as the originator of that 'discord' which will ultimately become 'evil' in the world of Arda. His pride, rebellion and attempts at the domination of his brethren produce great suffering among the greater and lesser creatures; however, as Tolkien is careful to repeatedly underpin, even Melkor "shall prove but [Ilúvatar's] instrument in the devising of things more wonderful, which he himself hath not imagined" (*Sil* 5). The Narnian character who most closely resembles Melkor (though with important differences) is Queen Jadis, the Witch of *The Lion, the Witch and the Wardrobe*, who introduces the Evil in Narnia. She "understood the music better than any of them", and "hated" (*MN* 116) this manifestation of Aslan's creative power. "She would have smashed that whole world, or all worlds, to pieces, if it would only stop the singing" (116). She also tries to kill Aslan, but though she manages to hit him with an iron bar, he remains unscathed (123-24); indeed, here too violence is turned into goodness and life by the divine character, as the iron bar becomes the seed of Narnia's iconic lamp-post (127). Just as Melkor's music is "more violent than before" and "loud, and vain, and endlessly repeated," like "a clamorous unison [...] of many trumpets" (recalling the typical traits of military music), which essays "to drown the other music by the violence of its voice" (*Sil* 5), so Jadis acts with physical violence in the attempt to silence Aslan's song. In the even more dramatic enactment of Aslan's self-sacrifice in *The Lion, the Witch and the Wardrobe*, Aslan will actually die (in a scene modelled upon Christ's passion and death), but the Witch's seeming victory will be a defeat:

> though the Witch knew the Deep Magic, there is a magic deeper still which she did not know. Her knowledge goes back only to the dawn of Time. But if she could have looked a little further back, into the stillness and the darkness before Time dawned, she would have read there a different incantation. She would have known that when a willing victim who had committed no treachery was killed in a traitor's stead, the Table would crack and Death itself would start working backwards (*LWW* 170-71).

If therefore Jadis shares with Melkor some important traits (a mysterious power, an exquisite beauty which reveals her original potential for the good, the hatred for the Creator's music, the capability to initiate the evil), the role of the Ainur seems to have no parallel in Lewis's Narnia. True, there is no Narnian character partaking of the role and of all the attributes of the Ainur. However, I would argue that some of their traits are shared by two categories of creatures.

Firstly, one of the most important Biblical inspirations for the Music of the Ainur is found in the Book of Job, where God evokes the beginning of all times as the moment "when the morning stars sang together / and all the heavenly beings shouted for joy" (38:7). And while the Ainur are not 'stars' in Tolkien's 'Ainulindalë,' in *Mythopoeia* there is a passage which suggests a meaningful connection between angelic creatures such as the Ainur and the stars:

> He sees no stars who does not see them first
> of living silver made that sudden burst
> to flame like flowers beneath the ancient song,
> whose very echo after-music long
> has since pursued (98).

In *The Magician's Nephew*, the voice of the as yet unnamed and unseen Aslan is

> suddenly joined by other voices; more voices than you could possibly count. They were in harmony with it, but far higher up the scale: cold, tingling, silvery voices. The second wonder was that the blackness overhead, all at once, was blazing with stars. [...] The new stars and the new voices began at exactly the same time. If you had seen and heard it, as Digory did, you would have felt quite certain that it was the stars themselves which were singing, and that it was the First Voice, the deep one, which had made them appear and made them sing (115).

In fact, the Narnian stars are not merely "the great flaming globes they are in ours. They are people" (*LB* 184), and their singing, caused by and attuned with the Creator's Voice, is their own and unique mode of being.[17]

On the other hand, the 'providential' dimension which motivates the interventions of the Ainur in Arda is echoed (rather paradoxically) by the role of the Children in Lewis's Narnia. When Prince Tirian despairs for his own life and especially for that of his country, he first begs Aslan himself to come – "Come and help us Now!" (*LB* 58) and then asks him to "send [...] the helpers from beyond the world" (58). Indeed, the children coming from 'our' world "have always come in" to Narnia "when things were at their worst" (*LB* 58). His prayer is fulfilled, as Eustace and Jill are sent to him, not unlike the archangel

17 I am unavoidably reminded of the creation of the angels as narrated in Dante's *Paradiso* (canto XXIX, ll. 13-18).

Raphael to Tobias (Tobit 3:17ff). And just as the Ainur witness the musically creative act of Ilúvatar, so Polly and Digory (another couple of children), along with the Cabby (who has just finished a religious hymn) are witnesses to Aslan's creation (*MN* 115-19).

In both accounts of the Creation, there is an initial Void, a Nothing; in both, the Creator makes everything "out of [his] head" (*MN* 123), and everything is an "offspring of his thought" (*Sil* 3). In both, the act of Creation has a kenotic dimension, as Aslan says to his creatures: "I give you yourselves; [...] I give to you forever this land of Narnia. I give you the woods, the fruits, the rivers. I give you the stars and I give you myself" (*MN* 134-35). Similarly, Ilúvatar invites the Ainur to "show forth your powers in adorning this theme, each with his own thoughts and devices, if he will. But I will sit and hearken, and be glad that through you great beauty has been wakened into song" (*Sil* 3). In both, Creation happens musically; the themes declared by Ilúvatar resonate in the great concert of the Ainur, while in Narnia it is Aslan himself who sings nature into being. Interestingly, and though both authors recount the might and power of the creating God, they also describe some of the divine music as "gentle [and] rippling" (*MN* 120), or "soft and sweet", as a "mere rippling of gentle sounds in delicate melodies" (*Sil* 4). In both cases, the aural precedes the visual, and causes the visual to come forth. As Polly observes, "when you listened to [Aslan's] song you heard the things he was making up: when you looked round you, you saw them" (*MN* 123). Similarly, Ilúvatar invites the Ainur to behold their music, showing "to them a vision, giving to them sight where before was only hearing; and they saw a new World made visible before them" (*Sil* 5). I have elsewhere discussed (Bertoglio 2021), the role of musical notation as a symbol for the eternal present, inasmuch as it allows the musician to contemplate simultaneously the unfolding of temporal events; the 'Vision' which parallels and complements the musical component of creation may be symbolized by a musical score describing Aslan's and the Ainur's song.

## Conclusions

Though these comparisons demonstrate the closeness of the two authors' perspectives and also of certain specific details of their narratives, there is a deeper level which still needs to be explored, and which is possibly the most important of all. As I have stated above, music is employed by both writers as a symbol for the unfolding of Time and History, and the Providence itself. Actually, the end of (Narnia's) Time is marked by Father Time's blowing of a horn (*LB* 182). In Tolkien's *Mythopoeia*, "Time unrolls / from dark beginnings to uncertain goals" and the task of the sub-creators is to "unfurl" the "involuted breath" of speech, while they may also "spin" the "wish-fulfilment dreams" which "cheat / [their] timid hearts and ugly Fact defeat" (97-99). These dreams may act as surrogates which immediately (and transitorily) quench the human beings' longing for the Infinite (as happens, for example, with Casella's singing in Dante's *Purgatorio*, canto II, ll. 106-20); however, they also do tell an important truth about our innermost nature, giving form and shape to that *Sehnsucht* which played such a crucial role in Lewis's theological and spiritual experience, and which was so bound, for him, to the ecstasy of music.

Indeed, the pleasure we receive from music[18] depends precisely on the well-known dynamics of expectation and fulfillment; our knowledge of the language of music allows us to imagine how the musical discourse will develop, and to feel relieved and comforted when the musical tensions reach the distension we expected and hoped for. This is, of course, a musical parallel for the *eucatastrophe*: by demonstrating that the musical events do not happen by mere chance, but rather are harmoniously, intelligently and intelligibly organized in time, the composer gives meaning to our time, and encourages us to believe that also the factual events of our lives are not haphazardly combined, but rather part of a 'story.' This in turn parallels the action of the author of fiction, of the 'sub-creator,' who announces the presence of a loving God by narrating a story which is intelligible as a sequence of causes and effects, and reveals a providential design behind the seeming chaotic events of our lives. Creation, as we have previously seen, is not something happening once and for all, but

18 At least in the case of tonal music, of course.

rather is the continuing life received as a Gift from God's eternal Will, from his benign and loving Providence. As Alison Milbank put it,

> To tell a story, whether one's own or a traditional tale, is to mediate the world in its intentionality and narrative character. [...] For to tell a story is to affirm that there is meaning to life, and that experience is shaped and has an entelechy. (2009: 11)

To 'compose' a piece of music, therefore, is to give order and a (symbolically) understandable meaning to musical events; and these musical events are not created *ex nihilo* by the musician, who receives them from his or her musical tradition and language. It is their combination, their 'composition' that we call musical art; and it is through their combination that we perceive the 'providential' dimension of music, and consequently of our personal and social life.

Since 'Ainulindalë' is considered by Tolkien as the creation myth transmitted by the Elves, it comes as no surprise that music has such a crucial role in its development. As Tolkien put it, "[The Elves'] 'magic' is Art, delivered from many of its human limitations. [...] And its object is Art not Power, sub-creation not domination and tyrannous re-forming of Creation" (*Letters* 145, #131). Longing, yearning, desire and nostalgia are rather typical feelings of Tolkien's Elves; and this too resonates with Lewis's view of the role of *Sehnsucht* as a mystical experience of joy symbolized by music.

Ilúvatar and Aslan are depicted as creating the universe through music; thus, the instantaneous, eternal and simultaneous view of the world which belongs outside time to the creating God unfolds in Time, in 'our' Time, with the same purposeful, graceful and harmonious beauty which we experience in an artfully composed piece of music. By contemplating our history and our story as a song, we may grasp that it will develop beautifully, even though our temporal experience, fragmentary and short-sighted as it is, may prevent us from glimpsing its ultimate beauty. As St Bonaventure put it in his 'Commentaria,' the "beautiful canticle" of the history of the universe and of God's judgements cannot be evaluated or appreciated by those who hear it only partially (625); however, if at least we perceive its "musicality", we may trust that a great symphony does exist, and that it will be revealed, in its providential beauty, when Time will cease and eternity begin.

## About the Author

Chiara Bertoglio (*1983) has a PhD in Music Performance Practice (Birmingham, 2012), postgraduate degrees in Theology (Nottingham 2018) and is a professional concert pianist. Among her publications, *Reforming Music. Music and the Religious Reformations of the Sixteenth Century* (Berlin: De Gruyter, 2017) is the recipient of the RefoRC Book Award. Her most recent publications include *Musical Scores and the Eternal Present* (Eugene OR: Pickwick, 2021) and vols. IV-V of her recording project *Bach & Italy* (Da Vinci Classics). She teaches at Italian Conservatories and Pontifical Universities. Her website is www.chiarabertoglio.com..

## Bibliography


Augustine of Hippo. 1887. 'Letter 166. From Augustine to Jerome, on the Origin of the Soul'. *Nicene and Post-Nicene Fathers, First Seris, Vol. 1.* Ed. Philip Schaff. Buffalo, NY: Christian Literature Publishing Co..

Bannister, Peter. 2017. 'Kenosis in Contemporary Music and Postmodern Philosophy.' *Contemporary Music and Spirituality.* Eds. Robert Sholl and Sander van Maas. Abingdon: Routledge, 54-81.

Bassham, Gregory. 2018. 'Lewis and Tolkien on the Power of the Imagination.' https://epistleofdude.files.wordpress.com/2018/11/lewis-tolkien-imagination.pdf, Accessed 2 March 2020.

Bergman, Jerry. 2016. *C.S. Lewis: Anti-Darwinist: A Careful Examination of the Development of His Views on Darwinism*. Eugene, Oregon: Wipf & Stock.

Bertoglio, Chiara. 2017. 'The Untimely Timeliness of Fides et ratio.' *Logoi.ph* II/7, 337-354.

2018, 'Dissonant Harmonies: Tolkien's Musical Theodicy.' *Tolkien Studies* 15, 93-114.

2021. *Musical Scores and the Eternal Present. Theology, Time and Tolkien.* Eugene (OR): Pickwick.

Bonaventure of Bagnoregio. 1934. 'Commentaria in IV libros Sententiarum.' *S. Bonaventurae Opera theologica selecta* Vol. 1. Quaracchi: Collegio San Bonaventura.

Caldecott, Stratford. 2014. 'A New Light: Tolkien's Philosophy of Creation in *The Silmarillion*.' *Journal of Inklings Studies* 4.2, 67-85.

Carpenter, Humphrey. 1977. *Tolkien: A Biography*. Boston: Houghton Mifflin.

Carswell, John M. 2018. *Tolkien's Overture. Concerning the Music of the Ainur.* Franklin Tennessee: True Myths Press.

Chesterton, 2017. Gilbert Keith. *Orthodoxy*. Edinburgh: CrossReach.

Christopher, Joe R. 1987. *C.S. Lewis*. Woodbridge, Connecticut: Twayne Publishers.

1988. 'J.R.R. Tolkien, Narnian Exile.' *Mythlore* 15.1, 37-45.

1988. 'J.R.R. Tolkien, Narnian Exile. Part II.' *Mythlore* 15.2, 17-23.

Coleridge, Samuel Taylor. 1997. 'The Eolian Harp.' *The Complete Poems of Samuel Taylor Coleridge*. London: Penguin Books, 87-88.

Coutras, Lisa. 2016. *Tolkien's Theology of Beauty. Majesty, Splendor, and Transcendence in Middle-earth*. New York: Palgrave MacMillan.

Dryden, John. 'A Song for St. Cecilia's Day, 1687.' *Selected Poems*. London: Penguin Books, 292-94.

Duriez, Colin. 1998. 'The Theology of Fantasy in Lewis and Tolkien.' *Themelios* 23.2, 35-51.

Eden, Bradford Lee. 2003. 'The "Music of the Spheres": Relationships between Tolkien's *The Silmarillion* and Medieval Cosmological and Religious theory.' *Tolkien the Medievalist*. Ed. Jane Chance. New York and London: Routledge: 183-93.

(ed.). 2010. *Middle-earth Minstrel: Essays on Music in Tolkien*. Jefferson North Carolina: McFarland & Company.

Eilmann, Julian and Friedhelm Schneidewind (eds.). 2019. *Music in Tolkien's Work and Beyond*. Zurich and Jena: Walking Tree Publishers.

Flieger, Verlyn. 2005. *Interrupted Music: The Making of Tolkien's Mythology*. Kent and London: The Kent State University Press.

Godwin, Joscelyn. 1992. *The Harmony of the Spheres. A Sourcebook of the Pythagorean Tradition in Music*. Rochester: Inner Traditions.

Halsall, Michael J. 2020. *Creation and Beauty in Tolkien's Catholic Vision. A Study in the Influence of Neoplatonism in J.R.R. Tolkien's Philosophy of Life as 'Being and Gift.'* Eugene Oregon: Pickwick Publications.

Hardy, Elizabeth Baird. 2007. *Milton, Spenser and The Chronicles of Narnia: Literary Sources for the C.S. Lewis Novels*. Jefferson, North Carolina and London: McFarland & Company.

Hess, Laura Ann. 2010. *Roads to the Great Eucatastrophe: The Christian Mythology of C.S. Lewis and J.R.R. Tolkien*. Honors College Capstone Experience/Thesis Projects, Paper 237.

Houghton, John. 1995. 'Augustine and the Ainulindalë.' *Mythlore* 21.1, 4-8.

Kilby, Clyde S. and Linda J. Evans. 1974. 'C.S. Lewis and Music.' *Christian Scholar's Review* 4.1, 1-15.

Larsen, Kristine. 2010. "'Behold Your Music!': The Themes of Ilúvatar, the Song of Aslan, and the Real Music of the Spheres." *Music in Middle-earth*. Ed. Heidi Steimel and Friedhelm Schneidewind. Zurich and Jena: Walking Tree Publishers, 11-28.

Leeming, David. 2010. *Creation Myths of the World: An Encyclopedia*. Santa Barbara: ABC CLIO.

Lewis, Clive Staples. 2004. *The Collected Letters of C. S. Lewis, Volume I: Family Letters 1905-1931*. New York: HarperCollins.

1959. 'Edmund Spenser.' *Major British Writers. Vol. 1*. New York: Harcourd, Brace & World, 91-181

2014. *The Last Battle*. London: HarperCollins.

2017. *Letters to Malcolm*. London: HarperCollins.

2014. *The Lion, the Witch and the Wardrobe*. London: HarperCollins.

2014. *The Magician's Nephew*. London: HarperCollins.

2017. *Mere Christianity*. London: William Collins.

1942. *A Preface to "Paradise Lost"*. London: Oxford University Press.

2015. *The Problem of Pain*. London: HarperCollins.

2017. *Reflections on the Psalms*. London: HarperCollins.

1998. *Studies in Medieval and Renaissance Literature*. Cambridge: Cambridge University Press.

2010. *Surprised by Joy*. London: HarperCollins.

1979. *They Stand Together: The Letters of C. S. Lewis to Arthur Greeves (1914-1963)*. London: William Collins.

2014. *The Voyage of the Dawn Treader*. London: HarperCollins.

Matheson, Sue. 1988. 'C.S. Lewis and the Lion: Primitivism and Archetype in the *Chronicles of Narnia*.' *Mythlore* 15.1, 13-18.

Milbank, Alison. 2009. *Chesterton and Tolkien as Theologians. The Fantasy of the Real*. London: T&T Clark.

Milton, John. 2014. *Paradise Lost*. London: Penguin Books.

Roberts, Alexander, James Donaldson and A. Cleveland Coxe (eds.). 1885. *Ante-Nicene Fathers, Vol. 1*. Buffalo, NY: Christian Literature Publishing Co.

SAYER, George. 1994. *Jack: A Life of C.S. Lewis*. Wheaton, Illinois: Crossway.

SCHAKEL, Peter. J. 2002. *Imagination and the Arts in C.S. Lewis. Journeying to Narnia and Other Worlds*. Columbia and London: University of Missouri Press.

TAYLOR, Jerome (transl.). 1991. *The Didascalicon of Hugh of St Victor: A Medieval Guide to the Arts*. New York: Columbia University Press.

TOLKIEN, John Ronald Reuel. 1981. *The Letters of J.R.R. Tolkien*. Edited by Humphrey Carpenter, with the assistance of Christopher Tolkien. London: George Allen & Unwin; Boston: Houghton Mifflin.

1988. 'Mythopoeia.' *Tree and Leaf*. London: Unwin Hyman, 97-101.

2008. *On Fairy-Stories*. Eds. Verlyn Flieger and Douglas A. Anderson. London: HarperCollins.

2006. *The Silmarillion*. Edited by Christopher Tolkien. London: HarperCollins.

WILLIAMS 'Ab Ithel', John. 1862. *The Barddas of Iolo Morganwg*. Llandovery: Roderic.

YOUNG, Edward. 1853. *Young's Night Thoughts*. Edinburgh: J. Nicholl.

Łukasz Neubauer 

# *Ex nihilo* or *ex materia*?: The Acts of Sub-creation in J.R.R. Tolkien's Arda and C.S. Lewis's Narnia


**Abstract**

The cosmogonic dramas that unfold in Tolkien's Arda and Lewis's Narnia easily rank amongst the most ingenious mythopoeic narratives of the twentieth century. Their ingenuity does not, however, arise solely from the authors' immense creativity and familiarity with various mythological systems, because at the core of their sub-creative efforts are always the biblical accounts of Creation as they appear in Genesis 1:1-2:25, complete with God's commanding *fiats* and the elemental forces brought about in their consequence. Yet another vital component in the rich cosmogonic mosaics of Tolkien and Lewis is the Christian doctrine of *creatio ex nihilo*, the notion that, by the Lord's command, the world came into being out of nothing, that is to say not out of any pre-existing material. Its fundamental tenets may not always be so easily detectible in the *Ainulindalë* (Tolkien) and chapters 8 and 9 of *The Magician's Nephew* (Lewis), where the respective worlds are conceived, yet they are, in fact, not quite palpable even in the first book of the Hebrew Bible, where some forces already seem to be in existence prior to God's first Creative act.


Once at the centre of intellectual discourse (or, at least, very close to it), the dispute over the origins of our world (including, amongst other vital issues, the very moment and mode of its creation) has, over the past few centuries, been gradually relegated almost to the margins of academic debate, theological, philosophical, and, to a certain degree, cosmological. The reasons for this tendency are, of course, manifold, but amongst the most important ones there appears to be the nowadays widespread conviction that the theories of the Big Bang and Evolution (particularly that formulated in the mid-nineteenth century by Charles Darwin)[1] constitute universal, all-embracing answers to the fundamental questions of not only our existence, but also the genesis of everything that either exists or has existed on Earth. Notwithstanding that

1 Following the work of Yuri Filipchenko, there has been a distinction between 'macroevolution' (changes occurring above the species level) and 'microevolution' (the changes that may be observed within the individual species). The latter may be caused by what Darwin called the 'natural selection,' but the causes of the former remain quite elusive (Sepkoski 2008: 214).

all these models are still essentially no more than theories (a fact that many people today seem unwilling to acknowledge), it should be borne in mind that the former only deals with the initial expansion of the Universe, while the latter is chiefly concerned with the cumulative changes occurring in species through successive generations. As such, then, they do not account for (1) why these changes actually come about and, most importantly as to the essence of the following discussion, (2) how, in the first place, the material Universe ever came into existence.[2]

The field of human inquiry which seeks to answer these two questions is metaphysics, in particular the ontological branch of it, whose focus is upon such issues as being (both material and non-material), becoming, existence, and reality. The reasons for the primacy of metaphysical considerations in dealing with, for instance, the act of Creation stem from the fact that, unlike empirical science, in its methodological approach, metaphysics has at its core the study of the ultimate causes, the principles of which are believed to be eternal and unchanging. The character of such investigation is therefore inevitably speculative, on the one hand dependent upon one's trust in the revelatory sources (such as the book of Genesis), and, on the other, derived from a logical assessment of the concept(s) in question.[3]

It would be incorrect, though, to think of the applicability of metaphysics only within the frameworks of fully-developed theological systems such as Christianity or Judaism. The ontological approach could also be applied to all sorts of mythical narratives (ancient as well as modern), including the stories of creation, where some kind of divine creator (or creators) bring(s) the world into being and populate(s) it with living creatures. These stories may perhaps lack the dogmatic reverence of the Judeo-Christian tradition, nonetheless, they could likewise be subject to serious academic inquiry, also within the scope of broadly understood philological studies, literary as well as linguistic. It is with

2 Interestingly, the idea that the universal expansion could be traced back in time to a single point called the 'primeval atom' originally came from the Belgian Catholic priest (and professor of physics) Georges Lemaître. It should be borne in mind, though, that the methodology he used as a physicist was, for the most part, empirical (though not devoid of some elements of speculative reconstruction) and, notwithstanding his priestly vocation, was not based upon Christian dogmas.

3 The two branches of academic study are not, however, mutually exclusive. Indeed, as has been postulated a number of times, empirical sciences and theology may well interact with each other, and, in this way, contribute to our better understanding of the world (Heller 2019: 5-10).

these mythical narratives (and the way in which they convey the moment of creation) that we shall now begin our exploration of the cosmogonic accounts in the works of Tolkien (*The Silmarillion*) and Lewis (*The Magician's Nephew*). Following that, we shall have a look at how the concept of Creation is tackled in the first book of the Hebrew Bible and why it is of such great significance (if seen from the doctrinal perspective) that Christians should see the universal genesis as stemming from the divine decree 'out of nothing' (*creatio ex nihilo*). This, in turn, should allow us to have a better grasp of the conceptual designs which are at work in the acts of creation in, first, Tolkien's Arda, and then, Lewis's Narnia.[4]

## Cosmogonic Myths and Cosmology

Even though they are quite commonly discredited as being illogical and scientifically unsound,[5] creation myths are, in fact, amongst the most universal and conceptually transparent narratives that mankind has ever produced. They are, in the first place, exceedingly inventive stories, abundant in symbolic meanings and dramatic intensity; stories whose ontological profile is generally coherent with the set of beliefs held by the followers of a particular creed. Whether they should be considered as literal depictions of how the world came into being ('Young Earth Creationism'),[6] splintered fragments of the True Light (Tolkien),[7] or downright lies (as was the case with Lewis

4 Throughout this chapter, I shall be using the form 'Creation' (with a capital 'C'), to refer to God's *fiats* in Genesis 1, and 'creation' (with a lower case 'c'), to mean the corresponding acts of Ilúvatar and Aslan in, respectively, *The Silmarillion* and *The Magician's Nephew*.

5 See, for instance, *Sapiens: A Brief History of Humankind* (2015), the pseudo-scientific bestseller by Yuval Noah Harari, in which the author seems to be unable to detect any universal features in myths (not merely cosmogonic, but myths in general), apart from the fact that they are no more than products of collective imagination (28). Tolkien famously discards any such (or similarly contemptuous) views in his lecture/essay 'On Fairy-stories,' where he argues that "Max Müller's view of mythology as a 'disease of language' can be abandoned without regret" (41).

6 The adherents of Young Earth Creationism interpret the six 'days' that Genesis speaks of (1:1-31) as six consecutive 24-hour periods. In contrast, Old Earth Creationists interpret these same days as vast stretches of many millions of years.

7 Tolkien obviously understood that, in the strict sense, myths are not free from all sorts of errors, but he certainly held on to the view that they are also perfectly capable of preserving fragments of Truth. This is, possibly, best reflected in the words of Humphrey Carpenter, who, in an effort to creatively reconstruct the fateful discussion between Tolkien, Lewis, and Hugo Dyson on 19 September 1931, puts in the Professor's mouth the following words: "Our myths may be misguided, but they steer however shakily towards the true harbour" (1977: 147).

prior to his spiritual awakening),[8] there could be no doubt that there are to be found in them recurrent themes and motifs meant to convey certain universal truths in the language and idiom characteristic of the people who came to preserve them. In this way, leaving aside their spiritual dimensions, they may be seen as culturally-specific narratives whose objective is to address the issues of deep social significance, stories providing frameworks for self-identification and awareness of one's place in the world.

In all the cosmogonic myths, perhaps one of the most intriguing aspects is the actual mode of creation. David and Margaret Leeming list several types of it, including various acts on the part of the world-creating deity (or 'demiurge,' as the supreme being has often been referred to since the days of Plato)[9] in which our earthly abode emerges from some primordial chaos, hatches from an egg, or is brought into existence by the divine word or thought (1994: 56-61). The world may come into being in a flash of a second, or it may emerge in stages. Moreover, its formation may be intentional, or it may come about by mere chance. Last but not least, the creation may stem from a sexual impulse, or it may involve a sacrifice.[10] However, what seems to be a common thread in the bulk of these narratives is that there is usually a deity or group of deities (of both sexes and various spheres of authority) who not only initiate(s) the actual process of creation, but also use(s) some pre-existing matter and/or energy to bring the world into being. In the Babylonian account of the *Enūma Eliš*, for instance, the god Marduk fashions both the sky and the earth from the dismembered body of Tiamat, the primordial sea goddess he previously slays. In Hesiod's *Theogony*, the 'pre-world' is said to be populated by personifications of various aspects of nature, but it is not before the emergence of primal Chaos that the generation of Gaia (the Earth) actually begins. Yet another ingenious mode of

8 A somewhat generalised understanding of Lewis's pre-conversion views upon myths (including, one may guess, the cosmogonic one) could be inferred from Tolkien's dedication of the poem 'Mythopoeia' to his friend and colleague, the "one who said that myths were lies and therefore worthless, even though 'breathed through silver'" (85).

9 The Greek word δημιουργός, whence the English 'demiurge' derives (via Latin *demiurgus*), appears several times in Plato's dialogue *Timaeus*. This is not to be confused, however, with the 'demiurge' of the Gnostic tradition.

10 Naturally, the creation motives do not have to be mutually exclusive. In some mythical accounts, such as the eddic poems *Vǫluspá* and *Grímnismál*, one could discern at least a few of these elements, including, first, the birth of a race of primordial giants, and then the fashioning of our world from various parts of the body of one of them. For a harmonised outline of the creation accounts in the *Poetic Edda*, see Davidson (1964: 197-202).

creation could be found in many myths of the Native Americans, where the so-called 'earth-divers' plunge into the depths of the primeval waters and bring to the surface the very first particles of earth which then subsequently grow into the physical world as we know it.

Of course, these mythical accounts may be quite easily dismissed today as lacking any solid, verifiable foundations. However, in most of them, there are at least two underlying principles which, notwithstanding one's faith (or lack of it), give the appearance of being in compliance with the logic of cause-and-effect. These are, first of all, the pre-existence of a mover,[11] a formidable being of supernatural and/or divine origin without whom the act of creation would be impossible, and, secondly, some primordial matter, which, if properly fashioned (by means of dissolution, extraction, dismemberment etc.), would serve as a material foundation of the world(s).[12] As we shall see in the ensuing section, the former tenet is roughly consistent with the Judeo-Christian concept of the Almighty God as the exclusive 'architect' of the "sky and earth and sea, and everything in them" (Acts 4:24),[13] while the latter principle is only superficially reasonable, inevitably assuming also the pre-existence of some matter, and, in consequence, perhaps causing one to call to question the actual primacy of the Creator.

The arguments for and against the necessity of a pre-existence of some *primum mobile*, that is to say, something (or someone) that must have been there in the first place to set the cosmic clock in motion, is also a fundamental issue in various cosmological disputes and provides a fertile ground for numerous models of the cosmic genesis. One of the earliest systematic attempts to shed some light upon this complex issue might be found in Aristotle's *Metaphysics*, where the Philosopher advocates that there must be something in the Universe, the ὃ οὐ κινούμενον κινεῖ (1072a) "unmoved mover," that causes everything

11 Whether the said mover ought to be a prime one or not is a different matter, not directly relevant to the topic discussed in this chapter. For the sake of the argument here, it should suffice to say that his existence predates at least the act of creation.

12 In some cosmological models of the past, there is more than just a single habitable sphere in which humans dwell. The Norse concept of the world-tree Yggdrasill, connecting the nine realms of the cosmos, is perhaps the best known example of such multi-layered depictions of the world in Indo-European mythologies.

13 Unless otherwise stated, all the scriptural quotations come from the *Catholic Bible: Revised Standard Version* (2006).

to move, despite being himself unmoved. He also argues, in the eighth book of *Physics*, that, at the outset of all things, there must have been something he calls the ἀρχή (251a) "first principle," by which he means the ultimate and unprecedented cause which set everything in motion. Naturally, this unprecedentedness is in clear conflict with the Parmenidean line of reasoning (likewise a fundamental principle not only in Ancient Greek cosmogony; Gregory 2013: 70), according to which nothing could be generated from nothing.[14] It should be observed, though, that while the position put forth by Parmenides gives the impression of being more 'scientific' (in the strictly physical sense of that word), it nonetheless fails to account for how the cosmic matter came to be there in the first place and whether its existence is, indeed, secondary to that of God.[15] To account for this, we now need to take a detour (or, rather, get back on the track) and see how this delicate issue is handled in the first book of the Hebrew Bible and, no less importantly, how it subsequently came to be reflected in Christian theology.

## Cosmogony in the Judeo-Christian Tradition

As has been observed, what is tolerated, indeed even expected, in such diverse fields of human inquiry as mythopoeism and empiricism, is not always supported in its entirety by dogmatic theology, the branch of theological study whose concern is the systematic exposition of the will of God, as it is revealed in Scripture. By definition, then, dogmatic theology places its emphasis upon the logical and the theoretical rather than the experiential, the truths of faith, rather than those of empirical data. In other words, while the mythical narratives once sought to explain certain cosmic mysteries and celestial phenomena by applying the knowledge that was available at the time of their observation, modern cosmology aims at studying the foremost astrophysical and astrochemical processes involved in the formation and evolution of planets, stars,

14 In medieval and modern scholarship this argument is typically rendered in its Latin version as *ex nihilo nihil fit*. The actual words of Parmenides are, unfortunately, lost to the mists of time, and one of the earliest references to them is to be found in Aristotle's *Physics*. It appears, however, that certain reverberations of the claim that nothing can come from nothing might be discerned in the work of the post-Paramedian pluralist Empedocles of Acragas (Palmer 2013: 14).

15 To be fair, Aristotle does not explain that either. He does, however, seem to be more affirmative in this matter, while Parmenides appears to be locked in his notion of unchanging permanence.

and galaxies. In contrast, dogmatic theology does not rely upon what (for the sake of terminological clarity) could be referred to as unrestrained ingenuity of interpretation, nor does it call for any hard facts or interpretive theories in the area of astronomical science.[16] Considered through the Christian lens, the groundwork of our understanding of how the world came into being should rest upon the faith in the primacy and omnipotence of God. That is to say, the Christian cosmogony does not discard the use of mythopoeic language, the highly conventionalised lexical substratum that the Israelites inherited from their Babylonian neighbours.[17] Likewise, in modern biblical exegesis (not necessarily very 'progressive'), it is no longer universal (with the exception of those who adhere to the concept of 'Young Earth Creationism') to read the first two chapters of Genesis literally, as a factual account of how the world began. Nonetheless, it does not (and should not, if the belief in the omnipotence of God were to be treated with due reverence) refute the assertion that, no matter how we actually envision the acts of Creation, the prime cause of all things is to be found in the divine יְהִי (*yehi*) "let there be" (Gen 1:3, 6 and 14).

So how then do the opening verses of Genesis actually depict the cosmic reality prior to the act of Creation? "In the beginning," we read in its very first sentence, "God created heaven and earth" (1:1).[18] Obviously, the phrase בְּרֵאשִׁית (*bereshít*) 'in the beginning' was not meant to determine any kind of chronological order of the cosmogonic events. Instead, it appears to say more about the primacy of the Creator than the actual sequence of Creation. It is also sometimes argued that, as in *Enūma Eliš*, the opening verse should be treated as some sort of a 'title' (Świderkówna 2009: 44; Lemański 2013: 144) or précis of the ensuing narrative, rather than part of the account proper.[19] Its actual significance, truly revolutionary in comparison with the polytheistic visions of the world that had

16 This does not mean, of course, that dogmatic theology should refute the empirical sciences. In fact, for several years now, Michał Heller, the Polish Catholic priest (as well as philosopher and theoretical physicist), has been one of the leading proponents of what he calls 'theology of science,' the reflection upon the nature of scientific cognition through the lens of Christian theology.

17 In the words of Paul M. Blowers, the Hebrew model of the cosmic genesis and evolution is "couched in mythopoeic language and drawn into diverse interpretative traditions internal to Scripture" (2012: 18).

18 The words הַשָּׁמַיִם וְאֵת הָאָרֶץ (*hashamayim ve'et ha'aretz*) "heaven and earth" should not be taken literally as two entities, each having a distinct existence of its own. Instead, they constitute a merismic expression which stands for the entire Universe.

19 Indeed, in Hebrew, בְּרֵאשִׁית (*bereshít*) 'in the beginning' is used as a title, the equivalent of Greek Γένεσις.

hitherto prevailed in the Middle East, is therefore that God is the sole Creator of all that is, regardless even of the intriguing fact that אֱלֹהִים (*Elohim*), the word used as many as thirty-two times to describe Him in Genesis 1, is grammatically plural.[20] In other words (should we, for the time being, allow for this unavoidably simplistic reading), God is a single being in existence before the formation of the world, and thus everything which comes to be in the first two chapters of Genesis – be it the more abstract dyads such as light and darkness, or the more concrete ones such as sky and sea, land and vegetation – is solely of His making and has its roots in the divine acts of Creation.[21]

Coming back to the core of the matter, a vital issue needs to be addressed at this juncture. What of the assumed nothingness of the pre-Creative state of our world? Where is this supposed *nihil* that precedes God's initial *fiat*? As we have seen, the biblical account in Genesis commences with a rather straightforward assertion that "[i]n the beginning God created heaven and earth" (1:1). The narrative then continues with a staggering vision of a dark, primordial chaos,[22] very likely modelled upon the Middle Eastern conception of the world emerging from a void:[23] "Now the earth was a formless void, there was darkness over the deep, with a divine wind sweeping over the waters" (1:2). At first glance, this image of the earth as "a formless void" (1:2) might seem to be a consequence of the creation process initiated by God in the opening verse. There is, however, more to it than meets the eye.

It has already been said that there are biblical scholars who read the first sentence of Genesis, "In the beginning God created heaven and earth" (1:1), as some sort

20 There have been several attempts to rationalise this ostensibly 'polytheistic' anomaly. It may be, for example, a case of the so-called *pluralis intensitatis*, expressing the fullness of the Divine power (Grzybek 1961: 320-21). A more Christian reading sees in the word *Elohim* a veiled reference to the threefold personality of God, the *pluralis trinitatis* (Gassmann 2008: 4). The limited framework of this chapter does not allow for a more detailed analysis of this fascinating theological issue.

21 To accentuate this, the author consistently uses the verb ברא (*bara)*, meaning 'calling into existence something marvellous' (cf. Yahweh's words in Ex 34:10, "I shall work such wonders at the head of your whole people as have never been worked in any other country or nation"), which always has God for its subject.

22 The word *chaos* is not normally used in the English translations of Genesis, but in its early, cosmogonical sense of the word (analogical to its Greek counterpart χάος) its meaning could be rendered as 'the primordial, unordered state of existence' perfectly corresponding to the two Hebrew words תֹהוּ (*tóhu)* and בֹהוּ (*vóhu)* meaning, respectively, 'lack of form' and 'void.'

23 Similar, though not necessarily analogical accounts to those related in the earliest texts of Babylonian and Sumerian provenance might also be found in some Hellenic cosmogonies. These, however, do not seem to have had any impact (in the imagistic sense) upon the first two chapters of Genesis.

of a title.[24] If such indeed was the intent of the author of the 'Priestly' strand of the opening chapter,[25] it would have to have a substantial effect upon the subsequent sentence, where both the 'void' and the 'darkness' are mentioned. Only after that does God utter His first *fiat*, the effect of which is the creation of light and its separation from darkness (1:3-4). Literally read, following the chronological sequence of events, we thus end up with a vision of the primordial state of the 'world' *prior* to the actual acts of Creation! In consequence, the passage in which "the earth" is depicted as "a formless void" and there is "darkness over the deep" (1:2),[26] could be understood as an attempt to vividly express what the 'Priestly' redactor saw as the closest equivalent of what in later doctrinal discussions came to be referred as *nihil*.[27] It does not, however, automatically mean creation *ex materia*, antithetical to that of *ex nihilo*. After all, in order to cause light to shine forth (1:3-4) God does not necessarily have to 'make use' of any 'pre-existing' (and, as yet, 'formless') "void" or "darkness" (1:2). On the other hand, though, if one were to push the boundaries of imagination (as many people of the past surely did), it would not be implausible to envision Him as giving shape to the "vault [...] to divide the waters in two" (1:6-7) or "the dry land" called "earth" (1:9-10) using some (or all) of the elements mentioned in the second verse.[28]

Naturally, this second mode of formation (terrestrial as well as celestial) is somewhat controversial from the Judeo-Christian standpoint. Over the centuries, there were numerous arguments concerning the way in which the world came into being, with some early Christian scholars, like Tatian the Syrian, claiming that the entire Universe was created out of some pre-existing matter

24 From the terminological perspective, it would be more correct perhaps to see it as an *incipit*.

25 According to the so-called Documentary Hypothesis, the 'Priestly' strand in the first two chapters of Genesis is prominent in 1:1-2:4b. The following subsection (2:4b-3:24) is generally attributed to the 'Yahwist' redactor.

26 The word תהום (*t'hóm*), here rendered as 'the deep,' does not necessarily have to mean 'water.' In fact, it is usually translated as 'abyss, chasm,' which may imply that it is roughly synonymous with בהו: (*vóhu*) 'void,' used in the first clause of Gen 1:2.

27 This is not to say, of course, that this was his foremost intention. After all, the dogmatic disputes concerning the pre-creative state of the Universe were yet to come. Nonetheless, it seems that in stressing the primacy of God he made an attempt to reduce to the very minimum everything that comes before the first divine *fiat*.

28 The very moment of Creation, with God operating a compass or dividers, was often captured in medieval and early modern art. According to Friedman, these images are based upon "a metaphoric conception of God as an architect or artisan forming the cosmos from unrecognized matter" (1974: 422-24).

(Maryniarczyk 2018: 21).[29] In some aspects analogous, though not exactly the same, were also the earlier theoretical inquires of Philo of Alexandria, who contended that God did indeed create the world *ex nihilo*, yet, at the same time, not going so far as to deny the pre-existence of some unformed eternal matter (20). Even if not always perfectly synonymous with what we today understand as creation *ex materia*, these assumptions drew a lot of critical fire from the subsequent generations of Christian scholars, in particular the three saints: Irenaeus, Theophilus of Antioch, and Augustine of Hippo, as well as John Scotus Eriugena, all of whom firmly rejected any such claims (21-25).[30] Perhaps an apt précis of these critical views would be the words of Saint Theophilus, who, in the second chapter of *The Apology to Autolycus* (written shortly before his death between 183 and 185), argues that "even a human artist, when he gets material from some one, makes of it what he pleases. But the power of God is manifested in this, that out of things that are not He makes whatever He pleases" (chapter 4). About a thousand years on, in 1215, these words would find their dogmatic confirmation in the Canons of the Fourth Lateran Council, where, right in the beginning, it is explicitly decreed that the whole world (with all of its numerous beings, spiritual as well as corporeal) was indeed created *ex nihilo* by the omnipotent power of God (25). Finally, and not long after that, in the mid-thirteenth century, in his *Summa contra Gentiles*, Saint Thomas Aquinas fully formulated and justified the doctrine of *Creatio ex nihilo*, claiming that the Creation does not mean a transformation of any pre-existing matter, but rather bringing it into existence by God along with the created being (book II, chapter 16).[31]

---

29 He does, nonetheless, argue that "matter is not, like God, without beginning, nor, as having no beginning, is of equal power with God; it is begotten and not produced by any other being, but brought into existence by the Framer of all things alone" (qtd. in Iammarino 2013: 44).

30 It is not improbable that, at least in the Christian tradition, the line of argument stemmed mainly from John 1:3 ("Through him all things came into being, not one thing came into being except through him") and Heb 11:3 ("It is by faith that we understand that the ages were created by a word from God, so that from the invisible the visible world came to be"). In the Hebrew Bible, the basis for such an interpretation might be the following passage from 2 Macc: "I implore you, my child, look at the earth and sky and everything in them, and consider how God made them out of what did not exist, and that human beings come into being in the same way" (7:28).

31 In the words of Aquinas, *Deus res in esse produxit ex nullo praeexistente sicut ex materia* (book II, chapter 16) "God brought things into being from no pre-existing material substance." Part of his argument rests upon the claim made in Genesis 1:1. It should be added, though, that, not only in the *Summa*, the assertion that God created the world out of nothing cannot be seen as stemming solely and directly from the first verses of the Hebrew Bible. Instead, it is more likely to have proceeded from theoretical deductions within the scope of dogmatic theology.

The significance of this doctrine, "developed as a guideline for rightly reading Gen 1 [and 2] and for talking rightly how God relates to the world" (Chambers 2020: 1), as well as its impact upon the subsequent Christian thought is hard to overestimate. Were we to see things differently, the creative role of God would have to be reduced to that of a skilled 'craftsman' who only uses some pre-existing matter to give the ultimate shape to our world, much as in the aforesaid mythical narratives, in which the Earth is brought into existence by a god (or group of gods) from the body of a giant (as in the Norse poem *Vǫluspá*), or shards of an egg (as in the opening *runo* of the Finnish *Kalevala*). Needless to argue, there is a fundamental logical flaw in this sort of reasoning, as it would have to make God, at least at some point, an integral part of the Universe (or any kind of physical reality), the Universe He Himself is reported to have created.[32] To counter any such claims, Aquinas also proposed and developed the notion which subsequently came to be known as *Creatio continua*, the kind of 'ongoing Creation,' which, in his view, is an extratemporal process that does not actually have a beginning in what we understand as time (Dzierżak 2021: 60).

This, once again, brings us to the opening chapters of Genesis. If we assume that the world was indeed created by God *ex nihilo*, and that nothing could be said to have existed prior to the Creation, why is actually something there ("a formless void," "darkness over the deep," and "the waters") before He utters His first *fiat*? There is no simple all-embracing explanation of that, of course. One reason might be that the biblical redactor had a somewhat different vision of the primordial state of the 'world,' to some extent modelled upon the Babylonian cosmogony. However, as we have seen, he also seems to be trying to reduce to the bare minimum everything which might suggest that there had actually been anything in existence prior to the first Creative act, anything that could defy the absolute primacy and omnipotence of God. Hence, in an attempt to do so, he condenses his vision of the primeval 'world' to what, turning a blind eye to

32 I am well aware of the fact that the whole issue is far more complicated than that. We could, for instance, assume that the Universe was created in two stages, the first of them being the creation of the matter and the second that of the world (out of the existing matter). This, however, would pose further interpretative difficulties in that the necessity to form this 'original matter' could be treated as a limitation to God's omnipotence.

the later doctrinal disputes, we could nowadays consider to be a resourceful, poetic depiction of *nihil*.

It cannot be denied, though, that to the modern readers of Genesis, this ingenious method may, in the long run, seem a bit suspicious on the grounds of some doctrinal inconsistencies, the two major problems being what I propose to call: (1) the 'nothing vs. something dichotomy,' and (2) the 'time before time paradox.'[33] However, some light upon this matter could be shed perhaps by Plato's theory of 'forms,' naturally well-known to both writers (Korpua 2021: 2-3; Brazier 2012: 7), and Tolkien's own concept of sub-creation. According to the Athenian, as he mouths his opinions through various speakers (most often Socrates), the εἴδη 'forms' (also referred to as ἰδέαι 'ideas') are the original, aspatial and atemporal, 'templates' of all the things (and more) that man can conceive in his mind. They are thus not only superordinate in their relation to everything that could be seen, heard, and in any way sensed or imagined, but also supramental in that we are systemically incapable of forming complete mental images of them. In other words, this unattainable sphere of 'forms' could only be transcendent to our own, physical sphere through their imperfect 'reflections.'[34] Naturally, the theory itself is not without its argumentative flaws, but as far as the following discussion is concerned its main premises seem to be at least roughly adequate.

Seen in a broader perspective, the application of Plato's theory of 'forms' does not have to be restricted to physical objects alone. In fact, it might as well be considered when dealing with the more abstract notions like unity, infinity, and eternity, or even such ostensibly mundane concepts like colours.[35] When it comes to the act of Creation, the very idea of the emergence of the world *ex nihilo* is, it seems, just as inconceivable to the human mind as the thought that the Universe should have no physical boundaries. Following, then, in the

---

33 These are not the only inconsistencies in the first chapters of Genesis. Another glaring example – doubtlessly stemming from the fact that it combines two separate traditions – might be that in Genesis 1 God creates all the living things before He creates man, while in Genesis 2 both flora and fauna are brought into existence after "Yahweh God shaped man from the soil of the ground and blew the breath of life into his nostrils" (2:7).

34 For a good introduction to Plato's theory of forms, see, for example, Penner (2009: 165-83) and Gill (2009: 184-98).

35 It is sometimes argued that, for instance, pure black and white colours do not really exist in the physical world, and so whenever we consider them, we only have in mind their various shades.

footsteps of Plato, it does not seem to be lacking logical grounds to suggest that the absolute *nihil* which, in the later dogmatic tradition, should precede God's first *fiat* is, in its purely semantic manifestation, that kind of an ideal, unattainable 'form.' Consequently, all those biblical images of the "formless void," "darkness over the deep," and "waters,"[36] ought to be seen as mere reflections of it, not quite precise in their doctrinal content,[37] but suggestive enough to be accepted as roughly adequate in their semantic aspect.[38]

Over the centuries, Plato's theory of forms came to be echoed in various metaphysical disputes, such as that over the existence of universals, and philosophical theories, like conceptualism or nominalism. In the twentieth century, perhaps most famously, it found its reverberation in Carl Gustav Jung's concept of the 'archetypes.' It should come as no surprise, then, that it ultimately made its way into the wide range of subjects discussed by the Inklings,[39] and, most importantly, into the works that came from the pens of Tolkien and Lewis. The most glaring example of that is, of course, Tolkien's concept of sub-creation, by which he understood a thoroughly derivative mode of creation as a result of which an imaginary (or secondary) world is invented, a world that is in some way different from the primary one, but remains internally consistent.[40] It is most notably developed in Tolkien's lecture/essay 'On Fairy-stories,' but certain

36 As has been observed, they all seem to have their conceptual foundations in the cosmogonic myths of the Middle East, quite possibly the Babylonian tradition which gave rise to the poem known to us as *Enūma Eliš* (Świderkówna 2009: 44).

37 Perhaps the same kind of cosmogonic 'inadequacies' shine through the words of God, as they are recounted in Job 38. There, speaking "from the heart of the tempest" (1), Yahweh recalls, for instance, laying "the earth's foundations" (4), or letting the sea burst forth "from the womb" (8).

38 Similarly limited is, for instance, our knowledge of God, and so must be all our attempts to put in words what cannot really be expressed through language. Cf. the *Catechism of the Catholic Church* (39-43).

39 An interesting conversation between Tolkien, the Lewis brothers, and their fellow Inkling 'Humphrey' Harvard, centred, amongst other things, upon the Platonic 'forms' and Jungian archetypes may be found, 'reconstructed' in Carpenter (1979: 138-39).

40 Sub-creation is also the highest form of human activity, inevitably echoing the original act of Creation (Phelpstead 2014: 88). This means that the former could only have the status of creation *ex materia*, while the latter, as the Creation proper, is naturally sustained *ex nihilo*. Sacrilegious as it may sound, then, it is hard to deny that, in some sense, the world depicted in the first two chapters of Genesis is indeed a secondary one, and that the mythopoeic efforts of the biblical authors to somehow outline the 'process' of its formation were genuine acts of sub-creation.

sub-creative elements might also be detected in his other works, including the poem 'Mythopoeia'[41] and the short story *Leaf by Niggle* (1945).[42]

Naturally, the idea of sub-creative powers in man, particularly in relation to the creative faculties of God, also came to be expressed in *The Silmarillion*, the book still far from being finished at the time of Lewis's death in 1963, but quite well known to him already in the 1930s, when parts of it were read to him during his regular meetings with Tolkien (Carpenter 1977: 148). As may be seen in *The Chronicles of Narnia*, the idea struck and soon came to be assimilated into Lewis's own fiction. However, certain glimpses of its impact may also be detected in his non-fictional works, such as *Reflections on the Psalms*, where he argues that the Christian truth is somehow encoded in the ancient beliefs (as well as rituals and practices), such as the "half articulate feeling [...] that man [...] must undergo some sort of death if he would truly live" (123-24), or when he maintains that "[t]he resemblance between [...] myths and the Christian truth is no more accidental than the resemblance between the sun and the sun's reflection in a pond" (124).[43]

Were they to be found in Plato, Tolkien, or Lewis, all these secondary images are practically by definition 'less real' than those we might consider to be their 'forms.' However, in some instances, "when the story-maker's art is good enough" (*TOFS* 52), they are also perfectly capable of being perceived by the reader as 'real-like.'[44] As we have seen, in the opening lines of Genesis, this is perhaps best exemplified by the images of "a formless void," "darkness over the deep," and "the waters" (1:2), neither of which is perfectly synonymous with what, in English, could be invoked by means of the *de facto* abstract noun 'nothingness.' Nonetheless, given the 'poetic-like' quality of Hebrew (as well as other Semitic languages), with its reliance upon sometimes elaborate images as conventional tools of expression, these phrases appear to be suitable enough to successfully

41 "The heart of man is not compound of lies, / but draws some wisdom from the only Wise, / and still recalls him" (*Myth* 87).

42 In *Leaf by Niggle*, Tolkien succeeds in giving a convincing literary form to what is, after all, a notional concept of sub-creation.

43 In a somewhat roundabout way, Lewis also seems to elaborate upon Plato's concept of forms in *Mere Christianity*, e.g. in the first chapter of book 4 entitled 'Making and Begetting' (158-59).

44 "This faculty," Tolkien says, "is [...] naturally called Imagination" (*TOFS* 59). Both Tolkien and Lewis (as well as, amongst others, George MacDonald and G.K. Chesterton) believed that all imaginative thinking originates in God.

get the main message through: there is only one, omnipotent, omnipresent, and omniscient God who created the world before anything else. For the Ancient Israelites, living in the land hitherto populated by various pagan peoples, this was perhaps enough, insofar as the acts of Creation were concerned. All the speculations concerning when or in what manner and order the world was actually brought into existence were to come in the subsequent centuries.

## Tolkien and Lewis Read the Book of Genesis

Given what has been outlined above, it seems a natural order of things now to turn our attention to the acts of creation (or, rather, sub-creation) in, first, Arda, and then Narnia, as they are brought to the pages of, respectively, *The Silmarillion* and *The Magician's Nephew*. Before that, however, we shall briefly take a look at the two authors and their attitudes to the scriptural texts, whether they considered them as more or less factual accounts, or whether their understanding of the Bible (and Genesis in particular) was more dynamic, taking into consideration its specificity as a culturally conditioned set of sacred texts. This should give us some idea of the 'dogmatic' foundations of their literary endeavours and what the above-listed images of *nihil* may have once invoked in the creative and philologically orientated minds of Tolkien and Lewis.[45]

As befits those who, like George MacDonald or G.K Chesterton, are rather consistently categorised today as 'Christian writers,'[46] both Tolkien and Lewis certainly knew their Bible. Indeed, they appear to have been well acquainted with its contents, their knowledge not only being deeply rooted in their personal faith, but also (and to a considerable degree) stemming from the academic work they did. Tolkien, for instance, regularly worked with a number of early English texts whose reliance upon the Scripture could vary greatly: from some indirect biblical allusions in *Beowulf* and explicit references in *Ancrene Wisse* to the more or less faithful paraphrases in *Exodus*. He is also known to have

45 Of the two scholars and writers, it is the former who is, of course, most frequently referred to as a language-genius (cf. the words of Lewis, who is reported to have said that his friend and colleague was "inside language" (Carpenter 1977: 139)). It should not be disregarded, though, that Lewis was also a philologically-trained scholar who knew, with varying degrees of fluency, French, German, Italian, Latin, Greek, Old English and Old Norse.

46 The term is, of course, rather vague and difficult to pin down with any greater precision. Needless to add, though highly relevant, the issue lays outside the scope of the present study.

read the New Testament in the original Greek and the whole Bible in its Latin Vulgate translation (Walton 2007: 62). He did not, however, know enough of Hebrew to be able to study the Old Testament in its primary form, and so, when, in the late 1950s, Tolkien took the task of translating the book of Jonah for *The Jerusalem Bible* (1966), he actually based it upon the French text of *La Bible de Jérusalem* (Wolfe 2014: 15).

For Lewis, it appears, the Bible was always a vital source of moral advice, even at the time when, prior to 1929, he still considered himself an atheist.[47] In the subsequent years, when he had set himself the task to become what, according to Carpenter, Tolkien scornfully called "everyman's theologian" (1977: 151), he would make a systematic use of it, quoting from or referring to it in his academic publications (e.g. *The Discarded Image*) and books of popular theology (*Mere Christianity*, *Miracles*, *Letters to Malcolm*, *Reflections on the Psalms*). This means that, apart from using it as a source of spiritual guidance, Lewis also studied the Bible (which he could read in Greek as well as in Latin)[48] as a text of its own, although, as pointed out by Duriez, he was, at the same time, quite "sceptical of a simple 'the Bible as literature' approach" (2013: 48) to it.

What is of a foremost significance here, however, is the question of their attitude to the reading of Genesis, in particular its two opening chapters relating the acts of Creation. When it comes to Tolkien, the matter may seem somewhat complex at first, but is, in fact, quite simple. On the one hand, given his theological orthodoxy, it is quite tempting to think of him as a diehard fideist, arguing that everything the Bible says (including the stories of the Creation, Adam and Eve, Cain and Abel, and other historically unverifiable accounts) should be taken at face value. This, however, is far from being true. In the letter he wrote on 30 January 1945 to his son Christopher, amongst other things, Tolkien discusses the veracity of Eden:

47 In the late 1910s, for instance, when his atheism appears to have solidified, he might be found quoting in his correspondence from the Epistles of Saint Paul (*CL I* 312, 362, 425, 444). It ought to be stressed, though, that this is not necessarily firm evidence of his ongoing search for God. A hundred years ago, far more people than today were acquainted with the words of the Bible, also, no doubt, on account of its cultural mandate.

48 Lewis, who in *Reflections on the Psalms*, openly admits that he is "no Hebraist" (1), nonetheless does appear to have had some basic knowledge of the language, just enough to give, for instance, one of his characters in *The Last Battle* the name of Emeth (meaning 'truth' in Hebrew).

> As for Eden. I think most Christians, except the v. simple and uneducated or those protected in other ways, have been rather bustled and hustled now for some generations by the self-styled scientists, and they've sort of tucked Genesis into a lumber-room of their mind as not very fashionable furniture, a bit ashamed to have it about the house, don't you know, when the bright clever young people called: I mean, of course, even the *fideles* who did not sell it secondhand or burn it as soon as modern taste began to sneer. In consequence they have indeed (myself as much as any), as you say, forgotten the beauty of the matter even 'as a story'. (*Letters* 109, #96)

Given his ironic remarks about 'the self-styled scientists' altogether rejecting any factual foundations of Genesis, and, in apparent contrast, the admittance that most of the *fideles* (himself included) no longer believe in its beauty 'as a story,' one may easily have a feeling that Tolkien is actually contradicting himself. Soon, however, he clarifies the whole matter by saying that

> partly as a development of my own thought on my lines and work (technical and literary), partly in contact with C.S.L., and in various ways not least the firm guiding hand of Alma Mater Ecclesia, I do not now feel either ashamed or dubious on the Eden 'myth'. It has not, of course, historicity of the same kind as the NT, which are virtually contemporary documents, while Genesis is separated by we do not know how many sad exiled generations from the Fall, but certainly there was an Eden on this very unhappy earth. We all long for it, and we are constantly glimpsing it: our whole nature at its best and least corrupted, its gentlest and most humane, is still soaked with the sense of 'exile'. (109-10)

The keys here, it seems, are the words 'myth' and 'historicity.' Not only in the above-quoted letter does Tolkien argue that myths (the Creation account in Genesis included) are not, as Lewis once believed, "lies breathed through silver" (Carpenter 1977: 147).[49] For him, they are narratives concerned not so much with specific historical facts, but the Truth behind the biblical imagery. Tolkien openly admits that for him Genesis does not have the same kind of 'historicity' as the New Testament, it does not, however, make it any less veritable than, say, the accounts of Christ's trial, condemnation, Crucifixion, and Resurrection. In other words, they may perhaps be "breathed through silver," (*Myth* 85), but they are certainly not lies. Nor are they fables or tall tales. For Tolkien, then, the Bible (and, consequently, the book of Genesis) is a vehicle of divine revelation, communicating to us some of the main dogmas, such as the

49 Cf., once again, the words of Tolkien in his poem 'Mythopoeia': "The heart of man is not compound of lies, / but draws some wisdom from the only Wise, / and still recalls him" (87).

one that, notwithstanding the number of days it may have taken,[50] the world was created by the one God in Holy Trinity.

Lewis's approach to reading the Bible appears to be, on the whole, quite similar to that of Tolkien. Notwithstanding that their pathways to God were rather different,[51] they could both be described as being rather orthodox, each of them, in his own way, actively standing up for the Christian Faith. Also, similarly to Tolkien, Lewis believed that the story of Creation, as related in the first two chapters of Genesis, is a myth "derived [at least in its visual form] from earlier Semitic stories" (*RP* 128). Here, however, it needs to be once again stressed that for the two Inklings the word 'myth' did not carry the same negative (or, at least, questionable) connotations as it does for many people, not only today. As we have seen, for Tolkien a myth is a story whose principal function is to convey the underlying truth. Likewise, for Lewis, whose notion of myths as narratives subservient to the Christian Revelation clearly owes a lot to the influence of his friend and colleague, it is "the mountain whence all the different streams arise which become truths down here in the valley" (*GD* 58).[52]

It should come as little surprise, then, that Lewis ultimately distances himself from what he refers to as a "belief that every sentence of the Old Testament has historical or scientific truth" (*RP* 127). Interestingly, in the very next sentence, he comes up with two, in his opinion, analogical examples of non-literal reading of the Hebrew Bible, one of which is the assertion that Moses, as the assumed author of the Pentateuch, related the Creation "after the manner of a popular poet" (127-28).[53] Naturally, the words, which Lewis erroneously puts in the mouth of Saint Jerome,[54] are not in any direct way supposed to voice

50 The meaning of יוֹם (*yōwm)*, used as many as eight times in Genesis 1-2, is rather clear and means the period of time between the dawn and the dusk. It need not, however, be taken literally, since, in the eyes of Israelites, the rhythmisation of the consecutive acts probably made the whole Creation process appear as more coherent and logical (Lemański 2013: 154).

51 Until his conversion to Catholicism in 1900, Tolkien had been a member of the Anglican Church. Lewis, on the other hand, was baptised in the Church of Ireland, but then fell away from the Faith in his teens, only to gradually return to it, in the Anglican tradition, in his early thirties.

52 Similarly, in his review of *The Lord of the Rings*, Lewis argues that "[t]he value of the myth is that it takes all the things we know and restores to them the rich significance which has been hidden by 'the veil of familiarity'" ('The Dethronement of Power' 14).

53 Notwithstanding that, as regards the cosmogonic sphere, Lewis does appear to be largely in favour of the creationist position. For an in-depth discussion of this fascinating issue, see Jerry Bergman's book *C.S. Lewis: Anti-Darwinist* (2016).

54 Arend Smilde (2014) convincingly argues that the said words should rather be attributed to the sixteenth-century humanist John Colet.

his own beliefs with regard to the historical veracity (or lack of it) in the first chapters of Genesis. However, given that his more general claim (concerning the Old Testament) is followed by a more specific one (relating to the story of Creation), it may be rather safely assumed that, to a certain degree, the latter was also meant to act as an intensifier, subtly implying that, if the Hebrew Bible is not always reliable (historically and/or scientifically), then the cosmogonic accounts in Genesis 1-2, so imbued with the mythical traditions of the Middle East, are even less so.

Once again, it needs to be stressed that, in saying so, Lewis does not in any way reject the authenticity of God's Creative acts *per se*. Instead, like Tolkien, he appears to be somewhat sceptical about the 'historical' accuracy of the narrative, not the Creation itself as a fact and as a product of the divine will. Moreover, it does not in the least mean that the two Inklings no longer treat Genesis (with its mythical imagery and symbolism) with any kind of reverence. Had it not been so, they would probably not have tried to replicate the primary act of Creation in their fiction. And, in fact, not just any kind of fiction. For Tolkien, *The Silmarillion* always remained the most important work (even when he seems to have lost any hope that it would ever be published)[55] and the core of his imaginative writing, one whose numerous narrative threads resonate in *The Hobbit* and *The Lord of the Rings*. Furthermore, the *Ainulindalë*, 'The Music of the Ainur,' whose earliest drafts probably date back to as early as 1917 (Garth 2019: 118-20), is also chronologically first of all the mythical narratives in Tolkien's fiction, and so its role is, at least in some degree, analogous to that which Genesis plays in the Bible.

When it comes to Lewis, *The Magician's Nephew* may not immediately spring to mind as his foremost literary achievement.[56] However, a quick look at his letter to an eleven-year-old girl named Anne Jenkins, one in which Lewis sheds some light upon the main themes of each of the seven books that make up *The Chronicles of Narnia*, allows us to see that, being a story which "tells the creation and how evil entered Narnia" (*CL III* 1244), it is,

---

55 The long and complex story of how *The Silmarillion* came to be written, revised and ultimately published Tolkien's son Christopher is masterfully summarised by Scull and Hammond (2017: 1153-82).

56 At least when it comes to its popularity, *The Magician's Nephew* is easily eclipsed by the enormous success of *The Lion, the Witch and the Wardrobe*, by far the most famous of the Narnia books.

as a matter of fact, a highly significant book, one which, not only in terms of its chronological place in the seven-book series, lays the foundation for the entire *Narniad*.[57] Having already written five volumes, Lewis decided to conclude *The Chronicles* with "the coming of Antichrist [...], the end of the world, and the Last Judgement" (1245). This thought probably incited him to consider what Alan Jacobs calls a "Creation-to-Apocalypse arc for the series" (2010: 270), which obviously means that Lewis first had to go back to the dawn of Narnian time, in some aspects (the musical one in particular) probably modelled upon Tolkien's own creation myth.[58] In effect, following the revised order in which the individual volumes ought to be read (269-70), *The Magician's Nephew* became the first in the sequence of seven books, a kind of 'Genesis' story of *The Chronicles of Narnia*.

Notwithstanding their attitudes to the 'factuality' and/or 'historicity' of Genesis, it cannot be denied that the first book of the Hebrew Bible did, in fact, have an enormous impact upon Tolkien and Lewis; an impact which certainly went beyond the narrative parallels that may be quite easily discerned in their sub-creative efforts in *The Silmarillion* and *The Magician's Nephew*. Some evidence of that is to be observed, for instance, in the stylistic 'modality' of the *Ainulindalë*, clearly recalling the elevated language of King James' Bible. This is far less apparent in Lewis's novel, written, as we known, with a very specific group of readers in mind, but it cannot be denied that certain passages in its eighth chapter, those which so vividly relate the creation of Narnia, sound a bit more formal (or, at least, more serious) than the rest of the book.[59] The reasons for these stylistic endeavours are, it seems, quite evident. In the words of Margaret Hiley, "[t]he register of biblical language has for centuries carried a power and influence greater than that of any other [text]. Tolkien is exploiting the reader's associations with this kind of language to give his own narrative, language, and myth greater resonance" (2004: 848). The same (though, understandably, to a

57 Besides that, as Lewis also remarks in the opening chapter of his book, "[i]t is a very important story because it shows how all the comings and goings between our own world and the land of Narnia first began" (*MN* 11).

58 The mode of creation of Narnia is, of course, highly reminiscent of the Music of the Ainur in Tolkien's *Ainulindalë*, the first book of *The Silmarillion*, parts of which were known to Lewis already in the 1930s (Hooper 2005: 16; Green and Hooper 202: 210).

59 Edith M. Humphrey also argues that, in *The Magician's Nephew*, "[t]he commanding Creator and the sub-created response of the stars recall the awe-inspiring majesty of Gen 1" (2017: 47).

somewhat lesser degree) could also be said about Lewis's sub-creative endeavours in *The Magician's Nephew.*

Any kind of attempt to emulate the style and/or language of Genesis does, of course, entail more or less deliberate efforts on the part of the author. This, in turn, implies a more-than-usual attention to detail, so as not to miss some fundamental tenets, such as, we might presume, the notion that the world came into being *ex nihilo.*[60] We have already seen, though, that, even in the Hebrew text, the story of Creation is not entirely devoid of certain semantic ambiguities, at least partly stemming from the fact that we, as humans, are not only systemically incapable of creating things 'out of nothing,' but also, in our meagre imitation of God's inventiveness, can merely try to replicate the act itself (and its consequences), to the effect that the very concept of *nihil* has to be rendered by means of various periphrastic synonyms such as "a formless void," or "darkness over the deep" (Gen 1:2). As we shall soon be able to see, consciously or not, the same principle could also be applied to the creation narratives in *The Silmarillion* and *The Magician's Nephew.*

## The Act of (Sub)creation in Arda

Practically any sort of research into Tolkien's creation myth (as it may be found in *The Silmarillion*) is, almost by definition, a delicate undertaking that requires a multifaceted approach, one which takes into consideration such matters as its continuous and, in a sense, never-ending development, as well as the question of its ultimate shape under the editorship of Christopher Tolkien (Leśniewski 2014: 5-32). This is, of course, too complex an issue to be addressed in here, but, just for the sake of clarity, it seems fair that we should first enumerate those texts (sometimes in more than one version) in which the creation of Arda is outlined in a more or less comprehensive fashion. For the overwhelming majority of readers of Tolkien, the primary text is, no doubt, that of the *Ainulindalë*, the first part of *The Silmarillion.* There exist at least nine versions of it, the

60 Both writers were, do doubt, aware of the disputes surrounding the mode of Creation, though only Lewis is known to have made any explicit comments concerning its *ex nihilo* character: "I know that to create is defined as 'to make out of nothing,' *ex nihilo*. But I take that to mean '*not* out of any pre-existing material.' It can't mean that God makes what God has not thought of, or that He gives His creatures any powers or beauties which He Himself does not possess" (*LM* 97).

oldest of which may have been written as early as 1917 (Garth 2019: 118-20). The one which ultimately found its way into the published *Silmarillion* is the so-called *Ainulindalë D*, in all likelihood written in 1951 (Kane 2009: 29). Four earlier versions of it are to be found in three different volumes of The *History of Middle-earth: The Book of Lost Tales Part One* (*The Music of the Ainur*), *The Lost Road and Other Writings* (*Ainulindalë B*), and *Morgoth's Ring* (*Ainulindalë C*, *C**, and *D*). There are also brief synopses of the creation myth in *Valaquenta* (*Sil* 13) and Tolkien's letter to Milton Waldman (*Letters* 146, #131).[61]

Likewise problematic could also be an attempt to point to the sources which provided Tolkien with the material for his creation myth. Surely, Genesis was one of them, but there are also certain elements he appears to have drawn directly from Saint Augustine (Houghton 2003: 176-77), and Plato's *Timaeus* (171). Clearly Augustinian is the idea of Creation as "a single moment of divine action with a five-part internal structure" (176) which the bishop of Hippo Regius outlined in *De Genesi*. Following this model, the foremost stages in the creation process in the *Ainulindalë* are as follows: (1) Eru brings to life the as yet non-corporeal spirits called the Ainur, "the Holy Ones [who are] the offspring of his thought" (*Sil* 3),[62] (2) he musically pre-figures in their minds the creation of Arda (3-4), (3) embodying his thoughts, the Ainur sing the Great Music, although a discord arises from Melkor, who has been "given the greatest gifts of power and knowledge" (4), (4) the Ainur are shown a vision of their song, without, however, its ultimate fulfilment (5-6), (5) having uttered but a single word "*Eä!*" (8),[63] followed, in the *Ainulindalë*, by its 'translation' "Let these things Be!" (8), Eru speaks the whole world into existence and sends to it the "Flame Imperishable" to make it live (8).[64]

As we can see, Tolkien's Arda is, in a sense, given some sort of existence twice: first in the minds of the Ainur (as a vision, and thus at least in a sense synony-

---

61 The process of Tolkien's composition of the *Ainulindalë* may be found meticulously outlined in the publications of Gießl (2006) and Devaux (2007).

62 In Tolkien's legendarium, Eru, "the One, who in Arda is called Ilúvatar" (*Sil* 3), is the mythical representation of the Almighty.

63 *Eä* is a Quenya verb meaning 'to exist,' but used as an imperative, it could be translated as *fiat* 'let there be.' In its substantival form, however, it means the whole creation, "Eä, the World that Is" (*Sil* 8).

64 According to Clyde S. Kilby, in his private conversation with Tolkien, the author made it clear that the 'Flame Imperishable' (also referred to as the 'Secret Fire') was originally meant to be synonymous with the Holy Spirit (1976: 59).

mous with the physical *nihil*), and then in the strictly physical sense (as the creation proper), coinciding with the incarnation of the "Holy Ones" (*Sil* 3).[65] Moreover, this as yet non-material "new World" is first made visible to the Ainur "globed amid the Void" (5), the mysterious space (or, rather, 'non-space') outside time and creation, and thus sometimes referred to as being 'Timeless' or 'Outer,' which, on the one hand, echoes the biblical וָבֹהוּ (*vóhu*) in Genesis 1:2, but, on the other, may recall the state of what physicists call 'perfect vacuum,' that is to say the ideal state devoid of any matter. Finally, even though in the *Ainulindalë* Tolkien is very careful not to use too many time-markers (either precise ones, such as 'on the first day,' or those which are imprecise, such as 'following,' or 'after that'), he is obviously unable to avoid providing his readers with an impression that, despite all of its being pre-temporal, some sort of 'sequence' of events is nonetheless at play.[66]

Naturally, we must not forget that *Ainulindalë* is, essentially, a work of fiction, a secondary myth written by an Oxford don with antiquarian interests. That very same don, however, happens to have been a devoted son of "Alma Mater Ecclesia" (*Letters* 109, #96), and so, notwithstanding the influence of various mythical narratives, his own *mythos* is also a fundamentally Catholic one.[67] If so, how does it fit within the dogmatic framework of Christian theology? To what extent does it comply with what Aquinas says about the Creation in his *Summa contra Gentiles*, namely that *Deus* [...] *est causa materiae primae, cui nulla praeexistit* (book XVI, chapter 11) "God is the cause of the prime matter, to which nothing is pre-existent"? Or, to put it bluntly, is the model of creation outlined in the *Ainulindalë* consonant with the doctrine of creation *ex nihilo*? This, of course, is a rather complex matter that needs to be approached with caution. After all, as we have seen, there are already some 'controversial' issues in the biblical narrative, where, (1) right from the beginning and prior to God's initial *fiat*, (2) explicit references are made to certain physical entities including

65 This might, but does not have to, reflect the fact that there are two Creation narratives in Genesis: 1:1-2:4a (the 'Priestly' strand) and 2:4b-2:24 (that of the 'Yahwist' tradition). Another possible, and, it seems, more likely, source of this intriguing duality is the concept of 'two creations' in the view of Gregory of Nyssa (Zachhuber 2014: 145-86).

66 See, for instance, the above-outlined five-stage sequence of 'events' before the creation proper.

67 At this point it is hard not to recall the oft-quoted words uttered by Tolkien in a letter to Father Robert Murray SJ: "*The Lord of the Rings* is of course a fundamentally religious and Catholic work" (*Letters* 172, #142).

the mysterious "formless void", "darkness over the deep" and "waters" (Gen 1:2). Both have already been addressed in this chapter, the former labelled as 'time before time paradox,' and the latter as 'nothing vs. something dichotomy.' Whether by conscious imitation or not, the same sort of 'inconsistencies' may also be detected in the *Ainulindalë*.

First, as the more tangible of the two, we shall consider the 'physical' properties of pre-creative 'reality' in Tolkien's myth as it is told in the opening part of *The Silmarillion*. Prior to the moment when, by the divine decree of Eru, the music of the Ainur takes its ultimate shape in the act of creation, there are already two distinct planes of what, for want of a better word, we may call 'existence.' These are: the Halls of Ilúvatar and the aforementioned Void. Whether they are in any way 'material' or not is difficult to tell with any degree of certainty. They are evidently both "Timeless" (*Sil* 8, *MR* 14, 42; *Sil* 234, *MR* 407), meaning 'eternal,' and, one may presume, also in some sense 'extratemporal,' yet it is their unexpected 'physical' dimension, antithetical to some of the tenets of the doctrine of *creatio ex nihilo*, that may first draw the attention of the more inquisitive readers.

Situated somewhere "beyond the confines of the World" (*Sil* 8), the Halls of Ilúvatar are not only to a certain extent spatially determined (even if only by the fact that they are unequivocally declared *not* to be part of our World), but also appear to be limited in terms of their 'physical' proportions. At any rate, that is what we may (perhaps erroneously) conclude from the fact that they appear to have at least a vertical dimension constrained between what Tolkien calls "the Abyss" and "the Firmament" (5). This is further supported by the implication that the primordial creative music of the Ainur is performed *inside* the Halls of Ilúvatar,[68] and thus it may be assumed that they are indeed in some sort of 'existence' prior to the emergence of the Universe. On the other hand, though, should we assume even some sort of 'physicality' of Eru's abode, any claim that it is actually "beyond the confines of the World" (8) could seem logically unsound. This intriguing 'physical' isolation may obviously bring to mind the various locations (both real and imagined) once thought to be

68 Once again, Tolkien seems to deliberately avoid using words like 'in,' 'inside,' or 'within,' yet it is clear from the context that the Halls of Ilúvatar is where the music is conceived.

the sacred dwellings of gods and goddesses, places like Mount Olympus or Asgarðr, in, respectively, Greek and Norse myths. However, what seems rather commonplace in the numerous belief systems of ancient and early medieval Europe (and beyond) cannot be so easily transposed into Christian theology, according to which God does not live in what we may understand as a spatially-defined 'place.'[69] Likewise, in the *Ainulindalë*, any such 'physical' limitation (self-)imposed upon Eru would make him merely a 'component' (albeit a vital one) of his own creation, a limitation Tolkien cleverly avoids by following the above-mentioned Augustinian model, in which all the phases are combined into a single Creative act that, leaving aside God's own will to bring things into existence, starts with passing on His vision to the angels (Houghton 2003: 176-77). In other words, both before and during the composition itself, the material dimensions of the world are yet to come, and so the Halls of Ilúvatar cannot be within its confines. Everything is as though within Eru's mind.[70]

However, even non-material concepts like thoughts or ideas are not exactly synonymous with *nihil* in the sense of not only the absence of any sort of matter, but, in fact, non-existence of anything at all. In other words, some kind of existence, not only purely cerebral (which, if we choose to be very precise, should also be in some way physically determined), appears to be 'expected' even from Eru who, in his anthropomorphic 'manifestation,' may, for instance, be heard speaking (*Sil* 3ff.), sits and listens (4), smiles (4), lifts his arms (4ff.) etc. This inevitably brings us to the perennial, but essentially flawed, question of God's existence (and whereabouts) prior to the acts of Creation.[71] However, not only does Tolkien avoid addressing some such complex theological issues in the *Ainulindalë*, but he also deliberately provides his narrative with certain traits universally found in the mythological canon, along with such 'essentials' as the anthropomorphisation of the divine, complete with the virtues and vices of gods

69 Of course, certain 'clues' concerning His 'place of residence' may be found scattered here are there in the Bible, as in 1 Kings: "listen from heaven where you reside" (8:43). These are, however, no more than culturally-determined projections of God's 'abode' which should not be given any dogmatic status.

70 The vision presented to the Ainur by Ilúvatar plays the part of an eternal, if, at that point, ostensibly *ex ante* framework of our worldly reality.

71 Naturally, any such discussion is fundamentally flawed in the sense that it is somewhat reductionist, as it assumes that God must be dimensionally and temporally limited.

and goddesses, as well as the places they allegedly inhabit.[72] Still, despite these theological 'flaws,' his vision is not only compelling from the point of view of mythopoeic tradition, but also quite convincing in what it was actually meant to be in the first place, that is to say, a literary rendition of the primordial reality in advance of God's first *fiat* in Genesis 1:3 and, in some measure, a creative reflection upon the *ex nihilo* doctrine.

Perhaps the most intriguing 'spatial' concept in the *Ainulindalë*, no doubt echoing the countless chasms in various mythological systems,[73] is, however, that of the Timeless Void, a mysterious region of non-existence which is outside both Time and Creation. It is at first bereft of everything, and most of all the Flame Imperishable sent by Ilúvatar to kindle the existence in Arda (*Sil* 8). In the vision he presents to the Ainur, they can see that the "new World" is "globed amid the Void and [that] it [is] sustained therein, but [is] not of it" (5). In one of his commentaries collected in 'Myths Transformed,' the fifth part of *Morgoth's Ring*, Tolkien describes the Timeless Void as "a conception of the state of Not-being, outside Creation or Eä," that Men and Elves are "inclined to confuse with the conception of vast space within Ëa, especially those conceived to lie all about the enisled 'Kingdom of Arda' (which we should probably call the Solar System)" (403). This means that in its 'erroneous' elucidation of Men and Elves, the Void is not unlike the outer space, which, with its low density and pressure, can bring to mind the so-called 'partial vacuum,' that is to say, the short-lived absence of matter obtainable by means of a vacuum pump.[74] In 'reality,' though, the elusive "state of Not-being" that Tolkien speaks of could perhaps be equated with what physicists call a 'perfect vacuum,' the as yet unattainable condition which, given the current state of our knowledge, appears to be situated solely within the sphere of theoretical discourse.[75] Needless to add, this makes Tolkien's Void a good, if not always perfectly

72 This last feature could also be found in the Hebrew Bible. Apart from the above-quoted words of 1 Kings 8:43, cf., for instance, the fourth verse of Psalm 3, in which David is heard "cry[ing] out to Yahweh" and "He answers from His holy mountain."

73 One such chasm, the gaping abyss of *Ginnungagap*, might be found in the eddic poem *Vǫluspá*. Its closest analogies in Classical mythology are Greek Χάος and Roman *Chaos*.

74 Partial vacuum can be created, if only for a brief moment, inside a vacuum pump. It is, however, always instantly filled by air pushed in by atmospheric pressure.

75 I am, of course, aware of the semantic limitations posed by a literal reading of these words. After all, the use of words like 'emptiness' or 'non-being' implies that there is some kind of enclosure within which there is a void. Similarly, 'darkness' does not really mean absence of matter, nor is 'deep' perfectly synonymous with 'bottomless.'

accurate, equivalent of what, following the arguments of Aquinas, we should understand as pure *nihil.*

At this point it might be worthwhile to have a look at the very word 'Void,' an intriguing noun also commonly used in the English translations of Gen 1:2 (albeit without the capital V) to render Hebrew בֹהוּ (*vóhu)* 'nothingness, void.'[76] *The Concise Oxford Dictionary of English* (2011) defines 'void' as "a completely empty space." It is, therefore, a space deprived of any matter, yet a space nonetheless; a multi-dimensional concept which could be rather hard to estimate in the physical domain, but, at the same time, one which does not give the impression of being purely immaterial. In other words, it is an entity which does exist, but, at the same time, does not have any determinable physical form, being thus at least in some measure antonymous to what we normally understand as pure 'nothingness.'[77] In the *Ainulindalë*, the Timeless Void is evidently that kind of entity, on the one hand, as its name implies, lacking any fixed 'dimensional' and/or 'temporal' qualities, but, on the other, 'substantial' enough to be penetrated (albeit in a vision) by Ilúvatar and the Ainur, and to provide a protective layer for the newly created World.[78] Moreover, it can be filled not only with music, but also its echo,[79] which means that, in the strictly physical sense, it is prerequisite that Tolkien's Void be in some measure tangible in its materiality, sonoric as well as spatial.

Seen from the mythopoeic angle, it is also interesting what Tolkien says about Men and Elves and their inclination to confuse the Timeless Void with the "vast space within Ëa" (*MR* 403). This seemingly casual remark expounds his acute awareness of the perennial inclination of man to label everything he can find around him, even (or perhaps especially) when certain phenomena still elude

76 Here, the Vulgate has the adjective *vacua* 'empty, vacant.'

77 In his most famous novel, *The Neverending Story* (*Die unendliche Geschichte*), Michael Ende comes up with a frightening concept of the formless entity called *Nichts*. Although it should actually be translated as 'nothingness,' it is, in fact, somewhat antithetical to the Christian idea of *nihil,* since, unlike perfect vacuum, it absorbs (or devours) everything that comes within its reach.

78 "But when they were come into the Void, Ilúvatar said to them: 'Behold your Music!' And he showed to them a vision, giving to them sight where before was only hearing; amid they saw a new World made visible before them, and it was globed amid the Void, and it was sustained therein, but was not of it" (*Sil* 5).

79 "[A] sound arose of endless interchanging melodies woven in harmony that passed beyond hearing into the depths and into the heights, and the places of the dwelling of Ilúvatar were filled to overflowing, and the music and the echo of the music went out into the Void, and it was not void" (*Sil* 3).

his understanding.[80] That is to say, by looking at a scene of natural wonder (such as an electrical storm), man can assign to it some, typically supernatural, meaning, thus giving rise to numerous mythical concepts and narratives. This, of course, roughly corresponds with what, in Plato's mind, came to be conceptualised as the theory of forms, with the combination of thunder and lightning (as it is nowadays understood with the application of modern scientific knowledge) playing the part of a quasi-'form' and the pre-modern perceptions of it (wrath of a thunder-god) as its 'appearances.' Likewise, in Tolkien's own world, the immaterial Timeless Void (in the sense, we might quite safely assume, of perfect vacuum devoid of any matter), which, in accordance with the *ex nihilo* doctrine, must have been (or rather 'not-been') there prior to Ilúvatar's creative act, would be tantamount to an idealised, and thus not fully conceivable, 'form.' Consequently, in the eyes of Elves and Men, the memory of the Void (as it seems to have been preserved in a chain of hypothetical narratives)[81] would take a more tangible 'shape' of roughly quantifiable 'emptiness' rather than the purely theoretical 'nothingness.' Or, in strictly biblical terms, בֹהוּ׃ (*vóhu)* rather than *nihil.* Whether in this way Tolkien actually wished to say that, not only in mythopoeic writings, certain abstract concepts cannot be so easily conveyed by means of the language we otherwise use to deal with the more material matters is not in the least clear. However, given his insightful nature and great attention to all sorts of details, not only philological, it cannot be ruled out as impossible.

As has been observed, the other major problem with the creation story in the *Ainulindalë* (as seen from the *ex nihilo* perspective and its various implication) has to do with its 'temporal' dimensions, in particular the things that come to pass before Ilúvatar utters his "*Eä!* Let these things Be!" (*Sil* 8). On the one hand, none of what is reported to be 'taking place' prior to the creation proper

---

80 Tolkien alludes to this human urge in his essay 'On Fairy-stories' (42-43) and poem 'Mythopoeia' (85-86).

81 Some parts of the earliest lore of Arda are, for instance, fictionally attributed to the Elvish Loremaster named Pengolodh (*WJ* 396-98), although in *The Silmarillion* index it is an earlier historian (and likewise an Elf), Rúmil of Tirion, who is credited with the authorship of the *Ainulindalë* (320). However, since all the 'extant versions' of the creation story are written in the Westeron language (i.e. Modern English), Agøy suggests that "the text as it now stands" should be understood "as a Mannish adaptation of Rúmil's original" (2007: 149). It should be borne in mind, though, that the Norwegian scholar does not actually explain how, thousands of years on, Rúmil came up with the idea of his narrative, but merely tries to reconstruct its subsequent stages of transmission.

can really be placed upon the timeline of Arda, the sequence of events whose 'primeval atom' is to be found in the command "*Eä!*," Tolkien's rendition of the divine יְהִי (*yehi)* "let there be" in Genesis 1:3.[82] On the other, though, it does not seem to be quite correct to claim that *nothing* actually happens in Tolkien's universe before the creative act of Ilúvatar. As in the first book of the Hebrew Bible, this ostensible chronological inconsistency could be referred to as the 'time before time paradox' and might have been a conscious choice on the part of the author in his attempt to get a better understanding of the opening verses of Genesis.

Perhaps to evade any fixed 'temporal' constrains, Tolkien may have also decided not to use any words or phrases that could imitate the rather specific biblical בְּרֵאשִׁית (*bereshít*) 'in the beginning' (Gen 1:1).[83] Instead, he opens his narrative with a straightforward declaration that "[t]here was Eru, the One, who in Arda is called Ilúvatar" (*Sil* 3), a declaration whose first two words might give the impression of being a deliberate amalgam of two different concepts: (1) the divine announcement "I am he who is" in Exodus (3:14), where the major stress lies upon the verb הָיָה (*haya*) 'be, exist,' and (2) the standard opening phrase "there was (once) X," commonly used in all sorts of narratives whose roots are to be found in the folk tradition (here, of course, without the temporarily declarative 'once'). However, with pure extratemporality being not only hard to conceive, but also practically impossible to be fully conveyed by even the most abstract metaphysical jargon, it should come as no surprise that in the subsequent part of the narrative Tolkien resolves to the more conventional means of sequencing the events. And so, even before the universe is ultimately set in motion (*Sil* 8), he repeatedly uses such indisputably temporal words as "[t]hen" (3ff.), "until" (4ff.), or "while" (3ff.), and, much less frequently, expressions like "it came to pass" (3) or "[n]ever since" (3). Moreover, on one occasion, when the Ainur are reported to be performing their musical themes, they are said to be doing it "for a long while" (3).

Naturally, all this may look rather suspicious from the purely doctrinal standpoint, the *ex nihilo* principle denying not only pre-existence of any physical

82 According to *The Annals of Aman*, "Time indeed began with the beginning of Eä" (*MR* 49).

83 However, in *Valaquenta*, he opens his narrative with the rather unequivocal words "In the beginning" (13).

entity, but also, less directly, any sign of 'temporal' progress. However, it should not be forgotten that, like the biblical accounts of Creation in the first two chapters of Genesis, Tolkien's *Ainulindalë* has the form of a mythical narrative and, as such, ought to follow some of the basic narrative conventions. One of these is obviously chronology, which does not necessarily have to be stringently linear, but should, at least in some measure, reflect the passage of time and/or sequence of events, even if, as in the case of precreative acts in Genesis and the *Ainulindalë*, the said 'sequence' "does not," to quote C.S. Lewis, "consist of moments following one another" (*MC* 167). In other words, notwithstanding its creative appeal, the 'genesis' story in *The Silmarillion* is inexorably imitative in its form and essence, for the most part drawing heavily upon the biblical accounts, where, as we have seen in the opening verses of Gen 1, even the causative וַיֹּאמֶר (*vayómer*) '[and God] said' (1:3) is not the first verb to be used by the narrator.[84] However, unlike the 'spatial controversy,' the 'temporal' one does not necessarily have to stem directly from Tolkien's conscious imitation of the Scriptural model, but may have been simply determined by the narrative conventions, whereby the plot usually unfolds as a series of related events.

All in all, it is hard to tell whether (and, if so, to what extent) Tolkien deliberately sought to incorporate certain elements of the *ex nihilo* doctrine in his account of creation in the *Ainulindalë*. That he was perfectly conscious of its significance hardly needs to be argued for. However, his insight into the doctrinal premises of Creation does not automatically denote Tolkien's willingness to replicate the core of the theological discussions that ensued in the early centuries of Christendom with regard to the actual time and mode of the universal genesis. After all, his foremost intention in writing *The Silmarillion* was "to create a mythology *for England*" (Carpenter 1977: 89; emphasis original), and in doing so he had to integrate a great number of features from various belief systems, both Christian and non-Christian, without, however, relying too much upon the later dogmatic legacy of the Church.[85] Like Georges Dumézil, Mircea

84 "In the beginning God **created** heaven and earth. Now the earth **was** a formless void, there **was** darkness over the deep, with a divine wind **sweeping** over the waters. God *said*, 'Let there be light,' and there was light" (Gen 1:1-3; emphasis added).

85 This is not to say, of course, that, in its essence, Tolkien's work could be described as being pagan. Indeed, much as in *The Lord of the Rings*, in *The Silmarillion*, the Christian element seems "absorbed into the story and the symbolism" (*Letters* 172; #142).

Eliade, Joseph Campbell, and other notable scholars in the field of mythological studies, Tolkien was well acquainted with the ways in which these early narratives develop, become sacralised, and function on a societal level. Such was, no doubt, the fate of all the *ur*-texts, ultimately merged in what we know today as Genesis, the book which combines the ancestral history of the Jewish people (12-50) and the primeval history of the world (1-11), both significantly enriched by the mythical traditions of the Middle East. Such, metatextually, of course, also seems to be the *modus nascendi* of Tolkien's *Ainulindalë*, often far more faithful to the general contours of the biblical account (along with its numerous mythical implications and semantic limitations) than to the principles and frameworks introduced and developed by Saint Thomas Aquinas and his predecessors (including a strict adherence to the *ex nihilo* doctrine).

Still, as was clearly expounded in a letter to Milton Waldman, Tolkien held a firm belief "that legends and myths are largely made of 'truth', and indeed present aspects of it that can only be received in this mode; and long ago certain truths and modes of this kind were discovered and must always reappear" (*Letters* 147; #131). No doubt, despite (or should we say owing to?)[86] the presence of the two major theological 'controversies' in his own story of creation (the 'nothing vs. something dichotomy' and the 'time before time paradox'), much of that 'truth' is also shrewdly preserved in the opening book of *The Silmarillion*, that is to say, (1) the primacy of God's Creation (despite the vision of the Ainur that 'precedes' it) and (2) the assertion that everything, literally everything, in the Universe is merely a reflection, a "refracted light [...] splintered from a single White" (*Myth* 87). None of his claims in this complicated matter could ever be seen in their full light without Tolkien's conviction that, in the words of Saint Thomas Aquinas, *Deus res in esse produxit ex nullo praeexistente sicut ex materia* (*Summa contra Gentiles* II.16) "God brought things into being from no pre-existing material substance," and everything man has ever done since then is a poor, if sometimes blessed, imitation of that first Creative Act.

86 Once again, we cannot rule out that both of them were in fact derived from Tolkien's careful reading of Gen 1-2.

## The Act of (Sub)creation in Narnia

Unlike Tolkien's Arda, whose musical cosmogony ultimately came to be recorded (or related) in a number of, for the most part unvarying, versions, the sequence of creative events in Narnia should not give rise to any chronological uncertainties, its single source being chapters 8 ('The Fight at the Lamp-post') and 9 ('The Founding of Narnia') of *The Magician's Nephew* (1955).[87] Certain glimpses into the primordial past of Narnia (and perhaps the entire Universe) could also be detected in *The Lion, the Witch and the Wardrobe* (1950), the first of the seven novels in the series to be written by Lewis.[88] There, in the heart-warming scene which follows his sacrificial death and resurrection, the Great Lion Aslan, the Narnian incarnation of Christ, explains why his antagonist, the White Witch Jadis, could not foresee the ultimate fiasco of her efforts to rule the world:

> Her knowledge goes back only to the dawn of time. But if she could have looked a little further back, into the stillness and the darkness before Time dawned, she would have read there a different incantation. She would have known that when a willing victim who had committed no treachery was killed in a traitor's stead, the Table would crack and Death itself would start working backwards. (*LWW* 171)

Naturally, the above-quoted passage, written at least three years before Lewis started to work on *The Magician's Nephew*,[89] does not say anything about the way in which Narnia came to be created. After all, the reason why Aslan raises the issue of the primordial laws which govern it stems from the necessity to accentuate the primacy of God's sovereignty, that, whatever they are, the rules which give the appearance of being eternal, are, in fact, subordinate to the law (or, rather, the Law) established "before Time dawned" (171).

---

87 In contrast with Tolkien, who is known to have preserved much of his oeuvre, both published and unpublished, Lewis habitually destroyed the manuscripts of those works which had already come out in print (Hooper 1971: 45). "By a most fortuitous case of survival" (48), there exists a single longer piece of narrative that appears to be an early version of *The Magician's Nephew* (48-65), without, however, a single mention of Narnia (let alone the moment of its creation).

88 There are two ways – both of which have their proponents – in which *The Chronicles of Narnia* might be read today: one that follows the order in which the individual volumes were written and published, from *The Lion, the Witch and the Wardrobe* (1950) to *The Last Battle* (1956), and the other one, from *The Magician's Nephew* (1955) to *The Last Battle*, whose sole determinant is the chronological sequence of events (Green and Hooper 2002: 320).

89 *The Lion, the Witch and the Wardrobe* was certainly completed by the Summer of 1948 (Duriez 2005a: 234), whereas the first chapter of *The Magician's Nephew* appears to have been written in May 1951 (247-48).

Nonetheless, as we may see, it does provide a few glimpses of that pre-temporal vacuum, where "stillness and darkness" (171) are the only anchor points for our deficient senses.

It might therefore be argued that the act of creation in *The Magician's Nephew* was intended by Lewis to add some 'historical' and spiritual depth to the world already well known to the readers of *The Lion, the Witch and the Wardrobe* (1950), to shed some light upon how, when, and in what form evil came into Narnia.[90] Indeed, amongst the foremost issues explored in the sixth (but chronologically first) book in the series are such fundamental tenets of Christian theology as primal innocence, ancestral sin, temptation, and forgiveness. However, as Lewis himself expounds in the afore-mentioned letter to Anne Jenkins, "*The Magician's Nephew* [primarily] tells [the story of] the Creation and how evil entered Narnia" (*CL III* 1244). Consequently, then, the bulk of Narnian scholarship today appears to be more focused upon that latter aspect of the novel, which should come as no surprise, given that, in the Christian thought, Redemption – the unfortunate prerequisite of which is sin – constitutes the central ground of our Salvation. To put it bluntly, there would be no Redemption without the ancestral sin, and, consequently, no sin without our prior innocence, that "native innocence" of man, to use the words of John Milton (*Paradise Lost* book IX, l. 193), which abounds in the Garden of Eden in the early days of our existence, the necessary precondition of which (chronologically as well as ontologically) is the very act of Creation.

The vivid account of how Narnia came to be is not perhaps something which would automatically appear (and not only to the first-time reader!) to be an inevitable consequence of the preceding chain of events. In fact, after their narrow escapes from, first, the dead world of Charn (*MN* 79), and then, late-Victorian London (110), Digory and Polly once again find themselves in the enchanted Wood between the Worlds (110-11), this time, inadvertently, in the company of the boy's Uncle Andrew, the astonished Cabby Frank with his horse Strawberry, and the temporarily incapacitated Witch. Determined to flee from especially that last companion of theirs, Digory and Polly grab the

90 Seeing it from a more general perspective, Chad Walsh argues that "*The Magician's Nephew* provides a theological and metaphysical background for the other tales" (2008: 136).

magical rings (made from Atlantean dust) that enable them to be transported from one world into another, and so, suddenly (and to everyone's surprise), they find themselves in utter darkness, in what Jadis declares to be "an empty world" (112), or, indeed, "Nothing" (112).[91]

Having come from the mouth of the Witch, a Satan-figure in the world of Narnia,[92] these words might perhaps be taken as being not entirely trustworthy or factually accurate. However, the narrator also seems to be following the same line of reasoning, by claiming that

> really it was uncommonly like Nothing. There were no stars. It was so dark that they couldn't see one another at all and it made no difference whether you kept your eyes shut or open. Under their feet there was a cool, flat something which might have been earth, and was certainly not grass or wood. The air was cold and dry and there was no wind. (*MN* 112)

It is only after some time that, in the utter darkness of some primordial Narnian night, "the darkness before Time dawned" (*LWW* 171), the powerful but, on the whole, gentle voice of Aslan, soon "joined by the other voices; more voices than you could possibly count" (115), begins to sing the new world into existence, with thousands of "stars, constellations, and planets" (115) suddenly appearing in the hitherto dark sky.[93] Before long, all these heavenly bodies are joined by a most magnificent sun, much younger and joyful than the one which they previously saw "above the ruins of Charn" (117).[94] Finally, still in consecutive stages, echoing (but not fully adopting) the order of Creation in the first two chapters of Genesis, trees, plants, and all sorts of creatures, real or imagined,

---

91 Colin Duriez actually calls it "a world of Nothing" (2005b: 201), which is only ostensibly a contradiction in terms, as already in the views of the atomists, like Leucippus, nothingness appears to have some sort of reality of its own (Zilioli 2020: 24-25).

92 These satanic features are, of course, reflected not only in what the White Witch does, but also, a number of times, in what she says and what kind of effect she wishes to achieve. For an in-depth study of the depictions of ultimate evil in the *Narniad*, see, for instance, the first chapter in Elizabeth Baird Hardy's book *Milton, Spenser and the 'Chronicles of Narnia': Literary Sources for the C.S. Lewis Novels* (2014: 17-50).

93 In its conceptual essence, the musical genesis of Narnia evidently echoes Tolkien's own cosmogonic myth in the *Ainulindalë* (Hardy 2014: 173). For an interesting examination of the power of Aslan's voice, not only in the process of creation, see, in particular, Stephen H. Webb's chapter in *The Chronicles of Narnia and Philosophy* (2005: 3-14).

94 The almost concurrent appearance of the sun (*MN* 117) and Aslan (118) could easily bring to mind the solar symbolism in early Christian art, where many an image of Christ gives the appearance of being a visual elaboration upon the *Sol Invictus* cult in the later Roman Empire.

gradually come into existence, emerging from the earth in a remarkable, primal fecundity of the new world.[95]

Highly imaginative as it is, if read chiefly for its narrative content and the role it plays within the larger Narnian framework, the above-outlined account in *The Magician's Nephew* should not raise many suspicions in the mind of an average, usually youthful reader. Indeed, as we already know, it does, for the most part, follow the sequence of Creative acts outlined in Genesis, including the separation of light from darkness, emergence of vegetation, and creation of living creatures.[96] Upon the second reading, though, it may also come to the reader's notice that there are certain discrepancies between the two narratives, perhaps the most obvious deviation from the biblical template in Lewis's novel being that, as Colin Duriez rightly observes, in the world of Narnia, the arrival of evil (in the person of Queen Jadis), in fact, antedates the creation itself (2005b: 98).[97] It is also striking (and directly relevant to the issue discussed in the present chapter) that, alongside the unequivocally 'non-existential' claims that the 'space' around "was uncommonly like Nothing," that "there were no stars" where the 'sky' should be, and that "[i]t was so dark that they couldn't see one another at all" (*MN* 112), Lewis also states that "[u]nder their feet there was a cool, flat *something* which might have been earth" (112; emphasis original). What is more, staying faithful to the laws of physics, if there were no atmospheric air (consisting of the right combination of nitrogen, oxygen, argon, carbon dioxide, etc.), it would be impossible for the sound waves to propagate. However, when Digory, Polly, and the rest of the cast find themselves in the "empty world" (112) that would be Narnia, they are not in any way prevented

95 This sequence of events clearly echoes the 'Yahwist' tradition, where the creation of man precedes that of the animals (Gen 2:19).

96 Clyde S. Kilby argues that the account of the creation of Narnia in *The Magician's Nephew* was not quite written "in imitation of the already sublime account recorded in early Genesis but rather presenting a warmly creative image in which the great golden Lion Aslan (Christ) sings into existence sun, water, grass, trees, birds – a whole world bursting with life" (1978: 56). In this, however, he seems to be only partly correct. After all, one does not have to exclude the other, and so Lewis's wish to give his creation myth a more 'warmly' touch does not quite rule out the more general influence of Genesis. Later on, Kilby is, nonetheless, right to point out that Lewis probably drew some of his imagery from elsewhere in the Bible, e.g. Job 38:7 (56).

97 So does, of course, man, but perhaps by bringing human beings to what soon will take the shape of Narnia, Lewis wanted to say that the Creation of the world was determined by the fact that God had already envisioned it as the abode of man.

from hearing one another, which, inevitably, signifies that 'something' is indeed 'in the air' (more than meets the eye perhaps, but still).

Interestingly, in his depiction of the pre-Narnian state of 'nothingness,' Lewis avoids such explicitly 'nihilistic' expressions like "formless void," or "darkness over the deep" (Gen 1:2).[98] From the very beginning, the impression of absence of any tangible physical phenomena is quite suggestively rendered by means of various remarks that come from the newcomers. Indeed, apart from Digory's casual observation that their escape from the Wood between the Worlds "was a bit of luck" (*MN* 111), the first words to be heard from anybody, as the party keep on "sinking into darkness" (111),[99] are Polly's question "Oughtn't we to be nearly there now?" (111). Naturally, it may be taken as a sheer expression of surprise that their coming from one space into another should take so long. At the same time, though, it is quite revealing of the girl's complete astonishment that the 'place' they find themselves in is so "uncommonly like Nothing" (112).[100]

But then, again, as we have seen, in a strict sense of the word, it is *not* exactly like nothing ('nothing,' this time, understood as genuine absence of any matter). Leaving aside the aforesaid atmospheric/acoustic quibble, there are to be experienced a number of sensations that, logically considered, should have no right to be felt if the words "uncommonly like Nothing" (*MN* 112) are to be taken literally. After all, not only do they all find themselves "standing on something solid," but the air in there is also described as being "cold and dry" (112). To see Lewis's intent more clearly, though, it must be immediately added that the way in which he depicts all these sensory phenomena is, in many ways, as close as can be to what, withholding, for a moment, our critical assessment (but without abandoning literary credibility), we may imagine as the elusive *nihil*.[101] To illustrate, what Digory reports to be standing on may be solid, but,

98 Of course, here I am not using the word 'nihilistic' in its primary sense of 'being universally senseless.'

99 This particular darkness does not, however, seem to be endemic of the pre-Narnian void. In fact, whenever Digory and Polly find themselves travelling from one world into another, they usually experience a sensation of being immersed into darkness (*MN* 39, 52).

100 It is interesting that the word 'Nothing' is spelt (twice) with a capital 'N.' Perhaps in this way Lewis wished to put more emphasis upon the fact that this is not just 'an ordinary nothing,' but the very kind that is synonymous with the *nihil* which should precede God's Creation.

101 In the words of Katherine Langrish, at that point Narnia "is a flat emptiness offering nothing but the basics: somewhere to stand and air to breathe" (2021: 51).

at the same time, it is also devoid of anything that could make it look and/or feel like earth. It is "cool," and so neither cold nor warm; and it is "flat" (112), and thus bereft of any undulation of the terrain. It is also not covered by any "grass or wood" (112). All this, if taken *en masse*, might recall in the minds of some readers the so-called 'white void' in George Lucas's film *THX 1138* (1971), a kind of prison-cum-limbo with no visible boundaries, in which the protagonist is trapped as if in his own mind. Of course, there is not any form of entrapment in Lewis's novel (physical, mental, or other). Nor is there any mention of white in it (or, as a matter of fact, any colour). However, much as in that famed scene in Lucas's early classic, and with only a handful of expressions deliberately avoiding any kind of physical concreteness, Lewis manages to draw very near the conceptual sphere which reflects what, in biblical scholarship is otherwise expressed by means of the word *nihil*.

As in Tolkien's *Ainulindalë* (and Genesis), another inconsistency which may be found in the account of how the Narnian world came to be created concerns its 'temporal' dimension. We have been told that what the Witch knows about Aslan's creation "goes back only to the dawn of time" (*LWW* 171). Indeed, she is then and there (along with Digory, Polly, Uncle Andrew, and the Cabby Frank with his horse) when the first sounds of the creation song are heard (*MN* 114). However, we are also informed that, "a little further back," there was only "stillness and darkness" (*LWW* 171), evidently the same stillness and darkness in which the 'first' humans find themselves in the eighth chapter of *The Magician's Nephew* (112). This, however, is a glaring contradiction in terms, as it all appears to happen *before* "the dawn of time" (*LWW* 171), earlier than the voice of Aslan is heard (*MN* 114), and prior to the first sunrise in the newly created world (117).[102] And yet, before all this happens, the newcomers are far from being restless, the 'chronological' order of the events in which they partake being as follows: (1) the speculations concerning the world they expected to find themselves in, (2) the words of anguish uttered by the Witch, in some sense prefiguring what will happen almost a thousand years later,[103]

102 As Maria Szamot rightly observes in her study of Genesis, any early measurement of the passage of time is wholly dependent upon the cyclicity of celestial phenomena (2020: 24-25).

103 According to the 'Outline of Narnian history,' year 1 marks the point of its creation, and 1000 the end of the Long Winter and the defeat of the White Witch (Hooper 1971: 41-42).

(3) the thanksgiving hymn of the Cabby, and (4) Uncle Andrew's attempt to leave the company and go back to our world (112-14).

Naturally, the word 'chronology,' derived (via Latin) from Ancient Greek χρόνος 'time,' is an oxymoron here (much as the adverbs 'then' and 'there' also appearing in the previous paragraph). It is not possible to arrange the events into any sort of timeline before the time (or, as a matter of fact, 'Time')[104] actually begins its ceaseless movement forward. Perhaps in this way Lewis wished to give more emphasis to the fact that, as Professor Kirke (i.e. Digory forty years later) argues in *The Lion, the Witch and the Wardrobe*, "the other world ha[s] a separate time of its own" (57).[105] However, it all sounds rather unconvincing and may, at best, reflect our wishful thinking that Lewis should add more realism to what is, after all, a series of fantasy novels written with the younger readers in mind, a series built upon 'suppositions' rather than irrefutable scientific facts.[106] Nevertheless, viewed strictly from the position of the *ex nihilo* doctrine, it should not escape the notice of a careful reader that, just as there is a certain problem with the 'spatial' issues in the depiction of the pre-Narnian 'void' (the 'nothing vs. something dichotomy'), there is also a 'temporal' one (the 'time before time paradox'), perhaps just as intriguing from the perspective of Lewis scholarship and criticism, and just as insufficient from the standpoint of biblical exegesis.

Again, as with Tolkien's *Ainulindalë*, we need to bear in mind that creating a work of fantasy means stretching (but not necessarily breaking) the boundaries of human imagination. Likewise, being in contact with it, requires from the reader (or film-viewer) that peculiar state of mind which, in his essay 'On Fairy-stories,' Tolkien calls, following in the footsteps of Coleridge,[107] "a willing suspension of disbelief" (52). Neither the events outlined in chapters 8 and 9 of *The Magician's Nephew*, nor the memorable words of the resurrected Aslan in *The Lion, the Witch and the Wardrobe* (171) were ever intended to give us

104 It is interesting to note that, in *The Silver Chair* and in *The Last Battle*, Time also appears, albeit briefly, as a character: a sleeping giant in the former novel and an awakened one in the latter.

105 For an interesting discussion concerning the 'Narnian' timelines see Oziewicz (2005: 122-28).

106 For a brief but highly informative explanation of what Lewis meant by 'supposition' and how it differs from allegory, see his 1958 letter to Mrs Hook (*CL III* 1004-05). This intriguing issue was later elaborated on by a number of scholars, including, perhaps most importantly, Lewis's own secretarial assistant Walter Hooper (2005: 422-29).

107 The expression was originally used by Samuel Taylor Coleridge in his book *Biographia Literaria* (1817).

the impression of being factual (factual, that is, in the sense that replicates the empirical method of observation and description). Instead, Lewis provides his readers with a highly imaginative account of the Narnian genesis (as a sub-creative analogy to the biblical depiction of how our own world came into existence). In this, despite the above-discussed inconsistencies, Lewis appears to be generally faithful to the mode and sequence of Creative acts in the first two chapters of Genesis, inasmuch, of course, as our insufficient human lexicon (where "stillness" and "darkness" stand for the otherwise inexpressible *nihil*) could allow us.

This, once again, brings to mind words uttered by the White Witch following her declaration that the darkness which she and her companions find themselves in is not Charn: "This is an empty world. This is Nothing" (*MN* 112). On the one hand, she is right, of course. The creation process is yet to begin. However, from the somewhat metatextual purview, it should not escape our notice that what the narrator says in the ensuing paragraph is that, indeed, "it was uncommonly *like* Nothing" (112; emphasis added). In other words, what surrounds the astounded party is not 'nothing' in a true and literal sense of that word, since this is not expressible in strictly human terms, but a semantic approximation of it. Somewhere along this line of reasoning, Colin Duriez argues that, in Lewis's mind, "[t]he natural world of God's creation [...] imposes a boundary to the human imagination" (2005: 47). This means that "[w]e cannot, like God, create *ex nihilo*, out of nothing. We can only rearrange [albeit imperfectly] elements that God has already made and that are overflowing with his meaning" (47). Rearrange and, one should add, find roughly synonymous substitutes for what cannot really be expressed, or, like 'nothing,' even properly imagined. In this sense, consciously or not, the musical genesis in *The Magician's Nephew* is merely an imperfect reflection of God's own Creative acts, purely derivative in its shape and essence, also, as we have seen, with regard to time and space.

These last two concepts, that is to say, 'time' and 'space,' once again bring us within the broad scope of Plato's theory of 'forms.' The fact that some sequence of events is scrupulously outlined *before* "something [...] happen[s] at last" (*MN* 114) in the hitherto obscure 'nothingness' of Narnian prehistory could provide yet another illustration of the above-discussed limitations of human cognition. In other words, seen from the purely human perspective, it is not quite conceivable that time should have a clearly defined beginning beyond which nothing has any quantifiable value. Likewise, the 'darkness perceptible,' to paraphrase the words of John Milton in his depiction of hell in the first book of *Paradise Lost* (l. 63), which surrounds Digory, Polly, and their companions upon the arrival to the as yet "empty world" (*MN* 112) of Narnia, is only a vague reflection of what in Christian theology is rendered by means of the word *nihil*. We might obviously have some faint notion of them on the purely theoretical plain (as Plato's 'forms'), but when it comes to the more tangible realisation of these abstract concepts we are, unavoidably, at a complete loss of words, and, in consequence, have to resolve to the nearest attainable substitutes ('ideas').

We have seen that in the *Ainulindalë* the practical application of the *ex nihilo* doctrine (provided, of course, that it was indeed a more or less conscious effort on the part of Tolkien) is somewhat less tangible than we may wish, stemming perhaps from the fact that in his mythopoeic efforts he was much more interested in drawing upon the earliest cosmogonic traditions (including Gen 1-2) than the later doctrinal pronouncements of Saint Thomas Aquinas and other Christian theologians. Lewis's vision was, however, markedly different. In each of the seven volumes comprising *The Chronicles of Narnia*, he sought to relate the biblical lore from a somewhat different angle, without, what he himself called, "stained-glass and Sunday school associations" ('Sometimes Fairy Stories May Say Best What's to Be Said' 58). This means that some of the most fundamental Christian principles had to be given less visibility and/or strict dogmatic contours. In consequence, the *ex nihilo* doctrine, otherwise fundamental to our understanding of the absolute primacy of God, appears to have been relegated to the background, even in the story of creation so vividly narrated in *The Magician's Nephew*. That is to say, it is still there, but its tenets are noticeably less rigorous than they otherwise would have to be, allowing much artistic freedom with regard to both 'spatial' and 'temporal' constraints of the doctrine. On the other hand, though, even in this less rigorous rendering of Gen 1-2, "casting all these things into an imaginary world" (58), Lewis nonetheless succeeds in creating a compelling, if not at all times 'accurate,' vision of the dark and almost non-sensorial pre-creative state that, for the lack of a better word, we may call 'pre-temporal *nihil*.'

## Conclusion

Well known (and not only to their immediate readers) for the immense creativity and ingenious use of various, usually pre-modern, texts as springs of inspiration, Tolkien and Lewis consistently strove to make their sub-created worlds as compelling and as complex as possible, also with regard to the very origins of their *mundi*. Steeped in the Christian tradition and worldview, it was but natural for them to incorporate in their visions of creation elements from the Hebrew Bible, in this way evidently accentuating the absolute primacy of the divine *fiat*, without, however, disregarding the mythological (sub)strata of Gen 1-2 (a notable trait particularly visible in the *Ainulindalë*). Evidently from there, or, more precisely, from the 'Priestly' notion of וָבֹהוּ (*vóhu)*, Tolkien must have got the idea of the Timeless Void and Lewis derived his vision of the unnamed primeval darkness, both entities in some quasi-existence before the creation proper. Interestingly, though, these fairly accurate emulations of the biblical account are not necessarily in full compliance with all the tenets of Christian theology, particularly as regards the *ex nihilo* doctrine. Nonetheless, in their respective accounts of creation, both writers seem to have resorted to other, often highly inventive, means of conveying this essential truth to their readers. Having, like all of us, but a faint notion of what the elusive pre-creative *nihil* could actually entail, Tolkien and Lewis turned to the boundless deposits of their unrestrained imagination. As in Plato's theory of 'forms' and 'ideas,' their concepts are, of course, less 'accurate' in what the *ex nihilo* doctrine prescribes, but, at the same time, in their sub-creative efforts, they remain highly suggestive to the readers, dexterously weaving into surprisingly concrete words what human mind must necessarily find hard to imagine.

## About the Author

Łukasz Neubauer received his PhD in English philology from the University of Łódź. He is a researcher and lecturer at the University of Koszalin, Poland, where he teaches courses on J.R.R. Tolkien and C.S. Lewis, Old English literature, and Arthurian romances. Apart from his publications dealing with various medieval as well as Christian influences and resonances in *The Lord of the Rings*, he has written papers on *The Battle of Maldon*, *Beowulf*, *Hêliand*, Icelandic sagas and the so-called 'beasts of battle' trope in, particularly but not exclusively, Old Germanic poetry. He is also a member of the British branch of the International Arthurian Society and a conceptual coordinator of the annual Medieval Fantasy Symposium in Mielno-Unieście, Poland. His most recent publications include *Middle-earth, or There and Back Again*, a collection of essays written by a group of Polish scholars, and a monograph *The Long Shadow of Fáfnir: Dragons in the Works of J.R.R. Tolkien and C.S. Lewis. A Christian Perspective.*

## Bibliography

Agøy, Nils Ivar. 2007. 'Viewpoints, Audiences and Lost Texts in *The Silmarillion*.' *The Silmarillion – Thirty Years On*. Ed. Allan Turner. Zurich and Jena: Walking Tree Publishers, 139-63.

Aristotle. 1989. *Metaphysics. Books 10-14. Oeconomica Magna Moralia*. Transl. Hugh Tredennick and George Cyril Armstrong. Cambridge, MA: Harvard University Press.

2008. *Physics*. Transl. Robin Waterfield. Oxford: Oxford University Press.

Bergman, Jeremy. 2016. *C.S. Lewis: Anti-Darwinist. A Careful Examination of the Development of His Views on Darwinism*. Eugene, OR: Wipf and Stock.

*The Bible: Authorized King James Version with Apocrypha*. 2008. Eds. Robert Carroll and Stephen Prickett. Oxford: Oxford University Press.

Blowers, Paul M. 2012. *Drama of the Divine Economy: Creator and Creation in Early Christian Theology and Piety*. Oxford: Oxford University Press.

Brazier, Paul H. 2012. *C.S. Lewis: The Work of Christ Revealed*. Eugene, OR: Pickwick Publications.

Carpenter, Humphrey. 1977. *J.R.R. Tolkien: A Biography*. London: George Allen and Unwin.

1979. *The Inklings: C.S. Lewis, J.R.R. Tolkien, Charles Williams, and their Friends*. Boston, MA: Houghton Mifflin Company.

*Catechism of the Catholic Church. Second Edition*. 2020. Huntington, IN: Our Sunday Visitor.

*Catholic Bible: Revised Standard Version*. 2006. San Francisco, CA: Ignatius Press.

Chambers, Nathan J. 2020. *Reconsidering Creation Ex Nihilo in Genesis 1. Journal of Theological Interpretation Supplement 19*. University Park, PA: Eisenbrauns.

Davidson, Hilda Roderick Ellis. 1964. *Gods and Myths of Northern Europe*. Harmondsworth: Penguin Books.

Devaux, Michaël. 2007. 'The Origins of the *Ainulindalë*: The Present State of Research.' *The Silmarillion – Thirty Years On*. Ed. Allan Turner. Zurich and Jena: Walking Tree Publishers, 81-110.

Duriez, Colin. 2013. *The A–Z of C.S. Lewis*. Oxford: Lion Books.

2005a. *The C.S. Lewis Chronicles*. London: Darton, Longman and Todd.

2005b. *A Field Guide to Narnia*. Stroud: Sutton Publishing.

Dzierżak, Piotr. 2021. 'Doktryna stworzenia z niczego – *creatio ex nihilo* u św. Tomasza (i nie tylko).' *Zawsze Wierni* 4 (215), 52-63.

Ende, Michael. 2018. *Die unendliche Geschichte*. Stuttgart: Thienemann.

Friedman, John Block. 1974. 'The Architect's Compass in Creation Miniatures of the Later Middle Ages.' *Traditio* XXX, 419-29.

Garth, John. 2019. 'Ilu's Music: The Creation of Tolkien's Creation Myth.' *Sub-creating Arda: World-building in J.R.R. Tolkien's Work, its Precursors, and its Legacies*. Eds. Dimitra Fimi and Thomas Honegger. Zurich and Jena: Walking Tree Publishers, 117-51.

Gassmann, Lothar. 2008. 'Vater, Sohn und Heiliger Geist. Der dreieinige Gott – menschliche Erfindung oder biblische Lehre? Eine Antwort an Zeugen Jehovas und andere Bestreiter der göttlichen Dreieinigkeit.' *Zeitjournal Durchblick im Zeitgeschehen. Vol. 2. Vater, Sohn und Heiliger Geist*, 4-31.

Giessl, Thomas. 2006. 'Ainulindalen.' *Hither Shore* 3, 151-64.

Gill, Mary Louise. 2009. 'Problems for Forms.' *A Companion to Plato*. Ed. Hugh H. Benson. Chichester: Wiley & Blackwell, 184-98.

Gregory, Andrew. 2013. *Ancient Greek Cosmogony*. London and New York: Bloomsbury Academic.

Grzybek, Stanisław. 1961. 'Biblia. Prawda czy legenda.' *Ruch biblijny i liturgiczny*. Vol. 6,, 312-22.

Green, Roger Lancelyn and Walter Hooper. 2002. *C.S. Lewis: A Biography*. Fully revised and expanded edition. London: HarperCollins.

Halsall, Michael John. 2020. *Creation and Beauty in Tolkien's Catholic Vision*. Eugene, OR: Pickwick Publications.

Hardy, Elizabeth Baird. 2014. *Milton, Spenser and the 'Chronicles of Narnia': Literary Sources for the C.S. Lewis Novels*. Jefferson, NC: McFarland.

*Hebrew English Interlinear ESV Old Testament*. 2014. Wheaton, IL: Crossway Books.

Heller, Michał. 2019. *Nauka i teologia – niekoniecznie tylko na jednej planecie*. Kraków: Copernicus Center Press.

Hiley, Margaret. 2004. 'Stolen Language, Cosmic Models: Myth and Mythology in Tolkien.' *Modern Fiction Studies* 50.4, 838-58.

Hooper, Walter. 1971. *Past Watchful Dragons. The Origin, Interpretation, and Appreciation of the Chronicles of Narnia*. London: Macmillan.

2005. *C.S. Lewis: The Companion and Guide*. London: HarperCollins.

Houghton, John William. 2003. 'Augustine in the Cottage of Lost Play.' *Tolkien the Medievalist*. Ed. Jane Chance. New York and London: Routledge, 171-82.

Humphrey, Edith M. 2017. *Further Up and Further In: Orthodox Conversations with C.S. Lewis on Scripture and Theology*. Yonkers, NY: St Vladimir's Seminary Press.

Iammarino, Darren. 2013. *Religion and Reality: An Exploration of Contemporary Metaphysical Systems, Theologies, and Religious Pluralism*. Eugene, OR: Pickwick Publications.

Jacobs, Alan. 2010. 'The Chronicles of Narnia.' *The Cambridge Companion to C.S. Lewis*. Eds. Robert MacSwain and Michael Ward. Cambridge: Cambridge University Press, 265-80.

Kane, Douglas Charles. 2009. *Arda Reconstructed: The Creation of the Published Silmarillion*. Bethlehem: PA: Lehigh University Press.

Kilby, Clyde S. 1976. *Tolkien and The Silmarillion*. Wheaton, IL: Harold Shaw Publishers.

1978. *Images of Salvation in the Fiction of C.S. Lewis*. Wheaton, IL: Harold Shaw Publishers.

Kocher, Paul H. 1980. *A Reader's Guide to The Silmarillion*. Boston, MA: Houghton Mifflin Company.

Korpua, Jyrki. 2021. *The Mythopoeic Code of Tolkien: A Christian Platonic Reading of the Legendarium*. Jefferson, NC: McFarland.

Langrish, Katherine. 2021. *From Spare Oom to War Drobe: Travels in Narnia with My Nine Year-Old Self*. London: Darton, Longman and Todd.

Leeming, David and Margaret. 1994. *A Dictionary of Creation Myths*. New York and Oxford: Oxford University Press.

Lemański, Janusz. 2013. *Księga Rodzaju. Rozdziały 1-11. Wstęp, przekład z oryginału, komentarz.* Nowy Komentarz Biblijny. Częstochowa: Edycja Świętego Pawła.

Leśniewski, Michał. 2014. 'O konstruowaniu *Silmarillionu* słów kilka, czyli jak wygląda, jak może wyglądać i jak powinien wyglądać „Silmarillion".' *Aiglos* 19, 5-32.

Lewis, Clive Staples. 2004. *The Collected Letters of C.S. Lewis. Vol. I. Family Letters 1905-1931.* Ed. Walter Hooper. London: Harper San Francisco.

2010. *The Collected Letters of C.S. Lewis. Vol. III. Narnia, Cambridge and Joy 1950-1963.* Ed. Walter Hooper. London: Harper San Francisco.

2004. 'The Dethronement of Power.' *Understanding The Lord of the Rings: The Best of Tolkien Criticism.* Eds. Rose A. Zimbardo and Neil D. Isaacs. Boston and New York: Houghton Mifflin Company, 11-15.

2014. *God in the Dock. Essays on Theology and Ethics.* Ed. Walter Hooper. Grand Rapids, MI and Cambridge: William B. Eerdmans Publishing Company.

2020. *Letters to Malcolm. Chiefly on Prayer.* London: William Collins.

2014. *The Lion, the Witch and the Wardrobe.* London: HarperCollins.

2014. *The Magician's Nephew.* London: HarperCollins.

2012. *Mere Christianity.* London: William Collins.

2020. *Reflections on the Psalms.* London: William Collins.

2017. 'Sometimes Fairy Stories May Say Best What's to Be Said.' *Of Other Worlds: Essays and Stories.* San Francisco, CA: HarperOne, 55-60.

Maryniarczyk, Andrzej SDB. 2018. *Dlaczego stworzenie »ex nihilo«. Teoria metafizycznego kreacjonizmu.* Lublin: Polskie Towarzystwo Tomasza z Akwinu.

Milton, John. 2014. *Paradise Lost.* London: Penguin Books.

Oziewicz, Marek. 2005. *Magiczny urok Narnii. Poetyka i filozofia „Opowieści z Narnii" C.S. Lewisa.* Kraków: Universitas.

Palmer, John. 2013. *Parmenides and Presocratic Philosophy.* Oxford: Oxford University Press.

Penner, Terry. 2009. 'The Forms and the Sciences in Socrates and Plato.' *A Companion to Plato.* Ed. Hugh H. Benson. Chichester: Wiley & Blackwell, 165-83.

Phelpstead, Carl. 2014. 'Myth-making and Sub-creation.' *A Companion to J.R.R. Tolkien.* Ed. Stuart D. Lee. Chichester: Wiley Blackwell, 79-91.

Sepkoski, David. 2008. 'Macroevolution.' *The Oxford Handbook of Philosophy of Biology*. Ed. Michael Ruse. Oxford: Oxford University Press, 211-37.

Scull, Christina and Wayne G. Hammond. 2017. *The J.R.R. Tolkien Companion and Guide. Reader's Guide. Part II*. London: HarperCollins.

Smilde, Arend. 2014. 'C.S. Lewis, St Jerome, and the Biblical Creation Story: The Background of a Recurring Misattribution.' *The Journal of Inklings Studies*. 4.2, 115-24.

Szamot, Maria. 2020. *Genesis. Czy ktoś w to jeszcze wierzy?* Poznań: Wydawnictwo W drodze.

Świderkówna, Anna. 2009. *Rozmowy o Biblii. Prawo i prorocy*. Warszawa: PWN.

Theophilus. 1885. 'Theophilus to Autolycus.' *The Ante-Nicene Fathers. Translations of The Writings of the Fathers down to A.D. 325. Vol. 2 Fathers of the Second Century*. Revised by A. Cleveland Coxe. Eds. Rev. Alexander Roberts and James Donaldson. Buffalo, IN: The Christian Literature Publishing Company, 85-122.

Thomas Aquinas. 1976. *Summa Contra Gentiles. Book Two: Creation*. Transl. James F. Anderson. Notre Dame, IN: University of Notre Dame Press.

Tolkien, 2016. John Ronald Reuel. *Leaf by Niggle*. London: HarperCollins.

1981. *The Letters of J.R.R. Tolkien*. Ed. Humphrey Carpenter with the assistance of Christopher Tolkien. London, Boston and Sydney: George Allen and Unwin.

1995. *Morgoth's Ring. The History of Middle-earth 10*. Ed. Christopher Tolkien. London: HarperCollins.

2001. 'Mythopoeia.' *Tree and Leaf*. London: HarperCollins, 83-90.

2008. *Tolkien On Fairy-stories*. Expanded Edition with Commentary and Notes. Eds. Verlyn Flieger and Douglas A. Anderson. London: HarperCollins.

2006. *The Silmarillion*. London: HarperCollins.

2002. *War of the Jewels. The History of Middle-earth 11*. Ed. Christopher Tolkien. London: HarperCollins.

*The Vulgate Bible. Vol. 1. The Pentateuch*. 2010. Ed. Swift Edgar. Cambridge, MA and London: Harvard University Press.

Walsh, Chad. 2008. *The Literary Legacy of C.S. Lewis*. Eugene, OR: Wipf and Stock Publishers.

Walton, Christina Ganong. 2007. 'Bible.' *J.R.R. Tolkien Encyclopedia: Scholarship and Critical Assessment*. Ed. Michael D.C. Drout. New York and London: Routledge, 62-64.

WEBB, Stephen H. 2005. 'Aslan's Voice: C.S. Lewis and the Magic of Sound.' *The Chronicles of Narnia and Philosophy: The Lion, the Witch and the Worldview.* Eds. Gregory Bassham and Jerry L. Walls. Chicago and La Salle, IL: Open Court, 3-14.

WOLFE, Brendan N. 2014. 'Tolkien's Jonah.' *Journal of Inklings Studies* 4.2, 11-26.

ZACHUBER, Johannes. 2014. *Human Nature in Gregory of Nyssa*. Leiden: Brill.

ZILIOLI, Ugo. 2020. *Atomism in Philosophy: A History from Antiquity to the Present.* London and New York: Bloomsbury Academic.

Joanna Łękawska



# The Interpenetration of Past, Present and Future in *The Chronicles of Narnia* and *The Lord of the Rings*

**Abstract**

The following chapter seeks to examine the interpenetration of past, present and future in *The Chronicles of Narnia* and *The Lord of the Rings* as an interesting backdrop for the development of the plot in each of these works. Of the two writers, Lewis makes this interpenetration more explicit, with the shifts of setting from the primary world of late-nineteenth and early-twentieth-century England to the secondary world of Narnia, where the passage of time is markedly different. Furthermore, in the *Narniad*, Time also appears as a character, first in *The Silver Chair*, and then in *The Last Battle*, at the end of the world, when the temporal realms pass away and something new, atemporal or eternal, begins. The interpenetration of past, present and future in *The Lord of the Rings* is, perhaps, just as considerable as in *The Chronicles of Narnia*, but in a less explicit way. There is a historical depth in it that is significant to the plot at every stage, as the characters and the events are not only steeped in the history of Middle-earth, but also forge it at the same time.

The question of time is a permanent reality of human existence and it is something that can be approached from different perspectives. The ever-increasing pace of life, the demands to be more efficient, and the irrevocable passage of time are experiences that mark individuals and societies. Indeed, the twentieth century is sometimes described as one obsessed with time (Mendilow 1976: 71), and this is often explicitly expressed in its art and literature, including the works of C.S. Lewis and J.R.R. Tolkien, both of whom delve into the question of time in their numerous writings. In her book *A Question of Time: J.R.R. Tolkien's Road to Faërie*, Verlyn Flieger points out that one motif "central to Tolkien's thought [is] the interpenetration and interdependence of all aspects of time" (1997: 22). Reading *The Lord of the Rings*, one may thus easily see that there is an ever-present awareness of the passing of time and its importance for the development of the plot. Something similar could also be observed in *The Chronicles of Narnia*, both in its primary world and the world that Peter, Edmund, Susan, Lucy, and other children find themselves in. The aim of this chapter is to briefly examine the interpenetration of past, present and future in *The Chronicles of Narnia* and *The Lord of the Rings*, considering it as an important backdrop for the plotlines of these works.

## The Reading Order of *The Chronicles of Narnia*

The reader of *The Chronicles of Narnia* should become aware of the mutual merging of temporal realities in each of the seven books already when faced with the dilemma of which reading order to follow: the order in which the books were published or the chronological sequence in which the events unfold. Even though literary critics and publishers may argue successfully for one or the other,[1] the reading order is certainly not irrelevant, as it also affects the reader's experience of the flow of time. The publication order is as follows: *The Lion, The Witch and the Wardrobe* (1950), *Prince Caspian* (1951), *The Voyage of the Dawn Treader* (1952), *The Silver Chair* (1953), *The Horse and His Boy* (1954), *The Magician's Nephew* (1955), and *The Last Battle* (1956).[2] The reader, thus, enters Narnia for the first time with Lucy during the reign of the White Witch, follows the adventures of the Pevensie children through the following two books, witnesses Prince Rilian's rescue from the Underworld by Eustace and Jill, then gets to know about what happens to Shasta and Aravis during the Golden Age of Narnia, when Peter is High King, and only then finds out how the Narnian world came to be created in *The Magician's Nephew*. The beginning of Narnia and its end in *The Last Battle* are placed side-by-side as 'companion pieces' and, consequently, contrast the original goodness of creation with the corruption of a tired world (Glover 1981: 179). Only towards the end of the series, in *The Magician's Nephew*, the narrator accounts for the magical nature of the wardrobe through which the Pevensies first enter Narnia, for the presence of the lamp-post in the Lantern Waste, and provides more insight into the identity of Aslan (Alan Jacobs 2010: 271). This original publication order allows the reader to be taken more by surprise and be in suspense when reading the books – especially *The Lion, the Witch and the*

---

1 See, for example, Glover (1981: 134 and 171ff), and A. Jacobs (2010: 269-71).

2 According to Walter Hooper, though, the chronological order as formulated and recommended by C.S. Lewis himself, should be as follows: *The Magician's Nephew, The Lion, The Witch and the Wardrobe, The Horse and His Boy, Prince Caspian, The Voyage of the Dawn Treader, The Silver Chair*, and *The Last Battle* (Green and Hooper 2002: 320).

*Wardrobe* – and thus experience the magic of Narnia and the interpenetration of time more intensely.

On the other hand, reading *The Magician's Nephew* as the first book in the series,[3] saves the reader some of the detective work and provides a more systematic account of the events. When it comes to time, perusing the books in the chronological order of events is also less confusing. The experience of time at the most basic level is, thus, as follows: (1) the creation of Narnia, (2) the end of its usurpation by the White Witch and the reign of the children as Kings and Queens, (3) the adventures of Shasta during the Golden Age, (4) the Pevensies' return to Narnia to restore Caspian to his throne, (5) the voyage on the Dawn Treader some years later, (6) the rescue of Caspian's son Rilian from the power of the Green Witch, and, finally, (7) the moral decomposition and temporal end of Narnia. There is, thus, not much movement back and forth when it comes to the fundamental flow of 'historical' time.[4] In a work so laden with time-warp experiences, and which spans over a long period of time, the reading order is certainly of significance and marks the reader's experience of time in both the primary and secondary worlds.

## The Temporal Structure of Narnia

When discussing the interpenetration of past, present and future in *The Chronicles of Narnia*, it is of foremost importance that the difference between the time in the primary world and that in the secondary one should be taken into consideration. Every time the children enter Narnia and return from it, which happens in all the books except for *The Horse and His Boy*, it seems to them that they come back into 'our time' at exactly the same moment they have left. A good illustration of this might be the words of Digory, who says at the end of *The Magician's Nephew* (once he has returned to England after being away for hours, witnessing the creation of Narnia and all that followed it), "I

---

3 It should be noted that some current publishers follow the original order. The movie series (2005-10), though only a trilogy, also stays true to the publication sequence, the first film being *The Lion, the Witch and the Wardrobe*.

4 The 'Outline of Narnian history so far as it is known,' comprising the events from both the primary and secondary worlds, is to be found in Walter Hooper's book *Past Watchful Dragons* (1971: 41-44). It is also included in Green and Hooper's *C.S. Lewis: A Biography* (2002: 316-20).

believe the whole adventure's taken no time at all" (201). This same Digory, as old Professor Kirke, uses the different flow of time as one of his arguments in support of Lucy's truthfulness:

> if, I say, she had got into another world, I should not be at all surprised to find that the other world had a separate time of its own; so that however long you stayed there it would never take up any of *our* time. On the other hand, I don't think many girls of her age would invent that idea for themselves. If she had been pretending, she would have hidden for a reasonable time before coming out and telling her story. (*LWW* 57)

Andrzej Wicher refers to this as a "reversed time loop effect" and juxtaposes this phenomenon with what is often found in folk literature, where characters experience that "the years spent in the Otherworld pass less quickly than the earthly years" (2013: 201). In *The Chronicles*, though the characters spend lengthy periods of time in Narnia, no time passes in the primary world. Wicher argues that it "seems to be [Lewis's] intentional device which is meant to show that the supernatural domain is a space where the limitations of the earthly time are overcome" (2013: 202). These limitations are overcome also because they are not fully understood by the characters and accepted by them as such. The children who enter Narnia and experience this phenomenon assume it as it is, without undermining it. Wicher further develops his idea when he says that, "it is surely only during the strongest and most intensive experiences, both positive and negative, that one feels as if the flow of time has slowed down, that one can experience more in a minute than one would have otherwise experienced in a year's time. Such experiences provide a greater physical sense of the reality of the real" (202). The children's experiences in Narnia are so intense that they fill their time with much more content than one minute of 'our time' is able to hold.

This 'reversed time loop effect' is present in every book in the series (the least so in *The Horse and His Boy*) and is also frequently referred to by its characters. The children who experience it are puzzled by it at the beginning, but then accept it; and they know that they cannot really figure out the time difference between the two realms. Eustace, for instance, explains it to Jill at the beginning of *The Silver Chair*, only a few months after he first came to Narnia with his cousins:

> this world has a different time from ours. [...] The time you spend here doesn't take up any of our time. Do you see? I mean, however long we spend here, we shall still get back to Experiment House at the moment we left it. [...] And

> when you're back in England – in our world – you can't tell how time is going here. It might be any number of years in Narnia while we're having one year at home. [...] And now apparently it's been about seventy years – Narnian years – since I was here last. Do you see now? And I come back and find Caspian an old, old man. (54-55)

Eustace at first does not recognize Caspian, because he himself is only a few months older, and the King of Narnia is now an elderly man. What is very significant is that there seems to be no clue as to how much time passes in Narnia while one is in the primary world. This "supernatural domain," as Wicher calls it (2013: 202), is somehow not accessible to them while the children are in England. Marek Oziewicz studies this phenomenon, and analyses with great detail the chronology of both Narnia and England as presented in *The Chronicles.* He transcribes the chart presented by Walter Hooper in *Past Watchful Dragons*, demonstrating a total temporal non-uniformity of the two worlds (2005: 123-25). He then quotes Hooper, who argues that Lewis was "convinced that other worlds could have different characteristics than in our world, such as the density and rarefaction of time" (125; Hooper 1971: 39). Oziewicz claims that the children can travel across the worlds which lack this uniformity, because Lewis accepts a pluralistic time-space model. This refusal to use only the linear concept of time as well as its slowing down, in turn, permits the author of *The Chronicles* to present a credible model of time travel (128). Both the reader and the characters simply accept the fact that "Narnian time flows differently than ours," as the narrator explains it at the beginning of *The Voyage of the Dawn Treader* (24).

The last thing to be considered in this section is the effect that the time in Narnia has on the characters, which further accentuates the mutual interpenetration of the two temporal realms. In *The Lion, the Witch and the Wardrobe*, Peter, Susan, Edmund, and Lucy spend fifteen Narnian years in the secondary world. They not only help Aslan to defeat the White Witch, but they also rule as Kings and Queens of Narnia for many years. In other words, they grow up and mature on the human level and take on the customs of their state. The narrator describes it in the following way:

> And they themselves grew and changed as the years passed over them. And Peter became a tall and deep-chested man and a great warrior, and he was called King Peter the Magnificent. And Susan grew into a tall and gracious woman with

> black hair that fell almost to her feet and the kings of the countries beyond the sea began to send ambassadors asking for her hand in marriage. And she was called Queen Susan the Gentle. Edmund was a graver and quieter man than Peter. […] So they lived in great joy and if ever they remembered their life in this world it was only as one remembers a dream. (191-92)

Their maturity is also seen in the way they speak, because they adopt the ways of the court and language that befits the royalty. Yet, they once again turn into 'normal children' when they are transported back to the primary world. They are, once again, of the same age as they used to be, which obviously has an influence on their appearance and behaviour. This is clearly visible at the beginning of *Prince Caspian* when they end up in Narnia again and wonder whether they can swim and ride horses, as they used to do when they were Queens and Kings. Peter tries to explain it to his siblings by saying, "but we were sort of grown-up then. […] We reigned for years and years and learned to do things. Aren't we just back at our proper ages again now?" (42). The answer to this question is not explicitly given in the books, although it is repeatedly stated that the Narnian air affects the children in a way that they quickly become stronger and somehow nobler.

An interesting exchange of opinions concerning the effects of Narnian life on the children may be found in *The Last Battle*, as Jill and Eustace prepare to help King Tirian in the battle. The boy then asks his friend, "What'll happen if we get killed here?' […] I mean, what will happen in our own world? Shall we wake up and find ourselves back in that train? Or shall we just vanish and never be heard of any more? Or shall we be dead in England?" (119). Such questions are not clearly answered in the books, just as it is not clear what effects the disappearance of Frank the Cabby and his wife Helen, who become the first monarchs of Narnia (*MN* 157-58), will have in the primary world. Eustace's musings about the possible death of the children in Narnia and, consequently in England, take on even more depth once the reader discovers that these characters indeed arrive in Narnia only after they have been killed in a railway accident (*LB* 221). Therefore, as they reflect on the possibility of dying in England as a result of their being killed in Narnia, they actually continue to live in the secondary world while being no longer alive in the primary one. This may also be Lewis's commentary on how the 'supernatural domain' surpasses the question of time, and it certainly underlines the interpenetration of the past, present and future in *The Chronicles*.

## Father Time as a Character in *The Chronicles of Narnia*

Notwithstanding all that has been said so far, the Narnian time also comes to be personalised in the figure of Father Time, the enigmatic character that appears in *The Silver Chair* and in *The Last Battle*. As Jill, Eustace and Puddleglum go through the Underworld led by the Warden, they come upon a sleeping figure said to be Father Time. The passage is set within the context of a long journey through a mysterious land without the sun:

> It brought them into a smaller cave, long and narrow, about the shape and size of a cathedral. And here, filling almost the whole length of it, lay an enormous man fast asleep. He was far bigger than any of the giants, and his face was not like a giant's, but noble and beautiful. His breast rose and fell gently, under the snowy beard which covered him to the waist. A pure, silver light (no one saw where it came from) rested upon him. 'Who's that?' asked Puddleglum. [...] 'That is old Father Time, who once was a King in Overland,' said the Warden. 'And now he has sunk down into the Deep Realm and lies dreaming of all the things that are done in the upper world. Many sink down, and few return to the sunlit lands. They say he will wake at the end of the world.' (*SC* 155-56)

Despite the Warden's explanation, the sleeping giant remains enigmatic. To some extent, he resembles Father Christmas, who appears in *The Lion, the Witch and the Wardrobe* at the end of the White Witch's reign (115-17), mainly on account of his size, friendly nature, and, most significantly, being a herald of important changes in Narnia. In the atmosphere of the Underworld and following the travellers' painful experiences with the giants in Harfang, Father Time evidently has the appearance of a positive figure, because of his "noble and beautiful" countenance and peaceful sleep. It is not very clear, however, why he is no longer "King in Overland" and what Lewis means by saying that Father Time "lies dreaming of all the things that are done in the upper world" (*SC* 156). It may mean that, since Father Time no longer rules in Overland, his time is drawing to an end; yet, at the same time, the world of Narnia is kept in existence because he continues to dream of all that happens there. What is hinted at here is that, paradoxically, time will end when Father Time wakes, as in fact happens in *The Last Battle*. Michael Ward argues that Father Time is the Roman god Saturn (2008: 200), whose Greek equivalent is Kronos, from whom the concept of chronological time derives. In an early draft of *The Silver Chair*, C.S. Lewis gives the following words to the Warden when describing the sleeping giant, "That is the god Saturn, who once was a King in Over-land. [...] They say he will wake at the end of the world" (Ward 2008: 200). Ward's thesis in his book is that each of the *Chronicles* corresponds to one of the seven planets, and that is the unifying backdrop of Lewis's work (22). He links *The Last Battle* with Saturn, because, among other things, of the prominent role that Father Time plays at the end of the book, as is foretold in the above-quoted passage of *The Silver Chair.*

The seventh novel in the series is marked from the very beginning by a sense of finality, which culminates with the end of time and the transformation of Narnia into a new reality. The book's title, *The Last Battle*, the opening sentence, "In the last days of Narnia" (11), and the introduction of Tirian as "the last of the Kings of Narnia" (24) all hint at the irreversible end that is fast approaching and is one of the main themes in this novel (Ward 2008: 199). The reader is presented with this idea explicitly and yet, at the same time, there is a strong desire to hope that the end may somehow be prevented. This wish may, for instance be detected in the following conversation between Jill and Jewel the Unicorn:

> 'Oh, I do hope we can soon settle the Ape and get back to those good, ordinary times. And then I hope they'll go on for ever and ever and ever. *Our* world is going to have an end some day. Perhaps this one won't. Oh Jewel – wouldn't it be lovely if Narnia just went on and on – like what you said it has been?' 'Nay, sister,' answered Jewel, 'all worlds draw to an end, except Aslan's own country.' 'Well, at least,' said Jill, 'I hope the end of this one is millions of millions of millions of years away.' (*LB* 111)

Jill's conviction that 'her world' will end is juxtaposed with her wish for Narnia to continue into infinity. Despite the sufferings and wrongdoings she has experienced in Narnia, perhaps she nonetheless sees it as somehow less prone to destruction than the world she comes from. Because it is more magical than Earth, Narnia can still be 'fixed' and somehow prevented from the chaos that seems to be approaching. Jill's noble wish that Narnia would continue for a long time, is abruptly shattered a few lines later when King Tirian learns of the take-over of Cair Paravel and the murder of his close associates, to which he exclaims, "Narnia is no more" (*LB* 114). The pathos that accompanies these events and all that happens up to the moment of "the last battle of the last King of Narnia" (158), is also marked by a subtle reminder that Aslan can set all things right and that his world shall not end.

The final chapters of *The Last Battle* describe what happens once King Tirian and the children go "through the stable door" to witness the end of Narnia and the beginning of a new reality, as they go "further up and further in" (200). Before this new realm is formed however, when all are gathered around Aslan, he summons the already-mentioned Father Time in a very dramatic way, "He raised his head and roared, 'Now it is time!' then louder, 'Time!'; then so loud that it could have shaken the stars, 'TIME.' The Door flew open" (181). There is a double-meaning in the words uttered by Aslan: he calls for Time and states that the time for the end has arrived. This is explained shortly afterwards with a reference to the events outlined in *The Silver Chair*:

> Then Jill and Eustace remembered how once long ago, in the deep caves beneath those moors, they had seen a great giant asleep and been told that his name was Father Time, and that he would wake on the day the world ended. 'Yes,' said Aslan, though they had not spoken. 'While he lay dreaming his name was Time. Now that he is awake he will have a new one. (182-83)

Aslan does not state, however, what Time's new name is. The giant wakes up and obediently carries out the orders which he receives from the Lion, and which result in the termination of Narnia. He no longer keeps the world in existence while he sleeps, but, rather, brings about its end by repeatedly blowing his horn.

The giant's destructive actions are not completely terrifying to the children, because of Aslan's presence. The narrator presents the scene of the final destruction of Narnia in a serious way, but accompanies it with some degree of humour. The scene unfolds in the following way:

> Then Aslan said, 'Now make an end.' The giant threw his horn into the sea. Then he stretched out one arm – very black it looked, and thousands of miles long – across the sky till his hand reached the Sun. He took the Sun and squeezed it in his hand as you would squeeze an orange. And instantly there was total darkness. (*LB* 191)

The allegorical language used in this passage underlines the inevitability of the passing of time and its relativity. The sun, which Polly and Digory see when Narnia comes into existence in *The Magician's Nephew*, is now squeezed like an orange and ceases to be, along with the entire world it illuminates. This scene is the last one in which Father Time appears, as he completes Aslan's will to bring the world to an end and thus fulfils his mission. The reader does not find out the giant's new name, but sees by his actions that he is the herald of destruction, which, according to Michael Ward, is a characteristic of Saturn in C.S. Lewis's other works (2008: 200). This allegorical depiction of Time, as one which keeps in existence, destroys or transforms into a new reality, is an underlying element in all the seven books that make up *The Chronicles*. In *Mere Christianity*, in the chapter aptly titled 'Time and Beyond Time,' Lewis states that "almost certainly God is not in time. His life does not consist of moments following one another. [...] every moment from the beginning of the world – is always the Present for Him" (143). Likewise, in the *Chronicles*, this idea of a Providence which guides and governs the world, appears to be atemporal, that is to say, not affected by the flow of time. In the above-discussed passage of *The Last Battle*, Time is therefore shown to be at the orders of Aslan, who, as a Christ figure, obviously stands outside of time, and is not in any way subject to it.

## The Historical Depth in *The Lord of the Rings*

The interpenetration of the past, present and future in *The Lord of the Rings* may be sensed by the reader already in the opening sentences of both the Prologue and the first chapter of Book One. In the former, the narrator states that the work is about hobbits and their history (*FR* 1), while in the latter he mentions the preparations for the eleventy-first birthday of Bilbo Baggins (21). Both sentences place the narrative within a larger scale and context of events, reveal the importance of time, and point to the historical depth of Middle-earth.[5] Each chapter of *The Lord of the Rings* is filled with sometimes multiple references to all sorts of significant places and events that took place in the past. Moreover, the story begins *in medias res* and the reader is quickly made

5 In 'Time and Tide – Medieval Patterns of Interpreting the Passing of Time in Tolkien's Work' (2011), Thomas Honegger provides a thorough examination of the medieval approach to time present in Middle-earth.

aware of the fact that the hobbits are part of something broader, something that exceeds their individual accounts. This 'something broader' is briefly outlined in the Prologue, where the hobbits are described as "an unobtrusive but very ancient people, more numerous formerly than they are today" (1). Already at this stage, the hobbits are provided with a complex historical background. The narrator then goes on to describe Dwarves, the Elves and Men, with numerous references to significant events from the history of Middle-earth, events which shed some light on the more recent past. This is a characteristic trait throughout the novel, not only in the Prologue. Colin Manlove says that in *The Lord of the Rings* "There is scarcely a mortal character whose descent is not chronicled or a racial history which is not mapped out either in the text or the appendices. [...] Remembrance of times past is pervasive" (qtd. in Garbowski 2000: 111). Despite the abundance of details and descriptions, it is difficult to find any inconsistencies or contradictions in *The Lord of the Rings*. The different races of Middle-earth all have their history, language(s), and legends, both on the macro (an entire people) and the micro (individual members) levels. It is a history to which they often refer in their conversations, and its memory is a guiding light in their actions. An example of this may be seen in the words of Gimli, spoken shortly after the formation of the Company:

> 'I need no map,' said Gimli, who had come up with Legolas, and was gazing out before him with a strange light in his deep eyes. 'There is the land where our fathers worked of old, and we have wrought the image of those mountains into many works of metal and of stone, and into many songs and tales. They stand tall in our dreams [...]. Only once before have I seen them from afar in waking life, but I know them and their names, for under them lies Khazad-dûm, the Dwarrowdelf, that is now called the Black Pit, Moria in the Elvish tongue. (*FR* 283)

Gimli then goes on to list the names of other places from the land of the Dwarves, which have been present in the memory of his people for generations. It is significant that the images of Moria have been engraved both materially and mentally into the culture of the Dwarves. Even though Gimli himself has never been to Moria physically, he knows it well; its images are part of his own personal story and that of his race. The fact that he names the places in various languages, not only in his own, is also an important feature. It shows the intricacies and complexity of the various inhabitants of Middle-earth, each with its own story and legacy. Tom Shippey observes that "the maps and the names give Middle-earth [an] air of solidity and extent both in space and time" (2012: 147). Although Gimli claims that he does not need a map to find his way to the land of Moria, the maps are an important asset to the reader and one of the chief features of the book.[6] As the characters advance in their quest to save Middle-earth, the maps included in *The Lord of the Rings* show the distance they have travelled and the time they needed to do that.

Furthermore, each member of the Company, each race, and, most importantly, the Ring itself, has a past, which is in some way significant to the development of the plot. This history connects the worlds of the past and the present, and has consequences for both the now and the future. The time gone by is not portrayed, however, as either superlative or inferior to the present; rather, it is shown as it is, with both its dark and light elements, not infrequently affecting the here and now. Indeed, *The Lord of the Rings* is not a book that glorifies the past over the present, nor is it an example of chronocentrism, which rejects the past as less developed than current times (Garbowski 2000: 34). Garbowski argues that for Tolkien the past "was alive and [...] an equal partner in a dialogue he was engaged in" (34). Verlyn Flieger further adds that "the past, with its ancient griefs and glories, was [for him] a part of the present, woven into its fabric and deeply influencing its actions" (1997: 2). This common-sense attitude towards the past and the present is reflected in the following conversation between Gandalf and Frodo, when the latter hears about the power of the Ring:

> 'I wish it need not have happened in my time,' said Frodo.
>
> 'So do I,' said Gandalf, 'and so do all who live to see such times. But that is not for them to decide. All we have to decide is what to do with the time that is given us. And already, Frodo, our time is beginning to look black. The Enemy is fast becoming very strong. His plans are far from ripe, I think, but they are ripening.' (*FR* 51)

Gandalf expounds to Frodo the hard facts about the current situation, showing him the extent of the power of the Ring, but does not permit him to look with pessimism either at the past nor at the present. Besides being a call to personal responsibility on the part of the Ring-bearer, the Wizard's words provide an

6 For more on maps in Tolkien and fantasy literature, see Stefan Ekman's *Here Be Dragons. Exploring Fantasy Maps and Settings* (2013).

insightful attitude towards historical time: the acceptance of the time period in which one lives, with both its negative and positive elements. Gandalf states that one's lifespan is a gift, and he thus implies that there is a Providence, which bestows it on all the living creatures and guides everything that happens. Shippey writes that Tolkien, "believes in the workings of Providence – the Providence which 'sent' Gandalf back, and which 'meant' Frodo to have the Ring [...]. But that Providence does not overrule free will, because it works only through the actions and decisions of the characters.[7] In Tolkien there is no chance, no coincidence" (2012: 562). The characters, therefore, either cooperate with Providence to fulfil the role that is appointed to them or refuse to carry it out. Gandalf himself, being one of the Wizards,[8] is assigned with a particular mission to accomplish and is an instrument of Providence in the struggle against the Dark Lord. The Wizards are described in *The Silmarillion* as "messengers sent by the Lords of the West to contest the power of Sauron, if he should arise again and to move Elves and Men and all living things of good will to valiant deeds" (277). While Gandalf remains ever attentive to fulfil his task, Saruman fails in this mission when he succumbs to corruption. Throughout *The Lord of the Rings* there is, therefore, a strong sense of a Providence which guides the events as they unfold, no matter how dark the times seem to be.

## The Time Factor in a Quest Narrative

In a quest narrative much depends on the timing with which the characters act and move towards their goal, for though it could take months or years for them to accomplish their objective, it is important that the protagonists always be in the right place at the right time. Writing about this aspect in *The Lord of the Rings*, Flieger observes: "if the Ring cannot be destroyed before Sauron's forces gain momentum, the whole enterprise will have gone for naught" (1997: 21). This is one of the reasons why time is such a significant factor in the novel. The narrator gives an example of the seriousness of right timing in the episode at the Prancing Pony Inn in Bree, when Frodo reads

7 Flieger meticulously discusses the question of free will in Tolkien's work in her article 'The Music and the Task: Fate and Free Will in Middle-earth' (2009: 151-81).

8 In *The Silmarillion*, in the 'Index of Names,' it is implied that Gandalf is also called Olórin, and that he is one of the Maiar (318).

Gandalf's letter written to him three months earlier. There are numerous temporal references in Gandalf's text: "Bad news has reached me here. I must go off at once. You had better leave Bag End soon, and get out of the Shire before the end of July at the latest. I will return as soon as I can; and I will follow you, if I find that you are gone" (*FR* 169). Finally, he closes the letter with "Yours in haste" (170). The hastiness of Gandalf's action is contrasted with the behaviour of the hobbits. Not only does Frodo not leave the Shire by the end of July, but three months later, but he also does not take the necessary precautions that should be taken by one who is pursued by the Black Riders. In the said scene, just before the reading of the letter, Frodo acts with great recklessness, when he allows the Ring to take momentary control over him, thus leading to his disappearance while performing a song (160). He is immediately reprimanded for this by Aragorn (at this point of the narrative known as Strider), but the damage is done and suspicion begins to grow around the hobbits. Even when they hope to leave the inn right after they have read Gandalf's letter, they are repeatedly delayed by all sorts of external events. Their departure is described in the following passage:

> It was close on ten o'clock before they at last got off. By that time the whole of Bree was buzzing with excitement. Frodo's vanishing trick; the appearance of the black horsemen; the robbing of the stables; and not least the news that Strider the Ranger had joined the mysterious hobbits, made such a tale as would last for many uneventful years. (180)

This above episode is a good example of the importance of right timing in the novel. The hobbits are being chased by the Black Riders, who seem to be almost ever-present at the beginning of their quest, and depending on whether they take the right steps at the right moment, they may be captured or not. The time-accuracy with which the characters act is, therefore, of prime significance.

Even after the destruction of the Ring and the presumed success of their quest, the hobbits' good timing remains to be very important upon their return to the Shire. Gandalf tells Frodo as they travel, "if I were you, I should press on now for home, or you will not come to the Brandywine Bridge before the gates are locked" (*RK* 996). As they get nearer to the Shire, they do not only notice the differences that have occurred since their departure (such as the gates that were built and the vegetation that disappeared) but they also experience a growing sense of urgency to get back. After he has learned of some of the troubles that have befallen the Shire before they even get there, Sam reprimands himself by saying, "I ought to have hurried back quicker" (995). Also Merry, once they finally do return home, repeatedly says that they have not come back "too soon" (999, 1006), seeing the devastation done to what used to be their peaceful and safe homeland.

However, notwithstanding the damage brought about by Saruman and his followers, the hobbits are able to prevent further destruction by acting on time. As Barliman Butterbur from the Prancing Pony Inn tells them when they depart, "you've come back changed from your travels, and you look now like folk as can deal with troubles out of hand" (*RK* 995). Frodo, Sam, Merry and Pippin are no longer the same hobbits who procrastinated and acted imprudently at the beginning of their quest. They are able to face their responsibility with the resolve and rhythm that turn out to be necessary.

Connected to the idea of acting at the right moment is one of the central notions of *The Lord of the Rings*, namely how personal decisions forge history and the future. There are many examples of this in the novel. Garbowski refers to it in the following passage:

> The problem of decision-making is one of the key themes of *The Lord of the Rings*. At a simpler level, some decisions are a matter of skill and experience. In one of the difficult situations he comes across, for the sake of appeasing Gollum Frodo has himself and Sam blind-folded by Faramir in Ithilien, a diplomatic strategy he has learned from Aragorn. Fully mature decisions need to be made alone: Aragorn must eventually make decisions without Gandalf; likewise Frodo without either Gandalf or Aragorn; and so must Sam without Frodo at a key juncture. Individual decisions are more carefully delineated in the novel than collective ones. (2000: 192-93)

What is apparent throughout the narrative is that all sorts of decisions, even, as it seems, the most mundane ones, made by its numerous characters turn out to be significant, even crucial, for the unfolding of history. When considering Gollum, for example, it is undeniable that he is a creature who is the product of his own decisions. These decisions, such as the killing of Déagol and stealing the Ring in the distant past (*FR* 53), or his final meeting with Frodo on Mount Doom (*RK* 943), have irreversible consequences not only for himself, but also, even more importantly, for others. They make him become the greedy and pitiful creature that he is, and finally lead to his death and the destruction of the Ring.

While those who choose evil abound in *The Lord of the Rings*, the actions of those who wish to bring about the destruction of the Ring are far more important for the development of the plot. Whereas it is quite predictable that the Black Riders, the Orcs or Saruman will cause harm, the same predictability cannot be applied to the characters who oppose the Dark Lord Sauron. Their minds are set on choosing the good; yet, their deeds are not predetermined, and they are, therefore, prone to weakness and error. Perhaps the most prominent example of such a moral deviation is the moment when Boromir partially succumbs to the power of the Ring at the end of Book Two. At first he himself thinks he is taking the right steps, when he tells Frodo that "[tr]ue-hearted Men [...] will not be corrupted. We of Minas Tirith have been staunch through long years of trial. We do not desire the power of wizard-lords, only strength to defend ourselves, strength in a just cause" (*FR* 398). As Boromir's mind gets more and more set on the Ring, he begins to lose the lucidity and presses Frodo with an increasing force. He may be a man of honour, who undergoes great sacrifices to join the Company and overcome evil, yet he is still not predestined to choose the right way. When he gets back to his senses, he admits to Frodo that he was overtaken by "a madness" (400). Yet, the damage has been done; Boromir's failure to reject the temptation right away has very significant repercussions not only for himself, but also for Frodo and the entire quest. This threat from Boromir, however, also produces a positive effect as it spurs Frodo to direct himself resolutely towards Mordor. After he has escaped from Boromir, he says to himself, "I must go now or I shall never go" (*FR* 402); Boromir's weakness, therefore, to some extent strengthens Frodo and helps him to carry on with his mission.

Throughout the novel, Frodo's decision-making is always of primary importance. Since he is the chosen Ring-bearer, his endeavours to complete the mission are invariably central to the plot. Frodo's freedom to accept his calling to destroy the Ring in the Cracks of Mount Doom is especially evident during the Council of Elrond, when he makes the determined decision to continue towards Mordor.

> Frodo glanced at all the faces, but they were not turned to him. All the Council sat with downcast eyes, as if in deep thought. A great dread fell on him, as if he was awaiting the pronouncement of some doom that he had long foreseen and vainly hoped might after all never be spoken. An overwhelming longing to rest and remain at peace by Bilbo's side in Rivendell filled all his heart. At last with an effort he spoke, and wondered to hear his own words, as if some other will was using his small voice. 'I will take the Ring,' he said, 'though I do not know the way.' Elrond raised his eyes and looked at him, and Frodo felt his heart pierced by the sudden keenness of that glance. 'If I understand aright all that I have heard,' he said, 'I think that this task is appointed for you, Frodo; and that if you do not find a way, no one will. [...] But it is a heavy burden. So heavy that none could lay it on another. I do not lay it on you. But if you take it freely, I will say that your choice is right.' (*FR* 270)

Dickerson points out that "Elrond's words [show] the double emphasis on Frodo's free will: that his action is done "freely" and that it is a "choice" (2003: 87). The Ring-bearer's decision here is entirely dependent on his effort to complete the quest and for the future of Middle-earth. He is perfectly aware of it, just as he is sure that he cannot take on this mission unwillingly because it is too difficult to be undertaken with reluctance, which is further made clear in the words of Elrond. This willingness on the part of Frodo shows a maturing in his understanding of the situation, when it is contrasted with his initial reaction to Gandalf's proposal to destroy the Ring at the beginning of the novel. He bluntly rejects it then and only agrees to leave the Shire and travel to Rivendell to keep the Ring safe (*FR* 66). The change in Frodo's attitude at the Council of Elrond also points to the sense of responsibility that begins to form in his mind after he has made a series of important decisions.

When considering the quest as a way to self-transcendence, Garbowski cites Willis B. Glover, who writes that in *The Lord of the Rings*, "the good characters usually choose to do good but the decisions they make are real; the possibility of evil, of betraying the good, is always there, and the reader is made conscious of it" (2000: 194). Once again, this can be seen with great clarity not only in the example of Boromir, but also Frodo. On the surface, the latter manifests itself in the already-mentioned episode at the Prancing Pony Inn, when Frodo puts on the Ring and becomes invisible, thus attracting unnecessary attention which could imperil his incipient quest. On a deeper level, there is the increasing desire to keep the Ring, which he experiences a number of times until the very moment of its destruction (*RK* 946-47). Frodo's autonomous decisions, made at a specific moment in the present, determine the plot and affect the future, gradually bringing about the success of the quest.[9]

Another significant element in the novel as regards the issue of temporality is the entrelacement of events. The *Encyclopaedia Britannica* defines it as "a literary technique in which several simultaneous stories are interlaced in one larger narrative."[10] One of its functions in *The Lord of the Rings* is to "coordinate the independent actions of the fragmented Fellowship as they unfold" at the same time (Flieger 1997: 21) from the last chapter of Book Two to the end of the novel in Book Six. Soon after Frodo and Sam separate from the rest, Boromir is killed, and Merry and Pippin are kidnapped by the Orcs. From then on, there is a "chronological overlapping" of separate strands of action (Shippey 2012: 224). The narrator follows each group separately, relating long episodes of their ventures and then returning to the other characters. Because of that, the chronological order of events is, at times, slightly warped for the reader, as he or she reads about the whereabouts of individual characters with great detail, sometimes much later than when they actually occur. Nonetheless, a temporal cohesion is created when some events are described as happening concurrently, without the characters actually realising it. When Frodo and Sam are held by Faramir in Ithilien, for instance, the Ring-bearer contemplates the night sky and recalls his friends, "Far off in the West the full moon was sinking, round and white. […] For a while Frodo stood there on the high stone, and a shiver ran through him, wondering if anywhere in the vastness of the night-lands his old companions walked or slept, or lay dead shrouded in mist" (*TT* 683-84). Afterwards, he and Sam continue on their perilous quest, and when the reader leaves them, they are in dire straits inside Minas Morgul. When the narrative resumes with Gandalf and Pippin, the latter also looks at the moon:

> The last thing that he remembered before he fell into deep dream was a glimpse of high white peaks, glimmering like floating isles above the clouds as they caught the light of the westering moon. He wondered where Frodo was, and if he was already in Mordor, or if he was dead; and he did not know that Frodo from far away looked on that same moon as it set beyond Gondor ere the coming of the day. (*RK* 748)

---

9 Nonetheless, the quest would still have not been completed if it had not been for the acts of Providence.

10 'Enterlacement.' *Encyclopaedia Britannica*, Encyclopaedia Britannica, Inc. https://www.britannica.com/art/entrelacement. Accessed 17 May 2019.

These mirroring scenes not only evoke pathos in the reader, but also create a sense of simultaneity and provide a temporal unity in what seems to be a fragmented storyline. As Richard C. West points out, "the narrative is not loose, except to a superficial view; everything is interconnected" (1980: 84). Even though the Fellowship is broken, the Companions remain united in their common goal to overcome the Dark Lord and through the bonds of friendship which surpass time and space.

## The Temporality of Tom Bombadil

Finally, there is the character of Tom Bombadil, a significant figure in *The Lord of the Rings* when it comes to the interpenetration of the past, present and future, one who seems to be both atemporal and immersed in the history of Middle-earth at the same time. He is commonly regarded as one of the most puzzling creations of Tolkien, even referred to as "an enigma" by the author himself (S. Jacobs 2020: 80), and whose longevity is one of his chief features.[11] When Frodo asks Tom Bombadil who he is, he is given the following reply:

> 'Don't you know my name yet? That's the only answer. Tell me, who are you, alone, yourself and nameless? But you are young and I am old. Eldest, that's what I am. Mark my words, my friends: Tom was here before the river and the trees; Tom remembers the first raindrop and the first acorn. He made paths before the Big People, and saw the little People arriving. He was here before the Kings and the graves and the Barrow-wights. When the Elves passed westward, Tom was here already, before the seas were bent. He knew the dark under the stars when it was fearless – before the Dark Lord came from Outside.' (*FR* 131)

Bombadil not only describes himself in terms of his age, but also claims he is the "Eldest;" he seems to be some sort of a primordial being, who predates the Elves and Men. As Robert E. Chapman-Morales points out, the "Eldest" is "capitalised to show that he is older than all living beings," and that he is "the very first being in Middle-earth" (2020: 64). Also, Elrond refers to Tom Bombadil at the Council held at Rivendell, when he says: "But I had forgotten Bombadil, if indeed this is still the same that walked the woods and hills long ago, and even then was older than the old. That was not then his name. Iarwain Ben-adar we called

11 A comprehensive list of some of the most common speculations concerning the nature of Tom Bombadil was summarised by Charles E. Noad (1991:79-83).

him, oldest and fatherless. He is a strange creature" (*FR* 265). What the reader learns from Elrond is not particularly revealing in the light of what Bombadil says about himself; however, it is intriguing that the master of Rivendell finds Tom Bombadil impenetrable. Elrond confirms what Tom says about himself and additionally calls him "oldest and fatherless" (265). Chapman-Morales argues that "Bombadil's function" in *The Lord of the Rings* is to show "Tolkien's belief in the ultimate power of expressing joy in the face of evil" (2020: 61). He suggests that Bombadil's age reveals that he can be considered "a character who knows the unique joy and peace of a time and land without Sauron or Morgoth and the despair they seek to bring" (74). This is revealed in what Tom Bombadil himself says about his knowledge of "the dark under the stars when it was fearless" (*FR* 131). As such, he is not touched by the Ring's power and remains practically indifferent to the Dark Lord's scheming.

Furthermore, Shippey juxtaposes Tom Bombadil's age with that of Treebeard, when he says:

> Tom shares the adjective 'oldest' with another being in *The Lord of the Rings*, Fangorn the Ent, whom Gandalf calls 'the oldest living thing that still walks beneath the Sun' [*TT* 499]. An inconsistency? It need not be so, if one accepts that Tom is not living – as the Nazgûl and the Barrow-wight are not dead. Unlike even the oldest living creatures he has no date of birth, but seems to have been there since before the Elves awoke, a part of Creation, an exhalation of the world. (2012: 152)

This is a very insightful statement as regards the nature of Tom Bombadil, whom Shippey further calls "a *genius loci* [of] [...] the river and willow country of the English midlands (2012: 153). As a spirit residing in and watching over the forest he predates, Tom is not bound by time, nor can he be affected by any external factors. Towards the end of the novel, when Frodo wonders about how Tom Bombadil is doing, Gandalf responds: "As well as ever, you may be sure. [...] Quite untroubled; and I should guess, not much interested in anything that we have done or seen, unless perhaps in our visits to the Ents" (*RK* 996). The wizard thus seems to be the one who knows Bombadil more than the other characters – as is evidenced by his quick and sure reply regarding the question whether Tom would have come to the Council of Elrond (*FR* 265) – and that is why his answer to Frodo seems accurate and convincing. In her analysis of Tom Bombadil, Suzanne Jacobs makes an analogy between him and the wind when she says that "a number of the epithets that Tom ascribes to himself are also used in medieval riddles as conventional epithets for the wind" (2020: 84). She uses a number of medieval texts to demonstrate that the wind could also be imagined as the "oldest and fatherless," present at the moment of creation, just as Tom witnessed "the first raindrop and the first acorn" (*FR* 131), as he himself claims (S. Jacobs 2020: 85). This parallel between Tom Bombadil and the wind is obviously in line with Shippey's description of him as "not living" and with Gandalf's claim that he is not much affected by the events of the world, both of which shed some light on his longevity.

## Conclusion

The aim of this chapter was to explore the interpenetration of the past, present and future in *The Chronicles of Narnia* and *The Lord of the Rings*. Upon examining Lewis's septology the question of time becomes significant from the very beginning of one's encounter with Narnia, when considering the reading order of the books, as it affects the reader's perception of the time and the unfolding of the plot. This temporal interpenetration is made more explicit with the continual shifts of setting through time travel, from the primary world of England in the 1940s to the secondary world of Narnia, where the passing of time is not equivalent to that of the "real time" in England. Furthermore, Time itself also appears as a character in *The Chronicles of Narnia*, first in *The Silver Chair*, and then in *The Last Battle*, at the end of the world, or rather worlds, when the temporal realms pass away and something new – atemporal and eternal – begins.

In *The Lord of the Rings* there is a historical depth that is significant to the plot at every stage, as the characters and the events are, on the one hand, steeped in the history of Middle-earth and, on the other, constitute it themselves. A good example of that is the character of Tom Bombadil, who is both intrinsic to the history of Middle-earth and, at the same time, remains unaffected by it, as he seems to be somehow outside of time. In his works, and *The Lord of the Rings* in particular, Tolkien also frequently shows the importance of the right timing in making personal decisions which affect the future of specific individuals and entire peoples. The interconnectedness of the past, present, and future is, therefore, an ever-present background in Narnia and in Middle-earth, which points to Lewis's and Tolkien's view of time and history as deep and meaningful realities guided by Providence.

There is a strong sense of the linearity of time in the above-discussed works, with a marked beginning, progression, and direction towards which the events unfold. In *The Chronicles*, there is a definite termination of the secondary world of Narnia and the beginning of what seems to be a timeless reality. Tolkien's novel, on the other hand, concludes with the Third Age drawing to an end and the dawn of the Fourth. In all these works, there is a tangible, though hidden, Providence behind the events that unfold, which does not, however, interfere with the decision-making of the characters. Along with this directed linearity, though, Lewis and Tolkien often hint at a temporal complexity in their created worlds. Not only is the guiding Providence outside of time, there are multiple temporal realities, such as the Elvish realm of Lothlórien in *The Lord of the Rings* or the land of Narnia itself, which seem to coexist with one another in their respective narratives. Their works demonstrate a clear vision of the interconnectedness, indeed interpenetration, of the past, present and future, but also imply that, as C.S. Lewis famously exclaimed, "some things are not in Time at all" (*MC* 143).

## About the Author

Joanna Łękawska graduated from the Faculty of Arts and Science of the University of Toronto and the English Institute of the University of Warsaw. She has taught English in Canada and in Poland and has been involved in formal and informal education as well as management for over a decade. Her current research interests include J.R.R. Tolkien, Susanna Clarke and the use of literature in teaching English as a foreign language.

## Bibliography

Chapman-Morales, Robert. B. 2020. 'Fearless Joy: Tom Bombadil's Function in *The Lord of the Rings*.' *Mythlore* 38.2, 59-79.

Dickerson, Matthew. 2003. *Following Gandalf. Epic Battles and Moral Victory in The Lord of the Rings*. Grand Rapids, MI: Brazos Press.

Ekman, Stefan. 2013. *Here Be Dragons. Exploring Fantasy Maps and Settings*. Middletown, CT: Wesleyan University Press.

'Enterlacement.' Encyclopaedia Britannica, Encyclopaedia Britannica, Inc. https://www.britannica.com/art/entrelacement. Accessed 17 May 2019.

Flieger, Verlyn. 1997. *A Question of Time: J.R.R. Tolkien's Road to Faërie*. Kent, OH: The Kent State University Press.

2009. 'The Music and the Task: Fate and Free Will in Middle-earth.' *Tolkien Studies* 6, 151-81.

Garbowski, Christopher. 2000. *Recovery and Transcendence for the Contemporary Mythmaker: The Spiritual Dimension in the Works of J.R.R. Tolkien*. Lublin: Maria Curie-Skłodowska University Press.

Glover, Donald E. 1981. *C.S. Lewis: The Art of Enchantment*. Athens, OH: Ohio University Press.

'Greek Names of the Planets'. Greek Names. <the-planets>. Accessed 17 March 2020.

Green, Roger Lancelyn and Walter Hooper. 2002. *C.S. Lewis: A Biography. Fully Revised and Expanded Edition*. London: HarperCollins Publishers.

Honegger, Thomas. 2011. 'Time and Tide – Medieval Patterns of Interpreting the Passing of Time in Tolkien's Work.' *Hither Shore* 8, 86-99.

Hooper, Walter. 1971. *Past Watchful Dragons: The Narnian Chronicles of C.S. Lewis*. Eugene, OR: Wipf and Stock Publishers.

Jacobs, Alan. 2010. 'The Chronicles of Narnia.' *The Cambridge Companion to C.S. Lewis*. Eds. Robert MacSwain and Michael Ward. Cambridge: Cambridge University Press, 265-80.

Jacobs, Suzanne. 2020. 'Tolkien's Tom Bombadil: an Enigma 'Intentionally.'' *Mythlore* 38.2, 79-108.

Lewis, Clive Staples. 2014. *The Horse and His Boy*. London: HarperCollins.

2014. *The Last Battle*. London: HarperCollins.

2014. *The Lion, the Witch and the Wardrobe*. London: HarperCollins.

2014. *The Magician's Nephew*. London: HarperCollins.

1977. *Mere Christianity*. London: Fount Paperbacks.

2014. *Prince Caspian*. London: HarperCollins.

2014. *The Silver Chair*. London: HarperCollins.

2014. *The Voyage of the Dawn Treader*. London: HarperCollins.

Mendilow, Adam Abraham. 1976. 'The Time-Obsession of the Twentieth Century.' *Aspects of Time*. Ed. Constantinos Apostolos Patrides. Manchester: Manchester University Press, 69-74.

Noad, Charles E. 1991. 'The Natures of Tom Bombadil: A Summary.' *Leaves from the Tree: J.R.R. Tolkien's Shorter Fiction*. London: The Tolkien Society, 79-83.

Oziewicz, Marek. 2005. *Magiczny urok Narnii. Poetyka i filozofia „Opowieści z Narnii" C.S. Lewisa*. Kraków: Universitas.

Shippey, Tom. 2012. *The Road to Middle-earth*. London: HarperCollins Publishers.

Tolkien, John Ronald Reuel. 2005. *The Lord of the Rings. Part 1. The Fellowship of the Ring*. Lon-don: HarperCollins.

2005. *The Lord of the Rings. Part 2. The Two Towers*. London: HarperCollins.

2005. *The Lord of the Rings. Part 3. The Return of the King*. London: HarperCollins.

2006. *The Silmarillion*. Ed. Christopher Tolkien. London: HarperCollins.

Ward, Michael. 2008. *Planet Narnia: The Seven Heavens in the Imagination of C.S. Lewis*. Oxford: Oxford University Press.

West, Richard C. 1980. 'The Interlace Structure of *The Lord of the Rings*.' *A Tolkien Compass*. Ed. Jared Lobdell. New York: Ballantine Books, 82-102.

Wicher, Andrzej. 2013. *Selected Medieval and Religious Themes in the Works of C.S. Lewis and J.R.R. Tolkien*. Łódź: Łódzkie Towarzystwo Naukowe.

Gabriel Schenk



# A Jumble of Unrelated Mythologies?: Cohesion and Consistency in *The Lion, the Witch and the Wardrobe* and *The Hobbit*

**Abstract**

The following chapter challenges the idea that Lewis's Narnia is an inconsistent muddle compared to Tolkien's Middle-earth. It first surveys the ways the two writers have been compared to each other as fantasy authors, and disputes the idea that Tolkien objected to Lewis's world-building in the Narnia series. Secondly, it analyses the levels of cohesion (elements fitting together seamlessly) and consistency (those elements being used in the same way throughout a book or series) in the works of Tolkien and Lewis, focusing, in particular, on *The Lion, the Witch and the Wardrobe* and *The Hobbit.*

It is a widely held view that Tolkien's Middle-earth is a coherent and consistent world in contrast with Lewis's Narnia, the latter of which Tolkien disparagingly characterised as "a jumble of unrelated mythologies" (Sayer 1988: 189). This chapter argues that, although this view has some factual foundations, the contrast is not as stark as it is often supposed to be. It analyses the two authors' earliest published accounts of their imaginary worlds (*The Hobbit* and *The Lion, the Witch and the Wardrobe*) in order to demonstrate that, on the one hand, Tolkien's setting is by no means free from inconsistency, anachronisms and anatopisms, and that, on the other, Lewis's tale is not a mere jumble.

Probably the first clear articulation of the view that the two authors took starkly different approaches to writing their fantasy novels is to be found in Humphrey Carpenter's *The Inklings*, published in 1978:

> [For Tolkien] every loose end, every detail of the story – the chronology, the geography, even the meteorology of Middle-earth – had to be consistent and plausible, so that the reader would (as Tolkien wished) take the book in a sense as history. *The Lion, the Witch and the Wardrobe* offended against all these notions [...] there were inconsistencies and loose-ends [...] [and it] borrowed so indiscriminately from other mythologies and narratives. (2006: 224)

Carpenter has an influential, authoritative voice, having written the first biography of Tolkien in 1977, overseen by the author's son Christopher and based on unpublished papers and interviews with Tolkien's peers. As a result, the idea that Lewis drew from multiple sources indiscriminately – resulting in a largely inconsistent fantasy world, as opposed to Tolkien's preference for unity and consistency – is sometimes repeated by other scholars. Alan Jacobs, for example, states that the Narnia novels contain a "promiscuous mixing of mythological elements," which is probably why Tolkien was "appalled" by them (198). A.N. Wilson argues that Narnia contains a "jumble of elements," unlike Tolkien's Middle-earth which was created by a "finished and enclosed imagination" and includes no moment "of two worlds jarring together" (225-26). The same idea has come to be replicated in numerous comparative studies of Lewis's and Tolkien's fiction, most recently, perhaps, in Martha C. Sammons's *War of the Fantasy Worlds* (12).

Part of the reason for this contrast is the assertion that Tolkien disliked Narnia because of its inconsistencies. This assertion, however, is difficult to verify. First-hand quotations from Tolkien concerning his opinion of the Narnia series come from only two sources: a letter to David Kolb, in which he describes Narnia as being "outside the range of [his] sympathy" without stating why (*Letters* 352, #265); and an unpublished 1971 letter to Eileen Elgar, in which he says that he does not like the books because he disapproves of "religious allegory of this kind" (Long 2013: 39). Second-hand accounts – summaries or quotations from Tolkien based on the memories of the people who knew him – provide more detail. George Sayer, a former student of Lewis's and later a close friend of both Lewis and Tolkien, further corroborates and expands the contrast made by Carpenter:

> [Lewis] was hurt, astonished, and discouraged when Tolkien said that he thought the book was almost worthless, that it seemed like a jumble of unrelated mythologies. Because Aslan, the fauns, the White Witch, Father Christmas, the nymphs, and Mr. and Mrs. Beaver had quite distinct mythological or imaginative origins, Tolkien thought that it was a terrible mistake to put them together in Narnia, a single imaginative country. The effect was incongruous and, for him, painful. But Jack argued that they existed happily together in our minds in real life. Tolkien replied, 'Not in mine, or at least not at the same time.' Tolkien never changed his view. (1988: 189)

Although there is nothing in Tolkien's published letters that directly supports the view Sayer describes, it is, of course, possible that he held this objection without explicitly stating it in any correspondence. In addition, Sayer repeats his summary of Tolkien's attitude in a 1996 article, where he refers to "frequent" conversations with Tolkien, on the subject of Lewis's books, as his source (25).

Some scholars have questioned the accuracy of these second-hand accounts. Joe Christopher analyses some of the reasons that Carpenter provides in his book for Tolkien's dislike of Narnia in an article titled 'J.R.R. Tolkien, Narnian Exile.' On the charge that Lewis mixed sources indiscriminately, Christopher notes that Lewis's approach is not indiscriminate at all, but follows a medieval literary tradition that mixes various classical, Northern, British, and Christian sources. In addition, although Tolkien achieves "a unity of tone" in *The Lord of the Rings* by focusing on Nordic sources, in *The Silmarillion* "Nordic" werewolves exist in the same world as "Eastern-European" vampires (1988: 40).[1] As Carpenter does not indicate his sources in the explanation of Tolkien's dislike for the Narnia books – unlike other parts of *The Inklings*, which do contain citations – Christopher concludes that the given reasons "should be taken more as Carpenter's interpretations" than the actual reasons ever given by Tolkien (38-39).

Eric Seddon's response to Christopher's argument identifies another problem with the idea that Tolkien rejected Narnia because of its eclecticism: if Tolkien had not really approved of different sources being mixed together, he would also have objected to Lewis's previous work, most notably his *Space Trilogy*, which is as much a 'jumble' as the Narnia books (2007: 63).[2] Instead, Seddon argues that it was Lewis's theological approach that led Tolkien to reject the Narnia series.

Josh B. Long suggests that Sayer may have been relying too heavily on Carpenter, instead of accurately remembering the words used by Tolkien, since he cites *The*

1 Tolkien would have been aware that werewolves and vampires are not merely 'Nordic' and 'Eastern-European,' respectively. A werewolf appears in the thirteenth-century French romance *Guillaume de Palerme*, for example, and vampiric, blood-sucking demons can be found in mythologies from India, Persia, Greece, and other places. Nevertheless, Christopher's point remains valid: Tolkien draws from legends which originated in different parts of the world, even if those legends also travelled widely or similar legends can be found in a wide range of places.

2 In fact, Tolkien seemed to enjoy *Out of the Silent Planet*, the first novel in the *Space Trilogy*. He encouraged Stanley Unwin to publish it, describing it as "an exciting serial" when read aloud in instalments, and "highly approved" by the Inklings who heard it (*Letters* 29, #24).

*Inklings* as one of his sources (2013: 35). However, unlike Christopher, Long defends Carpenter's account. In his view, Tolkien's objection to the mixture of mythologies in Narnia makes sense if the real issue is its incongruity rather than mere eclecticism. Middle-earth, he argues, contains a multitude of mythical races, but they do not come from such disparate traditions as the creatures in the Narnia series (38-39).

Most recently, Holly Ordway admits that it is "plausible" that Tolkien objected to Lewis's apparent "mixing of mythologies" (2021: 78) although a comment Tolkien made in later life, in which he calls the Narnia books "deservedly very popular" (unpublished letter to Eileen Elgar qtd. in Long 2013: 39) suggests that he might have eventually modified that opinion (Ordway 2021: 78-79). Ordway concludes that Tolkien's views on Narnia are at the very least "more complex and interesting" than Carpenter's contrast implies (88).

Other scholars have taken a different approach, contending that Narnia is not the jumble it appears to be. Michael Ward, for instance, argues that although the series appears to be a "hodgepodge," and Tolkien disliked Narnia because "Lewis had thrown together things from different traditions [...] without good cause," the series follow a secret pattern in which each book corresponds to a different planet in the Western medieval cosmos (2010: 7). In this reading, Father Christmas, the beavers, and fauns fit together in the same story because they contribute a sense of joviality, one of the aspects of Jupiter, whose presence runs through *The Lion, the Witch and the Wardrobe* (2008: 66-67). The effect of Ward's theory, if accepted, is that Narnia is as unified and ordered as Middle-earth, although this is only knowable when one is aware of Lewis's hidden logic.

The fantasy author Lev Grossman also sees Lewis and Tolkien as two writers working in a similar way, rather than being at odds with each other on the matter of unity and cohesion. Lewis and Tolkien, Grossman argues in a lecture available online, encountered the materials that inspired their fantasy worlds "at first as little fragments which they proceeded to restore and then extrapolate from, to recreate this whole lost world that had been shattered."[3] These materials included Anglo-Saxon literature (primarily when it comes to Tolkien) and

3 Lev Grossman, 'Fear and Loathing in Aslan's Land'. Available as part of the Tolkien Lecture series on YouTube. Grossman's words come between 03:30-45. Accessed February 2021.

Beatrix Potter's *Squirrel Nutkin* and Norse mythology (in the case of Lewis). Whether Narnia should be referred to as a "jumble" of mythologies is not important in Grossman's wide historical perspective, which positions both Lewis and Tolkien as amongst the first in a category of fantasy authors who created cohesive, detailed, and structured narrative worlds.[4]

This chapter does not argue that Lewis's Narnia is on the same level of cohesion and unity as Tolkien's Middle-earth; rather, it argues that Tolkien's subcreated world includes a similar muddle of disparate elements as there might be found in Lewis's Narnia. Whether Tolkien actually thought that Narnia was a jumble does not matter. Either he did hold that objection but was guilty of the same fault himself, or he did not think it was as much of an issue as Carpenter, Sayer, and others believe it to have been. It is more important to accurately compare Lewis and Tolkien side by side to identify the differences without disregarding the similarities. While doing this, we will first examine levels of cohesion and consistency across a wide selection of the works of Lewis and Tolkien, then in *The Hobbit* and *The Lion, the Witch and the Wardrobe* specifically, and finally in the sequels to those novels.

## Cohesion and Consistency in the Works of Lewis and Tolkien

Tolkien discusses the importance of developing internally-consistent details in Secondary Worlds in his essay 'On Fairy-stories,' first delivered as a lecture in 1939. If done right, he says, the art of turning imagination into a sub-created work creates the "inner consistency of reality" (*TOFS* 60) in a fantasy world. Thus, the events in *The Lord of the Rings* fit into the chronology established in *The Silmarillion*; the climatic features correspond so well to the geography that the weather in Middle-earth can be analysed using a climate model, as demonstrated by researchers at the University of Bristol (Brown); and the travelling distances are described accurately enough to be mapped against a consistent topography and phases of the moon, as Barbara Strachey does in *Journeys of Frodo.*

4 Lev Grossman, 'Fear and Loathing in Aslan's Land'. 20:40.

This attention to consistency and detail in *The Lord of the Rings* does not mean that Tolkien was not interested in fusing disparate sources in his wider fiction, however. Indeed, his work often synthesises different images, languages, mythologies, and periods of time. His poem 'The City of Present Sorrow' (1916), for example, combines the observations of Oxford in the present with descriptions of "forgotten days" (*BLT 2* 297). In an interview from 1964, Tolkien talks about a habit of fusing memories from different times and places together, like one photograph laid over the top of another in a double exposure, as a result of being born in South Africa, and then moving, at the age of three, to the alien environment of England. This resulted in hybrid memories, such as that of a house which combined the elements of his Bloemfontein home and his grandparents' house in Worcestershire (qtd. in Sibley, track 1, 09:56). John Garth describes this as "a kind of visionary superpower," also in use in his fiction, for example when the slow-running willow-lined river Ancre seems to appear in the 1917 version of *The Fall of Gondolin* (2020: 12, 106). Garth furthermore reveals the synthesising of different sources in Tolkien's 1914 poem 'The Voyage of Éarendel the Evening Star,' arguing that not only is the poem a response to the Old English *Crist*, but additionally a "reappropriation and response" to 'Arethusa' by Percy Byshe Shelley (2014: 23). The effect is that Tolkien takes "a piece of classically-oriented English poetry and rebuilds it as a vehicle for his speculations on a lost Germanic legend" (24).

Nor is this approach limited to Tolkien's early work. *The Fall of Arthur*, which he worked on in the 1930s and still intended to finish in 1955, is a reworking of an ancient British legend in the verse-form predominant in Old English literature. It takes plot elements from Malory, the alliterative *Morte Arthure*, the stanazaic *Morte Arthur*, and *Mort Artu*, as well as certain details from the *Mabinogion*, Geoffrey of Monmouth, and Middle English literature (*FA* 73-122). Tolkien even considered bringing the Arthurian legend into his own legendarium by connecting his Tol Eressëa to Arthur's Avalon (153-54) and Eärendil to Lancelot (136).

Lewis's combination of different sources in his work is easier to identify than Tolkien's because Lewis makes no effort to hide what he is doing. In fact, he actively avoided trying to be original, arguing that someone who tried to be original would inevitably fail and that it is better to just try to tell the truth

(1944: 64). In his final book, *Letters to Malcolm*, he argues that only God can truly create new things: all that we can do is "build" using the materials God has given us (97). This parallels Tolkien's concept of sub-creation – the name he gives to the act of creating myths and stories, a process derivative of God's primary art of Creation – although Tolkien does not seem to agree with Lewis's conclusion that true originality is impossible.

Lewis builds his arguments using disparate materials throughout his non-fiction. In *A Preface to Paradise Lost*, for example, he first discusses the critical approaches to Milton by Joseph Addison and E.M.W. Tillyard, and then moves on to likening the disobedience of Adam and Eve to God with that of Beatrix Potter's Peter Rabbit trespassing in Mr McGregor's garden (71-72). Lewis also builds his narratives using disparate materials, but the Narnia books are not the only works of fiction where he does this. His 1945 novel *That Hideous Strength*, for example, combines the Arthurian legend with a portrait of contemporary university life, told in the 'spiritual thriller' style of Charles Williams. Lewis even brings Tolkien's legendarium into the text, referencing Númenor (here misspelt as "Numnior") in a discussion of ancient history (x). The variety of sources in Lewis's work is matched by the variety of forms he uses in his writings: from literary criticism to children's fiction to Christian apologetics.

Lewis is not an inconsistent and scattershot author, however; there is a sense of purpose behind his variety of sources and images. As Jacobs notes, comparing Peter Rabbit to Milton's Adam and Eve does not merely demonstrate "considerable range," but also unveils a "*moral* unity" between the two, "far more important than those otherwise dramatic differences in time, genre, and purpose" (xvii). For the writer and fellow Inkling Owen Barfield, Lewis was such a multifaceted author that he sometimes seemed to be five separate people writing under the same shared name (1989: 121). Nevertheless, Barfield also considered Lewis to be a cohesive thinker united by a "presence of mind": that everything he thought was present in everything he wrote (122). Testing Barfield's assessment would take more space than this chapter allows, but the point remains that it is possible to see a cohesion running throughout Lewis's works even when they draw from a wide variety of sources.

## Cohesion and Consistency in *The Hobbit* and *The Lion, the Witch and the Wardrobe*

In his biography of Tolkien, Carpenter does not include inconsistencies and indiscriminative borrowing from various mythologies in his list of reasons why Tolkien apparently did not approve of Narnia (2002: 268). Instead, this reason was only included in *The Inklings* a year later, after Christopher Tolkien's edited and unified version of *The Silmarillion* had been published, establishing a detailed chronology and sense of history for Middle-earth.[5] A more accurate comparison between Lewis's and Tolkien's approaches would be based on similar works, however: not between fairy story and mythic history but between fairy story and fairy story.

Tolkien began writing *The Hobbit* in 1930 and finished it in January 1933 (Rateliff 2011: xxii). After a few years of revisions it was eventually published in 1937. One of the novel's main themes is that of displacement, the characters leaving the places where they come from and into which they fit, be it the dwarves who have lost their home kingdom, or Bilbo Baggins who has left his home to go on an uncomfortable adventure. This sense of displacement is temporal as well as spatial: although the story is set "long ago" there is a sense that elements of it overlap with our own time (*Hobbit* 7). Hobbits belong to a different age, needing "some description nowadays," but still exist as "rare" creatures in our world (10). The narrator also suggests that goblins may have "invented some of the machines that have since troubled the world, especially the ingenious devices for killing large numbers of people at once" (73). Occasionally the narrator brings the readers out of their own time and place into the setting of the story. Once the eagles have set Thorin's company down, so they can prepare a meal, the narrator speaks to the reader as though they were able to see what was to happen next: "Later on you might have seen a bright fire on the shelf of rock and the figures of the dwarves round it cooking" (120). Tinder-boxes are used there because, the narrator explains, "Dwarves have never taken to matches even yet" (121). All in all, Tolkien creates an impression of different times, places, and realities overlapping with one another. Not only do the hobbits, goblins, and dwarves co-inhabit the

5 Christopher Tolkien and Guy Gavriel Kay worked *The Silmarillion* into "a single text," with sections selected and arranged "to produce the most coherent and internally self-consistent narrative" (*Sil* 8).

same story, but they also exist in the mythic time of the narrative and, to some extent, in the contemporary world of the reader.

Even the writing process contained a sense of multiple, overlapping realities. Tolkien recalls writing the first line of the novel on a blank exam paper while he was marking exams, beginning the writing process on material, and in a time, not meant for novel-writing (*Letters* 215, #163). This first line, "in a hole in the ground there lived a hobbit," was an image not yet connected to a story, and came to Tolkien unexpectedly from nowhere (Rateliff 2011: xiv-xv). The novel was also separate from his developing legendarium when it was first written. In a letter to W.H. Auden, Tolkien says that it was "originally quite unconnected" to stories set in Middle-earth, which he had been working on throughout the 1910s and 20s (*Letters* 215, #163). Nor was the novel, in its initial form, a unified whole. Tolkien recalls that he "just spun a yarn out of any elements in my head: I don't remember organizing the thing at all" (qtd. in Anderson 2002: 8, from an interview in 1964). The initial impetus for the story was merely intellectual curiosity; once he had written the word "hobbit" on the blank exam paper Tolkien decided to "find out what hobbits were like" because "names always generate a story in my mind" (qtd. in Carpenter 2002: 230). The end result was an organised novel, but one "derived from (previously digested) epic, mythology, and fairy-story" (*Letters* 31, #25), made up of prose, songs, riddles, and the author's own illustrations. Douglas Anderson lists Beowulf, Andrew Lang, the Brothers Grimm, E.H. Knatchbull-Hugessen, Rudyard Kipling, William Morris, George Macdonald, and E. A. Wyke-Smith as among these "previously digested" literary elements (2002: 5-6).

Tolkien's rewriting process was partly concerned with organising the different elements of the story into a coherent whole. One early draft, for example, contains references to contemporary places including China and the Hindu Kush which were dropped in the final version, so that the geography is consistently separated from the Primary World (Rateliff 2011: 17). According to Carpenter, Tolkien also made numerous changes to the publisher's proofs in 1937, including fixing "inconsistencies in the description of the topography" (242). Changes for the benefit of consistency continued even after its publication. Chapter 5 was rewritten for a new edition published in 1951, in order to make the Ring an item difficult to part with, rather than just a birthday present that Gollum agrees to give up. While it may therefore be tempting to read *The Hobbit* as a consistent and cohesive work because of how it fits in with the later texts, doing so would disregard the multifaceted nature of the text as it was originally written and published. Tolkien himself saw *The Hobbit* as a multifaceted work, describing it, in the year it was first published, as a "rabble of Eddaic-named dwarves out of Völuspá, newfangled hobbits and gollums […] and Anglo-Saxon runes" in contrast to his own "mythology (which is just touched on) with its consistent nomenclature" (qtd. in *RS* 7). In another letter from the same year, he refers to it as "a comic tale" featuring "conventional and inconsistent Grimm's fairy-tale dwarves," only accidentally getting drawn into "the edge" of his legendarium (*Letters* 26, #19).

Lewis began writing the first of his Narnia books, *The Lion, the Witch and the Wardrobe* around 1939, most likely inspired by the experience of hosting evacuated children at the Kilns in September that year (Duriez 2005a: 183-84). He seems to have paused writing until 1948, finishing the text in 1949 (Hooper 1997: 402). Like Tolkien, Lewis drew on a long list of disparate literary traditions when forming his fictional world. As Colin Duriez writes, tracing "even the most significant stories and books" that Lewis drew on in his series would be "an enormous task," although he lists a selection: Plato, Spenser, Milton, George MacDonald, H. Rider Haggard, Robert Louis Stevenson, William Morris, Edith Nesbit, and G.K. Chesterton (2005b: 28-35). Additionally, like Tolkien writing *The Hobbit*, Lewis began with a single image from which a story later emerged. In Lewis's case, the image was not a hobbit in a hole but "a Faun carrying an umbrella and parcels in a snowy wood" ('It All Began with a Picture…'). Other images came to him – "a queen on a sledge, a magnificent lion" ('Sometimes Fairy Stories May Say Best What's to be Said' 310) – and in his essay, 'Three Ways of Writing for Children,' he wrote about the need to work these types of images into a narrative unity. "If you are very lucky […] a whole set might join themselves so consistently that there you had a complete story," but more often one has to "do some deliberate inventing" to fill in the "gaps" between the images (48). The title of the first Narnia novel reflects this image-based approach: the lion, the witch, and the wardrobe are three distinct images with no apparent connection, but they are brought together in the narrative.

The spatial and temporal displacement is as much a theme in *The Lion, the Witch and the Wardrobe* as it is in *The Hobbit*. The plot hinges on people being in their correct places; the White Witch claims Edmund because every traitor "belongs" to her, and Aslan's goal is for "all names" to be restored to their "proper owners" when the thrones of Cair Paravel are occupied by the rightful monarchs (*LWW* 148). The Pevensies are doubly displaced: first, by being "sent away from London" (11) because of the war, and, secondly, by travelling to another world almost entirely separated (save for a single doorway) from their own. The Pevensies are also displaced from their own timestream, separated from the moment they enter the wardrobe until they go back through it. Finally, there is a degree of temporal dissonance at the end of the novel when they become adult kings and queens but then return to their childhood selves upon leaving Narnia.

Lewis did not rewrite the *Chronicles* to the same extent that Tolkien rewrote parts of *The Hobbit*, but he did make minor, post-publication changes to the American edition of *The Lion, the Witch and the Wardrobe*. Two of these changes may have been to anchor specific elements of the story to a cohesive mythology. The name 'Maugrim' for the White Witch's wolf Captain of the Secret Police was changed to 'Fenris' (Hooper 1997: 412). 'Maugrim' may have been chosen for its connection to the word 'maugre' but 'Fenris' is a clear reference to the demonic wolf in Norse mythology (Ford 2009: 148). In addition, "The fire stones of the secret hill," where Aslan says the Deep Magic is written, was changed to "The trunk of the World Ash Tree," a much clearer allusion, again to Norse mythology (Hooper 1997: 412-13). The edits do not increase a sense of cohesion and unity by reducing the number of different sources that form the novel – in fact, they add another mythic source – but instead connect a character and location to a mythical tradition instead of leaving them as vague allusions.

The most incongruous elements of *The Lion, the Witch and the Wardrobe* and *The Hobbit* are the apparent anachronisms and anatopisms: items that belong to a later period than most items elsewhere in the text, and items that seem to belong to a different place than the world in the text, respectively. Father Christmas is a glaring example of both in *The Lion, the Witch and the*

*Wardrobe*, originating in the seventeenth century and a different culture.[6] Mr. Tumnus tells Lucy about Christmas, but it is never explained why the Narnians would celebrate that holiday when they have no Christian religion. Roger Lancelyn Green urged Lewis to remove Father Christmas from the narrative as he did not "seem to fit quite comfortably into his place," but Lewis retained him in the final version (Green and Hooper 2002: 307). Mrs. Beaver's sewing machine and Mr. Tumnus's foldable umbrella are two further anachronisms. The lack of guns and cannons, and the prevalence of swords and castles as defendable locations, when Aslan makes plans for "assaulting" the White Witch in her castle (*LWW* 154), suggests an early-medieval time period, predating the invention of the eighteenth-century foldable umbrella and nineteenth-century sewing machine.

Besides their being anachronistic, sewing machines and foldable umbrellas suggest other types of incoherence in the text: Narnia seemingly has no infrastructure for creating and distributing such items. As Peter Schakel notes, "The story presupposes factories, shops, farms, laborers, shopkeepers, and farmers: but they are invisible" (2002: 60). The poet Ruth Pitter points out yet another problem with some of the items in the novel. When she asked Lewis how the Beavers could consume the meal including potatoes, oranges, sugar, suet, flour, malt, hops, and milk – the Narnian climate being, of course, too cold to grow such ingredients and the Witch not allowing any foreign trade – Lewis was "stumped" (Hooper 1997: 721-22).

Middle-earth, like Narnia, is a pre-industrial world with medieval-era warfare. Despite this, Bilbo owns an eighteenth-century mantlepiece clock (*Hobbit* 13, 28, 247) and has access to nineteenth-century matches (66). Tolkien avoids the problems of a cold climate limiting certain food types, but not the issue of foreign trade; hobbits smoke tobacco and drink tea and coffee, a combination which implies an advanced global trade network that in our world did not exist until the seventeenth century. There are also glaring anatopisms in Middle-earth. In *The Hobbit*, the narrator explains that one of Bilbo's ancestors knocked a goblin

6 Although a personification of Christmas can be traced back to a fifteenth-century carol attributed to Richard Smart, the first recorded use of the term 'Father Christmas' is from 1646. See 'Father Christmas,' *OED Online*, Oxford University Press, December 2020, www.oed.com/view/Entry/68498. Accessed 9 February 2021.

king's head off down into a rabbit-hole, thus inventing "the game of Golf" (18). A few paragraphs later, Gandalf threatens the dwarves with removing Bilbo from the company, which means they would "stop at thirteen and have all the bad luck" associated with that number (19). Both golf and the superstition of the number thirteen are so specifically linked to cultures in our own world that they do not seem to fit in with the rest of Middle-earth. Some of these incongruities were removed during the rewriting process. Bilbo's tomatoes – a food that came to Europe from the Americas in the sixteenth century – were replaced by pickles in the 1951 edition, although some of the other anachronistic food items remained, including coffee (10, 12), scones (11), and porter beer (10). Finally, in an early draft of *The Hobbit*, Elrond is described as being "kind as Christmas," the last word soon to be altered to 'summer' (Atherton 2012: 139). However, later in the narrative, a larch tree growing in the place where the company is assaulted by the goblins is compared to "an enormous Christmas tree," even in the revised edition of the book (110).

Some scholars have attempted to explain or excuse Tolkien's anachronisms. For John Rateliff, Tolkien's inclusion of tobacco and tomatoes has a "good precedent," as the Brothers Grimm also referenced potatoes and other anachronisms in their fairy tales (2011: 43). Rateliff further notes that many of the anachronisms are not really anachronistic, as the narrator is only comparing items and sounds to those which are familiar to contemporary readers (43). Bilbo's scream, "like a whistle of an engine coming out of a tunnel" (*Hobbit* 17) is given as an example of this. The Christmas tree comparison might be considered another, but, even if coming solely from the narrator, the association with Christianity seems particularly incongruous, which is presumably why Tolkien removed it from his description of Elrond.

Potatoes and tobacco are less discordant, and could still be counted as the narrator's anachronism were the text to be considered a translation in which the actual objects are rendered by means of their English equivalents, contemporary with readers. This was the conceit Tolkien used in the first edition preface of *The Fellowship of the Ring*, the appendices for *The Lord of the Rings*, and *The Hobbit* in the author's note added to the 1966 Longmans and Unwin editions. However, Lynn Forest-Hill notes that both potatoes and tobacco cannot be treated as merely substitute words, at least, not in *The Lord of the Rings*, where both items are discussed in such detail that the words must refer to the same items the English words signify (2017: 78). Instead, Forest-Hill argues that anachronisms do exist in Middle-earth but they perform an important narrative function, creating a sense of familiarity (e.g. tobacco and nasturtians makes the Shire feel homely) and otherness (Gollum's ignorance of potatoes and common herbs makes him seem alien), when needed. This argument elaborates on Tom Shippey's idea that hobbits are intentionally anachronistic because they function as a bridge of familiarity, helping contemporary readers cross into the ancient Northern fairy-tale world of Middle-earth (2000: 6, 47-48).

Less critical attention has, so far, been paid to Lewis's anachronisms and anatopisms, but some of the arguments used to justify the ones found in Middle-earth could also be applied to the anachronisms in Narnia. Lewis, like Tolkien, uses temporally and culturally misplaced items for a purpose, creating a sense of familiarity or otherness for contemporary readers. The sardines on toast at Mr. Tumnus's house and the sewing machine at the Beaver's dam convey feelings of homeliness in contrast to the "strange" and "gloomy" home of the White Witch, with its towers compared to unpleasant dunce's caps or unfamiliar sorcerer's caps (*LWW* 100). The Witch tempts Edmund with two items of food – the anatopic Turkish Delight as well as a "very sweet and foamy and creamy" hot drink "he had never tasted before" (43) – and of these two, it is the Turkish Delight that makes the Witch's offer seem far more tempting to both Edward and, most likely, the readers.

Lewis's essay 'On Stories,' delivered as a talk in 1940 and published in 1947, helps to explain the mixing of images and sources in *The Lion, the Witch and the Wardrobe*. In it, Lewis argues that the Brothers Grimm and Kenneth Grahame did not use images arbitrarily, but always following "the logic of a fairy-tale" (99). Thus, the principal character in *The Wind in the Willows* is a toad, rather than a stag or a lion, because toads' faces resemble some of the facial features found in humans (99). What may have seemed a random jumble of different animals in Grahame's book is, instead, a collection chosen for a specific purpose: to evoke a sense of place or character. In *The Lion, the Witch and the Wardrobe*, the African lion belongs to the story just as much as the European wolves, because lions evoke a sense of majesty and power appropriate for Aslan, and wolves bring to mind a sense of danger and maliciousness appropriate for the White Witch.

In summary, the Middle-earth of *The Hobbit* is not the cohesive, unified world implied in some of the critical contrasts made between Lewis and Tolkien. Furthermore, neither *The Hobbit*, nor *The Lion, the Witch and the Wardrobe*, should be seen as jumbles of unrelated mythologies, but stories that use disparate images from different sources to lend more emphasis to their themes of displacement, and to help make their narrative worlds comprehensible to contemporary readers by drawing on familiar references.

## Cohesion and Consistency beyond *The Hobbit* and *The Lion, the Witch and the Wardrobe*

*The Lord of the Rings*, the 'sequel' to *The Hobbit*, further complicated the problem of anachronisms present in the Shire. In addition to the potatoes and matches, hobbits use foldable umbrellas (*FR* 37, 39), send letters through a postal service (10, 26, 65), and have access to a museum (5, 13). In his letter to Stanley Unwin, sent four years before the publication of *The Fellowship of the Ring*, Tolkien describes *The Lord of the Rings* "as indivisible and unified as I could make it" (*Letters* 138, #125), suggesting both an ongoing effort to force unity and cohesiveness, and a realisation that these could not be completely achieved. The novel, like *The Hobbit*, is concerned with displacement and multiple realities: the hobbits must leave their home in order to return an item to its place of origin, and, along the way, encounter different cultures and are threatened by supernatural powers.

The theme of displacement also carries through all seven Narnia novels, expressed through such concepts as the rings in *The Magician's Nephew*, which either want "to get back to [their] own place" or are "trying to get out of [their] own place" (50), and the characters trying to get back to their home countries (Shasta and Bree in *The Horse and His Boy*), or to be restored to their proper place in society (the non-human races in *Prince Caspian*). In *The Last Battle*, it is revealed that all the characters in both England and Narnia have lived displaced lives; their real 'home,' the land they have been looking for all their lives, is Aslan's country (219).

There is evidence that Lewis attempted to make Narnia a more cohesive and consistent world after he had finished writing *The Lion, the Witch and the Wardrobe.* In *Prince Caspian,* he develops the idea that our world and Narnia overlap: there are multiple places where it is possible to cross over from our world into Narnia, as the pirates who become the Telmarines once did (229). This explains why Professor Kirke knows about Narnia at the end of *The Lion, the Witch and the Wardrobe* and how "pictures of Father Christmas" (115) filtered to our world from Narnia, whence the real figure originates. The sequels to *The Lion, the Witch and the Wardrobe* also avoid some of the anachronisms from the first book, with, for instance, the anachronistic beavers said to be extinct by the time of *Prince Caspian* (180). In *The Voyage of the Dawn Treader*, the anachronisms and anatopisms are used to comic effect, when Eustace Scrubb wants access to the wireless and the British Consul to the bemusement of the other characters (37, 52, 72). *Prince Caspian* does mix mythologies even more than *The Lion, the Witch and the Wardrobe* – a Narnian river god, the Roman god Bacchus, and the Christ-figure Aslan are all included – but the later books demonstrate a more focused approach. In *The Lion, the Witch and the Wardrobe*, the White Witch is said to be "half a Jinn and half a giantess" (96). By the time Lewis finished writing *The Magician's Nephew* (1954), though, the character's lineage had been simplified, and Queen Jadis is only said to have "giantish blood" (83).

After including Father Christmas in the first book, neither he nor Christmas are mentioned in the series again. Instead, Lewis included references that reinforce Narnia as a separate, detailed world. In *Prince Caspian*, characters eat a Narnian fish called a pavender, and two stars are named – Tarva and Alambil – that do not exist in our world (58, 61, 69, 89). Additionally, multiple "trees, birds, and plants" unique to Narnia are referenced, although not named, in *The Last Battle* (109).

At least one change made during the writing process was intended to improve the unity of the narrative. A character named Piers (a reference to *Piers Plowman*), was cut from *The Magician's Nephew* after Roger Lancelyn Green told Lewis that it was "out of harmony with the rest of the book" (Hooper 1997: 405). With it gone, Green declared that the novel was "a single unity now" (405), suggesting that this was something his former tutor sought, even if he may have needed help to achieve it. Lewis also continued to think about how the books fitted together long after they had been published. In 1963, seven years after *The Last Battle* was published, Lewis created, for his own pleasure, a detailed 'Outline of Narnian History So Far As It Is Known' (Green and Hooper 2002: 316), treating the *Chronicles* as if they really were a historical record (316-20). He even agreed to re-edit the published Narnia chronicles to "connect the things that didn't tie up," but died before he could actually make the changes he had in mind (432).

## Conclusion

Should all the seven Narnia books be compared with all the published work of Tolkien set in Middle-earth, it would be clear that Lewis did not create a secondary world as detailed as that of his friend and colleague. This does not mean that Carpenter's contrast – between a meticulous Tolkien making "every loose end, every detail of the story [...] consistent and plausible," and a sloppy Lewis, including "inconsistencies and loose-ends" in his first Narnia novel – is accurate. When *The Lion, the Witch and the Wardrobe* is compared to *The Hobbit* instead of *The Silmarillion*, the two authors appear similar: both combine disparate sources, include anachronisms and anatopisms, and explore the themes of displacement and belonging. Neither Narnia nor the Middle-earth of *The Hobbit* is a mere "jumble of unrelated mythologies," (Carpenter 1988: 189) but, equally, neither is entirely cohesive or internally consistent.

### About the Author

Gabriel Schenk teaches literature at Signum University, specializing in cultural histories, Arthuriana, and the works of the Inklings. He holds a D.Phil. in Arthurian Literature from the University of Oxford and is one of the founders and organizers of the annual Tolkien Lecture on Fantasy Literature at Pembroke College, Oxford. In addition to that, he manages the websites for the Owen Barfield and the P.H. Newby literary estates.

## Bibliography

ANDERSON, Douglas. 2002. *The Annotated Hobbit: Revised and Expanded Edition*. Boston: Houghton Mifflin.

ATHERTON, Mark. 2012. *There and Back Again: J.R.R. Tolkien and the Origins of The Hobbit*. New York: I.B. Tauris.

BARFIELD, Owen. 1989. 'The Five C.S. Lewises.' *Owen Barfield on C.S. Lewis*. Ed. G.B. Tennyson. San Rafael: The Barfield Press.

RADAGAST the Brown. 'The Climate of Middle Earth.' https://www.bristol.ac.uk/university/media/press/10013-english.pdf. Accessed 30 September 2020.

CARPENTER, Humphrey. 2002. *J.R.R. Tolkien: A Biography*. London: HarperCollins.

2006. *The Inklings: C.S. Lewis, J.R.R. Tolkien, Charles Williams and Their Friends*. London: HarperCollins.

CHRISTOPHER, Joe. 1988. 'J.R.R. Tolkien, Narnian Exile.' *Mythlore* 15.1, 37-45; 15.2: 17-23.

DURIEZ, Colin. 2005a. *The C.S. Lewis Chronicles*. London: Darton, Longman and Todd.

2005b. *A Field Guide to Narnia*. Stroud: Sutton.

FORD, Paul F. 2009. *Pocket Companion to Narnia: A Guide to the Magical World of C.S. Lewis*. London: HarperCollins.

FOREST-HILL, Lynn. 2017. "Tree and Flower and Leaf and Grass': Anachronism and J.R.R. Tolkien's Botanical Semiotics.' *Journal of Inklings Studies* 5.1, 72-92.

GARTH, John. 2014. "The Road from Adaptation to Invention': How Tolkien Came to the Brink of Middle-earth in 1914.' *Tolkien Studies* 11, 1-44.

2020. *The Worlds of J.R.R. Tolkien: The Places That Inspired Middle-earth*. London: Lincoln.

GREEN, Roger Lancelyn and Walter HOOPER. 2002. *C.S. Lewis: A Biography. Fully Revised & Expanded Edition*. London: HarperCollins.

GROSSMAN, Lev. 'Fear and Loathing in Aslan's Land. Tolkien Lecture.' *YouTube*, 26 May 2015. <www.youtube.com/watch?v=EcIWgPvx41c>. Accessed 30 September 2020.

HOOPER, Walter. 1997. *C.S. Lewis: A Companion & Guide*. London: HarperCollins.

Jacobs, Alan. 2005. *The Narnian: The Life and Imagination of C.S. Lewis*. London: SPCK.

Lewis, Clive Staples. 1944. *Beyond Personality*. London: Bless.

2014. *The Horse and His Boy*. London: HarperCollins.

'It All Began with a Picture…' *Radio Times, Junior Radio Times*, CXLVIII, 15 July 1960.

2014. *The Last Battle*. London: HarperCollins.

1964. *Letters to Malcolm: Chiefly on Prayer*. London: Bless.

2014. *The Lion, the Witch and the Wardrobe*. London: HarperCollins.

2014. *The Magician's Nephew*. London: HarperCollins.

1969. *A Preface to Paradise Lost*. London: Oxford University Press.

1947. 'On Stories.' *Essays Presented to Charles Williams*. London, New York, Toronto: Oxford University Press, 90-105.

2014. *Prince Caspian*. London: HarperCollins.

'Sometimes Fairy Stories May Say Best What's to be Said.' *New York Times*. 18 November 1965, 310.

2014. *The Voyage of the Dawn Treader*. London: HarperCollins.

2005. *That Hideous Strength: A Modern Fairy-Tale for Grown-Ups*. London: HarperCollins.

2017. 'Three Ways of Writing for Children.' *Of Other Worlds: Essays and Stories*. London: HarperCollins, 33-54.

Long, Josh B. 2013. 'Disparaging Narnia: Reconsidering Tolkien's View of *The Lion, the Witch and the Wardrobe*.' *Mythlore* 31.3/4, 31-46.

Ordway, Holly. 2021. *Tolkien's Modern Reading: Middle-earth Beyond the Middle Ages*. Park Ridge: Word on Fire.

Rateliff, John D. 2011. *The History of the Hobbit*. London: HarperCollins.

Sammons, Martha C. 2010. *War of the Fantasy Worlds: C.S. Lewis and J.R.R. Tolkien on Art and Imagination*. Santa Barbara: Praeger.

Sayer, George. 1988. *Jack: C.S. Lewis and His Times*. San Francisco: Harper and Row.

1996. 'Recollections of J.R.R. Tolkien.' *Mythlore* 21.2, 21-25.

Schackel, Peter. 2002. *Imagination and the Arts in C.S. Lewis: Journeying to Narnia and Other Worlds*. Columbia: University of Missouri Press.

Seddon, Eric. 2007. '*Letters to Malcolm* and the Trouble with Narnia: C.S. Lewis, J.R.R. Tolkien, and Their 1949 Crisis.' *Mythlore* 26.1, 61-81.

Shippey, Tom. 2000. *J.R.R. Tolkien: Author of the Century*. Boston: Houghton Mifflin.

Sibley, Brian. 2001. *J.R.R. Tolkien: An Audio Portrait*. London: BBC Audiobooks.

Strachey, Barbara. 1981. *Journeys of Frodo: An Atlas of J.R.R. Tolkien's* The Lord of the Rings. London: HarperCollins.

Tolkien, John Ronald Reuel. 2015. *The Book of Lost Tales Part Two. The History of Middle-earth. Vol. II.* Ed. Christopher Tolkien. London: HarperCollins.

2013. *The Fall of Arthur*. Ed. Christopher Tolkien. London: HarperCollins.

2007. *The Hobbit, or There and Back Again*. London: HarperCollins.

2016. *The Hobbit, or There and Back Again (Facsimile First Edition)*. London: HarperCollins

1981. *The Letters of J.R.R. Tolkien*. Ed. Humphrey Carpenter with the assistance of Christopher Tolkien. London: George Allen & Unwin.

2005. *The Lord of the Rings. Part 1. The Fellowship of the Ring*. London: HarperCollins.

2008. *On Fairy Stories: Expanded edition, with commentary and notes*. Eds. Verlyn Flieger and Douglas A. Anderson. London: HarperCollins.

2015. *The Return of the Shadow. The History of Middle-earth. Vol VI.* Ed. Christopher Tolkien. London: HarperCollins.

2006. *The Silmarillion*. Ed. Christopher Tolkien. London: HarperCollins.

Ward, Michael. 2008. *Planet Narnia: The Seven Heavens in the Imagination of C.S. Lewis*. Oxford: Oxford University Press.

2010. *The Narnia Code: C.S. Lewis and the Secret of the Seven Heavens*. Milton Keynes: Paternoster.

Wilson, Andrew Norman. 2005. *C.S. Lewis: A Biography*. London: HarperCollins.

Hamish Williams



# Dionysiac, Apolline, Orphic, or...?: Nietzschean Conflicts in Representing the Natural World in Christian Fantasy

**Abstract**

Through their representations of the natural world, J.R.R. Tolkien and C.S. Lewis oppose Nietzsche's assertions of the death of God, the foundational truth of the Dionysiac, and the necessary illusion of the Apolline. In *Prince Caspian*, Lewis depicts the Dionysiac force of nature as built upon a Christian, 'Aslanine' foundation or divine order in Narnia; conversely, the Apolline attempts of the Telmarines to create order based on human, civilisational will alone, along with their scornful attitudes towards the divine order (and aesthetic beauty) of nature, lead to their destruction. Tolkien deviates somewhat from Lewis in showing notions of chaos and order in balance in the natural world, as aesthetic products of divine creation. Such a balance is best represented by the enigmatic character of Tom Bombadil in the Old Forest sequence of *The Fellowship of the Ring*. Tom, a kind of 'nature spirit,' opposes the Dionysiac chaos of the Old Forest (the devouring hunger of Old Man Willow) through the imposition of a shepherding, Orphic form of ordering, but such order does not try to assert its Apolline will to power over others (Sauron's One Ring has zero effect on Tom). Conversely, it is the precise fault – the evil – of Melkor, Sauron, the Witch-King and other wayward beings to not appreciate this balance: to despair at the Dionysiac void; to impose the illusion of Apolline will to counter this and control others.

## Nietzsche's Dionysiac and Apolline

In the course of modern philosophy and cultural scholarship, it has become fashionable to define and characterise fundamental aspects of human nature – or of universal experience, more broadly – through the personification of certain Greek gods: whether 'the Apolline,' 'the Dionysiac,' 'the Promethean,' and so on; these drives are often, moreover, conflictual – they are put in binary contrast with each other in terms of some particular domain of human experience or nature.

Nietzsche's' discussion of the Dionysiac and the Apolline in his work *The Birth of Tragedy: Out of the Spirit of Music* has undoubtedly been the most influential of these divine schematizations since the end of the nineteenth century:[1] "it was Nietzsche's singular contribution to classical philology that generations of literary scholars have explored the terrain that he exposed and that he later on described as *Das Dionysische*" (Del Caro 1989: 589-90).[2] While the German philosopher's discussion is, in part, an attempt to explain the roots of tragedy and the aesthetic components from which it was formed, it also provides broader commentary on man's experience in the universe. Most importantly, it pertains to the lack of greater purpose and, thus, the necessary illusion of will – "we must deceive ourselves in order to cope with this fact [i.e. the meaninglessness of existence]. Otherwise, we would be unable to function" (Blount 2013: 91). This lack of a higher purpose or meaning, of course, relates Nietzsche's famous proclamation as to the death of God:

> Nietzsche also boldly states that God is dead and life is meaningless – though, he assures us, that ain't all bad. When he announces God's death, he does not mean to be taken literally. For, of course, God has not actually died. Rather, Nietzsche means that humans can no longer harmonize God's existence with other things they know about the world, "that belief in the Christian God has become unbelievable." [Friedrich Nietzsche, *The Gay Science*, in *A Nietzsche Reader*, pp. 208-09.] According to Nietzsche, talk about God's dying does not

1 For the influences of German classicism and romanticism in the eighteenth and nineteenth century on the development of Nietzsche's Dionysiac/Apolline contrast, see Del Caro (1989: 590-603).

2 It is probably worth pointing out, from the start, that these divine states of being or experience are modern philosophical constructs and have little to do with the actual stories of classical mythology and our coherent interpretations of them. For example, in Ovid's tale of the poet-musician Orpheus in his *Metamorphoses*, there is an apparent Nietzschean conflict between the Apolline and the Dionysiac: while playing his music to his enchanted audience of trees, Orpheus, who is "Apollo's minstrel" (11.8), having been instructed by the god in the art of playing the lyre, is attacked by a group of maenads, whose advances he had earlier spurned: "And still his [Orpheus'] singing would have charmed every weapon, but the huge clamour, the drums, the curving Phrygian fifes, hand-clapping, Bacchic screaming drowned the lyre. And then at last, his song unheard, his blood reddened the stones" (book XI, ll.15-19). Nietzsche, a Classical philologist by training, would have pointed, surely, to the melodic order of the Apolline order versus the polyphonic cacophony of the Dionysiac chaos (*BT* 20-10). Despite the persuasive authority of Nietzsche's formulations (Del Caro 1989: 589-90), such broad systems of symbol are less certain in Classical mythology and literature. Although Apollo (along with Athena) might have been associated generally with the ordered and the civilised/urban and Dionysus with the barbarian or rural countryside, Apollo could also act as a terrifying god of destruction, the source, for example, of an infectious plague among the Achaean Greeks in book I of the *Iliad*. Moreover, in the tragedy of Orpheus' death at the hands of Bacchic worshippers, Bacchus himself is not terribly pleased: "Bacchus did not permit this crime to pass unpunished, unavenged. Distressed to lose the minstrel of his mysteries, at once he fastened in the woods by twisting roots all the women who had seen that wickedness" (Ovid *Metamorphoses* book XI, ll. 67-70). In short, classical mythology is not reducible to overarching symbolic systems; each story often maintains its own internal, often aetiological meaning without concern for grander connotations.

> refer to the deity's demise in fact; instead, it refers to the human realization that God never existed in the first place. (Blount 2013: 90)

In Nietzsche's discussion in *The Birth of Tragedy*, then, he defines two aesthetic principles which govern man's creativity:[3] every artist is "either an Apolline dream artist or a Dionysiac ecstatic artist or else [...] a dream artist and an ecstatic artist at one and the same time" (*BT* 18). For Nietzsche, the Apolline, on the one hand, invokes individual control and the exercise of will, symbolised by the metaphor of the calm boat riding the storm,[4] the image of the sun and light (thus, perhaps, the city and civilisation), and in art the controlled shaping of sculpture (16), epic poetry (19, 24), or melodic music (20-21);[5] the Dionysiac, on the other hand, is associated with a lack of control, when "subjectivity becomes a complete forgetting of the self" (17), and inspired intoxication (17), with art forms such as dance and polyphonic music (17, 20-21).

> Singing and dancing, man expresses himself as a member of a higher community: he has forgotten how to walk and talk, and is about to fly dancing into the heavens. His gestures express enchantment. Just as animals now speak, and the earth yields up milk and honey, he now gives voice to supernatural sounds: he feels like a god, he himself now walks about enraptured and elated as he saw the gods walk in dreams. (*BT* 17-18)

The Dionysiac state of mind frees the enchanted individual from his Apolline control and envelops him into a 'higher community,' a state of oneness with a broader environment, which is metaphorically revealed through, in part, an ontological confusion between man and beast – "he has forgotten how to

3 For art as the essential means for Nietzsche of dealing with such despair and with creating the necessary illusion, see Blount (2013: 91).

4 Nietzsche here quotes German philosopher Arthur Schopenhauer, namely his *The World as Will and Representation*: "Just as the boatman sits in his little boat, trusting to his fragile craft in a stormy sea which, boundless in every direction, rises and falls in howling, mountainous waves, so in the midst of a world full of suffering the individual man calmly sits, supported by and trusting the *principium individuationis* [i.e. the principle of individualisation]" (*BT* 16). Nietzsche further elaborates: "it might be said of Apollo that the unshaken faith in that *principium* and the peaceful stillness of the man caught up in it have found their most sublime expression in him, and we might even describe Apollo as the glorious divine image of the *principium individuationis*, from whose gestures and looks all the delight, wisdom and beauty of 'illusion' speak to us" (16).

5 "The music of Apollo was Doric architecture transmuted into sounds, but only suggestive sounds such as those of the cithara. Care was taken to ensure that the one element held to be non-Apolline was excluded, the very element of which Dionysiac music consisted – the overwhelming power of sound, the unified flow of melody and the utterly incomparable world of harmony. In the Dionysiac dithyramb, man's symbolic faculties are roused to their supreme intensity – a feeling never before experienced is struggling for expression – the destruction of the veil of Maya, Oneness as the source of form, of nature itself" (*BT* 20-21).

[...] talk," "just as animals now speak" (*BT* 17-18) – between the human and the natural. For Nietzsche, however, this transition to a quasi-natural state is not reflective of a pro-environmental, 'Buddhist,' enlightened, or essentially benevolent state of consciousness with one's surroundings; it is, rather, perilous in its descent towards chaos, anarchy, and a primordial state. Thus, "the highest impact of Apolline culture [...] must always overthrow a realm of Titans and slay monsters, and [...] must emerge triumphant over a terrible abyss in its contemplation of the world and its most intense capacity for suffering, by resorting to the most powerful and pleasurable illusions" (*BT* 24). A few paragraphs later, Nietzsche adds that the Dionysiac, the "primal Oneness, eternally suffering and contradictory, also needs the delightful vision, the pleasurable illusion for its constant redemption" (25). The Bacchic or Dionysiac mood (note that the god is always symbolic for Nietzsche) sends the man possessed by it, ultimately, into primitive anarchy, an abysmal chaos. More than that, though, for Nietzsche, the Dionysiac is the base, 'true' state of universal experience; the Apolline is, in contrast, an illusion which man imposes upon his surroundings: the Apolline entails a triumph of the will,[6] with the very *creation* of the gods providing "a justification for the life of man by living it themselves – the only satisfactory form of *theodicy*" (23). For Nietzsche, modern man has to move beyond God, not without a sense of mourning of course, and to create meaning through Apolline will alone.

Using Nietzsche's understandings of the Apolline and the Dionysiac as a comparative framework (though not a source), this chapter explores how two influential Christian writers of fantasy – J.R.R. Tolkien and C.S. Lewis – responded to the notion of a godless universe (an essentially modernist notion, whether or not they had close knowledge of Nietzsche)[7] and reframed the tension which Nietzsche introduced:[8] turning the contrast between the Dionysiac and the Apolline to that between the Bacchic and the 'Aslanine' (Lewis) or between

6 Popular analyses critical of Nietzsche's philosophy have often emphasised the hegemonic appeal of his ideas and the pragmatic result of this philosophy in the twentieth century: "German philosopher Friedrich Nietzsche [...] was an outspoken supporter of the quest for power" (Blount 2013: 89). There is a risk of reduction in such popular interpretations of Nietzsche's philosophy and of attributing posthumous events and ideologies to the German philosopher; for example, on the influence of Nietzsche's sister Elizabeth on his subsequent political appropriation, see Gere (2009: 38).

7 On Tolkien's possibly intentional reception of Nietzsche, see Blount 2013: 94-95, footnote 18.

8 Blount's (2013) study on Tolkien and Nietzsche provides the groundwork for this chapter's comparative approach.

the Dionysiac and the Orphic, with a marked rejection of the Apolline (Tolkien). In Lewis's *Prince Caspian*, such gods are literally embodied in the natural world; in Tolkien's *The Lord of the Rings*, they are symbolised as different agents or forces of the natural world. In both cases, therefore, the natural environment (particularly, forests) acts as the arena in which this 'Nietzschean contest' takes place.[9] Both Tolkien and Lewis respond to Nietzsche's modernist assertion of the substratal truth of the Dionysiac ('God is dead'), but they do so in different respects, as this chapter explores (Blount 2013: 95).

To give a brief structural outline of the argument: the second section of the chapter discusses C.S. Lewis's *Prince Caspian*, in particular the scene of natural liberation involving Bacchus, Maenads, and of course Aslan – a scene which owes much to the Greek playwright Euripides and his *Bacchae* – and analyses how Lewis contrasts, and indeed tames, the Bacchic with the 'Aslanine' or Christian. The third section discusses Tolkien's *The Fellowship of the Ring*, in particular the chapter 'The Old Forest,' along with some reference to the other 'Bombadil' chapters as well as Fangorn Forest and Treebeard in *The Two Towers*, and it analyses how Tolkien contrasts the Dionysiac with the Orphic. The fourth section discusses how the forces of evil in Tolkien's work can be defined by their (false) Nietzschean belief in the Dionysiac and their 'Apolline will.' Tolkien's reframing will also be put into conversation with his cosmogony, as revealed in *The Silmarillion*.

## Lewis's *Prince Caspian* and Euripides' *Bacchae*: Between the Bacchic and the 'Aslanine'

The second book in the Narnia heptalogy narrates the return of Peter, Susan, Edmund, and Lucy to Narnia, about a thousand 'Narnian years' after the events described in the first book.[10] During this interval Narnia has been colonised by a group of humans called the Telmarines, whose dominion has forced the sentient, original animal inhabitants into hiding, with their existence at the time of the story having already been mythologised. The Narnians, roused

9 For the importance of the natural world in Tolkien's works, see Curry (1998), Dickerson and Evans (2006), as well as Light (2013).

10 Any reference to the order of the Narnia books in this chapter refers to the original publication order: i.e. *The Lion, the Witch and the Wardrobe* (1950), *Prince Caspian* (1951), etc.

by Prince Caspian and inspired by the Pevensie children, fight back against the Telmarines. The resistance against the Telmarines takes two forms: first, under the leadership of Prince Caspian and High King Peter, the Narnians make a brave last stand at a great mound, Aslan's How; second, at the behest of Aslan, and with Susan and Lucy tagging along, the natural world (trees, plants, the river, nature beings such as dryads, etc.) is awakened and successfully fights back against the Telmarines. The latter resistance incorporates a notable classical element.

The roar of Aslan awakens not only Ent-like tree people – "pale birch girls," "shaggy oak men" (*PC* 168) – but also a vine-clad procession:

> One was a youth, dressed only in a fawn-skin, with vine leaves wreathed in his curly hair. His face would have been almost too pretty for a boy's, if it had not looked so extremely wild. You felt, as Edmund said when he saw him a few days later, "There's a chap who might do anything – absolutely anything." He seemed to have a great many names – Bromios, Bassareus, and the Ram were three of them. There were a lot of girls with him, as wild as he. There was even, unexpectedly, someone on a donkey. And everybody was laughing: and everybody was shouting out, "Euan, euan, eu-oi-oi-oi." (169)

This curly-haired youth is, as Lucy later identifies, "Bacchus and the old one on the donkey is Silenus" (*PC* 171). Lewis's Bacchus, like his source in Greek (Dionysus) and Roman mythology, is generically associated with viticulture and festivities, although, since *Prince Caspian* is a children's story, the "Romp" (169) and "laughter" (171) are engendered by copious, ecstatic ingestion of delicious grapes without any reference to fermentation (170-71). The wild girls with Bacchus are, of course, "Maenads" (209, 212, 223), most familiar to modern readers from the *Bacchae* by the Greek tragedian Euripides, one of Lewis's favourite writers,[11] and together with the Greco-Roman god of the vines these Maenads perform a number of emancipatory actions. First, they set free a river-god by destroying with magical vines the stone bridge which is hindering the god's river. Second, a repressive school, in the dour Victorian, institutional mould, is transformed into a natural terrain: "The walls became

11 "You ask whether I have ever been in love: fool as I am, I am not quite such a fool as that. But if one is only to talk from first-hand experience on any subject, conversation would be a very poor business. But though I have no personal experience of the thing they call love, I have what is better – the experience of Sappho, of Euripides, of Catullus, of Shakespeare, of Spenser, of Austen, of Bronte [sic], of, of, – anyone else I have read" (*CL I* 146).

a mass of shimmering green, and leafy branches arched overhead where the ceiling had been. Miss Prizzle [a history teacher] found she was standing on grass in the forest glade" (212). The teacher and the rest of the girls flee, but one, more enlightened girl, Gwendolen, joins the Maenads on their romp – so too do several beasts of burden and "chained dogs" (213).

Third, Bacchus and the Maenads punish a "man who was beating a boy. The stick burst into flowers in the man's hand. He tried to drop it, but it stuck to his hand. His arm became a branch, his body the trunk of a tree, his feet took root" (*PC* 213-14). The particular punishment of metamorphosis, specifically the transformation of a human into a tree or plant by a god, is the pervasive, unifying theme of Ovid's *Metamorphoses* – although many of the suffering, dendrified characters of Ovid's epic are not so guilty as Lewis's corporal-punisher. In addition to Ovidian metamorphosis, Lewis might also be drawing on and rewriting the punishment of Pentheus in Euripides' *Bacchae*. Pentheus, the irreligious ruler of Thebes, spies on the Maenads (a mob which includes his own mother) from the vantage of a tall pine tree; the Maenads, with the help of Bacchus-Dionysus, spot the Theban man, pull down the tree, and rip him to pieces limb from limb. Lewis's version is toned down somewhat, befitting a children's story: his Maenads do not dis-member their man after shaking him out of a tree but rather re-member him, so transforming him into a tree. Fourth, and last, Lewis's Bacchic romp sets free a work-stricken school tutor, whose abusive pupils are routed by Bacchus and, apparently, turned into swine: "it was said afterward […] that those particular little boys were never seen again, but that there were a lot of very fine little pigs in that part of the country which had never been there before" (214-15). The transformation of a group of inquisitive men into pigs is captured, most famously, in book X of the Homeric *Odyssey*, when the Ithacan *hetairoi* of Odysseus are turned into swine by the witch Circe in her island of Aeaea.

What can we take out of Lewis's reception and rewriting of Bacchus-Dionysus and his Bacchants? What particular role does this Greco-Roman procession play in Lewis's story? In Euripides' *Bacchae*, one of the major themes which flavours the quick exchanges between Dionysus and Pentheus as well as the god's own opening monologue (as given in the ensuing quotation) is the impiety of hubristic mortals: "Now Cadmus has given the kingship and its powers to

Pentheus, his daughter's son, who makes war on divinity in my person by thrusting me away from my sacrifices and making no mention of me in his prayers. Because of this I mean to reveal myself as a true god to him and everyone in Thebes" (*Bacchae* ll. 43-48). Pentheus is not the only disbeliever among the Thebans, but as the leader he is the object of the god's retribution. A similar irreverence is visible in Narnia, wherein the Telmarines, especially their leader Miraz, are guilty of impiety in relegating Aslan – essentially Narnia's Christ – to the realm of fairy tales; the following exchange between young Caspian and Miraz is indicative of this:

> [Caspian speaking…] "And so they [Peter, Susan, Edmund, Lucy] reigned for ever so long and everyone had a lovely time, and it was all because of Aslan—"
>
> "Who's he?" said Miraz. And if Caspian had been a very little older, the tone of his uncle's voice would have warned him that it would be wiser to shut up. But he babbled on,
>
> "Oh, don't you know?" he said. "Aslan is the great Lion who comes from over the sea."
>
> "Who has been telling you all this nonsense?" said the King in a voice of thunder. (*PC* 54)

The Telmarines' impiety is further displayed through their denial of the 'magic of creation' in Aslan's Narnia, of their antagonism towards the divine natural world: ""That's all nonsense, for babies," said the King sternly. "[…] fairy tales."" (*PC* 53). While human impiety (disrespect to/ignoring of the divine) and hubris (overweening pride) are present in both Euripides' *Bacchae* and Lewis's *Prince Caspian* and while Bacchus-Dionysus is an important, retributive figure in punishing this impiety in both narratives, the Christian structure of Lewis's story has subordinated Bacchus and his Bacchants to agents of Aslan-Christ, towards whom all piety is ultimately directed. The Narnian Bacchus is thus, in a clear sense, Christianised. He is not capable of the wild excesses of Euripides' Dionysus because Aslan is controlling him; Susan says, "I wouldn't have felt very safe with Bacchus and all his wild girls if we'd met them without Aslan" (171). There are, indeed, some innuendoes of the wild, chaotic Dionysus of Euripides and Greek myth, but these tokens are rewritten in a tamer form: for example, as has been observed, an allusion to bodily dismemberment, which is reconfigured by Lewis towards an eco-friendly re-memberment (214); orgiastic festivities, which are reconfigured into a childish 'romp,' with breathless laughter and grapes (170-71); and there is even a hint of female nudity, of Maenadic wildness: "Instantly she [Gwendolen] joined hands with two of the Maenads, who whirled her round in a merry dance and helped her take off some of the unnecessary and uncomfortable clothes that she was wearing" (212-13).

Lewis's taming of the Greek Bacchus-Dionysus renders the god acceptable for a Christian-oriented children's tale. He has also slightly altered the emancipatory function of Bacchus in a somewhat positivist fashion by reducing the god's role to a benign agent of the natural world. Lewis's Bacchus is, therefore, a pro-environmental figure: at the instruction of Aslan, he helps to set free a river (*PC* 210-11), and along with his Maenads, he twice transforms the urban institution of schools into a natural sphere.[12] It is worth pointing out, however, that while there is indeed a notable contrast in Euripides' *Bacchae* between the repressive urban sphere of Pentheus' Thebes and the rural, pastoralist haunts of the Bacchants,[13] the emancipatory function of the Greek Dionysus and his followers is not always so positivist in an pro-environmental sense in the tragedy and other classical representations; in fact, their actions often veer towards chaos and destruction. The maenads' apparent harmony with nature is a symbol of their devotion to the god Dionysus; it is not representative of a modern love of nature for nature's sake. Thus, Euripides' maenads, under the inspiration of the god, are as likely to coddle young animals (*Bacchae* ll. 699ff.) as they are to tear them apart: "the Bacchants [...] with weaponless hands, attacked the cattle that were grazing on the grass. One of them you might have seen using her hands to wrench asunder a young heifer with swollen udders – how the creature bellowed! Others were rending and tearing apart full-grown cows" (ll. 735-39).

In short, the natural world in *Prince Caspian* is overseen by two divine forces: a Bacchic and a Christian (Aslan); the former has the tendency towards wildness and anarchy, as Susan alludes to, but it is kept in check and kept from veering towards Euripidean chaos and anarchy by the latter. The wildness of Lewis's

12 The repressive nature of English schooling, and industrialised, urban England in general, had a lasting impression on the young Jack Lewis, coming from a greener landscape in Northern Ireland (Wilson 2005: 22ff.). "C.S. Lewis 'reacted with immediate hatred' to the sight of England. [...] [H]e felt he was entering a world of Stygian dullness" (22).

13 "A ravine, bound with cliffs, lay there, with pines casting their shadow over the stream that rushed through it. There the maenads were sitting, their hands employed in pleasant tasks. Some of them were restoring to a worn-out wand its crown of ivy locks, others, with the joy of young mares released from the painted yoke, were singing bacchic antiphonies" (Euripides *Bacchae* ll. 1050-57).

Bacchus and his maenads is just sufficient to reprimand the excessive 'Apolline' ordering of human urbanisation (the Telmarines) which threatens to destroy the natural world, but this Bacchic wildness does not descend into total chaos because of the rightful divine order imposed by Aslan – because the natural world is, in Lewis's view, an ordered product of the divine creation. Such a tension between an ordered, rational, controlling force within and outside the natural world (the lion Aslan) and a wild, irrational, anarchic force inside the natural world (Bacchus) contrasts sharply with Friedrich Nietzsche's understanding of the Dionysiac and the Apolline (*BT* 14-18). For Nietzsche, modern man has to move beyond God, not without a sense of mourning of course, and to create meaning through Apolline will alone; for Lewis, on the other hand, the leonine will which his protagonists experience entails no such illusion. Indeed, for this Christian writer, the potentially Bacchic mood of nature is, if anything, the illusion since it is created by a force of universal order, embodied in the powerful, regal natural symbol of the lion, which forms the substructure of existence. Between Nietzsche's Apolline and Dionysiac, or between Lewis's 'Aslan-ine' and Bacchic – how does the depiction of the natural world in Tolkien's writings respond to these tensions between irrationality and rationality, chaos and order?

## Dionysiac versus Orphic Nature in Tolkien's Old Forest

In *The Fellowship of the Ring*, the four hobbits are forced by necessity, in order to escape from the perilous Black Riders and leave the Shire (Buckland), to enter the Old Forest. As soon as they enter the woodlands, the hobbits become aware of a collective presence, the forest acting as a singular force rather than a collection of trees. This is revealed, for example, through the story of the trees having once collectively attacked the Hedge, the outer wall of Buckland (*FR* 110-11); through the hobbits' reacting to the Forest as a coherent entity, a proper noun, as in the words of Pippin, who says, "I am getting very suspicious of this Forest and everything in it" (115); through the sense in the narrative that they are being gradually steered towards the *centre* of the Old Forest; and, in the later skirmish with Old Man Willow, through the feeling that all the trees are communicating with one another:

> The branches of the willow began to sway violently. There was a sound as of a wind rising and spreading outwards to the branches of all the other trees round about, as though they [the Hobbits] had dropped a stone into the quiet slumber of the river-valley and set up ripples of anger that ran out over the whole Forest. (*FR* 118)

Tolkien's depiction of nature in the form of the Old Forest can be interpreted according to Nietzsche's description of the Dionysiac. It is governed by a "primal Oneness" (*BT* 25). The collective oneness has already been described above; the ancient, primordial aspect of Tolkien's forest is suggested both by its name and by the descriptions of the trees suggesting senectitude: "straight or bent, twisted, leaning, squat or slender, smooth or gnarled and branched; and all the stems were green or grey with moss and slimy shaggy growths" (*FR* 111). The 'shagginess' and the moss are suggestive of bearded old age; the references to the trees being twisted, bent, and gnarled suggest corporeal decay over time. Moreover, this "primal Oneness" is, at its core, a destructive force: Nietzsche speaks of the Dionysiac as entailing the disintegration of the individual (*BT* 20), a yearning for death, to not have been born (22-23), a substratal descent into chaos and destruction, spatially symbolised as "a terrible abyss," or mythically "a realm of Titans and [...] monsters" (24).

Such a spatial abyss is depicted in the hobbits' centripetal journey into the centre of the forest: a journey which is marked by a downward, hellish descent – "they [the hobbits] scrambled and stumbled into a fold that was wider and deeper than any they had met. [...] All they could do was to follow the fold – downwards" (*FR* 114-15); also by a movement from occasional light to increasing gloominess and darkness.[14] When they do reach the centre of the Old Forest, "they came quite suddenly out of the gloom. As if through a gate they saw the sunlight before them" (115); this physical brightness is, however, contradicted by the warm thickness of the air and acts as a soporific – "A golden afternoon of late sunshine lay warm and drowsy upon the hidden land" (115) – coercing the hobbits from wakefulness of a deceptive light to the darkness of sleep (116-17).

The climax of the hobbits' experience of the primal oneness of the Old Forest is, as already alluded to, the skirmish with Old Man Willow, from whom all

14 For comparison of the descriptions of the Old Forest with Mirkwood in *The Hobbit*, see Dickerson and Evans (2006: 136-37).

the malice of the woodlands seems to originate. Old Man Willow represents a dangerous slide from rationality to irrationality, as under his influence the hobbits gradually succumb to sleep and lose control of their minds: “Frodo lay for a while fighting with the sleep that was overpowering him. [...] Half in a dream he wandered forward to the riverward side of the tree” (*FR* 116-17); “Sam sat down and scratched his head, and yawned like a cavern. He was worried. The afternoon was getting late, and he thought this sudden sleepiness uncanny” (117). The loss of control of the mind, the slipping from rationality to irrationality, marks a transition away from individuality towards dissolution, towards being consumed, devoured, and ultimately destroyed by the primal Oneness of the Old Forest – thus, Merry and Pippin are literally eaten up by Old Man Willow and become part of him, hearing his voice and warnings to Frodo and Sam; Frodo is tied up by the roots of the willow and is almost drowned in the river (117). Both acts of destruction are further symbolically charged. The devouring of Merry and Pippin is a reverse of birthing out of a womb and, thus, a return to pre-individual origins, the Dionysiac drive to not be born (*BT* 22): “Merry was trapped: another crack had closed about his waist; his legs lay outside, but the rest of him was inside a dark opening, the edges of which gripped [him] like a pair of pincers” (*FR* 117). Frodo’s near death by drowning would match the drowning of his father and mother, who died in a boating accident in the Brandywine River.

Now, the Hobbits do try to fight back, and it is Samwise Gamgee, a culture hero and cultivator of nature – quite literally, in his role as a gardener, but also in his drive for order – who starts fighting back. Sam first wonders if they have an “axe among our luggage” (*FR* 118) and then hits upon a surer solution: “We might do something with fire! [...] We might try to hurt or frighten this tree to begin with” (118). The immediate recourse to axe and fire connotes a quite primitive response to the Dionysiac unknown, the all-consuming mass of chaos in the dark forest beyond the tribe; the fire, moreover, represents a particularly Apolline attempt to bring light to the darkness, to will order on chaos.[15] The attempt is, however, unsuccessful; Old Man Willow, far too strong for them, threatens to squeeze the life out of Merry, and Sam stamps out the

---

15 As Dickerson and Evans state, the menace of the Old Forest “seems to guide the hobbits in a certain direction against their will” (2006: 138).

fire. To oppose the Dionysiac nature of Old Man Willow, the hobbits will need to locate an opposing force, another 'god of nature.' Frodo, thus, quite inexplicably "ran along the path crying *help! help! help!*" (118). His plea is, oddly enough, answered, and the four hobbits are subsequently saved by the arrival of the enigmatic Tom Bombadil, who tames Old Man Willow and escorts the hobbits to his home in the forest, recounted in the subsequent chapter, 'In the House of Tom Bombadil.'

This sudden reversal of a plot towards an unexpected happy ending is typical of fairy tales; Tolkien regarded this as the dominant mode of the fairy story, in contrast to tragic catastrophe, and termed it the *eucatastrophe* (*TOFS* 75). Such eucatastrophes in Tolkien's stories often involve eagles, who are, in his legendarium associated with the divine, Zeus-like might of Manwë, the strongest of the Valar: thus, in the nick of time eagles save the tree-bound dwarves, Bilbo, and Gandalf from the wolves and orcs who are trying to burn them alive in the chapter of *The Hobbit*, 'Out of the Frying Pan and into the Fire'; eagles also arrive at the crucial moment in two battles, the Battle of the Five Armies and the Battle of the Black Gate.[16] The ability of Tolkien's eagles to arrive 'out of the blue,' and to offer a eucatastrophic plot resolution, has often mystified lay readers of the books and watchers of the films, appalled by the fact that the Fellowship could not simply have taken a first-class flight to Mount Doom directly and avoid all the fanfare along the route; such an interpretation misunderstands the divine symbolism of the eagles. Equally, does this sudden, unexpected happy-ending in the Old Forest narrative suggest that Tom Bombadil is also some kind of divine agent?

Is Tom Bombadil, like Lewis's Aslan, a figure associated with a superior divine, essentially Christian order who tames and restraints the potential Bacchic wildness of nature? Or is he like Nietzsche's Apollo, a god-like man who himself creates the will to provide a peaceful illusion over the chaotic Old Forest? Or is he a classical Orpheus, a magical human disciple of Apollo in Greek and Roman poetry? The answer to such questions is, in part, unsolvable because Tolkien has directly styled Tom Bombadil as an enigma, a riddle which the

16 For an in-depth examination of the role of the Eagles in Tolkien's fiction, see Neubauer (2021).

reader can never entirely resolve[17] – small wonder, then, that Peter Jackson chose to remove this strange figure from his movie trilogy, given the necessity to retain ethical simplicity in the depictions of an ordered battle between good and evil (in environmental terms: nature and industrialisation; Dickerson and Evans 2006: 18-19):[18] "even in a mythical Age there must be some enigmas, as there always are. Tom Bombadil is on (intentionally)" (*Letters* 174, #144).[19] The enigmatic status of Tom Bombadil is revealed by the complexity of his wife Goldberry's answer to Frodo's simple, 'foolish' question of identity:

> 'Fair lady!' said Frodo again after a while. 'Tell me, if my asking does not seem foolish, who is Tom Bombadil?'
>
> 'He is,' said Goldberry, staying her swift movements and smiling.
>
> Frodo looked at her questioningly. 'He is, as you have seen him,' she said in answer to his look. 'He is Master of wood, water, and hill.'
>
> 'Then all this strange land belongs to him?'
>
> 'No indeed!' she answered, and her smile faded. 'That would indeed be a burden,' she added in a low voice, as if to herself. 'The trees and the grasses and all things growing or living in the land belong each to themselves. Tom Bombadil is the Master. No one has ever caught old Tom walking in the forest, wading in the water, leaping on the hill-tops under light and shadow. He has no fear. Tom Bombadil is master.' (*FR* 124)

Goldberry's reply reveals how Tom Bombadil defies the typical, simple rubrics of identity which are used to establish and make sense of all other individuals in Tolkien's story (and, indeed, in our daily lives). For example, Tom Bombadil has no clear genetic identity, whether according to parental origins – Tom is revealed in the Council of Elrond as the "Iarwain Ben-adar [...], oldest and fatherless" (*FR* 265) – or ethnic, racial origins, since Tom is immortal but neither Elven nor apparently of the Maiar, a "strange creature" (265). He has no manifest political identity, according to power or ownership, in that he is both Master of the Forest, and yet, as Goldberry says, it does not belong to him. Lastly, he has no clear ethical identity, according to the scale between good and evil; Tom is, more than anything, indifferent to the evil invoked by

---

17 On the difference between an enigma and an anomaly, see Hargrove (1986: 20). In Hargrove's view, we are meant, then, to attempt to unravel the enigma, whereas an anomaly could be ignored.

18 "Tolkien admitted that during the writing of *The Lord of the Rings* he himself seemed unsure of who Tom Bombadil was or what he might represent in the overall fabric of the trilogy" (Dickerson and Evans 2006: 18).

19 "But many have found him [Tom Bombadil] an odd or indeed discordant ingredient. In historical fact I put him in because I had already 'invented' him independently (he first appeared in the Oxford magazine) and I wanted an 'adventure' on the way" (*Letters* 192, #153).

the Ring, wearing it without any effect.[20] Our inability to answer such basic questions of identity suggests that Tom Bombadil is to be understood by the reader, first and foremost, as a poetic riddle, fitting for a character who is best invoked through verse (Hargrove 1986: 20). Tom Bombadil, then, defies our attempts at understanding his personal, ethnic, political, or ethical identity – can we actually say anything *definite* about this enigmatic figure?

Most obviously, Tom, along with Goldberry (Dickerson and Evans 2006: 20), is associated with the natural world – trees, plants, rivers, and so on; his field of influence is restricted to non-urban, natural landscapes. Dickerson and Evans thus regard him in general terms as "the representation or personification of nature: an earth spirit" (19; Curry 1998: 76; Hargrove 1986: 21). The four travelling hobbits first encounter him once they have travelled to the very heart of the Old Forest, to the Withywindle Valley, where the enchantment of nature is greatest. Moreover, although Tom later saves the hobbits from the necrotic threat of the barrow-wights and steers them along their path, he is spatially limited to the non-urban sphere – their return to the east-west Road and their propinquity to the town of Bree is a threshold which Tom cannot cross:

> *Tom's country ends here: he will not pass the borders.*
> *Tom has his house to mind, and Goldberry is waiting!* (*FR* 148)

Tom has no great interest in what transpires beyond his natural domain; he has some knowledge of, for example, Farmer Maggot, whom he holds in high esteem, but this is unsurprising since that hobbit is associated with soil and land and has the 'earthy-wisdom' of a simple pastoralist (Dickerson and Evans 2006: 19-20). Later, in the Council of Elrond, Gandalf further endorses the restricted domain of Tom: "now he is withdrawn into a little land, within bounds that he has set, though none can see them, waiting perhaps for a change of days, and he will not step beyond them" (*FR* 265). Tolkien later wrote that Tom Bombadil represents a kind of 'allegory' of "pure (real) natural science: the spirit that desires knowledge of other things, their history and nature, *because they are 'other'* and wholly independent of the enquiring mind, and entirely unconcerned with

20 "The Ring has no power over him. He is his own master. But he cannot alter the Ring itself, nor break its power over others" (*FR* 265). An indifference which can be explained by his 'green time,' his perspective of the earth on a longer, non-anthropocentric timeline (Light 2013: 157-58).

'doing' anything with the knowledge: Zoology and Botany not Cattle-breeding or Agriculture" (*Letters* 192, #153; Dickerson and Evans 2006: 21-22).

Yet Tom is also an extremely *powerful* force within the natural world. His natural power is also much discussed in the Council of Elrond, where the counsellors discuss the possibility of leaving the One Ring to Bombadil. "'But within those bounds [of his domain] nothing seems to dismay him,' said Erestor" (*FR* 265). Glorfindel even compares Tom's power to that of Sauron, though ultimately unfavourably, as being the last likely to succumb to evil: "Could that power [of Sauron] be defied by Bombadil alone? I think not. I think that in the end, if all else is conquered, Bombadil will fall, Last as he was First; and then Night will come" (266). Lastly, the elven counsellor Galdor precisely links Tom's power to the natural world: "Power to defy our Enemy is not in him [Tom], unless such power is in the earth itself. And yet we see that Sauron can torture and destroy the very hills" (266). Gandalf and Elrond, undoubtedly the two wisest individuals in the Council, are in agreement with the assessments of Glorfindel and Galdor.

Dickerson and Evans write that "Bombadil's power is equated precisely with the natural potency of the earth – the brute fact of its existence and its resistance against forces of destruction" (2006: 20). Yet, it is worth noting that nature itself can represent a destructive sphere, as we have seen; Bombadil represents, then, a specific incarnation of nature which is opposed to the chaotic primal force of Old Man Willow, embodying the Dionysiac force of the Old Forest. What kind of 'nature god' is Tom then? To compare Tolkien's text with Lewis's *Prince Caspian*, for example, does Tom Bombadil represent a powerful leonine-Christian or 'Aslanine' force, which represents a substratum below the natural world, and which controls the natural world?

One recalls it is Aslan's divine roar, his command which sets in motion the narrative of environmental renewal and oversees the Bacchic fight back against urban colonisation and excessive human order and tyranny. On his possible symbol as the Christian God, there has been some speculation in Tolkien scholarship that Tom Bombadil might be a Vala or even the incarnation of the Ilúvatar himself, God in Tolkien's legendarium (Hargrove 1986: 21-23). There are some clues in the text which might (incorrectly, I would say) lead readers to such an assessment: firstly, the characteristic difficulty of defining God in concrete terms is manifest in Tom's enigmatic persona; secondly, the riddling contrast between being both a Master (with a capital M) and not domineering over his subjects is reflective of theological speculation as to how an omnipotent (and omniscient) being such as God can still allow free will over his subjects and not be tyrannical;[21] thirdly, there is Goldberry's simple description of who Tom is: "'He is,' said Goldberry, staying her swift movements and smiling." Similar allusive phrasing in Christian discourse suggests how God is the ontological essence of the universe; in other words, the mere presence of existence, the very word *is*, implies God – no further nominative complements, in grammatical terms, are necessary.[22] Tolkien, however explains this riddle of the pronouns differently:

> Goldberry and Tom are referring to the mystery of names. See and ponder Tom's words in Vol. I p. 142. You may be able to conceive of your unique relation to the Creator without a name – can you: for in such a relation pronouns become proper nouns? But as soon as you are in a world of other finites with a similar, if each unique and different, relation to Prime Being, who are you? Frodo has not asked 'what is Bombadil' but 'who is he'. We and he no doubt often laxly confuse the questions. Goldberry gives what I think is the correct answer. We need not go into the sublimities of 'I am that I am' – which is quite different from he is. She adds as a concession a statement of part of the 'what'. (*Letters* 191-92, #153)

Moreover, the attribution of God-like status to Bombadil raises far more problems than it solves as to the riddle of his identity. Why, for example, would Tom/God's power be considered deficient or in decline compared to that of Sauron, as Gandalf, Galdor, and Glorfindel assume? Admittedly, this assessment of Bombadil in Rivendell is through internal character focalisation (albeit three of the wisest characters in the epic); however, the sense that Bombadil's power is not as it once was is indicated by the waning of the forests since we know that his realm once extended much further (*FR* 265-66). Also, from a symbolic perspective, why would Tom/God dwell in the dark, Dionysiac realm of the Old Forest, surrounded by the chaotic, primitive tokens of nature? "He [Tom] hardly even judges, and as far as can be seen makes no effort to reform or remove even the Willow"

21 Tolkien downplays the theological implications when he writes that "lots of other characters are called Master" (*Letters* 191, #153).

22 "In terms of medieval philosophy this would mean that existence is a predicate of Tom Bombadil and that he is therefore God" (Hargrove 1986: 22).

(*Letters* 192, #153). Elsewhere in Tolkien's writings, the divine essence, whether of Ilúvatar or his angelic Valar, seems generally associated with lightness and the colour white. Lastly, it is noteworthy that unlike Lewis's Aslan, Tom Bombadil does not control or seem to hold sway over the Old Forest in any respect; rather, he co-exists with the Dionysiac force of the forest, which does not get the better of him; as Goldberry says, "No one has ever caught old Tom walking in the forest, wading in the water, leaping on the hill-tops under light and shadow" (*FR* 124). "He merely knows and understands about such things as concern him in his natural little realm" (*Letters* 192, #153).

The particular order which Bombadil imposes on the Old Forest might best be described as not essentially Christian in a Lewisian sense, nor Apolline, in the Nietzschean sense of a wilful illusion imposed over nature, but, as Peter Sundt (2021: 184-86) has discussed, *Orphic*. The figure of Orpheus in classical mythology (as in, for example, Virgil's *Georgics*, Ovid's *Metamorphoses*, and brief appearances in other ancient texts, including the Homeric *Odyssey*) was a musician-poet, who was associated both with the natural world, having powers to enchant and even animate trees with his song, and with his love for the nymph Eurydice, whom he tries to rescue, unsuccessfully, from the Underworld. Other scholars have viewed the elf Lúthien and perhaps also Beren as Orphic figures in Middle-earth (Beal 2014; Librán-Moreno 2007),[23] but there are definite Orphic elements in Bombadil's characterisation as a nature figure:

> Tom Bombadil introduces the hobbits to the magical powers of the older denizens of Middle-earth. His magical songs can sway the natural world, which is fortunate, since he appears exactly at the moment when the hobbits are under attack from a sentient willow tree, Old Man Willow, who has swallowed up Pippin, half-hidden Merry in a crack of its trunk, and thrown Frodo into a nearby body of water [...]. Like Orpheus, Tom Bombadil is almost constantly singing or speaking in a poetic, metrical fashion, and is introduced in the book singing a song [...], and he immediately uses a song to work his magic. In the encounter with the evil willow tree, Tom's solution to restrain the miscreant tree is to sing [...]. Similarly, when he later proceeds to rescue the hobbits a second time round [in the Barrow-downs], Tom and, indeed, all parties involved turn to song. (Sundt 2021: 184-85)

First and foremost, Tom Bombadil's use of poetry and music/song means that he can charm and so gain control over nature. Tom, as we have seen, subdues

23 For further classical, Ovidian analogues in the Beren and Lúthien story, see Stevens (2004).

the hostile Old Man Willow with his verses; in a somewhat different context, the classical Orpheus in Ovid's *Metamorphoses* mourns the loss of his beloved Eurydice in song, through which he gains an audience of trees, which are described in a long catalogue (book X, ll. 86ff..); his influence over the natural world extends beyond trees, moreover: "Orpheus sang his minstrel's songs and charmed the rocks and woods and creatures of the wild to follow […] as he swept his strings in concord with his song" (book XI, ll.1-5).

There are other Orphic characteristics to Tom Bombadil's character depiction. A further connection is the shared love of a female nymph-like character: "the biggest difference from Orpheus is of course the fact that Tom Bombadil never loses his wife. However, she [Goldberry] does parallel Eurydice in being associated with a river, but in reverse. For just as Virgil lets Eurydice die by a river, Tom Bombadil's Goldberry, who is alive and well, is born from one: "I am Goldberry, daughter of the River" […]" (Sundt 2021: 186). Similar to how the classical Orpheus endures a *nekyia*, travelling down to an underworld to rescue his beloved Eurydice, so too Tom Bombadil ventures into the underground of the barrows to save the four hobbits from the necrotic wights who dwell there; in both cases, the netherworlds are conquered through song (*FR* 142-43).[24]

It is, in summary, the tripartite association of nature, music (singing and poetry), and love which give Bombadil a particularly Orphic character (Sundt 2021: 180-81, 187). Tom Bombadil is not the only character in Tolkien's works to demonstrate this trio of associations – of natural magic/power, of musical abilities, and of love. Most notably, in *The Silmarillion*, Lúthien is first revealed as a songstress whose music can enchant nature and which engenders love in the beholder (Beren):

> [S]uddenly she [Lúthien] began to sing. Keen, heart-piercing was her song as the song of the lark that rises from the gates of night and pours its voice among the dying stars, seeing the sun behind the walls of the world; and the song of Lúthien released the bonds of winter, and the frozen waters spoke, and flowers sprang from the cold earth where her feet had passed. (*Sil* 149)

In *The Lord of the Rings*, Treebeard is vaguely Orphic as well, in his status as the greatest of the tree-herders – the Ents being shepherds of nature – and in

24 For further scholarship on the ancient theme of the journey underground (*katabasis*) in Tolkien, see Obertino (1993) and Stevens (2017, 2021).

his characteristic love of song-poetry; so too, the mournful loss of the Entwives, the spouses of the Ents, by Treebeard might reminds one of Orpheus' sad loss of his beloved Eurydice (Sundt 2021: 181-84).

On the subject of Treebeard, it is also instructive that Tolkien's Orphic characters communicate with and are involved in *shepherding* – a particular, quite Christian[25] form of *ordering* – what we have described as Dionysiac representations of nature. This is evident not only in the Tom Bombadil episode with Old Man Willow but also in the relationship between Treebeard and the Ents, as Orphic figures, and the Huorns, as Dionysiac figures:

> There is a great power in them [Huorns], and they seem able to wrap themselves in shadow: it is difficult to see them moving. But they do. They can move very quickly, if they are angry. You stand still looking at the weather, maybe, or listening to the rustling of the wind, and then suddenly you find that you are in the middle of a wood with great groping trees all around you. They still have voices, and can speak with the Ents – that is why they are called Huorns, Treebeard says – but they have become queer and wild. Dangerous. I should be terrified of meeting them, if there were no true Ents about to look after them. (*TT* 565)

The threat of the Huorns here, and their description, is a doubling of the threat of the Old Forest (Fangorn, of course, being part of an original primordial forest which was connected to the Old Forest), as the hobbits earlier experienced it; it is unsurprising, given the parallels, that Peter Jackson at least resuscitated some of Tom Bombadil's poetry through the words of Treebeard in the extended film edition of the *Two Towers* (2002).[26]

What is most interesting is that there is no obvious hierarchical distinction between the Orphic and the Dionysiac elements of nature – in landscape terms, we might frame this contrast in terms of the domesticated versus the wild. Whereas Nietzsche's analysis subordinates order to chaos and Lewis's chaos to order, there seems, for example, to be a symbiotic relationship between Tolkien's Ents and his Huorns. Moreover, Tom Bombadil is, apparently, Master of the natural world and cannot be trapped in the hills, river, and so forth; and yet he dwells in a realm where, more than anywhere else in Middle-earth, the primordial force

---

25 Such stewardship is also part of a Judaeo-Christian response to nature (McMahon and Csaki 2013: 183).

26 On similarities between Treebeard and Bombadil, see Dickerson and Evans (2006: 19).

of nature reigns supreme. In short, in Tolkien, we can find images of nature as chaotic (destructive, primal, and so on) and nature as ordered (shepherding, loving) side by side, coinhabiting the same space, whether in Fangorn or in the Old Forest. This notion is, essentially, linked to Tolkien's [Christian] cosmogony, which posits the existence of the world in musical terms, between harmony and disharmony (*Sil* 3-5), between order (beautiful, controlled music) and chaos (violent, overpowering cacophony, almost noise), both of which are required aesthetically (if not unproblematically, from a theological perspective) for narrative creation:

> And it seemed that there were two musics progressing at one time before the seat of Ilúvatar, and they were utterly at variance. The one was deep and wide and beautiful, but slow and blended with immeasurable sorrow, from which its beauty chiefly came. The other had now achieved a unity of its own; but it was loud, and vain, and endlessly repeated; and it had little harmony, but rather a clamorous unison as of many trumpets braying upon a few notes. And it essayed to drown the other music out by the violence of its voice, but it seemed that its most triumphant notes were taken by the other and woven into its own solemn pattern. (*Sil* 4-5)

The balance between the Orphic and the Dionysiac which we see in Tolkien's depiction of nature is an extension of this musical principle onto a spatial, ecological plane. Is it not appropriate, then, that both Old Man Willow and Tom Bombadil employ the soporific magic of music to achieve their ends – whether destructive or constructive?[27]

> They [Merry and Pippin] looked up at the grey and yellow leaves [of Old Man Willow], moving softly against the light, and singing. They shut their eyes, and then it seemed that they could almost hear words, cool words, saying something about water and sleep. (*FR* 116)

> Tom put his mouth to the crack [in the trunk of Old Man Willow] and began singing in a low voice. [...] 'You let them out again, Old Man Willow!' he [Tom] said. 'What be you a-thinking of? You should not be waking. Eat earth! Dig deep! Drink water! Go to sleep! Bombadil is talking! (*FR* 120)

---

27 Perhaps it is his whimsy and usage of poetic gibberish which has led some critics to refer to Tom Bombadil as "nonrational" (Hargrove 1986: 21); such an interpretation would characterise him more as a Bacchic-type figure than an Orphic. Against a view of Tom as nonrational, see Hargrove (22).

## The Problem of Evil and the Dionysiac: Melkor, Sauron, and Saruman as Apolline 'Gods'

Now while the origin of this musical, natural-world balance is, ultimately, a Christian-like creator figure, Ilúvatar, it is an indication of Tolkien's complex philosophical, theological worldbuilding – in contrast to Lewis's more militant, or, better, leonine, view of Christianity – that this resulting universal balance between order and chaos speaks to other, non-Western religions, vaguely comparable even to beliefs such as Taoism:

> According to Taoism, all things are comprised of the cosmic principles of yin and yang or some combination of the two. Yin and yang are opposites. Yin is associated with darkness, passivity, and femininity, whereas yang is associated with light, activity, and masculinity. Taoists maintain that harmony or goodness exists when the forces of yin and yang achieve the state of dynamic equilibrium illustrated in the symbol of the Tao. In the symbol, yin is portrayed as an internal element of yang and vice versa, illustrating that the relationship is a complex one. Taoists maintain that evil occurs as a result of an imbalance between yin and yang. (McMahon and Csaki 2013: 189)

It is, I believe, the error of Saruman, Sauron, and company to misunderstand such a Taoist-*like* balance between order and chaos, 'Apolline' and 'Dionysiac,' as will be discussed further below. It might be argued, of course, that darkness – the Dionysiac abyss – is essentially evil in Tolkien's symbolic system (McMahon and Csaki 2013: 189-90), if aesthetically necessary from a story perspective.[28] I would contend, however, that the evil in *The Lord of the Rings* resides rather in the despairing belief in such Dionysiac chaos and the consequent improper usage of order through the will to power, in Nietzschean terms: "St. Augustine and Tolkien both believe that ultimately all evil comes from the mind of some created person or other [...]. St. Augustine coined the phrase "inordinate desire" to describe the root of evil, which he identifies as the desire for something that violates the rightful order of things. [...]. In other words, evil comes from an exercise of free will" (Davison 2013: 103-04).

---

28 "Tolkien's negative characterization of the Dark Power also makes it evident that he privileges one of his two forces over the other. Clearly, Tolkien associates the Dark Power with evil and the forces of light with goodness. While the association of light with goodness and darkness with evil is commonplace in the West, Taoists do not characterize the cosmic forces of yin and yang in this manner. Though Taoists associate yin with darkness and yang with light, yin is not bad and yang good." (McMahon and Csaki 2013: 190).

If both order and chaos are aesthetically necessary, yin-and-yang constituents[29] for the song of [Christian] creation – in fact, the disharmonic element only serves to further enhance the beauty of Ilúvatar's orchestrated music (*Sil* 4) – we should be wary of critical attempts to equate chaotic elements in Tolkien's work with the ethical notion of evil, per se. With regard to representations of nature, critics such as Dickerson and Evans have, with this troubling assumption in mind, tried to exonerate or reduce the primal chaotic aspect of nature, especially in the Old Forest, through environmental positivism, by showing how nature is reacting against 'orcish' deforestation. Thus they characterise the Old Forest in different terms from the Dionysiac, restoring more rational agency to its actions by highlighting its 'victim status' in Middle-earth, taken as a historic, geographic whole:

> The Old Forest, however, once part of the vast forest of Eregion, displays a certain malevolent ill will toward destructive intruders. By the time Frodo and his companions enter it at the end of the Third Age, this forest has become suspicious of all outsiders – a trait also evident in Treebeard – and is hostile even to wandering Hobbits, who pose no genuine threat. (Dickerson and Evans 2006: 133)

Certainly, in the case of Fangorn Forest, such an interpretation of the Huorns seems valid, as Legolas identifies: "I catch only the faintest echoes of dark places where the hearts of the trees are black. There is no malice near us; but there is watchfulness, and anger. [...] But nonetheless it has suffered harm. There is something happening inside, or going to happen" (*TT* 491). In comparison with Fangorn, Dickerson and Evans posit that Old Man Willow was originally benevolent: "Old Man Willow, we may presume, is one of these: an originally 'good' tree that has gone 'bad'" (2006: 140). Their usage of a form of the word *presumption* is instructive because, read by itself as an isolated episode, the Old Forest does not appear to be 'fighting back' against a modernising, industrialising world; it is more the type of forest with which we are familiar from fairy tales (and the Old Forest is very much a fairy-tale aside in an otherwise historical, epic romance) and the pre-modern perceptions of nature as a dark unknown. The critical desire to 'positivise' the Old Forest, from an ethical perspective, is based on an unease which would follow from a depiction of nature as originally or innately evil; the destructive quality of nature (the Old Forest, Mirkwood)

29 For Taoist themes in Tolkien's work, see McMahon and Csaki (2013: 188-91).

must, therefore, in this interpretation, be secondary or a reaction to an external evil agency (Melkor, Sauron, orcs, industrialisation, and so on). This, in my opinion, reduces the symbolic value of nature (like music) for representing the two fundamental, symbiotic components of the created universe in Tolkien's works – order and chaos. Furthermore, it equates the destructiveness of Dionysiac chaos with the agency of evil.

While we might attribute the black mood of trees and nature in Mirkwood and Fangorn as reactionary, based on the evil influences of Sauron-Necromancer and Saruman-Orcs, there are other representations of nature in Tolkien which are not so clear cut. Apart from the Old Forest and Old Man Willow, we must consider the Stone-giants in *The Hobbit*, whose destructive hurling of rocks at one another cannot be attributed to their allegiance to some greater evil agency; they are merely a characteristic part of the wild lands: "the stone-giants were out, and were hurling rocks at one another for a game, and catching them, and tossing them down into the darkness where they smashed among the trees far below, or splintered into little bits with a bang" (53-55). In *The Fellowship of the Ring*, the encounter of the nine travellers with the mountain called Caradhras is somewhat more complicated, as the hostility of this peak, and the inimical weather, might have been provoked by Sauron or Saruman (Williams 2018: 181-88); yet, as Aragorn says, "[t]here are many evil and unfriendly things in the world that have little love for those that go on two legs, and yet are not in league with Sauron, but have purposes of their own. Some have been in this world longer than he" (*FR* 289). Aragorn's usage of the word *evil* for a destructive force of nature is focalised from the perspective of the Fellowship, who are being 'attacked' by the elements (McMahon and Csaki 2013: 184).

It is worth emphasising that in Tolkien's works, the major agents of evil such as Melkor, Sauron, and Saruman are not concerned with spreading chaotic destruction over their domains and ruin upon those whom they dominate for the aim or purpose of destruction (although this is often the terrible result of their actions);[30] their preoccupation is, by and large, rather with *order* of a cer-

30 "Sauron's quest to dominate, enslave, and establish his will over all others – even Ilúvatar – makes him the arch-enemy of all that is good in Middle-earth. Still, while it represents a deadly threat to others, the Dark Lord's power play represents to him the hope not merely of life but of abundant life" (Blount 2013: 89).

tain kind – with making rules, telling people what to do, with enforcing their will over their subjects, for which coercive purpose the One Ring is the greatest symbol (Vink 2020: 210).[31] We might, quite technically from a Nietzschean perspective, term this ordering of Melkor and Sauron[32] Apolline since it is an ordering which originates from the sheer will of individual agents[33] in a universe which, in the view of Melkor and Sauron, is originally godless and characterised by Dionysiac (or 'Ungoliant-like') blackness (void) and chaos (Blount 2013: 89, 94). Thus, Melkorian, Sauronian order is an illusion which must be inserted over the substratum of destruction which awaits orcs and men. Certainly, this fear of dissolution into nothingness is what induces many men to serve these dark lords; one notes, for example, the new theology and cosmogony which Sauron successful spreads among the Númenoreans in the decaying stages of their seafaring empire:

> Sauron with many arguments gainsaid all that the Valar had taught; and he bade men think that in the world, in the east and even in the west, there lay yet many seas and many lands for their winning, wherein wealth was uncounted. And still, if they should at the last come to the ends of those lands and seas, beyond all lay the Ancient Darkness. 'And out of it the world was made. For Darkness alone is worshipful, and the Lord thereof may yet make other worlds to be gifts to those that serve him, so that the increase of their power shall find no end.' (*Sil* 249)

This is a rather different kind of ordering than the 'natural' Orphic shepherding of Treebeard or Tom Bombadil.[34] The best opposition to the Nietzschean will of Sauron is, thus, none other than Tom Bombadil (Blount 2013: 88, footnote 2), over whom the will of the One Ring has precisely zero effect when he puts it on his finger (Davison 2013: 105), and who lives in ordered Orphic harmony (a shepherd or steward) in the Dionysiac realm of the Old Forest, without fear of being submerged into this chaotic abyss since, like many of Tolkien's

31 See also Blount (2013: 87-88). Vink (2020: 210) perceives a clear reference to Nietzsche in Tolkien's oft-cited letter to Milton Waldman: "the primary symbolism of the Ring, as *the will to mere power*, seeking to make itself objective by physical force and mechanism, and so also inevitably by lies" (*Letters* 160, #131; italics added).

32 Sauron, indeed, wishes to replace Ilúvatar as God on earth: "Sauron seeks to establish his will not only over his fellow creatures in Middle-earth but ultimately over Ilúvatar himself" (Blount 2013: 88).

33 "Sauron seems like a candidate for the title Übermensch (or overman)" (Blount 2013: 94).

34 An ordering which is without the imposition of power or control: "each side in the War of the Ring is struggling for power and control. Tom in contrast, though very powerful, has renounced power" (Hargrove 1986: 20).

positive characters such as Gandalf and Treebeard, he realises that darkness is itself an illusion.

The reader also realises, of course, through Tolkien's *eucatastrophic* moments of ultimate joy that such fears are misguided. Both order (harmony) and chaos (disharmony) are (musical) illusions which are the products of divine creation.[35] And yet, it seems that, in an apparent punitive eschatology (which might have the potential to undermine the creative principle of his universe), Tolkien's most evil agents must, ultimately, realise the dread of the original Dionysiac and the illusion of Apolline will; thus Gandalf says to the Witch King when he enters Minas Tirith: "You cannot enter here, [...]. Go back to the abyss prepared for you! Go back! Fall into the nothingness that awaits you and your Master. Go!" (*RK* 829).[36]

## Conclusions

In different ways through their representations of the natural world, both J.R.R. Tolkien and C.S. Lewis oppose Nietzsche's assertion of the death of God and the foundational truth of *das Dionysische*. Lewis depicts the Dionysiac force of nature as built upon a Christian, 'Aslanine' foundation or divine order, which is indeed no illusion but the true substratum of existence in Narnia. The Dionysiac component of nature in *Prince Caspian*, represented by sudden arrival of the Greco-Roman Bacchus himself, *could* be dangerous – as

35 I cannot answer the theological riddle as to why such disharmony/chaos (and thus the potential for evil) exists in Tolkien's universe in the first place: "where does evil come from? If the world was completely good at one point, then how could evil get started in the first place?" (Davison 2013: 103). See footnote below. There is, moreover, only a need for order, control, or design if there is some element which is chaotic. The best answer to this riddle is perhaps that it is necessary from an aesthetic perspective, in a story such as *The Lord of the Rings*.

36 In the sense that evil is a misguided understanding of the essential illusion of Dionysiac chaos in Tolkien's world (and a misguided imposition of Apolline will), I am in agreement with those scholars who have interpreted evil as nothingness, anti-creativity in Tolkien's writings: "The seminal arguments concerning the ontology of evil were forcefully laid out by Shippey (2005: 159ff.). The critic indicates the importance of the orthodox Christian, or Augustinian, view of evil for Tolkien, arguing the possible mediation of Boethius, an important author for medievalists, for whom "evil is nothing." The implications of this philosophy are that evil cannot create, only imitate and pervert the good. Consistent with this perspective, Elrond proclaims: "nothing is evil in the beginning. Even Sauron was not so" (*FR*, II, ii, 349)" (Garbowski 2014: 424; citations thus in Garbowski). For further discussion on the nature of evil in Tolkien (in particular, conflicts in Tolkien's representations between evil as Augustine/non-original and as Manichean/dualistic), see Davison (2013: 100-03) and Garbowski (2014: 424-29).

Lucy, Susan, and Edmund speculate, and as C.S. Lewis implies through his clever intertextualities to, in particular, the Greek playwright Euripides – but this potentially wild, pre-Christian, pagan element is tamed by the Christian Aslan and, in fact, becomes a force for the good, helping to restore order to Narnia, to return it to its natural beauty. The forces of evil in Lewis's novel are the Telmarines, a colonising, industrialising people who are concerned with exerting their control over nature – building bridges, for example, and besieging the last of the true Narnians; in a sense, their attitude to nature is that of a typical pre-modern, pre-environmental man who aims to civilise the wild unknown. Yet their error, in Lewis's mythologised world, is to not appreciate the symbolic value of nature in Narnia: a dangerous, chaotic Bacchic force which can undermine their Apolline attempts to create order based on human will alone (and nothing over and above that civilisational will), and, beyond or below that, an Aslanine force, an aesthetic, creative beauty in nature which connotes a divine order.

Tolkien deviates somewhat from Lewis in showing notions of chaos and order as being in balance in the natural world, as aesthetic products of divine creation. Such a balance is best represented by the enigmatic character of Tom Bombadil in the Old Forest sequence of *The Fellowship of the Ring* (but also by characters such as Treebeard and Gandalf); Tom is a kind of 'nature spirit' who opposes the Dionysiac chaos of the Old Forest through the imposition of a shepherding, Orphic form of ordering. Such order does not try to assert its Apolline will to power over others (Sauron's One Ring has zero effect on Tom), nor does the playful Tom take too seriously the terrible 'abyss' of the Dionysiac, represented by the devouring hunger of Old Man Willow. Tom's response to Old Man Willow is not to defeat the animated tree but merely to 'manage' or shepherd his dangerous actions by means of soporific song – in balance, incidentally, with the fact that Old Man Willow earlier used a different kind of music to send the Hobbits to sleep. Here, importantly, the symbolic value of nature and that of music intersect for Tolkien since, as is revealed by his cosmogonic myth in *The Silmarillion*, he regarded two musics as acting in tandem before the creation of the world: harmony and disharmony, or order (beautiful, controlled music) and chaos (violent, overpowering cacophony, almost noise). Both drives are subordinate to a divine creative being. It is the precise fault – the evil – of Melkor, Sauron, the Witch-King and other wayward beings to not appreciate this balance: to despair at the Dionysiac void; to impose the illusion of Apolline will to counter this and control others.

The implicit challenge of Lewis and Tolkien to Nietzsche's modernist assertion of the 'Apolline illusion' is a manifestly Christian one, appropriating the natural world as a symbol, along with music in the case of Tolkien. Further studies on nature in secular fantasy fiction, such as in the works of J.K. Rowling – the forest around Hogwarts attains a clear Dionysiac character in its darkness, its primitive secrets (undoubtedly enhanced by the film), its arachnid desire to consume the heroes – might provide some 'Apolline' alternatives to the Christian vision of Tolkien and Lewis in representations of nature. Is such Apolline control over nature in Rowling's works – over troublesome Hippogriffs and devouring, Shelob-like spiders, for example – garnered through magic? And if so, what does magic represent if not an ultimate supernatural, divine force? Sheer will alone (Harry's liberal, modern trust in himself as an *individual*)? The power of maternal love (the sacrifice of Harry's mother)? Conversely, in fantasy's cousin genre, science fiction, the challenge has often been between the Apolline will of science and the Dionysiac chaos of an alien natural world, with the latter often triumphing in contemporary, posthumanist-centred representations, as in the recent film *Annihilation* (2018), where the uni-cellular, thoughtless oneness of nature seems destined to take over humanity.

## About the Author

Hamish Williams (PhD in Classical Literature, University of Cape Town) is a guest researcher in European Literature and Culture at the University of Groningen, the Netherlands. He has previously held a Junior Fellowship at the Polish Institute of Advanced Studies in Warsaw and a Humboldt Postdoctoral Fellowship at the Institute of English and American Studies, Friedrich Schiller University Jena. His main research area is Classical Reception Studies, particularly post-classical afterlives in modern literature and popular genres, but he is broadly interested in modern literary studies, covering topics such as utopianism, decline, hospitality, and the sublime. His publications include *Tolkien and the Classical World* (ed.) (2021); *The Ancient Sea: The Utopian and Catastrophic in Classical Narratives and their Reception* (ed.) (2022); and *J.R.R. Tolkien's Utopianism and the Classics* (2023). His current project focuses on modern receptions of Minoan Crete. Outside of academic writing, Hamish tries keeping up with his polyglot family and is working on his own series of fantasy novels (see *The Southern Tide* (2021)).

## Bibliography

Beal, Jane. 2014. 'Orphic Powers in J.R.R. Tolkien's Legend of Beren and Lúthien.' *Journal of Tolkien Research* 1, 1-25.

Blount, Douglas K. 2013. 'Überhobbits: Tolkien, Nietzsche, and the Will to Power.' *The Lord of the Rings and Philosophy: One Book to Rule Them All.* Eds. Gregory Bassham and Eric Bronson. Chicago, LaSalle: Open Court, 87-98.

Curry, Patrick. 1998. *Defending Middle-earth. Tolkien: Myth and Modernity.* London: HarperCollins.

Davison, Scott A. 2013. 'Tolkien and the Nature of Evil.' *The Lord of the Rings and Philosophy: One Book to Rule Them All.* Eds. Gregory Bassham and Eric Bronson. Chicago, LaSalle: Open Court, 99-109.

Del Caro, Adrian. 1989. 'Dionysian Classicism, or Nietzsche's Appropriation of an Aesthetic Norm.' *Journal of the History of Ideas* 50.4, 589-605.

Dickerson, Matthew and Jonathan Evans. 2006. *Ents, Elves, and Eriador: The Environmental Vision of J.R.R. Tolkien.* Lexington: The University Press of Kentucky.

Euripides. 2005. *Euripides: The Bacchae and Other Plays.* Transl. John Davie. London: Penguin Books.

Garbowski, Christopher. 2014. 'Evil.' *A Companion to J.R.R. Tolkien.* Ed. Stuart Lee. Chichester: Wiley Blackwell, 418-30.

Gere, Cathy. 2009. *Knossos & the Prophets of Modernism.* Chicago, London: The University of Chicago Press.

Hargrove, Gene. 1986. 'Who is Tom Bombadil?' *Mythlore* 13.1, 20-24.

Lewis, Clive Staples. 2014. *Prince Caspian.* London: HarperCollins.

2004. *The Collected Letters of C.S. Lewis. Vol. 1. Family Letters 1905-1931.* Ed. Walter Hooper. San Francisco: HarperSanFrancisco.

Librán-Moreno, Miryam. 2007. '"A Kind of Orpheus-Legend in Reverse": Two Classical Myths in the Story of Beren and Lúthien.' *Myth and Magic: Art According to the Inklings.* Eds. Eduardo Segura and Thomas Honegger. Zurich and Berne: Walking Tree Publishers, 143-85.

Light, Andrew. 2013. 'Tolkien's Green Time: Environmental Themes in *The Lord of the Rings.*' *The Lord of the Rings and Philosophy: One Book to Rule Them All.* Eds. Gregory Bassham and Eric Bronson. Chicago, LaSalle: Open Court, 150-63.

McMahon, Jennifer L. and B. Steve Csaki. 2013. 'Talking Trees and Walking Mountains: Buddhist and Taoist Themes in *The Lord of the Rings.*' *The Lord of the Rings and Philosophy: One Book to Rule Them All.* Eds. Gregory Bassham and Eric Bronson. Chicago, LaSalle: Open Court, 179-91.

Ovid. *Metamorphoses.* 2008. Transl. A.D. Melville. Oxford: Oxford University Press.

Neubauer, Łukasz. 2021. '"The Eagles are coming!": A Pneumatological Reinterpretation of the Old Germanic 'Beasts of Battle' Motif in the Works of J.R.R. Tolkien.' *Journal of Inklings Studies* 11.2, 169-92.

Nietzsche, Friedrich. 2003. *The Birth of Tragedy: Out of the Spirit of Music.* Transl. Shaun Whiteside. London: Penguin Books.

Obertino, James. 1993. 'Moria and Hades: Underworld Journeys in Tolkien and Virgil.' *Comparative Literature Studies* 30.2, 153-69.

Stevens, Benjamin E. 2017. 'Ancient Underworlds in J.R.R. Tolkien's *The Hobbit.*' *Classical Traditions in Modern Fantasy.* Eds. Brett M. Rogers and Ben Eldon Stevens. Oxford: Oxford University Press, 121-44.

2021. 'Middle-earth as Underworld: From *Katabasis* to Eucatastrophe.' *Tolkien and the Classical World.* Ed. Hamish Williams. Zurich and Jena: Walking Tree Publishers, 105-30.

Stevens, Jen. 2004. 'From Catastrophe to Eucatastrophe. J.R.R. Tolkien's Transformation of Ovid's Pyramus and Thisbe into Beren and Lúthien.' *Tolkien and the Invention of Myth: A Reader.* Ed. Jane Chance. Lexington, Kentucky: University of Kentucky Press, 119-32.

Sundt, Peter A. 2021. 'The Love Story of Orpheus and Eurydice in Tolkien's Orphic Middle-earth.' *Tolkien and the Classical World.* Ed. Hamish Williams. Zurich and Jena: Walking Tree Publishers, 165-89.

Tolkien, John Ronald Reuel. 2007. *The Hobbit, or There and Back Again.* London: HarperCollins.

1981. *The Letters of J.R.R. Tolkien.* Ed. Humphrey Carpenter with the assistance of Christopher Tolkien. London: George Allen & Unwin.

2005. *The Lord of the Rings. Part 1. The Fellowship of the Ring.* London: HarperCollins.

2005. *The Lord of the Rings. Part 2. The Two Towers.* London: HarperCollins.

2005. *The Lord of the Rings. Part 3. The Return of the King.* London: HarperCollins.

2014. *On Fairy-Stories.* Expanded edition, with commentary and notes. Eds. Verlyn Flieger and Douglas A. Anderson. London: HarperCollins.

2006. *The Silmarillion*. Ed. Christopher Tolkien. London: HarperCollins.

VINK, Renée. 2020. *Gleanings from Tolkien's Garden: Selected Essays*. Beverwijk: Uitgeverij Ijmond.

WILLIAMS, Hamish. 2018. 'Caradhras: Savage Nature Warrior, Servant of Sauron, or Character Projection? A Spatial Study of a Mountain in *The Fellowship of the Ring*.' *Lembas* 183, 181-88.

WILSON, Andrew N. 2005. *C.S. Lewis: A Biography*. London: HarperCollins.

Andrzej Wicher 

# The Liminality of J.R.R. Tolkien's Non-human Species: A View through the Lens of C.S. Lewis

**Abstract**

The following chapter intends to analyse what might be called the ontological status of Tolkien's non-human species, particularly concerning liminality. Remarkably, C.S. Lewis provides us with four medieval conceptions of fairies, two of which have a liminal character, while the other two are far less liminal, e.g. fairies are thought of as "a third rational species distinct from angels and men" (*DI* 134). Bearing in mind Tolkien's great familiarity with medieval culture, and also with Lewis's ideas, this paper will examine whether Lewis's classification of magical creatures works in the case of Tolkien's non-human and para-human species.

## The Fairies of the Model

In *The Discarded Image*, C.S. Lewis devotes the entire chapter 6 to a discussion of supernatural creatures that, for the sake of terminological simplicity, can be called the fairies. Interestingly, that part of his book is entitled 'The Longaevi,' the long-lived ones, or long-livers, apparently because this is the way the fairies are often referred to in medieval, or late antique, sources, such as *De nuptiis Philologiae et Mercurii* ('On the Marriage of Philology and Mercury') by Martianus Capella (*DI* 122). Already this terminology problematizes the very mode of existence of the fairies: are they genuinely immortal, or perhaps only long-lived? In Tolkien, for instance, we see the elves, or rather the Elves, who never die of advanced age; indeed, they do not even seem to grow old, their bodies enjoying a kind of eternal youth, though they can still be killed, for example on the battlefield.

We are naturally talking here about liminality, a rather elusive and ambiguous term, which can be defined as follows:

> While on the one hand the term can and must be given an extremely narrow and technical delimitation as belonging to the middle stage in concretely acted out ritual passages, on the other hand, it is also evident that liminality lends itself to a wider application, as the term captures something essential about the imprecise and unsettled situation of transitoriness. (Thomassen 2014: 2)

The above passage implies two kinds of liminality. First of all, there is temporal liminality, which here seems to refer to a character's transformation of usually ritualistic nature, connected with the process of his or her initiation or maturation. Secondly, we have spatial liminality, where the word 'spatial' can be understood metaphorically, and which consists in a character, or group of characters, inhabiting some kind of paradoxical territory that can be defined as a borderland between opposite values or qualities, such as good and evil, light and darkness, human and non-human, and so on.

It could be suggested that Tolkien's Elves are 'liminal,' first of all, because their mode of existence represents an intermediate stage between mortality and immortality, between being a slave of time, which is part of our human condition, and a situation where the passage of time means little or nothing in one's life. But this does not mean that they cannot also represent some other kinds of liminality. For example, some of the High Elves, the Ñoldor, and, in particular, their king Fëanor, while being sublime and noble creatures, are also capable of being tempted by the spirit of darkness that inspires them with an impious, arrogant and rebellious disposition. Consequently, they may be thought of as inhabiting a transition zone between good and evil.

But the first kind of liminality distinguished by Thomassen, the one which might be called temporal, and which is derived from Van Gennep's concept of transition rituals which are the central part of the rites of passage, is either absent, or does not figure prominently in the stories concerning directly the elves[1] or fairies. Directly, because there are many stories in which these creatures are figures of secondary importance, and which are focused on a human hero who has some dealings with the fairies (or, at least, with one fairy). In such stories, the motif of the transition rite will often be clearly present. Thus, for example, in the Middle English romance of *Sir Launfal*, belonging to the genre

1 I mean here naturally the elves as they appear in folklore, not Tolkien's Elves.

of the Breton lays,[2] the eponymous hero undergoes a process of maturation, involving his paying dearly for the mistakes he has made, but the fairy lady he is in love with is immune to change, and the same is generally true of similar supernatural characters, both in traditional or medieval stories, and in fantasy novels, such as those of Tolkien.

In the same chapter, Lewis says something important about the relationship between the fairies and what, throughout the book, he calls "the Model," or "the Medieval Model," that is the medieval worldview conceived of as a grand design in which all the observable and non-observable phenomena that the medieval mind could think of are brought together in a harmonious, and hierarchic, whole. He calls fairies "marginal, fugitive creatures," which, in the context of the following passage, seems to mean creatures that escape any rigid classification or hierarchy (*DI* 11-12). This effect of 'escaping' is itself, of course, another dimension of liminality:

> They [the fairies] are marginal, fugitive creatures. They are perhaps the only creatures to whom the Model does not assign, as it were, an official status. Herein lies their imaginative value. They soften the classic severity of the huge design. They intrude a welcome hint of wildness and uncertainty into a universe that is in danger of being a little too self-explanatory, too luminous. (*DI* 122)

The "uncertainty" the author is talking about appears not to have posed any danger to the stability of the Model. But this was not, perhaps, necessarily so, considering that the said Model was always less stable and reliable than it may have appeared and that it eventually collapsed, being unable to account convincingly for the scientific discoveries made in the sixteenth and seventeenth centuries. The fairies, in their modest way, also may be thought of as undermining the Model because the Model could not effectively explain their nature, their place in the system, and their reason for being.

The new rational worldview is dealt with the problem of fairies much more ruthlessly, simply rejecting their existence as based on superstition. But the belief in their objective existence, both in the Middle Ages and also in post-medieval times, was very widespread, though it perhaps became less so, which

2 Thomas Chestre's *Sir Launfal* is based on Marie de France's *Lanval*, but it is neither a translation nor a paraphrase of it.

is reflected by the fact that even in modern literature fairies often appear as creatures whose existence can hardly be questioned.

In the sub-created world of Tolkien's novels, *The Hobbit* and *The Lord of the Rings*, nobody questions the reality of magical species, so there is no possibility of their being subsumed under Tzvetan Todorov's category of the fantastic, which implies an ontological uncertainty as to a given character being magical, or supernatural:

> The fantastic occupies the duration of this uncertainty. Once we choose one answer or the other, we leave the fantastic for a neighbouring genre, the uncanny or the marvellous. The fantastic is that hesitation experienced by a person who knows only the laws of nature, confronting an apparently supernatural event. (Todorov 1975: 25)

The Elves, and other fantasy races, in Tolkien do not evoke the above-described ontological uncertainty, which places his represented world firmly in the zone of the marvellous, perhaps because nobody in Tolkien's constructed world pretends to know much about 'the laws of nature.' This, however, does not mean that the Elves are not connected with the feelings of uncertainty and disquiet. They represent the spirit of adventurousness, the qualities of the unfamiliar and the exotic, which are generally inimical to a peaceful and conventional way of life. Thus Bilbo Baggins, the protagonist of *The Hobbit*, can become a questing hero largely owing to his being related to the rather unpredictable Took family, who are said to have had some dealings with the fairies:

> It was often said (in other families) that long ago one of the Took ancestors must have taken a fairy wife. That was, of course, absurd, but certainly there was still something not entirely hobbit-like about them, and once in a while members of the Took-clan would go and have adventures. (*Hobbit* 14)

This situation can surely also be interpreted in terms of liminality. In Tolkien, apparently, we have what might be called an echo of Todorov's ontological (or, alternatively, social) liminality, which consists in a tendency to overstep the boundaries of one's routine and well-established existence. The taste for 'adventures,' and the tendency mysteriously to appear and to disappear, is then, from the very beginning, associated with magical species, in this particular case with the fairies, a word that is actually only rarely found in Tolkien's works, being usually replaced by the Elves. This species then represents the call to adventure, the call that only heroes can heed, even though it may cost them a lot. It must be emphasized, at the same time, though, that the elves or fairies are, as such, only catalysts of heroic adventures, and rarely play themselves the roles of heroes or heroines.

## Varieties of Fairies

In *The Discarded Image*, C.S. Lewis puts forward the following classification of fairies, using, as guidelines, three quotations from Milton. First, he talks about the "swart Faery," that is, the black fairy, that can be "classified among horrors" (124), and is mentioned, "among bugbears used to frighten children" (125), which suggests a thoroughly negative, indeed demonic and devilish, perception of both fairies and elves. Every reader of Katherine Briggs's *The Fairies in Tradition and Literature* should be familiar with the folk stories about mortals visiting Fairyland, who either become fairies themselves (itself a kind of enslavement), or, even if they are lucky enough to avoid this fate (for example by refusing to eat the fairy food), and are allowed to return to the place of their origin, they tend to "lose all interest in life" to "pine away" and "soon die" (Briggs 2015: 20-22). This kind of fairies seems to consist of spirits of the dead, and any contact with them is deadly.

Secondly, Lewis talks about "the minute and almost insectal fairies [...] with their antennae and gauzy wings" (*DI* 127). Such fairies cannot, of course, be as dangerous as the fairies of the first type; in fact, "these creatures flee from man, not man from them" (129), and they are "the fairies whom children are supposed to enjoy" (130). It is only natural to mention in this context Shakespeare's plays, in particular *A Midsummer Night's Dream*, with its vision of diminutive fairies (with names like Peaseblossom, Cobweb, Moth, and Mustardseed), which clearly refer to the above-mentioned insect-like condition of existence. Also the vision of Queen Mab in *Romeo and Juliet* (act I, scene 4, ll. 53-67), clearly belongs here because Mab is indeed referred to as being small and insect-like. The common denominator of such fairies, along with their small size, is an inclination towards mischief, towards practical jokes of all kinds, naturally embodied not only by Queen Mab, but also by Puck from *A Midsummer Night's* Dream. Mischievous fairies and other small (or not so small), supernatural creatures, such as dwarfs or goblins, are also well known in the folklore of many countries. So, perhaps Lewis was not quite right in characterizing these creatures as "fleeing from man" (*DI* 129), since they often only seem keen to avoid being seen by humans, which does not necessarily mean that they do not want to meddle with them (naturally, on their own terms). Their smallness, which in practice often amounts to invisibility, gives them plenty of opportunities to make whatever mischief they may be intent on and get away with it.

Thirdly, Lewis mentions what he calls "the High Fairies" (*DI* 130), that is, the fairies as they appear in most medieval romances and ballads, works like *Sir Gawain and the Green Knight*, *Sir Orfeo*, *Sir Launfal*, and *Thomas the Rhymer*. They could be seductive (if female), or bullying and overbearing (if male), but they are invariably beautiful and attractive, and they like to make a show of their opulence. To the mortals of their choice, they offer a share in their material prosperity and magical powers. Regardless of whether they are male or female, though, they do not like being thwarted or contradicted, let alone cheated, and they may easily turn nasty. In the words of Lewis, "[t]he High Fairies are vital, energetic, wilful, passionate beings" (132). Naturally, then, they are not midgets of any kind, but powerful beings of human-like size.

It is clear enough that all three kinds of fairies are dangerous for humans. But it is only the High Elves who seem to represent a third way between the opposite values of good and evil; they promise paradise, and sometimes seem to be able to fulfil this promise, but they are also perfectly capable of creating for humans a kind of hell, or leaving them in the lurch. The first two kinds are only different from each other in that the former are lethal, while the latter may cause problems that usually can be sorted out. The three kinds of fairies can also be interpreted in the context of literary, or rather folklore, genres. The 'black fairies' are likely to appear in local legends, where the elements of horror can often be encountered. In contrast, the 'diminutive' ones, with their love of practical jokes, are characteristic of humorous tales and anecdotes. And it is only the 'High Fairies' that can be encountered in fairy tales proper, also known as wondertales or tales of magic. They will figure there, most likely, as supernatural wives or husbands that mortal heroes or heroines fall in love with and whom they, usually after a long series of trials and setbacks, eventually succeed in disenchanting, by turning them into ordinary humans. A good example of such a tale is *The King of the Golden Mountain* from the Brothers Grimm's collection. But, characteristically enough, in the medieval stories mentioned by Lewis, such as *Sir Gawain and the Green Knight*, *Sir Orfeo*, *Sir Launfal*, and *Thomas the Rhymer*, there is no chance of disenchantment. A fairy, or fairy-like creature, in these stories, is much more likely to turn a human into a fairy, which is what presumably happens in *Sir Launfal* and *Thomas the Rhymer*, rather than the other way round.

This division into three kinds of fairies is followed in Lewis's book by a list of four theories concerning the 'nature' of fairies. In three of these theories, fairies have a clearly liminal, borderline, character, appearing (1) as "a third rational species distinct from angels and men;" (2) as "demoted angels," (that is to say, creatures hovering on the borderland between the unfallen angels and the devilish fallen ones); (3) and as "the dead, or some special class of the dead," (they may in fact be called the undead, that is the creatures occupying the threshold between life and death). Finally, fairies are theorized (4) as "fallen angels; in other words, devils" (*DI* 134-37). Only the last theory, being apparently an echo of the previously mentioned conception of the black fairies, is unequivocally non-liminal, as it places the fairies firmly beyond a threshold, in this case, the threshold of moral acceptability. As such, then, the devilish fairies are shown as only superficially different from 'ordinary' devils. But, concerning the first three, we may see that they represent two kinds of liminality: a straightforward one, so to speak, that is, involving a zone of transition between two more or less defined conditions of existence; here belong the second and third theories listed above. In the case of the first theory, however, that is the one that defines the fairies as "a third rational species" apart from men and angels (*DI* 134), we come across what might be called the *tertium quid* liminality, with the *tertium quid* understood as: "Something indefinite or left undefined related in some way to two definite or known things, but distinct from both" (*The New Shorter* 3259). In this last case, fairies are not depicted as situated half-way between angels and men, but as a species that has a quality and individuality of its own, a quality that cannot be deduced from any study of the nature of either men or angels.

## Tolkien's Elfland

It is quite well-known that, on the one hand, in his fiction, Tolkien avoided the term 'fairy,'[3] and its derivatives, but, on the other, he wrote a theoretical essay under the title 'On Fairy-stories,' which opens with the following two sentences:

> I propose to speak about fairy-stories, though I am aware that this is a rash adventure. Faërie is a perilous land, and in it are pitfalls for the unwary and dungeons for the overbold. (*TOFS* 9)

We can see immediately that Tolkien is interested primarily in 'Faërie,' that is to say, fairyland, rather than the fairies themselves. He dismisses the definition of the fairy-story as "a tale about fairies, or generally a fairy legend," rightly pointing to the fact that "fairy-stories are not in normal English usage stories about fairies or elves, but stories about Fairy, that is Faërie, the realm or state in which fairies have their being" (*TOFS* 14).

Characteristically enough, Tolkien goes on to define the fairyland, in a liminal fashion, as neither this nor that, making use of the late medieval ballad of *Thomas the Rhymer*. In that ballad, we see a vision of three roads: the broad road to Hell, the narrow path to Heaven, and the winding road to Elfland:

> And see not ye that bonny road,
> That winds about the fernie brae?
> That is the road to fair Elfland,
> Where thou and I this night maun gae [must go]. (*TOFS* 10)

The enchanted realm of fairies, or elves, is then a *tertium quid*, the third option, or, rather, an unidentified third element in combination with two known ones. Indeed, from a theological point of view, Elfland is an unidentified place, a no-place rather than a place. In this context, one could certainly mention Thomas More's *Utopia*; the Greek name of this imaginary and idealised country is Utopia, that is οὐτόπος, meaning 'no place.' Naturally, from an atheistic point of view, heaven and hell would also be non-existent places, but even from that point of view, the non-existence of Elfland is, so to speak, deeper, because it

3 The problem of Tolkien's use of the terms 'fairy' and 'elf' is thoroughly discussed in the article by Helios de Rosario Martínez, 'Fairy and Elves in Tolkien and Traditional Literature' (2010).

is not guaranteed or motivated by an established world view, fallacious as that may be. Various elflands and fairylands can be found in folktales, of course, but their status has rather consistently been on the margin of the mainstream culture, especially the culture based on writing.

But what about the consequences of the 'winding' status of Elfland? Surely, a winding road, instead of referring to something that is *neither* this nor that, may imply a condition of being *both* this and that. Tolkien introduces the above-quoted passage from *Thomas the Rhymer* by the following sentence: "The road to fairyland is not the road to Heaven; nor even to Hell, I believe, though some have held that it may lead thither indirectly by the Devil's tithe" (*TOFS* 10). This reference to "the devil's tithe" is naturally an allusion to the motif that appears in the ballad itself: "Ilka seven year, Thomas, / We pay our teindings unto hell, [...] I fear, Thomas, it will be yerself" (*Thomas the Rhymer* stanza 18), that is, the custom of the fairies to pay every seventh year a tribute to the devil. This tribute is called a tithe, or a *teind*, and it was the tenth part of one's income, or possessions, which was a customary amount paid by the landowners to the Church. But the fairies pay it rather to the deadly enemy of the Church, and, moreover, the tribute consists usually in a living person who should be left to the devil's tender mercies. It is small wonder, then, that they are thinking of sacrificing Thomas, the human hero of the ballad, in this way, since he is a stranger to the fairies, and it is always more convenient to sacrifice such a person than one of one's own people. Thus, even the poem chosen by Tolkien to illustrate the neutrality of the fairies, suggests that this fair Elfland is closer to Hell than to Heaven, even though its paradisiac nature makes it similar to heaven, especially the heaven that is conceived of as an idealised garden.

An even more sinister vision of the fairyland appears in the ballad *Tam Lin*. *Thomas the Rhymer* and *Tam Lin* are often considered in tandem because they share the basic motif of a mortal seduced by a fairy, or fairies considered as a group. *Tam Lin* shows a young boy's adventure in Fairyland, while *Thomas the Rhymer* concentrates on an adult who has achieved some kind of fame. For Thomas, there is no hope; he has to stay with the fairies, or, perhaps, with the devils, while Tam Lin is saved by a girl who is in love with him and who can, through a heroic personal sacrifice, break the circle of enchantment that separates Tam Lin from the world of his fellow human beings. In both ballads, we also come across the motif of 'the devil's tithe;' in other words, there is a high likelihood that both Thomas and Tam Lin will be sacrificed to the devil on the strength of an ancient contract between Fairyland and Hell.

In this light, it seems possible to postulate that the liminality of Tolkien's Elfland is, so to speak, reduplicated. On the one hand, it has the nature of a *tertium quid*, something that escapes the traditional categorization. On the other hand, however, it is a liminality defined by a tendency to reduce this tertium quid to one of the familiar categories. We can see this phenomenon when we look at the status of Elfland and the Elves in *The Lord of the Rings*, as well as, of course, elsewhere in Tolkien. The enchanted land of Lórien has many paradisiac features. Urlin Milo Kaufmann, for instance, talks about "the presence of an all-sustaining spring, in a forest that never loses its mystery" (2003: 145). Clearly, this is a dynamic paradise, the inhabitants, far from being immersed in some kind of lethargic existence that the denizens of the Christian Heaven are often suspected of, often use their superior skills to fight off malicious orcs and other servants of Sauron. But, of course, fighting means that some of them may die, bearing in mind that, although they are essentially immortal, that is, incapable of dying either of illness or old age, the Elves can still be killed.

Besides fighting, Tolkien's Elves also pursue many other, more peaceful, artistic activities. They can create beautiful objects, such as the Silmarils but it is also the Elvish smiths of Eregion and their leader Celebrimbor who have forged many magical rings, with the exception of the sinister One Ring, forged in secret by Sauron. Yet even though, unlike the Ring, the Silmarils are not intrinsically evil, they are ultimately associated with envy and war. Fëanor, their creator, is devoured by pride and possessiveness and lets himself become an unwitting agent of Melkor, the spirit of darkness, who retains for some time his enchanting appearance, but eventually turns into Morgoth, whose outward form also becomes off-putting. In Fëanor, the beauty of the Elves becomes paradoxically synonymous with the ugliness of Morgoth and his servants. Instead of the 'devil's tithe,' that is the tenth part, we may feel that the whole of Elfland runs the danger of becoming the devil's own. A taste of this is included also in *The Lord of the Rings*, where we can observe a (potential) transformation of Lady Galadriel into an evil Empress of the World, in practice again associated with Sauron, who plays the same role as Melkor. Thus the 'thirdness' of the Elfland is being constantly threatened by forces that pull it in either the direction of Heaven, or that of Hell.

On the other hand, in 'On Fairy-stories,' Tolkien also launches the idea of *eucatastrophe*, which seems symmetrical and antithetical to that of 'the devil's tithe,' even though we also find there the notion of dyscatastrophe as its more obvious antithesis. Eucatastrophe is connected with "the Consolation of the Happy Ending," the exact opposite to a tragedy (*TOFS* 62), though, above all, it is "a sudden and miraculous grace: never to be counted on to recur" (62). Thus, we have, in *The Lord of the Rings*, visions of two very powerful champions of the cause, Gandalf and Galadriel, potentially joining the forces of evil, a possibility realized in the case of Saruman. Gollum, however, may serve as an example of a completely corrupt creature who is not redeemed, but still used, in a paradoxical way, to achieve the main eucatastrophe of the book, and whose contribution to this purpose is indispensable.[4]

## Liminality Reconsidered

But liminality is not only understood in spatial terms; it is also, more typically, a temporal phenomenon referring to a moral transformation or evolution, as in Van Gennep's classic interpretation of the rite of passage:

> Every rite of passage marking a person's change from one status to another [...] was outlined by the stages of separation, transition, and incorporation. During the transition phase one is in a liminal state, outside the margins of society, no longer one thing, but not yet another. Thus, separation from the group is necessary because, in the stage of transition, one may be ritually impure or dangerous. (Douglas 2008: 488n)

It seems that the last stage, that of incorporation, can sometimes be seen as re-integration, when the initiand, instead of joining a group he or she aspires to, wants to confirm or deepen his or her belonging to a group of which they are already members. It is clearly this, more conservative and more adult, model of initiation that can be seen in *The Hobbit* and *The Lord of the Rings*. Neither Bilbo nor Frodo are interested in joining any other society than that of the

4 David Callaway in his article 'Gollum: A Misunderstood Hero' (1984) sees this matter very differently, but I find it impossible to agree with him.

Hobbits, of which they already, even at the beginning of the plot, are long-standing members. But it can be argued that they want to prove to themselves, and to others, that they really deserve the privileges they already enjoy. Neither can we perceive any element of 'impurity' in their being separated from the Hobbit community, probably because during that separation they are not really isolated, but rather join other, equally or even more respectable, communities, those of Dwarves, Elves, heroic Men, or wizards. It is true, however, that neither Bilbo nor Frodo become fully re-integrated with the Hobbit society. They are respected, but feel ill at ease, which, in the case of Frodo, means actually falling seriously ill. The process of re-integration in the case of the other questing Hobbits, Merry, Pippin and Sam, is much successful.

Another well-known scheme that may be applied to the protagonists of Tolkien's novels is that of Joseph Campbell's monomyth, as expounded in his seminal book *The Hero with a Thousand Faces.* It is not essentially different from Van Gennep's tripartite conception, but it may be considered a little more useful, from my point of view at least, as it contains the notion of "the ultimate boon" (Campbell 1993: 172), or "the life transmuting trophy" (193), and defines the rite of passage as "a separation from the world, a penetration to some source of power, and a life-enhancing return" (35). Campbell's formulation allows us to realize the paradoxicality of Tolkien's version of the monomyth, especially as it appears in *The Lord of the Rings*, and also its paradoxical liminality. In Tolkien, the matters are, to a large extent, turned upside down. The task of the hero is not to find, but rather to lose, and to be freed from a 'source of power,' while his return is not so much 'life-enhancing' as 'life-diminishing.'

As has been indicated, at the beginning of *The Hobbit*, Bilbo is described as a person internally divided, disintegrated, torn between the style of life prevalent in the family of his father, the Bagginses, and that of the Tooks, the slightly unpredictable Hobbits on his mother's side of the family:

> Still, it is probable that Bilbo, her only son, although he looked and behaved exactly like a second edition of his solid and comfortable father, got something a bit queer in his makeup from the Took side, something that only waited for a chance to come out. (*Hobbit* 5)

The ritual of initiation he undertakes as a member of a very dangerous expedition organized by the wizard Gandalf and a group of adventurous Dwarves is thus not merely a test of his prowess and maturity, but also a way for him to become a more integrated personality, with his solid and 'queer' side made to cooperate with each other, rather than having, as is the case at the beginning of the story, one of them almost completely suppressed by the other. In this way, Tolkien emphasizes a psychological dimension of the ritual of initiation, which is usually seen from a sociological point of view.

Bilbo could thus be seen as a liminal character, since he undergoes a transformation from a comfort-loving middle-class Hobbit to a daring, but not foolhardy, 'burglar.' However, there is nothing in his portrait that shows him as a supernatural character who inhabits or represents an essentially different zone of existence. He may rub shoulders with magical characters and monsters of all kinds, but this does not make him in any way similar to them; he remains eminently identifiable as 'one of us,' even though, strictly speaking, he is not a human being.

Moreover, the 'Took side' of Bilbo's ancestry may be connected with his being of partly Elvish descent. In the represented world of Tolkien's books, there is naturally nothing absurd about a mortal hero falling in love with a fairy (or, rather, Elvish) woman. One may easily recollect the stories of Beren and Lúthien, or Aragorn and Arwen, where the decision of the Elvish (or half-Elvish, in the case Arwen) heroine to marry a mortal is connected with her renunciation of immortality, an essential part of her Elvish nature. The Hobbits may be thought of as too prosaic (and, perhaps, also too short), to attract the erotic interest of a female Elf, or of one of Lewis's High Fairies, but the branch (or race) of the Hobbits known as Fallohides, to which both Bilbo and his nephew Frodo belong, is known to have some friends among the Elves.

What, however, makes the Hobbits less exotic than other non-human species in Tolkien's legendarium is the fact that they are mortal, even though they usually live a little longer than the humans, and can easily survive in good health until they are about 120. Consequently, Bilbo's and Frodo's adventures may be regarded as liminal only in the psychological, rather than ontological, sense. This psychological liminality seems capable of turning at least some of Tolkien's characters into what E.M. Forster called "round characters" as opposed to "flat" ones: "The test of a round character is whether it is capable of surprising in a convincing way. If it never surprises, it is flat. If it does not convince, it is a flat pretending to be round" (1962: 85). It is naturally impossible for everybody to agree that a given character "surprises in a convincing way." And, generally speaking, the mythological and folkloristic characters that undergo something similar to the initiation ritual can hardly be called round in the Forsterian sense. But matters may be different in the case of Tolkien's protagonists. This difference is probably connected with their being genuinely unprepared and rather poorly qualified to perform the role of heroes. Eventually, they do become heroes, but in a slightly paradoxical sense of the word because they never become great fighters, and, if they sometimes perform magic, using for example the One Ring, they never do it to gain some worldly success.

It is not so, however, with the mythological or folkloristic heroes, who are only apparently unsuited to fulfil their heroic roles, even though they may resort to cunning, rather than to physical strength. In Vladimir Propp's formulation:

> The hero is the one who wins, irrespective of the means, especially if he defeats a stronger opponent. Perhaps this is why most of such tales turn on making a fool of someone. The same holds true for animal tales and partly for wondertales. Intellect and cunning are the strength of a weak person: with these qualities, the hero overcomes a stronger enemy. (1984: 28)

Max Lüthi emphasizes the hero's weakness even more strongly:

> It is the poor peasant boy, who sets out without any help, any preparation, any special qualities, to solve unsolvable problems, that becomes the object of interest of powerful forces that lead him to his destination. The blind, the disinherited, the youngest, the orphan, the one who has got lost, these are the true heroes of the wondertale, for their isolation makes them open to really essential contacts. (1985: 61)[5]

And yet, in spite of their paradoxicality, all these heroes are, from Forster's point of view, 'flat characters,' in that they do not significantly change. Once their often hidden heroic potential is revealed, they behave in a perfectly predictable way and follow the shortest possible route to the final success.

---

5 The translation of this passage from the German is mine.

Tolkien's Hobbit heroes are then liminal and "round" in that they represent unlikely heroes. A good illustration of that may be the character of Frodo, who becomes even more fundamentally liminal when he refuses to fulfil his task at the Crack of Doom and claims the Ring for himself. Frodo's mission is thus nearly completed, happening, as it were, in spite of himself, even though it would be unfair to say that he did not contribute to the success of this mission. Evidently, the scheme proposed by Van Gennep fails to function in Frodo's case. After all, how can the hero be 'incorporated' or 're-incorporated' if he actually falls short of the expectations of those who entrusted him with a difficult task?

And, indeed, following his return to the Shire, Frodo is hardly capable of once again becoming a regular member of the Hobbit society:

> 'Alas! there are some wounds that cannot be wholly cured,' said Gandalf.
> 'I fear it may be so with mine,' said Frodo. 'There is no real going back. Though I may come to the Shire, it will not seem the same; for I shall not be the same. I am wounded with knife, sting, and tooth, and a long burden. Where shall I find rest?' (*RK* 989)

The wound that Frodo is suffering from is clearly both physical and psychological. His predicament may easily remind one of the already mentioned fate of those mortals who, after their return from Elfland, "pined and lost all interest in life" (Briggs 2015: 22) and died very soon. However, such figures are typical of local legends; this is not the fate of mythological and folktale heroes who, like Orfeo (in the anonymous Middle English poem *Sir Orfeo*), or *Beowulf*,[6] return from the Otherworld with renewed strength, even though folktale heroes often have problems connected with their coming back home. For example, the rather naïve protagonists of the well-known Grimms' tale 'The Table, the Ass, and the Stick'[7] are regularly cheated by a dishonest inn-keeper on their way home, so that they arrive without the magic object, or animal, on which their reputation rested. Frodo also returns without the magic means he previously possessed (though it would perhaps be more correct to say that it possessed him). But his having successfully got rid of it, is not a token of shame. It is his crowning glory.

---

6 Beowulf's descent into the underwater cave is meant here. The cave, where he kills Grendel's Mother, may not be the Otherworld in the strict sense of the word, but it is a very exotic and strongly magical place, where Beowulf finds a magic sword

7 The tale is also known in English as 'The Wishing-Table, the Gold-Ass, and the Cudgel in the Sack.'

It is the awareness of the value of self-denial, rather than of personal, or even interpersonal, aggrandizement, that apparently gives Frodo this aspect of a round character, a character that changes rather unexpectedly and significantly, and not merely by revealing his hidden possibilities. Saruman, the wise, if also evil, wizard, seems genuinely surprised (though it is certainly not a pleasant surprise) by Frodo's evolution, a symptom of which is Frodo's merciful decision to let Saruman go, in spite of his malicious nature and even more malicious deeds, one of which is an attempt to murder Frodo:

> Saruman rose to his feet, and stared at Frodo. There was a strange look in his eyes of mingled wonder and respect and hatred. 'You have grown, Halfling,' he said. 'Yes, you have grown very much. You are wise, and cruel. You have robbed my revenge of sweetness, and now I must go hence in bitterness, in debt to your mercy. I hate it and you! Well, I go and I will trouble you no more. But do not expect me to wish you health and long life. You will have neither. But that is not my doing. I merely foretell.' (*RK* 1019)

This act of pardon may be naturally seen as a symptom of Frodo's diminished vitality, but Saruman is probably right when he attributes it to the Hobbit's increased wisdom. It should clearly be seen in conjunction with a similar display of magnanimity towards Gollum, a creature of a lesser order than Saruman, and someone whose harmfulness is more potential than real, but who is still dangerous enough, especially if he were to succeed in his obsessive ambition to get back the Ring. Frodo spares Gollum, having been previously encouraged to do so by Gandalf, and we may assume that Gandalf would have also advised Frodo to show some mercy to Saruman, who, despite his degeneration and moral corruption, is still, like Gandalf, a Maia, that is a superhuman being, and, again like Gandalf, a member of the order of wizards, the so called Istari.

Saruman's words, quoted above, are also interesting in that he foretells Frodo's approaching and untimely death. Strictly speaking, Frodo departs, after two years, to Valinor, a kind of earthly paradise, belonging to the so-called Undying Lands of the Uttermost West. Frodo is accompanied in his voyage to Valinor by Bilbo, the protagonist of *The Hobbit*, and a host of supernatural and magical figures, the most prominent among them being Gandalf, Galadriel and Elrond. It may be considered unwise to say that they all just die, and the whole voyage is merely an elaborate metaphor invented to somehow sweeten and obfuscate the prosaic fact of their demise, but there is little doubt that this departure is felt like death by those who stay alive and witness it. The last words said by Gandalf in the book are addressed to them: "Go in peace! I will not say: do not weep, for not all tears are an evil" (*RK* 1030). But it would not be quite adequate to say that the book ends then with a tearful scene of parting, of disintegration, rather than anything resembling Van Gennep's integration. After all, the very last words in *The Lord of the Rings*, uttered by Sam, Frodo's closest friend, are: "Well, I'm back" (1031), which suggests an interplay of integration, re-integration, and disintegration. It seems legitimate enough to conclude that this complex interplay is an important aspect of Tolkien's rethinking of the idea of liminality.

## Conclusion

Let us now try to draw some conclusions from the foregoing discussion of liminality in Tolkien's work. Liminality itself is not always easy to define or grasp. It can be looked upon in predominantly temporal (dynamic) or spatial (static) terms. Liminality involves a movement, or a state of affairs, between two notions logically opposed to each other, such as life and death, youth and maturity, heaven and hell, mortality and immortality, East and West, femininity and masculinity. Usually, one of those opposites is treated as, in some sense, 'better' or 'superior' to the other, for example, life is commonly (though not always) regarded as infinitely preferable to death.

The liminality of Tolkien's Elves, with respect to their mortality or immortality, is, to some extent, paradoxical, first of all, because they cannot be thought of as completely mortal or immortal. To understand this, it may be helpful to refer to the medieval notion of the 'Longaevi' (long-livers), used by C.S. Lewis in *The Discarded Image*. Secondly, the notions of life and death in Tolkien's work, even though, in a way, they do not seem to be quite compatible with mainstream Christian (or Catholic) theology, are not so neatly opposed to each other as we might expect: death may be represented as a gift, and immortality as a curse, associated with weariness, which itself may be described as a liminal state of affairs between life and death.

The reflections of the Longaevi that could be glimpsed in the works of Lewis and Tolkien may lead to the conclusion that liminality, particularly that of the static and spatial kind, may be divided into further two varieties:

(1) The straightforward liminality where the element of 'in-betweenness' is emphasized. For example, Tolkien's Ents inhabit the conceptual space between human beings and trees; the Ents also show that spatial and temporal liminality may be combined, since they are sometimes observed to be in the process of becoming ordinary trees.

(2) The *tertium quid* liminality where the element of 'being between' is pushed into the background, as it were, and what we have in the foreground is a new 'third' quality that cannot be accounted for as a mixture or amalgamation of the two opposites. For example, the Elfland in the Middle English romance *Sir Orfeo* shares some features of both heaven and hell, and yet combines them in an unexpected way. Tolkien's vision of the enchanted Land of Lórien in *The Lord of the Rings* is different because the paradisiac elements are predominant there, though not in full, since Lórien is, in a sense, besieged by the forces of darkness, while the queen of Lórien, the mighty 'witch' Galadriel, even though a very positive character, feels in herself the potential and temptation to turn this heaven into hell, or even to become a demonic ruler of entire Middle-earth.

Also very important for a proper understanding of Tolkien's approach to liminality is also his essay 'On Fairy-stories,' and, particularly, the vision of the three roads based on the popular Scottish ballad *Thomas the Rhymer.* Of particular importance here seems to be the notion of 'the devil's tithe,' that is the sacrifice of an outsider, deemed less valuable, to the forces of darkness. On a more theoretical plane, it may denote an admixture of the sinister in a seemingly idealised environment. This sinister element may be represented as a person, such as the doomed hero Túrin in the Elvish kingdom of Nargothrond.

The notion of the devil's tithe has its counterpart in the concept of eucatastrophe. First introduced in the same essay, it may perhaps figuratively be called the angel's tithe, as it involves an apparently doomed and unredeemable character or cause. A good example, in *The Lord of the Rings*, is the figure of Gollum, who, in spite of his 'utter depravity,' is essential in achieving the world-saving mission of the Ring-bearer.

As regards what has been called the dynamic liminality, it is also worth emphasizing the permutations, sometimes quite radical, of such schemes as Van Gennep's rite of passage, and Campbell's monomyth. It is largely owing to these permutations, consisting in amalgamating various fantastic genres, such as the fairy tale and the local legend, that Tolkien's works, especially *The Lord of the Rings*, gain in psychological depth, something that is not so frequently achieved in fantasy literature.

Finally, it should be remarked that various characters and species in the works of Tolkien may represent not only a different kind but also a different degree of liminality. These factors condition the quality of Tolkien's Legendarium, which could be compared with C.S. Lewis's conception of the Model, where supernatural, and liminal creatures, are also included as the most dynamic and unpredictable ingredient. Hence, the Elves may seem more liminal than either Dwarves or Hobbits, in the sense, first of all, that they are more mobile, mysterious and versatile. A connection with the Elves usually does good to the other two non-human races, who often tend to be too well set in their ways. Generally, interspecial (or interspecific) links are shown in a positive light in Tolkien, as long, however, as they concern the Free Peoples of the West. If not, we get, for example, the orcs, whose condition is also liminal (they may be thought of as a cross between the Elves and some artificial 'robots'), but, from Tolkien's point of view, there is nothing positive in this liminality.

## About the Author

Andrzej Wicher is professor in the Institute of English Studies at Łódź University where he lectures on the history of English literature and literary theory. His academic interests include medieval and Renaissance studies, cultural studies and modern fantasy literature. He published three monographs, including *Archaeology of Sublime, Studies in Late Medieval English Writings* (1995), *Shakespeare's Parting Wondertales: A Study in the Elements of the Tale of Magic in William Shakespeare's Late Plays* (2003) and *Selected Medieval and Religious Themes in the Works of C.S. Lewis and J.R.R. Tolkien* (2013). In 1997, he also published a volume of Polish translations of Middle English literary works including *Sir Gawain and the Green Knight* and *Pearl*. Andrzej Wicher took part in many international conferences and various academic exchange programmes as a visiting lecturer at a number of British universities. He is also a member of the International Shakespeare Association, PASE (Polish Association for the Study of English), and the Scholarly Society in Łódź.

## Bibliography

Briggs, Katharine. 2015. *The Fairies in Tradition and Literature.* London and New York: Routledge.

Callaway, David. 1984. 'Gollum: Misunderstood Hero.' *Mythlore 10.*3, 14-22.

Campbell, Joseph. 1993. *The Hero with a Thousand Faces.* London: Fontana Press.

De Rosario Martínez, Helios. 2010. 'Fairy and Elves in Tolkien and Traditional Literature.' *Mythlore* 28.3, 65-84.

Douglas, Mary. 2008. 'External Boundaries.' *Anthropological Theory: Introductory History.* Eds. R. Jon McGee and Richard Warms. San Marcos: McGraw-Hill Publishing, 484-93.

Forster, Edward Morgan. 1962. *Aspects of the Novel.* Harmondsworth, Middlesex: Penguin Books.

Grimm, Jakob and Wilhelm Grimm. 1993. *Grimms' Fairy Tales.* Ware, Hertfordshire: Wordsworth Editions.

Kaufmann, Urlin Milo. 2003. 'Aspects of the Paradisiacal in Tolkien's Work.' *A Tolkien Compass.* Ed. Jared Lobdell. Chicago and La Salle, IL: Open Court Publishing, 141-58.

Lewis, Clive Staples. 1964. *The Discarded Image. An Introduction to Medieval and Renaissance Literature.* Cambridge: Cambridge University Press.

Lüthi, Max. 1985. *Das europäische Volksmärchen. Form und Wesen.* Tübingen: Francke Verlag.

*The New Shorter Oxford English Dictionary On Historical Principles.* 1993. Ed. Lesley Brown. Oxford: Oxford University Press.

Propp, Vladimir. 1984. *Theory and History of Folklore.* Transl. Ariadna Y. Martin and Richard P. Martin. Ed. Anatoly Liberman. Manchester: Manchester University Press.

*Tam Lin.* https://en.wikipedia.org/wiki/Tam_Lin. Accessed 1 Aug. 2020.

'Thomas the Rhymer.' *The English and Scottish Popular Ballads.* 1892. Part VIII. Ed. Francis James Child. Boston: Houghton Mifflin, 455.

Thomassen, Bjørn. 2014. *Liminality and the Modern: Living Through the In-Between.* Farnham: Ashgate Publishing.

Todorov, Tzvetan. 1975. *The Fantastic: A Structural Approach to a Literary Genre.* Transl. Richard Howard. Ithaca, New York: Cornell University Press.

Tolkien, John Ronald Reuel. 2007. *The Hobbit, or There and Back Again*. London: HarperCollins.

2005. *The Lord of the Rings. Part 3. The Return of the King*. London: HarperCollins.

1992. 'On Fairy-Stories.' *Tree and Leaf (Including the Poem 'Mythopoeia')*. Ed. Christopher Tolkien. London: Grafton, 3-81.

Van Gennep, Arnold. 1960. *The Rites of Passage*. Transl. Monika B. Vizedom and Gabrielle L. Caffee. Chicago: University of Chicago Press.

Franz Georg Árpád Klug

# "Ye are of your father the devil": Satanic Figures in Arda and Narnia

**Abstract**

The main purpose of this chapter is to establish how far the major villains in the works of J.R.R. Tolkien and C.S. Lewis such as, for instance, the dark Vala Morgoth and the White Witch Jadis might be viewed as satanic figures, in varying degrees inspired by the Christian tradition of the devil. In doing so, this chapter will highlight the similarities and differences between Tolkien's and Lewis's devilish archvillains, while investigating the different diabolical aspects of the characters in question. Examining in what manner Tolkien and Lewis have these evildoers influence their fictional worlds of Arda and Narnia might shed more light on this topic of investigation. The archvillains in those worlds do not only seem to pursue typically satanic activities, corrupting lands, nature and peoples alike, but they also appear to inadvertently act as eucatastrophic vehicles which, in contrast to their evil intentions, contribute to the triumph of the side of Good. In this spirit, the chapter at hand is also devoted to analysing how Tolkien's and Lewis's diabolic evildoers might reflect the two authors' respective conceptions of the nature of Evil. Finally, this chapter is concerned with the question of how far such satanic figures reflect Tolkien's and Lewis's distinctive approaches towards sub-creation.

"Ye are of your father the devil, and the lusts of your father ye will do" (John 8:44). With this rebuke, delivered against the religious leaders who rejected His teachings and were guilty of lies, resistance to the truth, and murder – deeds typically associated with devilry – Jesus consequently marks His enemies as the spiritual children of the devil. In a transferred sense, one thus could argue that the infamous figure of Satan spawned many diabolical characters in literature who share common traits with their 'father,' the epitome of Evil. Perhaps it is because the devil and his henchmen are invariably central to the questions regarding the origins and nature of Evil that such devilish characters[1] never cease to fascinate authors and readers alike.

In the course of their artistic pursuit, Tolkien and Lewis seem, to varying degrees, to have been inspired by notions of the very personal devil and the diabolical in general when creating their highly memorable archvillains. In fact, the fantasy worlds of Arda and Narnia each appear to be infested by a triplicity of satanic figures. Tolkien presents us with the sinister Vala Melkor-Morgoth, the corrupted Maia Sauron and the fallen Istar Saruman in *The Silmarillion* (1977) and *The Lord of the Rings* (1954-55), whereas in *The Chronicles of Narnia* (1950-56) we encounter Jadis the White Witch, the Lady of the Green Kirtle and the vulture-like demon god Tash. This chapter is concerned with highlighting the similarities and differences between Tolkien's and Lewis's devilish archvillains. With this in mind, it will seek to investigate the extent to which these prominent villains in the Secondary Worlds of Arda and Narnia were modelled on the figure of Satan as he came to be portrayed in the Christian tradition. Moreover, it will reflect upon how these diabolical villains mirror Tolkien's and Lewis's views on the nature of Evil, and how their composition also reflects the authors' techniques of sub-creation.

---

1 Examples for such prominent diabolical characters would be, for instance, Professor Woland in Bulgakov's *Master and Margarita*, Lord Voldemort in the *Harry Potter* series, the Emperor Palpatine from *Star Wars*, or Baron Lived in James Krüss' *Timm Thaler*. Concerning direct inspirations for Tolkien's work in terms of diabolical figures he might have been familiar with, the following characters from mythology, legend and folklore are worth mentioning: the Formorian ruler Balor of the Evil Eye from Celtic mythology and Janibas the Wizard from the Dietrich of Bern cycle, both of whom might have served as models for Sauron. Also, the Norse trickster Loki and Milton's Satan from *Paradise Lost* may have influenced the depiction of Morgoth. In the case of Morgoth, his theft of the Silmaril might also point to the witch Louie from the *Kalevala* as a possible source of inspiration. Finally, the evil wizard Archimago from Spenser's *Faerie Queene* might have served as a model for Saruman.

## The Satanic Fall in Tolkien's and Lewis's Realms of Imagination

One might pose a question why, as Christian authors, Tolkien and Lewis appear to have shown such great interest in the powers of darkness and their devilish representatives. The answer to this question seems to lie in the two authors' attempt to engage with the nature of Evil and the reasons for human sinfulness. Both Lewis and Tolkien appear to have been regularly preoccupied with the concept of the Original Sin, the Fall of Adam and Eve. Lewis's speculative consideration of the scenario – "Suppose, even now, in some other planet there were a first couple undergoing the same that Adam and Eve underwent there, but successfully" (qtd. in Hooper 2005: 424) led to the novel *Perleandra* in which the Fall on the planet Venus is successfully averted by the protagonist Elwin Ransom. Lewis also appears to allude a number of times to the Fall of the first human couple within *The Chronicles of Narnia*. Tolkien viewed the Fall as a central and common element of fiction, stating that there could not "be any 'story' without a fall – all stories are ultimately about the fall – at least not for human minds as we know them and have them" (*Letters* 147, #131). In keeping with the important role Tolkien assigns to the Fall, he alludes to the Original Sin several times within his work, where the Elves and Men are guilty of comparably fatal misconducts. The very first being to fall by disobeying divine authority is the Vala Melkor who opposes his Creator already in the first book of *The Silmarillion*.

In some of his letters, Tolkien refers to Melkor as "the Diabolus" (*Letters* 195, #153; 283, #211) or "satanic demon" (206, #156). Indeed, he appears to be the Tolkienian archvillain most closely modelled on Satan. He classifies Melkor as a character type from mythology, "the inevitable Rebel and self-worshipper of mythologies that begin with a transcendent unique Creator" (259, #200). Thus, Tolkien clarifies that Melkor's bearing is that of a rebel against the order of the Maker, Eru Ilúvatar, which makes him comparable to Satan and his rebellion against God. Melkor is one of the Ainur, angel-like[2] entities created by Eru

2 For a more in-depth examination of the Ainur, see, in particular *Letters* (131, #117); cf. Wood (2003: 13).

and might be said to resemble the Choirs of Angels[3] in the Christian tradition. Much as Satan, who is often interpreted as the former leading archangel, Melkor is originally the greatest and most powerful among the Ainur.[4] In *The Silmarillion*, it is during the Great Music of the Ainur that Melkor disobeys Eru by introducing what he perceives to be his own melodies into the themes predetermined by the father of gods. Tolkien emphasizes the similarity between Melkor's and Satan's uprising by referring to the disobedience of the former as an act of "Satanic rebellion" (*Letters* 202, #156). As is the case with Satan, Melkor's act of disobedience seems to have been motivated by his pride and self-love. Melkor hungers for personal fulfilment as a creator and seeks to obtain the Flame Imperishable,[5] the power of creation wielded by Eru.

Melkor tries to challenge the Music of the Ainur but fails to dominate let alone surpass the musical themes of Ilúvatar, and is thus reprimanded by Eru (*Sil* 5). Tolkien stresses the fact that whereas Satan fell when the world had already been brought into being by God, in his myth Melkor fell before the Creation

3 The Choirs of Angels constitute the so-called celestial hierarchies. In the Bible, nine groups of angels are mentioned. The best-known Christian hierarchy of angels was listed by Pseudo-Dionysius (Dionysius the Areopagite). In her *Encyclopedia of Angels*, Rosemary Guiley elaborates that according to the "Pseudo-Dionysian scheme, the hierarchy of nine choirs is split into three tiers. The higher tiers possess all of the wisdom, abilities, and illumination of the lower tiers, which in turn depend upon the immediate higher choirs for dispensation of the light and love of God. In the highest tier, the seraphim, cherubim, and thrones receive illumination directly from God and send it down through the layers. The second tier of virtues, dominions and powers are concerned with heavenly order, the ruling of other angels and miracles. The third and lowest tier of principalities, archangels and angels are concerned with the affairs of humanity" (2004: 79). Thomas Aquinas, one of the most influential theologians of the Church, adopted Pseudo-Dionysius's celestial hierarchy several centuries later suggesting that Satan was a fallen cherub. The Bible seems to give no definitive answer as to whether the Choirs of Angels actually sing, as Tolkien's Ainur do. There are, however, several passages which are frequently interpreted in that way including Rev 5:9 and Luke 2:13-14. The most succinct passage in this respect would be Job 38:7, which reads that at the Creation of the world "the morning stars sang together and all the angels shouted for joy." If the morning stars are interpreted as angels, then this scene might be viewed as the original song of the spheres which inspired Tolkien's music of the Ainur and Lewis's creation scene which depicts the Lion Aslan shaping the world through his divine songs.

4 Tolkien later states that the Ainur Manwë, Melkor's brother, was equally powerful, but this power relation seems not to have been in place from the beginning and might rather be viewed as the result of Melkor's gradually dwindling powers after his Fall (*Sil* 19). Similar to the Archangel Michael, who became the most powerful angel after Satan's banishment and to whom Manwë is often compared, took the place of the now corrupted head of the Ainur.

5 In this respect, Melkor might be said to vaguely resemble the Titan Prometheus from Greek mythology who successfully stole the element of fire from Zeus and gave it to mankind as a gift. Fire was viewed as a divine and creative force that the Olympian god intended to keep from the humans. Like Melkor, Prometheus was a rebel figure against the divine rule, disobeying the orders of the father of gods. In that way, Prometheus is portrayed as a regular trickster in *Theogony*. However, in some later versions of the story, Prometheus is presented in a far more positive light, bestowing the gift of fire on mankind out of compassion.

of the physical world (*Letters* 243, #183). He does not further specify the exact moment of Melkor's Fall, so that "before the Creation of the physical world" could either refer to Melkor's actual act of disobedience during the Great Music or to the moment when he consciously decided upon "bring[ing] into Being things of his own" (*Sil* 4). In contrast to Satan, however, there is no discernible Fall in the form of Melkor's expulsion from the heavenly kingdom, and his transformation into the "Prime Dark Lord" (*Letters* 191, #153) is not as abrupt as that of Satan's, but is, instead, spread over several phases of corruption.

It is Melkor's own, Eru-given free will that makes him progressively descend "through fire and wrath into a great burning, down into Darkness" (*Sil* 19), and he turns out to be the instrument of his own punishment. Consequently, one could argue that Melkor's Fall is continuous, each new malfeasance plunging him deeper into the abyss. Having already sown the seeds of discord prior to the actual creation of Arda, by introducing disharmony into Eru's musical themes, Melkor seeks to impose his rule on the other Valar, exclaiming "this shall be my own kingdom; and I name it unto myself" (*Sil* 8). His hubristic attitude, therefore, resembles that of Satan who, according to Isaiah, exclaimed: "I will ascend into heaven, I will exalt my throne above the stars of God: I will sit also upon the mount of the congregation, in the sides of the north" (14:13). Melkor's claim is, however, rejected by his brother Manwë. Being truly fascinated by the glorious incarnations of his fellow Valar and the fruits of their labour, Melkor is, therefore, like Satan, roused by the feeling of envy (*Sil* 9). He then sets about disrupting the work of the Valar, taking on a dark and terrible form that reflects the "malice that burned in him" (9).

Melkor's desire to create gradually turns into a violent passion, bent solely on destruction and the reconstitution of the primal Chaos, embracing an ideology of "sheer nihilism" (*MR* 396). His goal is to turn Arda into his hellish domain even if, in doing so, he would destroy the fruits of his own labour. Like Milton's Satan[6] who would rather "reign in hell than serve in heaven" (*Paradise Lost*, book I, l. 263), Tolkien's Melkor would apparently prefer ruling over a totally destroyed Arda to assuming his rightful place as a servant of Eru. First, he makes open war on his fellow Valar (*Sil* 62), then seeks to extinguish all light

6 Cf. Mosley (2016).

in Valinor by bringing down the enormous Lamps Illuin and Ormawith and then, with the help of the primaeval giant spider Ungoliant, withering the Two Trees of Light, Telperion and Laurelin in Valinor (62). After that, he sinks even lower by stealing the Silmarils (66) and, in the process, viciously murdering Finwë, the High King of the Ñoldor (66).

Melkor then earns the epithet of *Morgoth*, the name he would subsequently be known by, whose meaning in Sindarin could be rendered as "Dark Enemy" (*MR* 120), "Black Foe" (194), or "Black Foe of the world" (294). He is also known by two other Sindarin names: *Bauglir*, meaning "Tyrant," "Oppressor" (*LR* 414) and *Belegurth* which translates into English as "Great Death" (*PME* 358). Other titles used by Tolkien to refer to Melkor-Morgoth are the "Master of Lies"[7] (*Sil* 131), the "Dark Power" (*MR* 124), the "King of the World" (*MR* 110) and "Black Enemy" (421).[8] The host of names and titles he invented for the original Dark Lord seems to constitute a deliberate allusion to the multiplicity of Satanic appellations in the Primary World. These include, most notably, the names of Lucifer (Isaiah 14:12), Beelzebub (Matt 10:25), Beliar, and Belial (2 Cor 6:15); he is also referred to as "the Prince of Darkness", "the Evil One" (Matt 13:19), "the father of lies" (John 8:44), "the Ruler of This World" (John 12:31), and, simply, the Enemy (1 Pt 5:8). Especially the last three titles seem to have directly influenced Tolkien's choice of names for Morgoth. His former, still honorary name *Melkor* – in Quenya, "He who arises in might" (*Sil* 19, 314) – thus comes to be substituted by a host of vile monikers and titles, all of which mark his Fall and stress his irreversible transformation into a dark, corrupted being consumed by the psychotic desire to destroy (*MR* 396).

---

7 This title bears similarities to the idea of the devil as the Great Deceiver. He is, for example, portrayed as such in Rev 12:9: "[…] that old serpent, called the devil, and Satan, which deceiveth the whole world" (12:9). Satan also prominently acts the part of the deceiver when tempting Jesus in the wilderness in form of a spirit. He attempts to make Jesus renounce God and accept him as His master instead (Matt 4:1-11). Shippey pays attention to a similar scene from the *Narn i Hîn Húrin*. Although he compares the scene in which Morgoth "debates with his captive Húrin on top of the 'Hill of Tears,' looking over the kingdoms of the world" (1992: 232) with the one featuring Christ and Satan (in *Paradise Regained*, though, rather than the Gospels), it also bears some resemblance to Matt 4:1-11. In his last attempt to sway the Son of God, Satan takes Christ to "an exceeding high mountain, and sheweth him all the kingdoms of the world" (Matt 4:8), comparable to Morgoth who tempts Húrin and wants to convince him of his superior power on the 'Hill of Tears' (*Sil* 180; *UT* 187).

8 Robert Foster supplies a comprehensive list of Melkor's names and epithets in his *The Complete Guide to Middle-earth*. Among them are also, for example, the "Dark King," "Lord of the Dark," and the "Dark Power of the North" (1993: 254).

Concerning Morgoth's host of names and his twisted nature, he might be said to resemble the spirit dwelling within the Gerasine demoniac, whom, in the Gospel According to Mark, Jesus asks "What is thy name?" (5:9), only to hear the bold reply: "My name is legion: for we are many" (5:9). It thus conspires that the spirit is twisted and houses a multitude of demons. Similarly, Morgoth's power is backed by the armies of vile demons and creatures and, in his desire to destroy (even though the destruction could also take its toll on him), he is as self-destructive as the demoniac "beating himself with stones and howling among the tombs and on the mountains" (Almond 2016: 24).

In their time, both Sauron and Morgoth held positions of primacy among the ranks of their followers, yet the former began his career as the latter's "satellite" (*Letters* 202, #156) and, in this way, he might be resemblant of Gog, the individual who, according to Joachim of Fiore's reading of Rev 20:8, served as the commander of Satan's army (Almond 2016: 181). Sauron was once a Maia of the Vala. Before he became Morgoth's lieutenant, he and Aulë used to be called *Mairon*, Quenya for 'the Admirable' (Giraudeau 2007: 31). Driven by the desire to impose his own sense of order in the world, Mairon wanted to partake in Morgoth's power, which would help to "effect his [i.e. Mairon's] designs quickly and masterfully" (*MR* 396). Tolkien clarifies that it was chiefly the Maia's "admiration of Strength" that made him follow Morgoth (*Letters* 243, #183). Like his master, Mairon was given a new name that marked his fall, and was henceforth called *Sauron*, a Quenya name meaning 'the Abhorred' (*Sil* 320).

Sauron's role begins to change after Morgoth's ultimate defeat. "By the end of the Second Age he assume[s] the position of Morgoth's representative" and then "claim[s] to be Morgoth returned" (*Letters* 243, #183), as he takes the place of his former master and becomes the satanic archvillain in *The Lord of the Rings*. His role as a devil figure becomes even more apparent in the light of Tolkien's comment that the conflict in *The Lord of the Rings* is about "God and his sole right to divine honour" (*Letters* 243, #183). Sauron thus challenges this "right to divine honour" and assumes the part of the Creator's adversary,[9] similar to the part which Satan plays in Christian theology.

Tolkien's original concept and choice of name for the figure of Morgoth's lieutenant appears to indicate that Sauron may have been envisioned as a satanic figure by Tolkien from the very beginning. Before Sauron surfaces in Tolkien's creation, his place as Morgoth's right hand in *Beren and Tinuviel* (1917), the very first version of the Beren and Lúthien tale from *The Silmarillion*, is filled with the character Tevildo, a giant, black tomcat known as the "Prince of Cats" (49, 69). His name appears to rather explicitly allude to Satan, especially that its Gnomish form *Tifil* (derived from the root *tif* 'resentment, ill-feeling' (*BLT2* 356)), appears to bear an even stronger resemblance to the English word 'devil.'[10] Also, the physical appearance of Tevildo links him even more strongly with the devil, since, for many centuries, black tomcats have traditionally been strongly associated with Satan.[11] A prominent trace of Sauron as a devilish cat is still discernible in *The Lord of the Rings*, in the form of Sauron's Great Eye,[12] which Tolkien likens to those of a cat: "The Eye was rimmed with fire, but was itself glazed, yellow as a cat's, watchful and intent, and the black slit of its pupil opened on a pit, a window into nothing" (*FR* 364). This evocative description bears testimony to Tolkien's virtuoso talent for powerfully com-

---

9 Eru Ilúvatar, of course, removes himself from Middle-earth at the time of that struggle and neither he nor the Valar seem to intervene in the affairs of its peoples any longer. Nonetheless, Middle-earth remains his work and is still filled with the spirit of the father of gods and the Ainur who shaped Arda. Meanwhile, Sauron challenges this Creation by seeking to impose his will and tyrannical rule on the Free Peoples. The Valar do not actively intervene, but they send "Emissaries" (*Letters* 180, #144) in the form of the Istari to strengthen the native energies of the peoples of Middle-earth and oppose the Dark Lord. This means that Sauron is not only in conflict with these representatives, but also, indirectly, in conflict with the Creator himself.

10 This, again, becomes even more apparent when one takes into consideration the fact that some of its cognates, for example Old High German *tiufal* and Scots *divil* look and sound very much like *Tifil.*

11 Brewer explains that the cat was "called a familiar, from the medieval superstition that Satan's favourite form was a black cat. Hence witches were said to have a cat as their familiar" (1992: 49). According to Becker, the black tom cat was viewed as an image of the devil during the Middle Ages (2010: 45).

12 In this respect, Sauron also strongly resembles the Old Norse father of gods, Odin. For one, both Sauron and Odin dwell in towers from where they have a wide view over the world (Odin's Hliðskjálf and Sauron's Barad-dûr). More importantly, however, both of them draw a considerable amount of their power from an 'Eye of Knowledge'. In exchange for omniscience, Odin had to sacrifice one of his eyes: "He [Odin] is full of learning because he drinks of the well from the horn Giallarhorn. All-Father went there and asked for a single drink from the well, but he did not get one until he placed his eye as a pledge" (Snorri Sturluson, *Edda*, 'Gylfaginning,' chapter 15). Sauron, in contrast, is not omniscient, but, nonetheless, demonstrates great power by being able of watching the whole world through his burning Eye.

pressing a complex artistic message into a single, haunting image, in this case, the sinister, cat-like eye.

As "a shadow of Morgoth and a ghost of his malice" (*Sil* 19), Sauron is, like his master Morgoth and their mutual inspiration the devil, given many names and titles by his enemies. He is, for instance, known by the Sindarin names *Gorthu* 'Mist of Fear' (Giraudeau 2007: 30) and *Gorthaur* "The Cruel" (*Sil* 19). Among others, Robert Foster lists some more diabolic epithets including "'Sauron the Deceiver,' 'the Lord of the Earth,'[13] 'the Enemy,' 'the Black One'" (2000: 438). As in the case of Morgoth, Sauron's Fall is also progressive. Having fallen under his lord's spell, he further incriminates himself as Morgoth's warlord, corrupts the Ñoldor of Eregion, kills their Prince Celebrimbor and causes the physical separation of Valinor from Middle-earth following which he is made to assume his dreadful shape as a hideous monster.

Having been himself corrupted by Morgoth, Sauron, in turn, causes Saruman, a third powerful being of evil inclination, to become a 'fallen angel' figure. In this respect, Tolkien's satanic figures appear to have a highly infectious influence on each other, which might give the impression of a diabolical domino effect. Saruman the White, one of the Istari sent to Middle-earth by the Valar to counteract Sauron, succumbs to his thirst for knowledge and lust for power. He perverts his proper function as an emissary of the Valar (*Letters* 180, #144) and becomes Sauron's pawn, which does not, however, in due time, prevent him from double-crossing his new master. Saruman thus appears to form a kind of satanic triplicity, along with Morgoth and Sauron. Like the two of them, he also progressively descends into darkness, tainting his original 'whiteness' by conducting immoral experiments, despoiling the Garden of Orthanc and its surrounding lands, and leading a reckless war of aggression against the Rohirrim. Some weeks after Gandalf deposes Saruman as the head of the Istari and causes his staff to break, Saruman commits his last atrocity. He journeys to the Shire and starts enslaving the guileless Hobbits with the help of his ruffians. Saruman's reign of terror over the Shire is only broken when he is defeated by a Hobbit army under the command of Frodo, Merry, Pippin and

13 The analogous epithet used in the Bible would be "the ruler of this world" (John 14:30; 12:31-32; and John 16:11).

Sam. Finally, Saruman finds a miserable end, dying at the hands of his own, maltreated servant Gríma Wormtongue.

In *The Chronicles of Narnia*, the closest equivalent to the satanic figures in Tolkien's oeuvre is undoubtedly Queen Jadis,[14] also known as the White Witch. Jadis makes her first appearance in *The Lion, the Witch and the Wardrobe* (1950) and is subsequently given more background in the prequel *The Magician's Nephew* (1955). There, she is introduced as the Queen of Charn, a great but corrupt city reminiscent of ancient Babylon. In contrast to all the diabolical archvillains in the works of Tolkien, Jadis does not begin her existence as a quasi-angelic being[15] but is already tainted by virtue of her ancestry. She is purportedly descended from the race of giants and Lilith, the first wife of Adam, frequently interpreted as a night demon and identified by Lewis as one of the Jinn.[16]

Having previously belonged to a society that kept slaves and practised human sacrifices, Jadis is, of course, far from being without blemish, but if one wanted to pinpoint a single moment that could clearly denote her irreversible Fall, it would be her annihilation of the City of Charn (as well as the world of the same name). In chapter 5, she is reported to have fought a war against her sister over the dominion of Charn. When Jadis's forces had lost the last great battle, rather than submit to her sister, in her pride, she used a tremendous curse of destruction referred to as "the Deplorable Word" which, in the global sense, annihilated all the life in Charn (*MN* 75), and, on the more personal level, constituted the moment of her Fall.[17] After this hideous act of mass destruction is revealed, Lewis begins referring to her as "the Witch" (80 ff.), thus stressing

14 In *The Magician's Nephew*, Jadis finds a willing servant in Digory Kirk's Uncle Andrew, a character who could also be viewed as a kind of Saruman figure. Uncle Andrew shares this scientific interest and misguided thirst for knowledge with the wizard of Orthanc. They are also both interested in magic ring(s). Digory's uncle actually creates two magic rings which allow the wearer to travel through different dimensions and Saruman also appears to be able to craft magic rings thanks to his close study of the subject (Honegger 2021: 6). In the same way that Saruman is attracted to the power of Sauron, Uncle Andrew feels drawn to the might of Jadis. However, in contrast to Saruman, he learns the error of his ways, gives up magic and becomes "a nicer and less selfish old man than he had ever been before" (*MN* 208).

15 Her appearance could be viewed as angel-like in all its commanding beauty and grace, but, as with many evil enchantresses, her superficial handsomeness is only a veneer.

16 The Jinn is a spirit from Islamic tradition. Shaitan (or Iblis, as the devil is called in Islam) is thought of as either a fallen angel or a Jinn. It appears that Lewis consciously chose the latter image in order to re-enforce her diabolical nature.

17 The Deplorable Word might be viewed as a satanic antithesis to the Word of God in that whereas the Word of God carried the power of Creation, the Deplorable Word could only mar and destroy.

her amoral nature as a practitioner of dark arts. By identifying her as a witch, Lewis also immediately associates her with the servants of the devil, since, traditionally, they have been believed to owe their sinister powers to the pact and illicit communion with Satan and/or his demons.

Notably, both Tolkien and Lewis tie the act of Creation to powerful, primal melodies that weave the fabric of their worlds, and satanic characters are already present, partaking in the performance of these songs of the spheres. Similarly to Tolkien's idea of the creation myth, the *Ainulindalë*, Lewis ties the act of Creation to divine songs that call his imaginary world into being. Lewis describes how the Lion Aslan shapes the whole of Narnia through his divine music, apparently consisting of at least two songs[18] (*MN* 119-20). As in the case of Tolkien's satanic Morgoth, Jadis is also there, during the performance of these songs of the spheres. Both authors seem to have wanted to supply an answer to the question of how Evil came to enter their worlds, and they chose to concretely embody Evil in the form of a satanic presence. Ultimately, the figure of Satan himself might be viewed as humanity's attempt to explain the origin of Evil: the devil brought Evil to Earth by contriving the Original Sin. Morgoth brings Evil into Arda by interfering in its creation. In *The Magician's Nephew*, the boy Digory Kirk acts the part of Pandora, unwittingly freeing Jadis and then bringing her evil presence to Narnia prior to its creation.

In the creation scene, it becomes apparent that Jadis, similarly to the biblical Satan and Tolkien's Morgoth, is driven by pride and the desire to rule as a usurper. First, she is filled with envy and hatred upon encountering a power superior to her sorcery in the form of Aslan's "Magic different from hers and stronger" (*MN* 116). Similar to Tolkien's diabolus Melkor, Jadis then tries to disrupt the heavenly music. However, while Melkor's disruption of the music serves his superordinate goal of becoming an independent creator and is thus a rebellious, creative intervention, Jadis merely resorts to a blunt, but at the same time, completely ineffective act of violence, which is only an end in itself, hitting Aslan with an iron bar (without, however, the powerful Lion even noticing it).

---

18 The end of chapter 8 relates that the "song had now changed" (*MN* 119) and at the beginning of chapter 9, the Lion is said to sing a new song (120). It is, however, left ambiguous whether the songs belong to a single great song or not. They could be interpreted as different themes/melodies within a great musical composition or indeed as separate, independent songs that work different kinds of magic on the newly created realms.

Following that, Jadis's envy is also directed at the rightful human sovereigns of Narnia, the cabman Frank and his wife, whose rulership the Witch refuses to accept. Instead, she styles herself queen of Narnia (*LWW* 40ff.) in the manner of a pretender. In this respect, Jadis is again comparable to Satan who is envious of man's God-given dominion over the Creation and refuses to be subordinate to the first human couple of Adam and Eve.

As is the case of Tolkien's diabolic villains, Jadis's Fall is also continuous in that, following her first encounter with Aslan, she keeps on sinking ever lower. After her monstrous destruction of Charn, Jadis suffers a Second Fall which is constituted by her violation of the taboo against eating from the Tree of Immortality in the Garden of Youth.[19] This scene naturally conjures up powerful associations with both Satan and, peculiarly enough, also the first victim of Satan's guile, Adam's wife Eve. Like Satan, Jadis invades the Eden-like garden and tempts a mortal, in this case the boy Digory, to take the 'forbidden fruit'. Simultaneously, Jadis's behaviour triggers evident associations with Eve,[20] to that extent that she actually eats the 'forbidden fruit' herself, in spite of the explicit warning placed at the gates, informing everyone that those who were to take an apple for themselves would not only "find their heart's desire," but also, most importantly "find despair" (*MN* 178). The association with Eve makes even more sense, given the fact that Jadis is a she-devil, a satanic figure in a female form, and, as such, she might be said to stand for the satanic corruption, coupled with stereotypical feminine weaknesses such as vanity, fickleness and duplicity. Having eaten the apple, Jadis is stigmatized by a "horrid stain" on her mouth from the fruit's dark juice (181), a kind of 'witch mark' that signifies her sinfulness and renewed Fall. The stain is the first sign of the curse which seems to come with Jadis's newly-gained immortality and

19 The invasion of an Edenic place is of course also present in Tolkien's *Silmarillion* in the form of Melkor's destruction of the Two Trees of light, Telperion and Laurelin. It has been noted that there is a strong similarity between Lewis's golden and silver tree in the Garden of Youth and the two trees in Tolkien's work, which also happen to be golden (Laurelin) and silver (Telperion) (Christopher 1988: 39). It cannot be ruled out that, in fact, Lewis borrowed this idea from Tolkien (39). Lewis might also have got the idea from the Alexanderian tradition. According to the fictional fourth-century *Epistola Alexandri*, King Alexander the Great encountered two holy trees of the sun and the moon in an Indian grove (https://blogs.bl.uk/digitisedmanuscripts/2020/01/the-trees-of-the-sun-and-the-moon.html).

20 Jadis appears to be a conflation of several literary, mythological and biblical figures who served as a model for her. Thus, she is a great example of how multi-faceted Lewis's process of sub-creation could potentially be. Apart from bearing a strong resemblance to Satan, Jadis is also reminiscent of Eve, the demoness Lilith, the Whore of Babylon, and Hans Christian Andersen's Snow Queen.

marks the beginning of her transformation into a restless, dwindling shadow of her former magnificent self.

## Satanic Scourges: Devastation and Diabolical Corruption

The satanic figures in the works of Tolkien and Lewis naturally have a profound effect on the imaginary worlds of the two authors. This part of the chapter will focus on different aspects and effects of their powers both on the natural world and on the peoples and protagonists populating the realms of Arda and Narnia. On the one hand, it will demonstrate that the satanic archvillains blight nature by destroying its beauty and bringing the seasons out of balance. On the other, this section will elaborate on the way in which the diabolical antagonists appeal to and exploit the weaknesses of their victims. Finally, it will demonstrate how these devilish villains tempt the protagonists into committing different kinds of sins, often guided by the seductive powers of their charm and beauty.

The hatred of Tolkien's Morgoth infests the world of Arda. Tolkien explains in his 'Notes on motives from the Silmarillion' that in order "[t]o gain domination over Arda, Morgoth had let most of his being pass into the physical constituents of the Earth – hence all things that were born on Earth and lived on and by it, beasts or plants or incarnate spirits, were liable to be 'stained'" (*MR* 395). As Christopher Tolkien puts it, the poisonous power of Morgoth was "dispersed or disseminated into the very matter of Arda" (xi). This tainted Earth is then referred to by him as "'Arda Marred,' that is Arda with a Melkor-ingredient" (396). Morgoth's influence on Arda is thus reminiscent of Satan's Kingdom of Darkness, such as it is envisioned in the New Testament. The Gospel of John, for instance, depicts it as casting its shadow over the earth: "The whole world lies under the power of the evil one" (5:19). Likewise, Morgoth casts his titanic shadow over Arda as a self-proclaimed "King of the World" (*MR* 110). Tolkien seems to stress Morgoth's lasting influence by etymologically linking his name to the blighted places of Middle-earth. Thus, we encounter the Sindarin root *mor* meaning "dark," "black" (*Sil* 334) in places like Moria, Morgul, Morannon and most prominently the Land of Shadow, Mordor.

Lewis depicts Jadis as having a destructive impact on the natural world, although she does not seem to have as profound or harrowing an effect on Narnia as Tolkien's satanic figures have on Arda and Middle-earth. Comparably to Tolkien's Morgoth, who threatens Arda with eternal winter by engulfing the world in the deadly chill radiated by the hellish Utumno, Jadis, the White Witch, conjures up a harrowing winter that covers the whole of Narnia and lasts for a hundred years. One could also argue that, like Morgoth, Jadis pours her essence into Narnia, infecting the land with her inner coldness that becomes directly palpable in the form of a stifling winter. Lewis, in fact, puts strong emphasis on the fact that Jadis's reign entails that it is "always winter and never Christmas"[21] (*LWW* 27, 114). The season of winter is traditionally associated with death and the stand-still of life, but winter can also function as a Christian symbol of faith and hope, since it is also the season during which Jesus is traditionally believed to have been born and brought light into the dark winter world. Moreover, winter is also the season that precedes spring[22] and allows nature to recuperate.

Jadis suppresses the Christmas season in Narnia, and her cruel disruption of a small Christmas party highlights her Antichristian nature, namely that of a fiend devoid of compassion. From the eleventh chapter of *The Lion, the Witch and the Wardrobe* we learn that the talking animals have been given "decorations of holly" (123) for their party by Father Christmas himself. In the Christian tradition, the prickly leaves of the holly are associated with the crown of thorns worn by Jesus at the Crucifixion, and its red berries symbolize the blood He shed to lead the Christians out of the darkness of sin into the light. Not surprisingly, then, the devilish Jadis is enraged at such outward signs of the festive season that already foreshadow the end of her wintry reign of stifling snow. Concerning the symbolism of snow, Michael Ferber points out that "the pre-Christmas snow [...] suggests death, the state from which Christ comes to redeem us. As a symbol of half-life or hibernation, snow might imply the spiritual paralysis or stasis of a whole society" (2017: 207). The snow masses with which Jadis covers the land of Narnia might therefore be said to symbol-

21 This statement is uttered as many as four times (albeit on three occasions slightly modified) in total in *The Lion, the Witch and the Wardrobe*. Mr. Tumnus tells Lucy and she then twice repeats it to Edmund and later Peter, and Mr. Beaver echoes the statement just before he shows the children the sledge of the White Witch.

22 Cf. the oft-quoted words of Percy Byron Shelley in *Ode to the West Wind*: "If Winter comes, can Spring be far behind?" (l. 70).

ize the spiritual paralysis and stasis of the Narnian realm under her rule. The country is in a state of suspended animation, one which is, however, about to be broken by the return of the Lion Aslan.

In the works of Tolkien and Lewis, the archvillains also appear to be distinctively satanic in that they are known to be tempting the inhabitants of, respectively, Arda and Narnia into sin. Tolkien's Morgoth is, unfortunately, the first to get in contact with the newly created race of Men and it is hinted at that something dark and terrible happened during that encounter. Shippey goes so far as to suggest that Tolkien "left a gap in *The Silmarillion*, or designed a dovetail, for the Fall of Man as described in the Old Testament" (1992: 209), so that unspecified further "exploit of Morgoth [might have been] the traditional seduction of Adam and Eve by the serpent" (210). Many tribes of Men joined Morgoth and, afterwards, mankind remained susceptible to the lure of darkness with, for example, the Dark Númenoreans, the Easterlings and the Haradrim later following the call of Sauron in the same way that the Dunlendings become a willing tool of Saruman.

While tempting Elves or humans into sin, Tolkien's satanic villains at times infect their victims with their own vices. Melkor exploits the thirst that the Ñoldorin Elves have for knowledge in order to exert more control over them, and thus turns them against the Valar. Moreover, Melkor also infects the Ñoldorin Elf Fëanor with a destructive rage similar to that of the dark Vala himself. His thirst for revenge makes Fëanor unwittingly as reckless and self-destructive as Melkor, so that he turns into a mirror image of the very person he seeks to defeat. Maddened by the murder of his father and the theft of the Silmarils by Melkor, Fëanor stops at nothing to have his revenge and commits the act of kin-slaying at Alqualondë, commanding a murderous attack on the Teleri Elves, a heinous crime that might be seen as the Fall of the Ñoldor.[23]

Sauron, in turn, poisons the mind of the Númenorean king Ar-Pharazôn, infecting him with his own avarice and the envy of the Valar, thus encouraging him to attack the Undying Lands. In this way, the satanic Sauron brings about the destruction of Númenor by Eru and, so to speak, the Second Fall of

---

23 For a detailed discussion of the repercussions of this act, see Gallant (2014).

Man, after which the Straight Road to the earthly paradise of Valinor is lost to mankind. Sauron continues to manipulate the Númenoreans through the power of his Master Ring and the rings he bequeathed to the mortal kings. These rings could be compared to the tools of satanic possession. Like the serpent in Paradise who only feigns to be able to bestow immortality on humans in order to lure them into selling their souls, Sauron's rings promise immortality but, at the same time, gradually turn their wearers into the shadowy, undead Nazgûl Ringwraiths, bestowing on them what might be described as a 'prolonged death' rather than endless life. Their rings of power, and, especially, the One Ring directly appeal to the human greed for power and immortality. The ones who fall victim to the possession of the Master Ring exhibit behaviour similar to that of being possessed by the devil. To give a prominent example, the mighty warrior Boromir undergoes an uncanny change when the power of the Ring affects him. Before Frodo realizes that Boromir is standing behind him, he feels as if "unfriendly eyes were upon him" (*FR* 397). Following that, during his fateful conversation with the Gondorian, he notices "the strange gleam in Boromir's eyes" (398). Like the distorted face of one possessed by the devil, Boromir's "fair and pleasant face was hideously changed; a raging fire was in his eyes" (399). It is as if, at that moment, his eyes reflected the evil stare of Sauron's Great Eye rimmed by fire.

In Lewis's book *The Magician's Nephew*, the sin of wrath causes Digory Kirk to unwittingly release an ancient Evil in form of the irascible Jadis. The evil Witch herself powerfully embodies the sin of wrath but also those of pride, avarice and envy. Edmund Pevensie, the Judas-like character in *The Lion, the Witch and the Wardrobe*, shares some of her traits. He is a proud little boy, full of anger, and subject to greed, who envies his older brother Peter, often seeking to elevate himself over him and the rest of his siblings, in which he is not unlike Jadis wishing to unjustly elevate herself over Aslan. Jadis exploits Edmund's gluttony and envy by feeding him the enchanted Turkish delight and promising him the rule over Narnia and his siblings as her successor to the throne. According to Luke,[24] the Devil entered into Judas Iscariot and made him betray Jesus.

24 Whereas the other gospels are silent on that matter, the Gospel of Luke depicts Judas' betrayal as a direct work of the devil: "Then entered Satan into Judas surnamed Iscariot, being of the number of the twelve" (22:3).

Owing to their allegiance with Satan, witches were commonly believed to have the power to project demons into their victims. Jadis the White Witch, in a way, possesses Edmund, symbolically, taking hold of him by putting "a fold of her fur mantle round him" (*LWW* 42), and then directly controlling him by exploiting the boy's insatiable gluttony for her dangerous sweets. Similarly to Eve, who falls under Satan's power by eating of the forbidden fruit, Edmund falls by consuming the seemingly harmless Turkish delight. The boy's subsequent betrayal of his siblings leads to his being condemned as a traitor. He is, however, saved from death by Aslan's self-sacrifice.

Tolkien's and Lewis's devilish villains also seem to rely much on their outward appearance to hold sway with their victims. According to the Judeo-Christian tradition, Satan used to be an angel of great beauty and magnificence and still has the ability to conjure up the illusion of goodliness, an ability he shares with his demons and followers. From 2 Cor we learn that "Even Satan disguises himself as an angel of light. So it is not strange if his ministers also disguise themselves as ministers of righteousness" (11:14). Likewise, both Jadis and, in particular, the Lady of the Green Kirtle[25] are depicted by Lewis as female beings of great beauty, and it is this superficial pulchritude which helps them to ensnare their unwary victims. In contrast, no such devilish temptresses appear in the works of Tolkien, and, consequently, the aspect of feminine attractiveness is not to be detected in his archvillains. As a rule, Tolkien's villains are marked by their distinct ugliness, although his Morgoth is, at first, still able to take on a pleasing shape, and Sauron appears as the handsome and charming Annatar "the Lord of Gifts" to Celebrimbor and the Ñoldor of Eregion (*Sil* 265). Saruman, in turn, relies on his aura of grandeur and benevolent wisdom, even after his treachery has become known.

There are, in fact, some remarkable parallels between the depictions of Tolkien's Saruman and Lewis's Lady of the Green Kirtle. To begin with, both of them hold a royal person captive in a throne room. With the help of his spy Gríma Wormtongue, Saruman weakens King Théoden of Rohan and makes him slothful (Treloar 1989:40), so that the monarch withers away on his throne, remaining

25 The Lady of the Green Kirtle is suggested to be "of the same crew" (*SC* 71) as Jadis, implying that she, too, comes from a union between the race of giants and Lilith.

inactive in spite of the great danger his country finds itself in. Prince Rilian is likewise enchanted so that he succumbs to the sin of sloth (King 1984: 16) which, in his case, is a kind of enforced recreancy,[26] and at night, he is bound to the Silver Chair that keeps him prisoner. Furthermore, much like Saruman, the Lady of the Green Kirtle has a pleasing, melodious voice with which she casts spells on her victims. Like Satan, the "father of lies", both of them are serpent-like deceivers. The Lady of the Green Kirtle can, in fact, take on the form of a serpent,[27] while Tolkien's Saruman is, at one point, likened to "a snake coiling itself to strike" (*TT* 581). Also metaphorically, both Saruman and the Lady of the Green Kirtle reveal their true nature by 'shedding their skin', that is, by being openly confronted by those who have seen through their guise. Théoden calls out Saruman by exclaiming: "You hold out your hand to me, and I perceive only a finger of the claw of Mordor. Cruel and cold!" (580). The "claw of Mordor" that the king of Rohan speaks of is, of course, intriguingly reminiscent of the devil's cloven hoof that, in various folktales, often gives him away, even when he is otherwise disguised in a pleasing shape.

## Re-imagining Satan's Binding and Final Defeat

The struggle between the forces of Heaven and Hell resonates just as much in the works of Tolkien as in those of Lewis. One motif strongly connected to that struggle, the Harrowing of Hell, is also present in *The Silmarillion* and *The Lion the Witch and the Wardrobe.* In the former, the binding of Satan seems to be recalled in the image of Morgoth being tied with the chain Angainor, following his first great defeat and the levelling of Utumno (*Sil* 104). In the latter, following his resurrection, Aslan comes to revive the petrified victims of

26 The term *recreantise* is used in French in connection with lazy knights. In medieval romances, the state of recreantise is often caused by the hero's overwhelming and disproportionate love for his lady which leads him to neglect his knightly duties. A good example may be provided by Chrétien de Troyes' romance *Erec and Enide.* Erec's all-consuming love for the fair Enide makes him forget about his duties as a knight. At the end of the poem, Erec has overcome his recreantise and has to fight a knight by the name of Maboagrain. Maboagrain, who has been put under a spell by his sorceress lady and thus also suffers from an extreme kind of *recreantise,* is an exaggerated mirror image of Erec. He is imprisoned in her garden where he is doomed to fight and kill any knight who enters his lady's retreat. In his enchanted state, Prince Rilian appears to bear some resemblance to Maboagrain.

27 The Lady of the Green Kirtle's strongest link to Satan evinces in her ability to transform herself into a monstrous, basilisk-like serpent, taking on the same form that Satan does in Eden, and thus associating herself with "the old serpent" of Rev 20:2. See also Hardy (2007: 41).

Jadis, freeing them from the White Witch's castle, in which the Lion resembles Christ descending into hell to free the righteous dead and lead them to Heaven. The defeat of Jadis in her final battle with Aslan is therefore reminiscent of Christ's victory over both death and the devil.

Moreover, both Lewis and Tolkien introduce a number of apocalyptic motifs into their Secondary Worlds, and some of their satanic figures also play an important role in the two authors' eschatology. One such character is the envious ape Shift in Lewis's *The Last Battle* who, acting as an Antichrist figure, attempts to usurp Aslan's righteous place by using the gullible donkey Puzzle as a false prophet and the diabolical ape's mouthpiece. Dressed up in a lion's skin, Puzzle is presented to the inhabitants of Narnia as Aslan returned. Much as the Antichrist in the Book of Revelation, Shift starts persecuting the true believers. His ultimate heresy is constituted by confounding the divine person of Aslan with the ghastly demon god Tash from Calormen, calling the false Lion "Tashlan." During the climactic last battle of the book, when the dreadful Tash himself makes his appearance, the Calormenes act the part of the heathen nations Gog and Magog at the time of the Last Judgement.

Tash is the only satanic figure in the works of Lewis that does not have a personality of his own and seems to cover the brutish, feral aspect of Satan as "the beast" (Rev 13:1). Tash might have been modelled on the Arabian vulture god Nasr but his four arms also recall Kali, the Hindu goddess of death and destruction. Milton, whose *Paradise Lost* Lewis had intimate knowledge of, likened Satan to a vulture, thereby implicitly comparing his search for victims to corrupt to the vulture's pursuit of prey. In the words of Karen Edwards "[t]he vulture's reputation for ferocity was such that it was often depicted as pursuing live prey, although most vultures feed exclusively on carrion" (2009: 264). Similarly, Tash pursues and captures heretics. The ones guilty of blaspheming against Aslan, Shift and the Calormene Rishda Tarkaan, are thus both seized and carried away by Tash after having taken the demonic god's name in vain. They had literally talked of the Devil and thereby summoned the fiend Tash. Shift and Rishda are, as High King Peter puts it, Tash's "lawful prey" (*LB* 163). Tash's double function as an enemy of Aslan and his father, the Emperor-over-the-Sea, and, at the same time, an enforcer of the divine punishment might be said to resemble the paradoxical role of Satan as, at the same time, the divine enforcer and the divine opponent (Almond 2016: 165). In this respect, Lewis's choice of Tash's vulture aspect is striking as well, since "Isaiah 34.15 places [that] bird in the context of God's vengeance" (Edwards 2009: 264).

Whereas Lewis seems to have limited his use of apocalyptic themes to his final Narnia novel *The Last Battle*, Tolkien interspersed with apocalyptic elements not only his vision of an eschatological battle in *The Silmarillion*, but also the plot of *The Lord of the Rings*. As is the case with Lewis's *The Last Battle*, Satanic figures also play a decisive role in Tolkien's apocalyptic scenarios. *The Silmarillion* relates how Morgoth is enchained for three hundred years after his defeat at the Siege of Utumno until he is set free again (*Sil* 39, 53), in which he is similar to Satan, imprisoned[28] for a thousand years prior to the Second Coming (Rev 20:1-3).[29] Tolkien envisioned two further great conflicts between the Valar and Morgoth, each labelled *Dagor Dagorath*, the 'Battle of Battles' in Sindarin.[30] The first of them results in Morgoth's capture, renewed binding, and his being "thrust through the Door of Night beyond the Walls of the World, into the Timeless Void" (*Sil* 234). This fate is also reminiscent of Satan's defeat at the Last Judgement: Satan would, together with his angels and the wicked in their resurrected bodies, "be consigned to the punishment of everlasting fires in indestructible bodies" (Almond 2016: 172). The second *dagor dagorath* at the end of times takes place after Morgoth has succeeded in returning and ends in the final destruction of Morgoth and the renewal of Arda. Michaël Devaux refers to this splitting of Tolkien's eschatological battles as "the scattering of

28 The motif of a rebel deity or angel being put in chains as a punishment for their transgressions is also present in the stories of Loki and Prometheus in, respectively, Norse and Greek mythologies. Loki is bound with the innards of his own son for having killed the light god Balder, and Prometheus is chained to a rock for stealing fire from the gods.

29 I am here purposefully referring to a particular theological reading of Rev 20:2-3 according to which Satan is actually bound twice. This reading posits that Satan was bound for the first time for a millennium after his defeat following the resurrection of Christ and he will be bound again (this time for good), after the Second Coming of Christ. The most prominent advocate of this reading was Saint Augustine. Almond expounds that this "was an interpretation of Revelation that was resonate throughout the medieval period, primary as a result of its endorsement by Augustine. [...] [A]ccording to Augustine, the binding of Satan had already happened as the result of the victory of Christ, and he had already been thrown into the bottomless pit. [...] [F]or Augustine, at the end of time, Satan would be loosed again. [...] After Christ comes in judgement, the Devil and his angels, together with the wicked in their resurrected bodies, would be consigned to the punishments of everlasting fires in indestructible bodies" (2016: 171f.).

30 Michaël Devaux points out that the first *Dagor Dagorath* is an equivalent to the battle otherwise referred to as the War of Wrath: "Tolkien uses it [*Dagor Dagorath*] to refer to both to the Last Battle at the end of the First Age and to speak about the last battle at the end of times" (2010: 110).

the *Apocalypse* in Middle-earth" (2010: 110), which is also discernible in the Christian tradition, as Joachim of Fiore maintained that there would be two battles against the Antichrist and Satan, with the second clash being also the final one (Almond 2016: 180f.).

Other apocalyptic themes in which some satanic figures can be discerned are to be found in the *Akallabêth* and *The Lord of the Rings*. In the former, Sauron acts as an Antichrist figure who corrupts many of the Númenoreans and persecutes the Faithful. Establishing a quasi-Satanist cult around his former master, Sauron has a temple for Morgoth[31] built on Númenor, a hideous act which may also reflect the re-erection of the temple in Jerusalem by the Antichrist. This motif appears to be more strongly present in the re-erection of the Dark Tower of Barad-dûr at the beginning of *The Lord of the Rings*. With Sauron playing there the role of the devil, his mouthpiece Saruman, a "liar [...] and a corrupter of men's hearts" (*TT* 580), appears to be an Antichrist figure. The Eastern and Southern tribes of men supporting Sauron in his war might therefore be interpreted as the heathen nations of Gog and Magog that inflict war on the lands of the Earth in Rev 20.

During the Siege of Gondor, Gandalf confronts the Witchking, who might recall the figure of Satan's general Gog, particularly when it comes to the fate that awaits the Dark Marshal (and Sauron): "Go back to the abyss prepared for you! [...] Fall into the nothingness that awaits you and your Master" (*RK* 829). These words appear to echo the verse from the Gospel of Matthew concerning the Last Day and the punishment of the devil and his minions: "Go you accursed into the eternal fire, which has been prepared for the Devil and his angels" (25:41). In the way which is reminiscent of that of Satan, believed to rage most strongly prior to his nearing defeat (Almond 2016: 169f.), Sauron musters his whole strength against the Free Peoples towards the end of his reign. Likewise, in the Christian tradition, the possessed ones are said to grow particularly wild as Satan's defeat approaches (171). This particular satanic effect might have inspired the corruptive powers of the Ring which grow most

31 This account is also strongly reminiscent of the Children of Israel being seduced by Satan to worship the dark Canaanite deity Baal (e.g. Judg 2:11-13). A temple called the House of Baal was erected where the Israelites practised idolatry of Baal and sacrificed children to him. Similarly, Sauron has the righteous sacrificed to Morgoth.

intense towards its nearing destruction. Frodo is already nearly possessed by the Ring, leading a ghostly life of its own, carrying a particle of Sauron's spirit. When the Hobbit is about to cast the Ring into the fires of Mount Doom, the satanic spirit within the Ring seems to brace itself and finally corrupts Frodo, driving him insane.

## The Masks of the Devil

The satanic villains that came from the minds of Tolkien and Lewis also appear to reflect the two authors' views on the nature of Evil. Tolkien shared a view on Evil with Lewis which was very similar to the stance on Evil embraced by St. Augustine and Boethius. According to St. Augustine,[32] the world and humanity as God's Creation are originally good by nature, and Evil is nothing more than a parasite, a corruption of spiritual and natural good. Considering that existence itself is innately benevolent, Evil is not a presence but an absence. Augustine identifies the misuse of free will as the cause of sin, and thereby Evil. In keeping with that Christian view, "the Devil did not sin at the instant of creation; this would have been tantamount to his not having had the opportunity to have exercised his free will and to his having been created Evil (which would deny God's goodness)" (Almond 2016: 64). As a corrupted archangel, Satan is "an Unangel. He is a parasite on the good of angel existence he has been granted" (Duriez 2015: 195). Tolkien's original Dark Lord, Melkor-Morgoth, as well as his successor Sauron, start out with good intentions, desiring to create order (*Sil* 4; *Letters* 243, #183). Tolkien explains "the problem: that this frightful evil can and does arise from an apparently good root, the desire to benefit the world and others – speedily and according to the benefactor's own plans – is a recurrent motive" (*Letters* 146, #131). The beings allured by Tolkien's satanic figures thus often go down that same road into darkness.

Both Melkor-Morgoth and Sauron misuse their free will by giving in to their inordinate sub-creative desire and thus oppose the divine authority of Eru Ilúvatar. However, both Morgoth and his lieutenant are unable to call into

---

32 Shippey predominantly refers to the Boethian opinion on evil which he sums up as follows: "[T]here is no such thing as evil. What people identify as evil is only the absence of good… [and Evil is] 'a parasite, not an original thing'" (2001: 130f.).

existence independent creations in keeping with the Christian/Catholic view of Evil as a perversion of what is good. Consequently, the sinister creatures serving Morgoth and Sauron are merely horrid travesties that mock the act of Creation. Only the Creator can give form to independent beings. As Lewis puts it in *The Pilgrim's Regress*, "Form [...] belong[s] to the good" (203).

Although Lewis would probably whole-heartedly agree with Tolkien's Augustinian outlook, neither the Satanic villains from his *Narniad*, nor the majority of their minions reflect it in any direct way. Instead, they often inadvertently convey an impression of dualism, a religious doctrine which stands in stark contrast to Augustine's view.[33] The type of dualism meant here would be Manichaeism or Cosmological dualism. Manichaeism was a religious doctrine founded by the Parthian prophet Mani (ca. 216–47). The Manichean creed is based on the belief in a primordial, universal conflict between two equal and competing forces of Good and Evil, represented by light and darkness, respectively. Shippey defines Manichaeism as "the belief that the world is a battlefield, between the powers of Good and Evil, equal and opposite" (2001: 134). The principles of Cosmic Dualism, as Almond points out, were first stated in an ancient Jewish religious manuscript, the Qumran *Rule of the Community* scroll (100–150 BC) according to which "God created the spirits of light and darkness. [...] Thus, reality was determined from the beginning by the opposition between spirit and matter, light and darkness, justice and evil, truth and falsehood [...] within an overarching pattern predetermined by God" (2016: 20). Cosmological dualism need not be as absolute or as radical as Manichaeism. *The Rule of the Community* scroll, for instance, does not view Belial, the prince of darkness, as God's equal but as his inferior adversary (20). However, what the different kinds of Cosmological dualism have in common is that they view Evil not as a corruption but as an independent principle which was created next to the principle of Good at the beginning of time. Radical dualism, in contrast, often maintains that there is an evil and equal counterpart to God. The more extreme Cathars, for instance, went so far as to adopt the heretical view that an evil 'god' existed next to the Creator and equalled Him in might.

---

33 Shippey draws attention to the apparently deep-seated contradiction between the Boethian/Augustinian view, on the one hand, and the dualist/Manichean view, on the other hand, in Tolkien's work and offers an in-depth discussion in his book *J.R.R. Tolkien. Author of the Century* (135).

Tolkien's work is at times thought of as embracing a dualistic, or even Manichean philosophy regarding the nature of Evil (Shippey 2001: 129). Manichaeism adopts a similar view to Evil as Cosmological dualism by supposing that "Good and Evil are locked in a struggle for world domination, and since they are equally balanced in power, it is not clear which, if either, will win in the end" (Davison 2004: 100). Colin Duriez points to the view that Evil in Tolkien's world is already present before the act of Creation in *The Silmarillion* in the form of Melkor (2015: 73), which suggests a Cosmological dualistic or Manichean worldview, yet the impression turns out to be erroneous. On the one hand, Melkor, like his fellow Ainur, came into existence by the power of Eru's thoughts and was thus not created evil. On the other hand, though, Evil is later depicted as being overcome and is, therefore, only temporary. However, according to Shippey, Tolkien reconciled the Boethian and Manichean stance as complementary worldviews. Shippey argues that Evil is neither simply an absence ('the Shadow'), nor merely an external force ('the Dark Power') (2001: 135, 142).

The satanic villains in Tolkien's work are doomed to oblivion because of their disobedience to and rejection of the Creator, echoing the devil's rejection of God ultimately leading to his being condemned to eternal imprisonment and suffering in the burning pit. Tolkien maintains that "[t]he Enemy in successive forms is always 'naturally' concerned with sheer Domination" (*Letters* 145, #131), and, indeed, in their pursuit of power, both Morgoth and Sauron even go so far as daring to turn their back on the divine goodness of Eru Ilúvatar. According to Tolkien, the Enemy, disobeying the Creator, will use "Magic" in order to gain "Power" and tyrannically "re-form Creation" (146, #131). Satan's pride,[34] which manifests itself in his hubris and pursuit of power, leads to his Fall. In a similar vein, Tolkien's satanic archvillains are corrupted by their craving for power and incriminate themselves by abusing the power given to them by their Creator.

34 Almond points to the Latin translation of the *Life of Adam and Eve*, a group of Jewish apocryphal manuscripts, as first describing Satan's pride as the direct origin of his downfall (2017: 39 ff.). *The Life of Adam and Eve* relates how Satan refused to worship the first human couple, Adam and Eve, as the image of God. Satan then exclaimed that he would rather attempt to place himself above God than obey his command, and Satan was subsequently expelled from heaven as punishment for his pride and disobedience. Satan's sin of pride as the direct cause of his Fall was later also prominently depicted in Milton's *Paradise Lost*.

Instead of becoming more powerful by turning away from their Maker, Morgoth and, subsequently, Sauron pay for their crimes by being continuously drained of their essence. They are subjected to a descent into oblivion similar to what Shippey refers to as the "'wraithing' process" (2001: 243), which may be observed in the Nazgûl. Morgoth "squandered his power (of being) in the endeavour to gain control of others" (*MR* 394) and Sauron invested so much of his power into the Ring that its loss left him weakened. In doing so, Morgoth and Sauron ultimately head for the emptiness of the Void.

In a vein similar to Tolkien, Lewis seems to have inadvertently made his archvillains appear dualistic. Upon having re-examined Lewis's work, Tolkien commented on "how dualistic Lewis' mind and imagination [were], though as a philosopher his [Lewis's] reason entirely rejected this" (*Letters* 371, #291). The circumstance which might have contributed to Tolkien's assessment is that Lewis does not provide an explicit history of corruption for his satanic archvillains who seem to enter his stories as fully formed evil characters. The same could largely be said of various satanic minions[35] in the *Narniad*. Although there are those servants of the White Witch, in *The Lion, the Witch and the Wardrobe*, who defect from the good side, thus becoming traitors, most of her minions appear to be innately evil creatures, never reported to have been created by Aslan in the beginning of the Narnian world. On the other hand, there is no evidence of their ever having been corrupted. This might give the impression that some sort of dualistic tendency was present in *The Chronicles of Narnia* from the beginning, since Cosmological dualism views Good and Evil as primordial principles created concurrently at the moment of Creation. Lewis may never have intended this, but the reader might be left with the impression that his satanic archvillains and their minions were in fact created evil.

Similarly to the diabolical villains in Tolkien's oeuvre, the satanic archvillains in *The Chronicles of Narnia* also seem to represent, to use Shippey's words, both "evil as an absence" and "evil as a force" (2001: 135). On the one hand, evil may seem to be an external force, manifesting itself in the archvillains and

---

35 The Earthmen from *The Silver Chair* are, of course, an important exception since they are benign creatures who only serve the Lady of the Green Kirtle as henchmen because they are under her spell. Yet another creature forced to work for the powers of darkness is, for instance, Mr. Tumnus from *The Lion, the Witch and the Wardrobe*.

monsters who give the impression of being tainted from the very beginning. On the other hand, Lewis's devilish archvillains are considerably less powerful[36] than their main opponent, Aslan, who represents the forces of light, and they are far from the power of the mighty Lion. Instead, they most strongly rely on phantasmagoria, trying to conceal the truth behind cunning lies. *The Chronicles of Narnia* pick up on the biblical theme "of evil as illusion and deception (and not an equal reality to good)" (Duriez 2015: 140f.). Thus, Evil is portrayed as an absence of truthfulness, with the satanic characters like the Lady of the Green Kirtle acting as agents of deceit.

Like Tolkien's Morgoth and Sauron, Jadis, the Lady of the Green Kirtle and Shift turn their backs on the goodness of the divine Creator. They all disrespect Aslan and his father, the Emperor-over-the-Sea, calling their divine authority into question. As Joseph Loconte argues both Lewis and Tolkien share the "Christian belief that evil represents a rejection of God and the joy and beauty that originate in him" (2017: 148). Lewis appears to be of the opinion that disobedience to the will of God causes misery (qtd. in Hooper 2005: 467). Though the reasons for their corruption are never explicitly named, one could argue that, like Tolkien's Sauron and Morgoth, the White Witch and the Lady of the Green Kirtle also fall on account of their unbridled yearning for domination. This wicked desire does not gain them extraordinary power or immortality but, instead, leads to their doom. Indeed, Jadis's descent into darkness clearly runs parallel to her pursuit of power, first in the world of Charn, and then as the White Witch in Narnia. By wishing to become immortal, Jadis rebels against the laws of the Creator, and, having gained a state of pseudo-immortality,[37] she is also cursed with discontent and misery. The more her powers as a sorceress grow, the more she dwindles,[38] turning from a tall, majestic enchantress into a shadow of her former self with a "dead-white face" (*LWW* 149). This dwindling process appears to be perfectly in line with Lewis's views on the nature of Evil. In Lewis's opinion, Evil appears to be "fissiparous", an opinion he has

36 Importantly, this holds true for the sphere of Narnia. Within the boundaries of Charn, Jadis appears to be so powerful that she is able to totally obliterate her native world through the unhallowed Deplorable Word.

37 This means that Jadis cannot die a natural death anymore. She can, however, be killed, unlike, for instance, the Greek gods who can suffer injuries and bleed but cannot be killed.

38 In that way, the dwindling of Jadis is reminiscent of the wraithing process undergone by Tolkien's Nazgûl.

one of his characters express in *The Pilgrim's Regress* (203). As Andrzej Wicher explains, Evil is "'fissiparous' because it reproduces itself by self-division and cannot stop reproducing itself, its expansion is then related to a process of vaporization, of becoming insubstantial, in other words, the greater it grows, the smaller it becomes" (2013: 138).

In the same way that the devil's plans frequently rebound on himself, the schemes of Tolkien's and Lewis's diabolic archvillains turn on their originators. According to the ransom theory as put forth by Irenaeus, Origen and Gregory of Nyssa,[39] the devil caused the death of Christ and thought of himself as victorious only to be defeated by the resurrected Messiah releasing mankind from the power of the devil by virtue of His sacrifice. Thus Satan, unwittingly, helped bring about his own defeat. Striving to do evil, the satanic figures in Arda and Narnia inadvertently act as eucatastrophic vehicles. Goethe's Mephisto famously utters that he was "A humble part of that great Power / Which always means Evil, always does the good" (ll. 1368-69). In a similar vein, Lewis expressed the opinion that "all, either willingly or unwillingly, do the will of God: Judas and Satan as tools, or instruments, John and Peter as sons" (qtd. in Hardy 2007: 38).

Inadvertently, the authors' devilish characters are strongly involved in the ultimate victory of the forces of light. This gives rise to the question whether the satanic villains in Arda and Narnia actually act as if they were truly Mephistophelian figures. Tolkien's eucatastrophies[40] are partly brought about by the machination of evil beings, most prominently, perhaps, Gollum, who inadvertently partakes in the destruction of the One Ring. In general, evil deeds might often unexpectedly lead to a turnaround of the events to the better in Middle-earth. Randel Helms provides a formula for this effect mechanism applying to Middle-earth: "(1) The cosmos is providentially controlled. (2) Intention structures result. [...] a good action with a good intent will have a good result; an evil action with an evil intent will also have an ultimately good result" (1971: 75). Melkor-Morgoth's disruptive influence on Arda mars the Earth but, also unintentionally, makes some aspects of Arda even more beautiful (*Sil* 8). Sauron's haughtiness and

---

39 For an elaborate discussion of the ransom theory see, for example, the subchapter 'Paying off the Devil' in Philip C. Almond's *The Devil. A New Biography* (2017: 49-53).

40 For some of the most recent studies on eucatastrophe, see Thayer (2016), Spirito (2017), and Gamble (2019).

disregard of those he perceives as weaklings lead to his miscalculation at the Siege of Gondor and, not long after that, his ultimate defeat. Saruman's Orcs contribute to the splitting of the Fellowship at Amon Hen and, as long-term consequences, Merry and Pippin stir the Ent Treebeard into action, thus bringing about the destruction of Isengard and Saruman's defeat which, in turn, enables the Rohirrim to play a crucial role in the War of the Ring.

Likewise, the sudden triumph of Good is often brought about by the originally evil intentions of satanic archvillains in Narnia. Jadis's corruption of Edmund in *The Lion, the Witch and the Wardrobe* results in Aslan's death and resurrection, paving the way for ultimate defeat of the White Witch. In *The Last Battle*, Shift's blasphemous crimes in the end lead to the creation of a new and unspoilt Narnia, more glorious and real than the old one, indeed, Lewis's own vision of the Kingdom of God. One the one hand, then, the sudden joyous turns in the works of Lewis and Tolkien bear witness to the resilience of goodness and godliness in the face of Evil – the Good triumphs over the Evil caused by the likes of Sauron, Saruman, and the White Witch. On the other hand, though, these satanic characters seem to act as an important device in the narrative technique employed by Tolkien and Lewis, in that they, quite ironically, prove to be the instruments of their own undoing and, at the same time, unwittingly contribute to the triumph of the side of Good. Therefore, the diabolic archvillains in Arda and Narnia indeed appear to act as truly Mephistophelean figures.

The devil and his demons are ultimately irredeemable. Already the early Christian scholar Origen of Alexandria (184–253) "seemed to believe that, by virtue of the devil's continually choosing evil, [...] [h]e had become 'natured' to evil and thus would, in fact, never choose the good and would never be saved" (Almond 2016: 45). Likewise, the satanic archvillains in the works of Tolkien and Lewis come to a bad end due to their unwillingness to repent, and are thus excluded from redemption.[41]

Those who are misled by Evil in Tolkien's Middle-earth seldom survive their flirtation with the satanic archvillains. In this respect, Wicher points out that

41 Such is also the ultimate fate of most of their monstrous minions.

in Tolkien's Secondary World "a thorough transformation of the moral nature of a character seems possible only in the direction of evil, and it takes place in the form of going down the slippery slope" (2013: 50). Wicher's observation would also apply to Tolkien's satanic figures who, having succumbed to the temptation of Evil, go down the same 'slippery slope.' Melkor feigns humility but does not repent on account of his pride. Similarly, Sauron "was given an opportunity of repentance [...] but could not face the humiliation of recantation; and suing for pardon" (*Letters* 190, #153). Last but not least, Saruman is conquered by his pride and hatred (*TT* 581-82), and thus, the Undying Lands remain out of his reach at the time of his death: "For a moment it [Saruman's spirit] wavered, looking to the West, but out of the West came a cold wind, and it bent away, and with a sigh dissolved into nothing" (*RK* 1020).

In contrast to those who are misled by Evil in Tolkien's Middle-earth, Lewis's child protagonists and other characters such as Uncle Andrew succeed in seeing the error of their ways. However, exactly like Tolkien's satanic archvillains, the White Witch Jadis, the Lady of the Green Kirtle, and Shift remain obstinate to the end, never attempting to make amends for their despicable behaviour. Both sorceresses thus dissolve into nothingness, while the Ape is carried away by Tash to his dark realm.

## Crafting Devils in Tolkien's and Lewis's Sub-creation

The composition of Tolkien's and Lewis's satanic figures appears to give some indication of their strategies of worldbuilding in general and their approaches to creating evil characters in particular. Lewis worked with 'supposals' which could be viewed as thought experiments or what-if scenarios on his part. To give an example, he meant Aslan to be "an invention giving an imaginary answer to the question, 'What might Christ become like if there really were a world like Narnia and He chose to be incarnate and die and rise again in that world as He actually has in ours?'" (qtd. in Hooper 2005: 424). Lewis strictly separated his way of thinking via supposals from finding allegorical representations of certain Christian themes. However, although Lewis would have us believe otherwise, he did, inadvertently or not, make use of Christian allegory while writing *The Chronicles of Narnia*, and his tendency to use allegories as templates for worldbuilding, viewed as a kind of sub-creative shortcut, is hard to be denied. This tendency becomes especially apparent in *The Lion, the Witch and the Wardrobe*, clearly elaborating on the themes of Christ's Crucifixion and Resurrection, and in *The Last Battle*, which uses the Last Judgement as a template. In the former novel, for example, Jadis allegorically represents Satan in the Passion of Christ. Consequently, with his simplified allegorical templates, Lewis does not seem to have the potential to deliver as convincing a portrayal of corruption as Tolkien does in the cases of Morgoth, Sauron and Saruman. Nevertheless, he still managed to create some compelling images of Evil in *The Chronicles of Narnia*.

Tolkien, on the other hand, was not particularly fond of allegories, mainly because they restricted the meaning of a text to a single reading. For his part, Tolkien "much prefer[red] history, true or feigned, with its varied applicability to the thought and experience of the readers" (qtd. in Shippey 1992: 152). Even though, then, Tolkien seems to have drawn on the concept of the devil in a similar way to that of Lewis, he does not at any point appear to have placed Morgoth, or Sauron and Saruman, within an allegorical frame.[42] This means that, whereas one can interpret Tolkien's satanic archvillains against the background of the devil's development in the Christian tradition, there is no one-to-one correspondence between the actions of these diabolical characters and the story of Satan. Nonetheless, Tolkien's satanic figures appear to be more closely modelled on the devil than Lewis's diabolic villains with regard to their Fall and the fact that they actually rebel against the work of their Creator.

For several reasons, Lewis's satanic archvillains appear to be considerably less rounded than those in the works of Tolkien. To begin with, in contrast with the more static archvillains in Narnia, the Fall of the devilish characters in Arda is more comprehensible, involving the evolution of three angelic entities from virtuous beings to malicious fallen angels. The impression that Lewis's satanic figures are devious from the very beginning seems to be largely due to the limited amount of worldbuilding that Lewis invested in their background. Furthermore, Lewis did not provide his diabolic archvillains with any more

42 For a critical commentary on Tolkien's aversion to allegory see, for instance, Petty (2007), Flieger and Shippey (2001), Craven (2002), Weidner (2002), Geier (2008), Segura (2010), and Honegger (2011).

complex motives beyond the basic categories of vices like envy, pride and the pursuit of power. They are neither corrupted by a desire to create (Melkor), nor by a desire for order (Sauron), nor thirst for knowledge (Saruman). Concerning the complexity of the *Narniad*, its novels seem to operate on the level of well-crafted literary fairy tales, with Lewis valuing story-telling above worldbuilding, the fact which might explain why he, to some extent, lacks the encyclopaedic impulse and attention to sub-creative detail so typical of the build-up of Tolkien's Secondary World.

Apart from Lewis's tendency not to overinvest in sub-creative detail, his dispensing with creating rather more complex and rounded portrayals of satanic figures might be constituted by his apparent discomfort with the creation of evil characters. Lewis commented on his work on *The Screwtape Letters* that he "never wrote with less enjoyment. Though it is easy to twist one's mind into the diabolical attitude, it was not fun, or not for long. The strain produced a sort of spiritual cramp" (qtd. in Hooper 2005: 268). In a similar vein, Lewis did not want to give a colourful portrayal of hell in his *Great Divorce* because he did not want to rouse fascination for the demonic, and he warned against showing "an excessive and unhealthy interest in [devils]" (268).

In contrast, Tolkien, who, in his youth "desired dragons with a profound desire" (*TOFS* 55), could barely conceal his fascination with envisioning monsters and especially their diabolic overlords. Tolkien's statement on the central role of the monsters from *Beowulf* could just as much apply to his satanic archvillains, being "fundamentally allied to the underlying ideas of [his work], which give it its lofty tone and high seriousness" (*BMC* 7). Tolkien even appears to have shown sympathy for his devils in that he understood their inordinate sub-creative desire, although he did condemn it at the same time.

Shippey argues that "Tolkien could not help seeing a part of himself in Fëanor and Saruman, sharing their perhaps licit, perhaps illicit desire to 'subcreate'" (1992: 214). I would argue that this applies even more to Melkor than Fëanor, or Saruman, since Melkor, like Tolkien, wanted to shape a whole world. It almost appears to be with some kind of admiration for the dark Vala's creative energies that Tolkien (*Letters* 190, #153) calls Melkor the "Prime sub-creative Rebel." It has to be noted, though, that, at this point, by calling Melkor a "sub-creative Rebel," Tolkien stresses that Melkor *strives* to be a sub-creator but, due to his hubristic and evil intentions, never quite reaches his goal. On a meta level, Melkor thus appears to be Tolkien's comment on the dangers of abusing one's sub-creative talent. Shippey makes the supposition that the sin of craving for illicit sub-creation was a "special variety of pride" in the form of "a restless desire to make things" aimed at the eternal reflection and incarnation of one's personality (1992: 214). Sub-creation should not serve narcissistic self-fulfilment and the sub-creator should, instead, show humility in the face of God's Creation, the Creation which holds the sum-total of the concepts that Man as sub-creator can draw on. If wholly independent man-made creations were possible, they would not be in accordance with God's Creation on the level of the human author. On the level of Tolkien's story, such acts would constitute absolute abominations in the face of the Creator. In this respect, Tolkien elucidates that "if Morgoth broke the supreme ban against making other 'rational' creatures like Elves or Men[,] [...] they would be Morgoth's greatest Sins, abuses of his highest privilege, and would be creatures begotten of Sin, and naturally bad" (*Letters* 195, #153) .

## Conclusion

Both Tolkien and Lewis incorporated into their sub-creative compositions of satanic archvillains a number of elements and themes from the biblical Christian tradition concerning the devil. Especially Tolkien seems to have been directly inspired by the Fall of Satan in his creation of the major villains in Arda: Melkor, Sauron and Saruman, each of them a fallen angelic being that rebelled against the work of their Creator. In the case of Lewis, these diabolic archvillains are more strongly associated with the Original Sin in man, whereas in Tolkien's world, they are directly complicit in causing the Fall of its inhabitants. Some of these Satanic figures, however, bring Evil into their respective worlds at the very outset of their existence. Others play a key role in the apocalyptic scenarios envisioned by the two authors. In the works of both writers, they also turn or attempt to turn the Secondary Worlds they inhabit into a Kingdom of Darkness which they intend to rule as usurpers. Finally, they engage in typical satanic activities, causing their victims to sin or even directly taking possession of them.

Concerning the nature of Evil, there appears to be a notable tension between the dualist and Augustinian/Boethian views in the portrayal of satanic figures in the works of Tolkien and Lewis. Nonetheless, both authors for the most part portrayed Evil as a parasite that lives on divine goodness and continuously dwindles. Ultimately, the satanic figures prove to be not only eucatastrophic vehicles, but also the instruments of their own destruction. In general, Tolkien modelled his archvillains more closely on the figure of the devil, although he did not adopt the allegorical approach that may be found in *The Lion, the Witch and the Wardrobe* and *The Last Battle*. On a meta level, the evil sub-creator Morgoth might, in fact, be viewed as Tolkien's comment on the pitfalls of inordinate sub-creative desire.

Both Tolkien and Lewis envisioned highly memorable satanic figures. The fiendish witch Jadis is a very prominent and popular villainess from Lewis's *Narniad*, not least due to the stunning portrayal of this character by Tilda Swinton in the film adaptation of *The Lion, the Witch and the Wardrobe* (2005), although the highly positive hero Aslan is indisputably Lewis's best-known character. Tolkien, in turn, succeeded in creating satanic villains who constitute truly iconic images of Evil, more strongly rooted in the collective consciousness than his best-known heroes such as Frodo or Gandalf, be it Sauron's Ring and his Great Eye in *The Lord of the Rings* or the dark Vala Melkor-Morgoth who casts his titanic shadow over the entire book of *The Silmarillion*.

The legacy of Tolkien and Lewis is that they not only helped to put a face to the figure of Satan in postmodern literature (although the works of Tolkien and Lewis are, of course, in themselves, not postmodern), but also inspired and continue to inspire a host of other satanic figures. Stephen King, for instance, an ardent admirer of Tolkien's work, seems to have based his Crimson King in *The Dark Tower* series, an evil figure who wishes to destroy the multitude of universes and rule the primaeval chaos, on Saruman, Sauron and Morgoth. Like the fallen Istar Saruman and the disgraced Maia Sauron, the Crimson King dwells in a dark tower and unites Sauron's desire to rule and Morgoth's desire to destroy in one person. The destruction of the beams supporting the *Dark Tower* by the Crimson King mirrors Morgoth's destruction of the Two Lamps. In a possible allusion to Saruman, he confronts the hero taking on the form of an old, white bearded man imprisoned in his own tower. As an undead

Dark Lord who loses his physical form and is bound to his tower in the form of two glowing red eyes, the Crimson King at the same time also points to the figure of Sauron.

Sauron also seems to have been a prominent source of inspiration for J.K. Rowling's Lord Voldemort. Similar to Sauron as the Necromancer who dwells in Mirkwood after his defeat, Voldemort recuperates in the forests of Albania, corrupting the area he inhabits, turning it into his haunted abode. Reminiscent of Tolkien's Sauron, Voldemort pours his life force into demonic talismans. The unbeatable weapon called Elder Wand which Voldemort seeks to ensure his ultimate triumph resembles Sauron's desire to reclaim the One Ring. At the same time, Saruman could also have served as a model for Rowling's Dark Lord, in that Voldemort, like Saruman, is a brilliant wizard gone over to the dark side who devotes himself to the study of magic artefacts which will grant him great power. Rowling greatly admired C.S. Lewis and some of the capricious she-devil characteristics of Jadis seem to have been passed on to Voldemort. Like Jadis, Voldemort condemns himself in his pursuit of immortality and dwindles into a pale shadow of his former handsome self.

Last but not least, there is the horned Night King from the HBO series *Game of Thrones* (based on George R.R. Martin's *A Song of Ice and Fire*). The crown of spikes protruding from his skull seem to point to Satan's horns and his icy homeland recalls the cold regions of hell. Similar to Sauron and Morgoth, he practices necromancy and attempts to engulf the world in an endless winter in the manner of Morgoth and Jadis. All these diabolic archvillains following in the footsteps of Tolkien's and Lewis's sinister and glorious rulers of darkness continue to fascinate the readers all over the world and constitute ever new attempts of approaching the shadowy enigma called Evil.

## About the Author

Franz Klug is a PhD student at the Friedrich Schiller University in Jena. He studied English there and at the University of Zurich, as well as Art at the Bauhaus University in Weimar. Between 2016 and 2020, he worked as a student assistant for the Department of English Studies in Jena, where he was a tutor in the History of English, Old and Middle English, and Diachronic Linguistics. His research areas include the linguistic and artistic components of literary worldbuilding, the works of William Shakespeare, J.R.R. Tolkien, George R.R. Martin, and James Joyce, as well as the impact of mythology on modern fiction.

## Bibliography

Abbott, Joe. 1990. 'Tolkien's Monsters: Concept and Function in *The Lord of the Rings* (Part III): Sauron.' *Mythlore* 16.3, 51-59.

Alberto, Maria. 2017. '"It had been his virtue, and therefore also the cause of his fall": Seduction as a Mythopoeic Accounting for Evil in Tolkien's Work.' *Mythlore* 35.2, 63-79.

Almond, Philip C. 2016. *The Devil. A New Biography*. London and New York: I.B. Tauris.

Auden, Wystan Hugh. 1967. 'Good and Evil in *The Lord of the Rings*.' *Tolkien Journal* 3.1, 5-8.

Blacharska, Katarzyna. 2013. 'The Fallen: Milton's Satan and Tolkien's Melkor.' *O What a Tangled Web*. Ed. Barbara Kowalik. Zurich and Jena: Walking Tree Publishers, 115–43.

Becker, Udo. 2010. *Lexikon der Symbole*. Freiburg im Breisgau: Verlag Herder GmbH.

Bender, Melanie. 2011. *Auf den Spuren von Narnia: eine religiöse Weltgeschichte*. Paderborn, Munich, Vienna and Zurich: Schöningh.

*The Bible: Authorized King James Version with Apocrypha*. 2008. Eds. Robert Carroll and Stephen Prickett. Oxford: Oxford University Press.

Bowman, Mary R. 2003. 'A Darker Ignorance: C.S. Lewis and the Nature of the Fall.' *Mythlore* 24.1, 62-78.

Chrétien de Troyes. 2004. 'Erec and Enide.' *Arthurian Romances*. London: Penguin Books, 37-122.

Christopher, Joe. 1988. 'J.R.R. Tolkien, Narnian Exile.' *Mythlore* 15.1, 37-45.

Cooper, John Charles (ed.). 1992. *Brewer's Myth and Legend*. London, New York, Sydney and Toronto: BCA.

Craven, Ken. 2002. 'A Catholic Poem in Time of War: *The Lord of the Rings*.' *Chesterton Review* 28, 246-66.

Daigle, Marsha Ann. 1985. 'Dante's *Divine Comedy* and C.S. Lewis's *Narnia Chronicles*.' *Christianity and Literature* 34, 41-58.

Davison, Scott A. 2004. 'Tolkien and the Nature of Evil.' *The Lord of the Rings and Philosophy. Popular Culture and Philosophy*. Eds. Gregory Bassham and Eric Bronson. Chicago and La Salle, IL: Open Court.

Devaux, Michaël. 2009. 'Dagor Dagorath & Ragnarök: Tolkien & the Apocalypse.' *Hither Shore* 6, 102-15.

Duriez, Colin. 2015. *Bedeviled. Lewis, Tolkien and the Shadow of Evil*. Downers Grove, IL: InterVarsity Press.

Edwards, Karen. 2009. 'Milton's Reformed Animals: An Early Modern Bestiary: T-Z.' *Milton Quarterly* 43, 241-308.

Ferber, Michael. 2017. *A Dictionary of Literary Symbols*. Cambridge: Cambridge University Press.

Fisher, Jason. 2008. 'Tolkien's Fortunate Fall and the Third Theme of Ilúvatar.' *Truths Breathed Through Silver: The Inklings' Moral and Mythopoeic Legacy*. Eds. Jonathan B. Himes, Joe R. Christopher and Salwa Khoddam. Newcastle: Cambridge Scholars Publishing, 93-109.

Flieger, Verlyn and Tom A. Shippey. 2001. 'Allegory Versus Bounce: Tolkien's *Smith of Wootton Major*.' *Journal of the Fantastic in the Arts* 12, 186-200.

Foster, Robert. 2001. *The Complete Guide to Middle-earth*. New York: Ballantine Books.

Freeman, James A. 2014. 'Satan the General.' *Milton and the Martial Muse*. Ed. James A. Freeman. Princeton, NJ: Princeton University Press, 113-85.

Gallant, Richard Z. 2014. 'Original Sin in Heorot and Valinor.' *Tolkien Studies* 11, 2014, 109-29.

Gamble, Chance. 2019. "New Hope in the Midst of Darkness': Eucatastrophe as Kairos in *The Lord of the Rings*.' Master Thesis. Texas: Scholar Works at UT Tyler.

Geier, Fabian. 2009. *J.R.R. Tolkien*. Hamburg: Rowohlt.

Giraudeau, David. 2007. 'Words, Phrases and Passages in Various Tongues in *The Lord of the Rings* by J.R.R. Tolkien.' *Parma Eldalamberon* 17, 1-69.

Glover, Willis B. 1971. 'The Christian Character of Tolkien's Invented World.' *Criticism* 13, 39-53.

Goethe, Johann Wolfgang von. 2014. *Faust. A Tragedy, Parts One and Two.* New Heavens, CT and London: Yale University Press.

Guiley, Rosemary Ellen. 2004. *The Encyclopedia of Angels.* New York: Facts on File Inc.

Hardy, Elizabeth Baird. 2007. *Milton, Spenser and the Chronicles of Narnia: Literary Sources for the C.S. Lewis Novels.* Jefferson, NC: McFarland.

Hartley, Gregory. 2012. 'A Wind from the West: The Role of the Holy Spirit in Tolkien's Middle-earth.' *Christianity and Literature* 62, 95-120.

Helms, Randel. 1974. *Tolkien's World.* Boston, MA: Houghton Mifflin.

Hood, Gyneth. 1993. 'Nature and Technology: Angelic and Sacrificial Strategies in Tolkien's *The Lord of the Rings*.' *Mythlore* 19.4, 6-12.

Hooper, Walter. 1998. *C.S. Lewis: The Companion & Guide.* San Francisco, CA: HarperSanFrancisco.

Honegger, Thomas (ed.). 2011. *Tolkien in Translation.* Zurich and Jena: Walking Tree Publishers.

2021. '"What have I got in my pocket?": Tolkien and the Tradition of the Rings of Power.' *Journal of Tolkien Research* 13.1, article 1.

King, Don. 1984. 'Narnia and the Seven Deadly Sins.' *Mythlore* 10.4, 14-19.

1987. 'The Wardrobe as Christian Metaphor.' *Mythlore* 14.1, 25-7, 33.

Lense, Edward. 1976. 'Sauron is Watching You: The Role of the Great Eye in *The Lord of the Rings*.' *Mythlore* 4.1, 3-6.

Lewis, Clive Staples. 2014. *The Last Battle.* London: HarperCollins.

2014. *The Lion, the Witch and the Wardrobe.* London: HarperCollins.

2014. *The Magician's Nephew.* London: HarperCollins.

2014. *The Pilgrim's Regress. Wade Annotated Edition.* Grand Rapids, MI: Wm. B. Eerdmans Publishing Co.

2014. *The Silver Chair.* London: HarperCollins.

Lloyd, Paul M. 1976. 'The Role of Warfare and Strategy in *The Lord of the Rings*.' *Mythlore* 11.3, 3-7.

Loconte, Joseph. 2015. *A Hobbit, a Wardrobe, and a Great War.* Nashville, TN: Nelson Books.

Long, Josh B. 2013. 'Disparaging Narnia: Reconsidering Tolkien's View of *The Lion, the Witch and the Wardrobe*.' *Mythlore* 31.3, 31-46.

Miller, Jennifer L. 2009. 'No Sex in Narnia? How Hans Christian Andersen's "Snow Queen" Problematizes C.S. Lewis's *The Chronicles of Narnia*.' *Mythlore* 28.1, 113-30.

Milton, John. 2014. *Paradise Lost*. London: Penguin Books.

Mosley, David Russell. 2016. *Being Deified: Poetry and Fantasy on the Path to God*. Minneapolis, MN: Fortress Press, 75–76.

Patterson, Nancy-Lou. 1990. 'The Bolt of Tash: The Figure of Satan in C.S. Lewis' *The Horse and His Boy* and *The Last Battle*.' *Mythlore* 16.4, 23-26.

Petty, Anne. 2007. 'Shakespearean Catharsis in J.R.R. Tolkien's Fiction.' *Tolkien and Shakespeare: Essays on Shared Themes and Language*. Ed. Janet Brennan Croft. Jefferson, NC: McFarland.

Randolph, Burt. 1968. 'The Singular Incompetence of the Valar.' *Tolkien Journal* 3, 11-13.

Rutledge, Fleming. 2007. 'The Battle for Middle-Earth: Tolkien's Divine Design in *The Lord of the Rings*.' *Nova Religio* 10.3, 124-25.

Sandner, David. 2006. 'Between Eucatastrophe and Grace: J.R.R. Tolkien and Flannery.' *An Interdisciplinary Journal* 89, 171-98.

Seachris, Joshua and Linda Zagzebski. 2007. 'Weighing Evils: The C.S. Lewis Approach.' *International Journal for Philosophy of Religion* 62, 81-88.

Segura, Eduardo. 2010. "Secondary Belief": Tolkien and the Revision of Romantic Notion of Poetic Faith.' *Hither Shore* 7, 123-35.

Shelley, Percy Bysshe. 2009. 'Ode to the West Wind.' *The Major Works Including Poetry Prose and Drama*. Oxford: Oxford University Press, 412-14.

Shippey, Tom. 1992. *The Road to Middle-earth*. London: HarperCollins.

2001. *J.R.R. Tolkien. Author of the Century*. London: HarperCollins.

Snorri Sturluson. 1987. *Edda*. Transl. Anthony Faulkes. London: Everyman.

Spirito, Guglielmo. 2017. 'Eucatastrophe and Tolkien's world building: "*a ray of light through the very chinks of the universe about us.*" A Theological Reading.' *Hither Shore* 14, 158-70.

Tolkien, John Ronald Reuel. 2006. '*Beowulf*: The Monsters and the Critics.' *The Monsters and the Critics and Other Essays*. Ed. Christopher Tolkien. London: HarperCollins, 5-48.

2018. *Beren and Lúthien*. Ed. Christopher Tolkien. London: HarperCollins.

2015. *The Book of Lost Tales. Part Two. The History of Middle-earth 2.* Ed. Christopher Tolkien. London: HarperCollins.

1981. *The Letters of J.R.R. Tolkien.* Ed. Humphrey Carpenter with the assistance of Christopher Tolkien. London, Boston and Sydney: George Allen and Unwin.

2005. *The Lord of the Rings. Part 1. The Fellowship of the Ring.* London: HarperCollins.

2005. *The Lord of the Rings. Part 2. The Two Towers.* London: HarperCollins.

2005. *The Lord of the Rings. Part 3. The Return of the King.* London: HarperCollins.

1993. *The Lost Road and other Writings. The History of Middle-earth 5.* Ed. Christopher Tolkien. London: HarperCollins.

1994. *Morgoth's Ring. The History of Middle-earth 10.* Ed. Christopher Tolkien. London: HarperCollins.

1997. *The Peoples of Middle-earth. The History of Middle-earth 12.* Ed. Christopher Tolkien. London: HarperCollins.

2006. *The Silmarillion.* Ed. Christopher Tolkien. London: HarperCollins.

2008. *Tolkien On Fairy-stories.* Expanded edition with commentary and notes. Eds. Verlyn Flieger and Douglas A. Anderson. London: HarperCollins.

2001. *Unfinished Tales of Númenor and Middle-earth.* Ed. Christopher Tolkien. Chicago, IL: Houghton Mifflin Harcourt.

Thayer, Anne. 2016. *On Eagles' Wings: An Exploration of Eucatastrophe in Tolkien's Fantasy.* Edinburgh: Luna Press Publishing.

Toner, Christopher. 2008. 'Catastrophe and Eucatastrophe: Russell and Tolkien on the True Form of Fiction.' *Journal Compilation.* Oxford: Blackwell Publishing.

Treloar, John L. 1988. 'Tolkien and Christian Concepts of Evil: Apocalypse and Privation.' *Mythlore* 15.2, 57-60.

1989. 'The Middle-earth Epic and the Seven Capital Vices.' *Mythlore* 16.1, 37-42.

Watkins, Zachary. 2005. 'Satan and *The Silmarillion*: John Milton's Angelic Decline in J.R.R. Tolkien's Melkor.' *The Grey Book: Online Journals of Middle-earth* 1.

Watson, George. 2009. 'The High Road to Narnia: C.S. Lewis and His Friend J.R.R. Tolkien Believed that Truths Are Universal and that Stories Reveal Them.' The *American Scholar* 78, 89-95.

Weidner, Brian. 2002. 'Middle-earth: The Real World of J.R.R. Tolkien.' *Mythlore*, 23, 45-57.

Wicher, Andrzej. 2013. *Selected Medieval and Religious Themes in the Works of C.S. Lewis and J.R.R. Tolkien*. Łódź: Łódzkie Towarzystwo Naukowe.

Wood, Ralph C. 2003. *The Gospel According to Tolkien*. Louisville, KY: Westminster John Knox Press.

Wytenbroek, Lynn J.R. 1988. 'Apocalyptic Vision in *The Lord of the Rings*.' *Mythlore* 14.4, 7-12.

Kris Swank



# The Nostalgic Fantasy of "Good Plain Food" in Narnia and Middle-earth

**Abstract**

Meals in Narnia and Middle-earth feature an abundance of local, simple, natural fare. C.S. Lewis and J.R.R. Tolkien stated their own preferences for eating in just such a fashion. "Good plain food," Tolkien called it, while Warren 'Warnie' Lewis, describing his brother's tastes, used the similar term, "plain domestic cookery." Some commentators connect Lewis's and Tolkien's affinity for plain food to the food of their childhoods, as both men spent some time in idyllic rural settings, although those days ended for both in tragedy. Yet, before either author was born, the Victorians had effected radical transformation in the food supply: local fare had been supplemented, and even supplanted, by imported foods; homemade goods had largely been abandoned in favor of time-saving, cheap processed foods. By the time Tolkien and Lewis were creating meals in their secondary worlds, "good plain food" had been disappearing from English culture for over a hundred years. Like the homely fare of Narnia and Middle-earth, similar food is depicted in fantasy classics from 'The Golden Age' of British children's literature by authors Kenneth Grahame (1859-1932), Beatrix Potter (1866-1943) and A.A. Milne (1882-1956). Like Tolkien and Lewis, these Golden Age authors spent some of their childhoods in rural idylls; they also experienced the tragic loss of those innocent childhood days. The use of nostalgically simple and natural food by all five authors fulfils a similar longing, not necessarily for their actual childhoods, but for an imagined time and space, an Edenic England as it might have been.

An image of living off the land pervades the stories of Narnia and Middle-earth. Mr. Beaver ice-fishes for trout just outside of his comfortable house. Hobbits pick and eat mushrooms fresh from Farmer Maggot's field. Sméagol catches a brace of rabbits which Sam cooks over an open campfire. Celebratory meals feature an abundance of simple, natural fare. Goldberry serves the Hobbits "yellow cream and honeycomb, and white bread, and butter; milk, cheese, and green herbs and ripe berries gathered" (*FR* 124). The feast created by Bacchus and Silenus in *Prince Caspian* consists of roasted meat, grain cakes, and "pyramids and cataracts of fruit" (223). C.S. Lewis and J.R.R. Tolkien stated their own preferences for eating in just such a fashion. "Good plain food," Tolkien called it (*Letters*

288; #213). Warren 'Warnie' Lewis, describing his brother's tastes, used a similar term: "plain domestic cookery" (*Letters of C.S. Lewis* 35).

Some commentators connect Lewis's and Tolkien's affinity for plain food to their youths. Nancy-Lou Patterson characterizes Lewis's Narnian cuisine as "the food of one's happiest memories of childhood" (1998: 74). In nearly identical language, Chris-Rachael Oseland connects the "authentic period recipes from Tolkien's youth" in her Hobbit-themed cookbook with "the happiest days of his childhood" (2014: back cover). Both Tolkien and Lewis were born at the tail-end of the Victorian era: Tolkien (1892) in Bloemfontein, Orange Free State, southern Africa; Lewis (1898) in Belfast, Northern Ireland. Both relocated to England when they were boys. In April 1895, Tolkien's mother brought him and his brother to England for a visit. His father died in Bloemfontein during their absence and Tolkien never returned there. He said in an interview, "my earliest memories are of Africa, but it was alien to me [...] I had for the countryside of England both the native feeling and the personal wonder of somebody who comes to it" (Resnick 1967: 41). The few years Tolkien spent in rural Sarehole with his mother and brother were, indeed, among the happiest of his life, though short-lived. By the end of 1904, the boys were living in industrial Birmingham, and their mother had sickened and died. Thereafter, Tolkien had no permanent home until he settled down with a wife and children of his own in the 1920s. The rest of his youth was spent shuttling between the homes of friends and relations, and various boarding houses. Unlike Tolkien, England did not produce love at first sight for Lewis. After his mother died of cancer in 1908, Lewis was sent to a series of English boarding schools, which he hated. In *Surprised by Joy*, Lewis recounts

> No Englishman will be able to understand my first impressions of England [...] The strange English accents with which I was surrounded seemed like the voices of demons. But what was worst was the English landscape [...] I have made up the quarrel since; but at that moment I conceived a hatred for England which took many years to heal. (25-28)

For both authors, a short, happy childhood was shattered by the deaths of their mothers, the death of, or separation from, their fathers and home, and relegation to a series of temporary and disagreeable living arrangements. Later, both men attended Oxford University and served in the British Army in World War

I (1914-18) where both suffered from trench fever and Lewis was injured. Both men also lost close friends in the war. Oseland writes, "After losing all but one of his friends in World War I then living through the horrors of World War II, it's no surprise [Tolkien] wanted to celebrate and venerate a gentler way of life he saw rapidly disappearing as the world around him grew smaller and bleaker" (2014: 7). She contends that something of that way of life is expressed in the food of the Shire. Patterson similarly pronounces Narnian food "good" because it is familiar from Lewis's childhood (1998: 73).

Such suggestions may not be wholly inaccurate. Yet, as this study argues, even before either author was born, the Victorians had effected radical transformation in the food supply: local fare had been supplemented, and even supplanted, by imported foods; homemade goods had largely been abandoned in favor of time-saving, cheap processed foods. By the time Tolkien and Lewis were creating meals in their secondary worlds in the 1930s and 1950s, respectively, the practice of eating off the land and eating natural foods had been disappearing from English culture for over a hundred years.

The homely fare of Narnia and Middle-earth, on the other hand, bears close similarities to homely food in fantasy classics from 'The Golden Age' of British children's literature, that is, works written from the mid-nineteenth century until World War I and its aftermath, represented by such authors as Kenneth Grahame (1859-1932), Beatrix Potter (1866-1943) and A.A. Milne (1882-1956). Tolkien, Lewis, and these three Golden Age authors all spent some of their childhoods in idyllic rural settings, and all five experienced the loss of those innocent childhood days. Their collective sense of nostalgia for old-fashioned English food is bound up in those idylls and losses. Svetlana Boym observes, "Modern nostalgia is a mourning for the impossibility of mythical return, for the loss of an enchanted world with clear borders and values; it could be a secular expression of a spiritual longing, a nostalgia for an absolute, a home that is both physical and spiritual, the Edenic unity of time and space" (2002: 8). As will be discussed, the Edenic times and spaces of Narnia and Middle-earth (and the River Bank, the world of Peter Rabbit, and the Hundred Acre Wood) act as nostalgic counterpoints to the adult modern world. Within these idyllic spaces, idyllic comfort food – *good plain food* – exists in contradistinction to the modern world's disruptions of industrialization, warfare, and parental loss.

## Literature Review

Several scholars have previously written about the cuisines of Narnia and Middle-earth through a variety of critical lenses. Often, *what* is being eaten is equated with the morality of *who* is doing the eating. The earliest commentator on the relationship between diet and morality in Middle-earth may have been Patricia Meyer Spacks whose 1959 essay notes, "the difference between good and evil seems rather simple [...] The good love nature, the evil destroy it. The good eat good food, the evil eat bad food" (1959: 55-56). Marjorie Burns also observes that Tolkien uses "food as a means of alluding to moral issues" (2005: 157). She argues that "virtue or corruption [...is] measured through dietary preferences" (Burns 2005: 164). She and Spacks both relate virtue with vegetarianism. Burns writes that the highest and most virtuous have "fleshless (or nearly fleshless) diets [...] The highest and best [i.e. the Elves] eat no meat at all" (2005: 166). Spacks writes, "the representatives of Good tend to be vegetarian" (1959: 55). Thomas Honegger agrees that Tolkien establishes a "relationship between what (and how) a protagonist eats and what he or she is" (2013: 77). However, he disagrees on the subject of vegetarianism, writing, "As a matter of fact, elves are not vegetarians, and we have several texts mentioning their hunting and, in *The Hobbit*, the starving dwarves perceive the 'smell of roast meats' wafting from the fires of the Wood-elves" (2013: 7). Janka Kaščáková reasons, although "it is a tempting assumption, taking into consideration the fact that there is no evidence that [Elves] ever eat meat; yet there is likewise no proof to the contrary, and such a claim can therefore be challenged on the basis of the fact that the absence of a thing in the story does not necessarily mean it does not exist" (2010: 95). As for Lewis, Matthew Dickerson and David O'Hara found that "in all the Narnia stories, the only professed vegetarians are Eustace's modern and ridiculous parents. Even the beavers eat ham (as well as trout)" (2009: 172).

Food has also been analyzed as religious symbolism in both Tolkien's and Lewis's works. Both Jonathan Langford and Kaščáková, for example, note the Eucharistic aspect of Tolkien's Elvish *lembas* cakes (Langford 1996: 123; Kaščáková 2010: 96). Langford observes the "overtly sacramental [...] effects of the Elvish miruvor" (1996: 122). Meanwhile, Patterson maintains, "all or at least many of Lewis's homely meals in his fantasies are meetings with the Creator in the Creation" (1998: 62). As such, food miraculously provided on a journey recalls the biblical Exodus and the manna provided in the wilderness, as well as the Seder which celebrates the Last Supper (Patterson 1998: 83). Martindale and Welch write, "[Lewis] tantalizes our taste buds with vividly described spreads of food but also gives us many symbolic scenes ranging from devouring demons to sacramental moments echoing the Lord's Supper, addressing the gamut of spiritual significance" (2005: 103).

Some commentators examine the nature of communal feasting in Middle-earth and Narnia. Susan Navarette argues that

> Among the hobbits and elves of Lorien [sic], food – the sharing of it and the providing of it – functions as an expression of kindness, good will, and generosity [...] Succor, strength, and sympathy prevail in those communities of men and women (and hobbits) who dine together, who together regenerate the soul by nourishing and renewing the body's life force. (1996: 100)

Langford also notes in *The Lord of the Rings*, "the sharing of food becomes an important cultural metaphor for social and spiritual communion indicating membership in a common group" (Langford 1996: 120). Guglielmo Spirito and Emanuele Rimoli point out that "fellowship in Italian is *compagnia*, from the Latin *cum-panis*, literally: 'those who share bread'" (2011: 250). Indeed, there are numerous examples of the revivifying effect of food shared along the way: food provided by the Beavers, Father Christmas, and Bacchus in Lewis's Narnia, and by Beorn, Gildor, Tom Bombadil, and Faramir in Tolkien's Middle-earth. Furthermore, Tolkien depicts the simple pleasures of normal, earthly 'hobbit-like' life because "food – and drink – matters, as pleasure and joy matters" (Spirito and Rimoli 2011: 245). As the dying Thorin tells Bilbo, "If more of us valued food and cheer and song above hoarded gold, it would be a merrier world" (*Hobbit* 263).

Some commentators have put the focus on the preferred cuisines of the authors themselves. Oseland writes, "The Shire represented everything Tolkien loved about English country life" (2014: 7). Patterson notes, "Readers of Lewis's letters, diaries, and biographical works will recall that to call food 'plain' is to pronounce it good" (1998: 53). Yet, there is still work to be done regarding the concept of *good plain food*: what exactly is it? And, what role does it play in Narnia and Middle-earth? Are Lewis's and Tolkien's depictions realistic representations of food from their childhoods? Or, should we even expect the food of fantasy worlds to be 'realistic'? And, if their food is not meant to be realistic, then what does *good plain food* represent?

## Defining 'Good Plain Food'

Both Lewis and Tolkien professed a preference for 'plain food.' Warnie Lewis wrote of his brother that "Plain domestic cookery was what he wanted [...] What he really disliked was 'messed-up food', by which he meant any sort of elaborately dressed dish: he could never be persuaded to experiment with new foods" (*Letters of C.S. Lewis* 36). In *The Fellowship of the Ring*, Tolkien wrote, "[Hobbits] love peace and quiet and good tilled earth: a well-ordered and well-farmed countryside was their favourite haunt" (*FR* 1). He compared himself to a Hobbit in a 1958 letter, writing "I like gardens, trees and unmechanized farmlands; I smoke a pipe, and like good plain food (unrefrigerated), but detest French cooking" (*Letters* 288-9, #213). He used the same phrase fifteen years later in a letter to his son Christopher upon returning from Bournemouth where he "had some good plain food" (430).

It is not only Lewis and Tolkien who express a preference for eating plainly, but also their fictional heroes. In fact, as shown in the two examples below, the provision of 'good' food is one way that good characters in Narnia and Middle-earth can identify one another. The Dufflepods in Lewis's *The Voyage of the Dawn Treader* at first appear nefarious when they abduct Lucy, but they prove to be good-at-heart by providing Caspian's landing party a "good meal" of "mushroom soup and boiled chickens and hot boiled ham and gooseberries, red currants, curds, cream, milk, and mead" (*VDT* 155). Tolkien's Sam Gamgee is suspicious of the people in Bree, but he is satisfied that the innkeeper Barliman Butterbur is trustworthy when he serves the Hobbits, "hot soup, cold meats, a blackberry tart, new loaves, slabs of butter, and half a ripe cheese"; Sam Gamgee deems this "good plain food, as good as the Shire could show and homelike enough to dispel the last of Sam's misgivings" (*FR* 154).

But what, precisely, constitutes *good plain food*? Using the preceding quotations from Warren Lewis and Tolkien together with supporting passages from C.S. Lewis's and Tolkien's fiction and letters, a clear and consistent picture emerges.

*Good plain food* has three essential qualities: it is simply-prepared, locally-sourced, and served as close to its natural state as possible. The opposite, then, is food which is elaborately-dressed, foreign and/or mechanically-processed.

***Simple.*** Both men expressed preferences for simple foods. In a 1920 letter to his father from a vacation in Somerset, Lewis writes, "We are quite alone and live an idyllic life on eggs, bully beef and–divine treasure–an excellent ham" (*CL I* 479). In a long account to his brother of a 1927 walking tour, Lewis writes of lunching admirably on "beer and bread and cheese followed by a pot of tea" (691). He is likewise pleased to get a meal of "boiled eggs and bread and jam" from a country postmistress on the same walking tour (692). Warnie Lewis describes, "a royal feast of the sort we both liked: no nonsense about soup and pudding, but a sole each, cutlets with green peas, a large portion of strawberries and cream, and a tankard of the local beer which is very good" (*Letters of C.S. Lewis* 246). These are largely simple foods, that is, dishes which are not 'messed-up' with elaborate sauces or composed of numerous ingredients.

Lewis provides a relevant contrast between elaborate and simple food in *The Horse and His Boy* in his descriptions of Calormene and Narnian meals. The silly Tarkheena Lasraleen of Calormen serves a meal "chiefly of the whipped cream and jelly and fruit and ice sort" (*HHB* 110). Like Lasraleen, the food is delightful and frothy, but insubstantial. The hero, Shasta, a foundling raised in the land of Calormen, similarly dines on a "fine meal after the Calormene fashion [...of] lobsters, and salad, and snipe stuffed with almonds and truffles, and a complicated dish made of chicken-livers and rice and nuts, and there were cool melons and gooseberry fools and mulberry fools, and every kind of nice thing that can be made with ice" (86). The food, like Calormen, is exotic and decadent. Patterson observes, "The operative word here is 'complicated'; as we have seen, simple, homely food is what Lewis prefers and values" (1998: 74). Later, Shasta enjoys a traditional Narnian breakfast of porridge with cream, bacon, eggs, mushrooms, and buttered toast. Although these are all foods instantly recognizable to the English reader, Shasta finds the food "new and wonderful [...] for Calormene food is quite different" (185). After eating, Shasta "gave a great sigh of contentment" and fell fast asleep (186). The lesson here is that Calormene meals may be impressive, but the simple Narnian breakfast is *satisfying*. In a similar vein, Prince Caspian contrasts his former life in the palace, with its silk sheets and "meals laid out on gold and silver dishes" to his new life living rough in the forest "on nuts and wild fruit"; Caspian finds his new life strange, "but he had never enjoyed himself more" (*PC* 95).

Tolkien, in his 1958 letter, linked *good plain food* to fresh-picked mushrooms and unmechanized farmlands. In *The Lord of the Rings*, Farmer Maggot's wife feeds the Hobbits exactly such food: "There was beer in plenty, and a mighty dish of mushrooms and bacon, besides much other solid farmhouse fare" (*FR* 96). In Mordor, Sam Gamgee's "mind was filled with the memories of food, and the longing for simple breads and meats" that remind him of the Shire (*RK* 936). In *The Hobbit*, Bilbo fantasizes more than once about bacon frying back home in his kitchen. Honegger suggests that in Middle-earth, good food "is typically simple food forgoing the use of sauces, condiments etc. that would alter or even cover completely the original taste (which is believed to be a typical characteristic of the traditional French haute cuisine)" (2013: 85). Both Lewis and Tolkien highlight fresh mushrooms, bacon, and bread as representatives of 'simple' foods.

***Local.*** Warnie Lewis wrote that his brother did not like 'new' foods, and Tolkien explicitly detested French cooking. Both men preferred locally-produced fare. The Pevensie children express this view when Mr. Beaver, in *The Lion, the Witch and the Wardrobe*, catches trout for dinner right out of the stream. The children think, "there's nothing to beat good freshwater fish if you eat it when it has been alive half an hour ago and has come out of the pan half a minute ago" (*LWW* 82). In a 1930 letter to his friend Arthur Greeves, Lewis wrote

> There is certainly something attractive about the idea of living as far as may be on the produce of the land about you: to see in every walk the pastures where your mutton grazed when it was sheep, the gardens where your vegetables grew [...] to feel that bit of country actually and literally in your veins [...] We of course who live on a standardised international diet (you may have had Canadian flour, English meat, Scotch oatmeal, African oranges, & Australian wine to day) are really artificial beings and have no connection (save in sentiment) with any place on earth. We are synthetic men, uprooted. (*CL I* 909)

For Lewis, local foodstuffs are a person's natural diet, while a diet based on foreign, imported fare is artificial.

This contrast between local and foreign food is clearly delineated in *The Last Battle* where Shift the Ape becomes the epitome of a "synthetic man" with his human affectations and obsession with exotic fare, like oranges and bananas (*LB* 18ff.) "from the towns further down the river" (11). Shift fantasizes that when he is in charge, "There'll be oranges and bananas pouring in – and roads and big cities and schools and offices and whips and muzzles and saddles and cages and kennels and prisons – Oh, everything." The morally-good animals object. "But we don't want all those things," says an old Bear (46). Puzzle the donkey observes, "there aren't many people – in fact, I don't think there's anyone but yourself – who wants those sort of things" (22). Dickerson and O'Hara note, "It is bananas and oranges in the first chapter, but later it becomes nuts and other foods he extorts from squirrels even though his demands may result in their starvation. The ape is prepared to manipulate the world to satisfy his lusts" (2009: 127).

Similarly, in *The Lord of the Rings*, Saruman seizes the best of the Shire's goods for export. When Merry finds Shire-grown Longbottom Leaf in Isengard, he says, "How it came here, I can't imagine. For Saruman's private use, I fancy. I never knew that it went so far abroad" (*TT* 562). The result of this exportation is exploitation. Back in the enemy-occupied Shire, the returning Hobbits find no beer, very little food, and no pipe-weed. Old Hob tells them, "There isn't no pipe-weed now [...] All the stocks seem to have gone. We do hear that waggon-loads [*sic*] of it went away down the old road out of the Southfarthing" (*RK* 1000).

Outside of their fiction, Lewis and Tolkien discussed their shared preference for local fare. In the same 1930 letter to Arthur Greeves where Lewis complained of the international diet, he wrote

> Tolkien once remarked to me that the feeling about home must have been quite different in the days when a family had fed on the produce of the same few miles of country for six generations [...] there was in a sense a *real* (not metaphorical) connection between them and the countryside. What had been earth and air & later corn, and later still bread, really was in them. (*CL I* 909; emphasis original)

This is what Sam finds at the Prancing Pony Inn when he pronounces Butterbur's provisions "homelike" (*FR* 148). Dickerson and O'Hara predict that, if they were writing today, both Lewis and Tolkien would be considered proponents of "local food consumption," or "locavorism": the preference for food that is produced locally, rather than moved long distances to market (2009: 297).

There are obvious exceptions to this rule in both Narnia and Middle-earth. Tea forms the centerpiece of three homely and revivifying meals in *The Lion, the Witch and the Wardrobe*: at Mr. Tumnus's house when he invites Lucy in from the cold; in the wilderness provided by Father Christmas; and, at the party of the forest animals who the White Queen turns to stone. Lewis was dedicated to tea. Warnie (who called him 'Jack') recounts, "When we were off on a walking tour together, or out on my motor-cycle with Jack in the sidecar, the whole day had to be planned around the necessity of finding ourselves at four o'clock in some place where afternoon tea would be available" (*Letters of C.S. Lewis* 36). Walter Hooper quotes Lewis as saying, "You can't get a cup of tea large enough or a book long enough to suit me" (*Of Other Worlds* vii). Tea was first imported into England in the early seventeenth century by the East India Company, and it grows in China, India and other tropical or subtropical regions in *our* world. Aslan only knows where it grows in the world of Narnia, but it was unlikely to have been cultivated in the country of Narnia itself, for tea plants cannot survive in prolonged cold or heavy freeze. Yet, at the time of *The Lion, the Witch and the Wardrobe*, Narnia had been enchanted by the White Queen to be "always winter and never Christmas" (*LWW* 27).

Tolkien also included some favorite crops in Middle-earth which are not native to England. In *The Hobbit*, Bilbo's larder at the Unexpected Party contains tea and coffee and tomatoes (*Hobbit Facsimile Gift Edition* 21).[1] Gaffer Gamgee's potatoes in *The Lord of the Rings* are likewise not native to the British Isles. Tobacco in *The Hobbit* was changed to the more ambiguous pipe-weed in *The Lord of the Rings* and given a mysterious provenance in order to justify its existence in the Shire: it was said to have been discovered by Tobold Hornblower, and "how Old Toby came by the plant is not recorded, for to his dying day he would not tell" (*FR* 8). In Tolkien's notes to Charlotte and Denis Plimmer, he wrote, "The action of the [*Lord of the Rings*] takes place in the North-west of

1 Tomatoes are mentioned in the first edition, only; Tolkien changed "tomatoes" to "pickles" in the second edition of *The Hobbit* (12).

'Middle-earth,' equivalent in latitude to the coastlands of Europe [...] Hobbiton and Rivendell are taken (as intended) to be at about the latitude of Oxford [...]" (*Letters* 376, #294). Like the country of Narnia, the Shire appears to be in the wrong geographical location to grow tea and coffee and tobacco, and so such crops may appear to be foreign imports.

How are readers to reconcile the contradiction of Lewis's and Tolkien's preferences for local foods and devotion to a few foreign imports? And how could such crops be available in Narnia and Middle-earth? There is a simple solution if one lets go of the notion that Narnia and Middle-earth represent real historical places. Instead, they are idealized countries of the mind. As my British friend, Gabriel Schenk, explained to me, tea and potatoes were so ingrained in the English and Irish cultures of Tolkien's and Lewis's day that they *seem* to fit into the category of 'good, local food.' And ultimately, Narnia and the Shire do not represent *our* world as it is, but the world as Tolkien and Lewis would have it be. Lewis was devoted to tea, so Narnia contains tea. Tolkien was a pipe smoker, so the Shire contains tobacco. But, by-and-large, the good food of Narnia and Middle-earth is such food as could be locally-produced in England.

***Natural.*** The preference for locally-produced fare is closely related to a preference for simply-prepared, natural foods. Honegger writes of Tolkien, "The description of good food suggests that it is prepared from chosen basic constituents, 'elaborated' to some degree, but not overly so, retaining a close affinity to and reflecting the flavours from the original ingredients. This agrees substantially with Tolkien's own culinary predilection" (Honegger 2013: 85). Descriptions by Lewis of good food is likewise natural food: the fresh trout from Mr. Beaver's pond, Caspian's wild fruit and nuts, Shasta's porridge, bacon, eggs, mushrooms, and buttered toast. Some of these are elaborated somewhat, but they still retain an affinity with their base constituent ingredients.

Conversely, Lewis and Tolkien both decried processed food, and equated its unnaturalness with spiritual corruption. The Plumptree's Vitaminised Nerve Food which Eustace Scrubb demands at the start of his adventures in *The Voyage of the Dawn Treader* is treated with revulsion (*VDT* 25). In *Out of the Silent Planet* (1938), the first novel of Lewis's *Space Trilogy*, the wicked Weston and Devine litter their country house with "condensed milk and opened sardine-tins" (*OSP* 13). For the trip to Mars, they pack World War I "trench rations" consisting of "tinned meat, biscuit, butter and coffee," which Ransom does not so much enjoy as eat mechanically, "almost unnoticed" (26). In the second novel, *Perelandra* (1944), Weston again brings tinned food with him to Venus. This forgettable processed food is contrasted against the local green berries which Ransom picks and eats. These are "memorable" and they provide him with "the specific pleasure of *plain food* – the delight of munching and being nourished" (*Perelandra* 188; emphasis added).

Despite Lewis's early letter relating the consumption of "bully beef" to an idyllic lifestyle, he later panned exactly the same sort of food. From the French *bouilli* 'boiled,' bully beef is a processed and tinned corned beef packed with gelatin. In *The Last Battle*, Eustace frees the young Narnian king, Tirian, from captivity and offers him "grub" in a "greasy and squashy packet" (64). This grub is, in fact, two hard-boiled egg sandwiches, two cheese sandwiches, and two sandwiches with "some kind of paste in them" (65). Diane Duane describes the paste as one of the "pestilent proto-sandwich spreads of Lewis's youth," and a cheap attempt at *paté* (2010: 96). Lewis writes, "If [Tirian] hadn't been so hungry, he wouldn't have thought much of the paste, for that is a sort of food nobody eats in Narnia" (*LB* 65). Along the same vein, when Jill Pole is rescued from Underland in *The Silver Chair*, she is delighted by "the hissing, and delicious smell of sausages, and more, and more, and more sausages. And not wretched sausages half full of bread and soya bean either, but real meaty, spicy ones, fat and piping hot and burst and just the tiniest bit burnt" (*SC* 238). In Narnia, real meat is wholesome and revivifying while processed meat blends are grotesque substitutes.

Tolkien indicated a similar sentiment in a letter to his son Christopher on the geo-political situation in 1943. Tolkien lamented the diffusion of a mass culture where, "even the unlucky little Samoyedes, I suspect, have tinned food and the village loudspeaker telling Stalin's bed-time stories about Democracy" (*Letters* 64). Tolkien's distaste for industrialization is well known. In *The Hobbit*, the goblins who "make no beautiful things" are delighted instead by "wheels and engines and explosions" (*Hobbit* 59). John and Priscilla Tolkien wrote of their father's sadness, "driving to Birmingham in the mid-1930s [where] he saw the whole region being built over and his beloved fields disappearing" (1992: 20).

In an early draft of the chapter, 'The Mirror of Galadriel,' Tolkien indicates that Frodo will see in her prophetic basin the scouring of the Shire as an industrial nightmare with trees being felled, factories belching smoke, and the tall biscuit factory of Sandyman & Son standing in place of the Old Mill (*TI* 216, 249, 264 fn. 16). In Middle-earth, as in England, factories and the food they produce are ugly things.

***Abundant.*** Closely associated with the qualities of *good plain food* (simple, local, and natural) are the quantities. Lewis and Tolkien frequently depict their morally good characters sharing abundant feasts with friends, allies, or even strangers. Shasta is routinely "given a hunk of bread and turned out of the cottage" by the Calormene fisherman who raised him (*HHB* 17). But, his Narnian breakfast is a revelation, with "a great many helpings, so that Shasta's plate or cup was being filled every moment, and every moment the Dwarfs themselves were saying, [...] 'I'd like a few more mushrooms,' or 'What about frying another egg or so?' [...] at last they had all eaten as much as they possibly could" (186). Tolkien does not detail what food was offered to the Fellowship in the Elvish haven of Lothlórien, yet "it seemed to them that they did little but eat and drink and rest, and walk among the trees; and it was enough" (*FR* 358). Mrs. Maggot's supper in *The Lord of the Rings* is equally "generous," "plenty," and "mighty" (*FR* 95-96). This is strong praise indeed from Hobbits who prefer to "eat, and drink, often and heartily [...] six meals a day (when they could get them)" (*FR* 2). This appetite is on show at Bilbo's Long-Expected Party in *The Lord of the Rings*, where the Hobbit guests engage in "that delightful stage which they called 'filling up the corners'" with numerable sips and nibbles of drinks and dainties following the feast (*FR* 28-29).

Taking all the evidence together, *good plain food* to Lewis and Tolkien is essentially simple, local, fresh and natural food which is plentiful (and shared). These are the qualities that define the most homely and congenial meals in their fantasy novels, and it describes the authors' own dietary preferences. These are also the very characteristics of food which were scarce throughout much of Lewis's and Tolkien's lifetimes.

## English Cuisine in Transition

The diary of Parson James Woodforde reveals much about eighteenth-century English cuisine. A party for his tenants in 1776 included roast beef, leg of mutton, and plum puddings (Dickson Wright 2011: loc. 3573). Celebrity cook and food writer Clarissa Dickson Wright observes, "for those with money, at least – the Georgian [1714-1830s] larder was always full" (loc. 3527). She writes, "Even less festive meals were pretty substantial [...] ham, fowls, tripe, green peas, a hare and a raspberry tart. Woodforde didn't just consume food; he went out and caught it, too" (loc. 3583). The food in Woodforde's diary is echoed by the simple, natural, and local fare in Bilbo's larder and at the Prancing Pony in Middle-earth, and at Mr. Tumnus's and the Beavers' homes in Narnia.

However, both Lewis and Tolkien identify their secondary worlds, not with the Georgian era, but with the late Victorian. Lewis triangulates *The Magician's Nephew* with the stories of Sherlock Holmes and Edith Nesbit's Bastable children in the latter part of the 1890s (*MN* 11). Tolkien also situates the Shire in that period. He wrote in a 1955 letter to his publishers, Allen & Unwin, "It is in fact more or less a Warwickshire village of about the period of the Diamond Jubilee," that is, 1897 (*Letters* 230, #178).

Yet, the cuisine of the 1890s into which Lewis and Tolkien were both born looked vastly different from Parson Woodforde's Georgian larder a hundred years earlier. The Victorians were great innovators and had revolutionized the food supply with advances in processing and global trade. Food historian Derek J. Oddy writes, "Simple meals made from a limited range of industrially processed foodstuffs constituted the 'plain fare' which most people in Britain ate from the 1890s until after the Second World War" (2003: jacket flap, emphasis added). Though using a similar phrase to Tolkien's and Lewis's "plain food," Oddy's "*plain fare*" is specifically *industrial* and *processed*. From the 1840s onward, urban growth and the development of railways, steamships, and refrigeration led to an increasingly processed and foreign character of English and Irish food. Dickson Wright notes, "Meat could be brought in from as far away as Canada, America, Australia and New Zealand, frozen beef and mutton first arriving from Australia in the *SS Strathleven* in 1880" (2011: loc. 4538). This is highly reminiscent of Lewis's complaint about the synthetic international diet, and here it is explicitly established in England by 1880. French preparations and foods from Jewish Eastern Europe (such as fried fish) became ubiquitous. Later in the nineteenth century, Queen Victoria's fascination with curries propelled Indian cuisine to the forefront of English food culture (loc. 4503). Dickson Wright notes, "By 1914, Britain was importing more than 60 per cent of its food supplies and 80 per cent of its wheat" (loc. 4908).

Nineteenth-century improvements in bottling and canning processes also soon found England "awash with tinned Pacific salmon, corned beef, sardines, condensed milk, green beans, peas" (Dickson Wright 2011: loc. 4547). New products also included potted meats, meat pastes, fish pastes, tinned soup, tinned fruits and vegetables, jams, salad creams, chutneys, pickles, relishes, mincemeat, marmalade, lemon curd and jellies with cheap, imported sugar (Oddy 2003: 4, 36, 96). Oddy writes,

> from the mid-nineteenth century, only pockets of resistance to shop products remained. Cooking and meal preparation became more modest in rural districts as the nineteenth century progressed and this was mirrored in the newly urbanized areas by the disappearance of home-made soups, broths and pottages where these had formerly been traditional. (4)

Oseland argues, "Country food in the 1890's bore little resemblance to the city food we associate with wealthy Victorians. While the wealthy would enjoy internationally inspired dishes like Kedgeree [...] their country cousins had to make do with old fashioned staples like bacon, eggs, and toast" (2014: 8). However, Oddy contends that even "the local area of country around any British town provided very little of its food supply other than some seasonal fresh meat, poultry, eggs, fruit and vegetables" (2003: 7).

Two travel writers document this change. Touring England in the 1720s, Daniel Defoe was "fascinated by the range of local foods in England: Essex fish, Cheshire cheeses, Norfolk cattle and pheasants, Kentish hops, Wirksworth ale" (Dickson Wright 2011: loc. 3542). Touring England one hundred years later, in 1820, William Cobbett, "was horrified to find that people in the countryside were now eating the same diet as their brethren in the towns: potatoes, bread from the baker's and tea" (loc. 4381). Furthermore, by the early part of the nineteenth century oranges, tomatoes, mangos and pineapple – the very exotic produce that

Puzzle the donkey claims no one in Narnia wants – were commonly available in England for those who could afford them (loc. 3552, 4445).

As for Northern Ireland, while the Irish climate was always well-suited to the rearing of cattle and the production of milk and butter, following the failure of potato crops and the Great Famine of 1845-49, less food was grown in Ireland: nutritious home-produced oatmeal and potatoes were increasingly abandoned "for less nutritious shop-bought foods: tea, white bread, commercially-produced jam, biscuits, and fatty American bacon" (Murphy). More food "came from abroad and was purchased from shopkeepers and dealers [...who] in their turn relied on the transportation links provided by steam trains, steam ships, better roads, and, eventually, bicycles, motor trucks, and motorcars" (Clarkson and Crawford 2001: 90).

None of this suggests that Lewis and Tolkien never ate simple meals made from local products, nor foraged for mushrooms; they clearly did so and preferred this sort of eating. Nevertheless, the English way of life which revolved around eating off the land, and which the two authors portrayed in Narnia and Middle-earth, had been vanishing long before either man was born.

Food scarcity was also an issue for much of Tolkien's and Lewis's lives. England's heavy dependence on imported foods meant that an effective naval blockade by German U-boats during World War I was able to choke the entire food supply. Writing from England to his father in Northern Ireland in March 1917, Lewis wrote

> The food allowances are beginning to be short enough here. Like you, we find the meat plenty, but the bread rather short. Potatoes have almost disappeared among the poorer people and are no longer an every day dish anywhere. Of course it would be absurd to complain at present but it looks very black for the future, if this submarine business goes on. (*CL I* 291)

Sugar was rationed from 1916. General rationing began in February 1918, with meat among the first items to be controlled.[2] Oddy writes, "Almost immediately, queues for other imported foods, particularly tea and margarine, reached 'gigantic proportions'" (2003: 78).

---

2 The meat ration lasted in Britain until 1954.

Wartime diets were heavily dependent on factory-processed, packaged and canned foods. Dickson Wright notes that packaged biscuits and tinned, processed "'bully beef' […] was central to most meals" in the trenches (2011: loc. 4923).[3] The British Army-issue ration biscuit, "Huntley & Palmers Army No. 4," was notoriously hard and "could crack teeth if not first soaked in tea or water […] which was often transported to the front line in petrol tins" ('Food That Fuelled the Front' 2020). These products were memorialized in a popular soldier's song from the war:

> Sing me to sleep where the bullets fall –
> let me forget the war and all;
> Damp is my dugout, cold my feet –
> nothing but bully and biscuits to eat.
> (Canadian Legion 1939: 6)

The idea of fresh produce from the English countryside or fresh-baked bread must have formed the substance of many a soldier's dreams.

After the lifting of the blockade, food importing returned. Shops filled up with new pre-packaged foods such as breakfast cereals and crisps [i.e. potato chips] (Dickson Wright 2011: loc. 5026).[4] A wide variety of chocolate bars and confections were also introduced in the interwar years, including the Turkish Delight that Edmund requests from the White Queen in *The Lion, the Witch and the Wardrobe* (Oddy 2003: 104-05). Notably, these new-fangled foods lacked much nutritional value.

While the 1920s and 1930s were times of general prosperity, with the advent of World War II (1939-45) rationing returned with severe limitations on meat, bacon, sugar, tea, margarine, and lard. Dickson Wright says, "Ask people who lived through the Second World War [in England] what they remember about wartime food, and they'll probably come up with a list of the things they had to go without" (2011: loc. 5161). Duane notes that butter was limited to two ounces per person *per week* (2010: 93). This casts new light on meals in *The Lion, the*

---

3 Away from the front lines, food could be considerably better. One soldier in the catering corps recorded a typical day's menu filled with items that Bilbo Baggins could easily find in his pantries: bacon, tomatoes, bread, jam, tea and cocoa, shepherd's pie (though made with tinned beef and potato), oxtail soup, roast beef, leeks, and rice pudding (Dickson Wright 2011: loc. 4932).

4 While crisps were a Victorian invention, they became commercially viable when a packaging method was discovered which could preserve their crunch (Dickson Wright 2011: loc. 5022).

*Witch, and the Wardrobe*, set during World War II. The Beavers' dinner features a "great big lump of deep yellow butter in the middle of the table from which everyone took as much as he wanted to go with his potatoes" (*LWW* 82). The high tea that Mr. Tumnus serves to Lucy would have been considered lavish. Duane writes, "It would be years before any Oxford don or little English girl could sit down to the delights of a meal that featured fresh eggs and real sardines, a meal in which there was [real] butter for the toast, and actual honey, and cakes with sugar on them" (2010: 93). Written before World War II, the feast at Beorn's house in Tolkien's *The Hobbit* would sound nostalgically extravagant to wartime readers, for Gandalf is able to enjoy "two whole loaves (with masses of butter and honey and clotted cream)" (*Hobbit* 121).

The government's 'Dig for Victory' campaign used a series of patriotic posters and instructional pamphlets to encourage citizens to grow vegetables and raise livestock ('Dig for Victory' 2020). Dickson Wright notes, "Even the grounds of Buckingham Palace were dug up to make room for food production" (2011: loc. 5529). In a 1940 letter to Arthur Greeves, Lewis wrote, "I think a great deal of nonsense is talked about the food shortage: at least I have never yet had a meal from wh[ich] I rose unsatisfied" (*CL III* 1538). Yet, Lewis was the regular recipient of food parcels from American fans during and after the war. Additionally, the Lewis brothers also kept nine acres of orchards and vegetable gardens on the grounds of their house, the Kilns (Jacobs 2006: 263). Tolkien's brother Hilary bought a small orchard and market garden after serving in World War I, and Tolkien and his family "were pressed into service to help on the land" whenever they visited (Carpenter 2000: 113). John and Priscilla Tolkien recall that during World War II their father turned a "rather decrepit tennis court" into a vegetable garden. It was, "an important asset during the war years [...] the aviary was turned into a hen-house and the fowls and their eggs became an important part of the household economy" (Tolkien and Tolkien 1992: 55).

Such self-sufficiency is reflected both in Middle-earth and Narnia. Tolkien's Hobbits spend most of their time "growing food and eating it" (*FR* 9). The characters who live off the produce of their own land are invariably virtuous characters who provide sustenance to travelers in Middle-earth. In addition to Farmer Maggot, Tom Bombadil and Goldberry tend a kitchen-garden with "a tall line of beans on poles" (*FR* 128). Beorn keeps dairy cows and hives of honey bees (*Hobbit* 109). Likewise, the importance of living close to the land is woven into the very foundations of Narnia. Aslan selects London cabby Frank to be the first king of the newly-created land, in part, because he can "use a spade and a plow and raise food out of the earth" (*MN* 158).

By the early 1950s, when Lewis was publishing *The Chronicles of Narnia* and Tolkien was publishing *The Lord of the Rings*, food shortages and rationing were finally easing in England. Yet, there is no doubt that one could (and still can) eat simple meals of bread and cheese, or ham and apple tarts there. It is likely that these types of homely meals were indeed served in the boyhood homes of Lewis and Tolkien. But such meals would not have been purely simple, local, and natural; they would have also consisted of factory-made marmalade, imported fish, and store-bought cakes (not to mention naturalized tea and potatoes). During Lewis's and Tolkien's lifetimes, food was increasingly imported, processed, rationed, and often scare. Thus, the plain and simple, local, natural and abundant meals in Narnia and Middle-earth do not so much represent the realistic Victorian/Edwardian childhood memories of Lewis or Tolkien, nor do they represent English food during much of the twentieth century. Rather, the *good plain food* in Narnia and Middle-earth is idealized food, English cuisine as it was nostalgically conceived by those who longed for an earlier, more innocent age.

## Food in Arcadia

The term *nostalgia* – from the Greek *nostos* (return to one's native land) and *algos* (suffering or grief) – was first employed by Swiss physician Johannes Hofer in the seventeenth century to describe the severe homesickness suffered by his countrymen living abroad (Hofer 1934: 381). As a medical condition, the symptoms included melancholy, hostile mood, disturbed sleep, physical weakness, loss of appetite, heart palpitations, and mental fog (386). It could be incapacitating or even fatal if untreated. The doctor mused, "it is not at all difficult to infer that the subjects of this state are principally young people and adolescents sent to foreign regions" (383). Hofer wondered if Swiss expatriates were particularly susceptible to nostalgia because they missed their native foods, "whether it is because the Helvetian has to search about for the morning broth, or by the scarcity of the milk of this tribe, or because he is suddenly deprived of his own manner of feasting" (384).

Focusing on the psychological and emotional aspects of nostalgia, Boym argues, "At first glance, nostalgia is for a place, but actually it is a yearning for a different time – the time of our childhood, the slower rhythms of our dreams" (2002: xv). Linda M. Austin argues that nineteenth-century romantic desire likewise produced a longing for childhood which manifested itself "in nostalgic images of children" (2003: 75-76). She continues later,

> The innocent child of nature – 'concocted,' Kincaid has observed, by late Victorians (72-73) – likewise signified the adult's past [...] The repertory of images from which an adult could choose to represent a personal past included nonhuman figures like fairies and animals [...] The particular past these diminutive creatures evoked in the beholder's imagination was usually undelineated; the figure mediated an inchoate nostalgia, the *experience* of memory rather than its content. (Austin 2003: 86; emphasis original)

Jean Starobinski also concludes that nostalgia is less about a particular place than a particular state, writing, "it is rather the conflict between the exigencies of integration into the adult world and the temptation to conserve the unique status of the child. The literature of exile [...is] a literature concerned with the loss of childhood" (1996: 103). Robert Hemmings similarly argues that nostalgia for "childhood signifies escape from the pressures of a modern, industrialized, polluted, and exploitative adult world" (2007: 56-57).

Hemmings explicitly links talking animals, fairies, and food with the nostalgic longing to recover lost childhood in 'Golden Age' British children's literature, that is, works published from the mid-nineteenth century until the First World War. He writes,

> The kind of childhood invoked by key texts from the golden age of children's literature [...] is profoundly nostalgic along these very lines. The interiorized village to which the adult writer, and also the reader, regresses is not only the imaginative space but also the time of the childhood. More specifically, it is not their actual childhood but an impossibly sanitized and Edenic time and space. (Hemmings 2007: 55)

In *Secret Gardens: The Golden Age of Children's Literature from Alice in Wonderland to Winnie-the-Pooh* (1985), Humphrey Carpenter examines a subset of Golden Age children's authors he calls "Arcadians" – including Kenneth Grahame,

Beatrix Potter, and A.A. Milne – who each incorporate "the symbol of a garden or Enchanted Place in their writings (1985: 9). Carpenter observes, "By Grahame's day, hatred of urban life, and of the harm that the industrial revolution had steadily done to English society during the previous hundred years, had become a major theme in English writing" (121). These English children's writers set their stories "in a distant era when things were better than they are now. And childhood itself seemed a Golden Age to many of these writers, as they set out to recapture its sensations" (x).

Like Lewis and Tolkien, Kenneth Grahame lost his mother in childhood. His father, who had a drinking problem, sent the children to be raised by their grandmother in the small rural village of Cookham Dean, Berkshire. But the idyll was short-lived as Grahame and his siblings (like Tolkien and Lewis after them) were moved from place to place. Grahame was also the survivor of adult trauma, although in a London workplace shooting rather than war. In the incident's aftermath, Grahame moved his family to Cookham Dean, escaping to "the setting of the happiest part of his childhood" (Carpenter 1985: 153).

Hemmings argues that Grahame's *The Wind in the Willows* (1908) is fixated "upon the associations of food and the powerful draw of home" (2007: 65-66). When Mole first arrives at the River Bank, he meets the Water Rat who shares his picnic luncheon "with its catalogue of good food" (Carpenter 1985: 156). Among other items, there is cold chicken, ham and beef, pickled gherkins, salad, sandwiches, ginger beer and lemonade (*Wind in the Willows* 8). Rat then invites Mole to stay at his home, where they tell stories until supper-time which is "a most cheerful meal" (20). When Rat and Mole are later caught in a snowstorm, they find "safe anchorage" at Badger's warm and inviting house where they are given a generous breakfast of bacon, eggs, and fried ham (64, 69, 73). Like the homely shared meals in Lewis and Tolkien, Grahame's fare is simple, local, natural, and abundant. After several adventures with Rat and his friends, Mole becomes homesick – or nostalgic – for his own cozy hole. He invites Rat to return with him, but is then horrified to discover his cupboards are bare. Plucky Rat turns up "a tin of sardines – a box of captain's biscuits, nearly full – and a German sausage encased in silver paper" (94). But Mole bemoans the lack of bread and butter. Such tinned and processed food is no substitute for simple, homemade fare. Hemmings asserts that *The Wind in the*

*Willows*, in addition to being a children's story, "is also for those adults who embrace a nostalgic reconstruction of childhood" (2007: 67). He argues that "in such an Edenic space, the taste and smell of comforting foods at once infuse the nostalgic vision with fond longing" but it may also "threaten to disrupt it with the incursion of traumatic knowledge," that is, memories of parental loss, the lack of a stable home, and violence (71).

Beatrix Potter also regarded parts of her youth as a personal golden age, though most of it was drear. She once referred to her London family home as "my unloved birthplace" (qtd. in Carpenter 1985: 140). Although Carpenter paints a slightly rosier picture of Potter's family life, Matthew Dennison's later biography describes the family routine as "stultifying" and portrays Potter's parents as social wannabes and emotional leeches who never wanted her to leave them or become an independent adult (Carpenter 1985: 138-43; Dennison 2017: 11). However, Potter seems to have relished time spent at her grandmother's country house or the childhood summers in a rental house along the River Tay (Carpenter 1985: 140). In 1905, a year before Grahame returned to Cookham Dean, Potter used the royalties from her first few books to make her escape from the family home and purchase her own Eden: Hill Top Farm in the Lake District. Carpenter argues, "her search for Arcadia, like Kenneth Grahame's, was no doubt partly motivated by the desire to return to what she called 'that peaceful past time of childhood'" (1985: 147). But if Dennison is even partially correct, Potter sought a childhood as she wished it had been, or that existed only part of the time, as when she was visiting her grandmother. Also like Grahame, Potter's depictions of food are homey and nostalgic. In *The Tale of Peter Rabbit* (1901), for example, Farmer McGregor's garden is filled with lettuces, French beans, radishes, parsley, cucumber and young cabbages (33-34). Mrs. Rabbit brings home brown bread and currant buns from the bakery (32), and Peter misses a delightful supper of "bread and milk and blackberries" (42). Like Lewis's and Tolkien's ideal food, this is simple and natural fare, and there is no indication that the baker's goods are anything but freshly-baked.

A.A. Milne, like Lewis and Tolkien, was a World War I veteran and, like Tolkien, was a signals officer. Milne was injured in the Battle of the Somme in July 1916 and invalided back to England where he spent the rest of the war working for Military Intelligence. Humphrey Carpenter regards Milne "as a survivor of the

Edwardians rather than belonging truly to the post-war world" despite his Pooh books being published after the war (1985: 210). Milne's vision was consonant with "the Victorian and Edwardian cultural movement that embraced the myth of an Arcadian rural England, a pastoral counterpoint to industrialization and modernization" (Hemmings 2007: 54). After the war, Milne purchased a Sussex farmhouse near an area where "at about age eleven he himself had begun a very happy period living in that part of England" (Carpenter 1985: 201). This Edenic setting became the model for the Hundred Acre Wood in *Winnie-the-Pooh* (1926) and *The House at Pooh Corner* (1928) where a fictionalized version of Milne's son, Christopher, had adventures with woodland friends based on Christopher's stuffed animals. These adventures often revolved around the finding and eating of food: honey, most memorably, but also other homey victuals like cakes, bread, milk, and Pooh's "simple meal of marmalade spread lightly over a honeycomb or two" (*Winnie-the-Pooh* 99).

Hemmings writes, "Children's books from the golden age are nostalgic [...] in retrospective longing for a past not as it was, but as it might only have been" (2007: 57). The nature and abundance of the food depicted in Grahame's, Potter's, and Milne's fantasies might hearken back to actual memories of the authors' respective childhoods, and they may have eaten such food some of the time, but the food of their Victorian childhoods was, like the food of Lewis's and Tolkien's later Victorian/Edwardian childhoods, largely the antithesis of *good plain food*. Increasingly, it would have been shop-bought, processed and imported. Rather, the food that Grahame, Potter, and Milne depict in their fantasies is as idealized as Lewis's and Tolkien's.

Carpenter marks the end of the Arcadians with Milne and designates Tolkien's *The Hobbit* as the start of "a very different era of children's books" (1985: 209). He argues that although Tolkien's story is set in an idealized landscape, it "shows the mark of [Tolkien's] own experiences in the trenches in 1916" (211). Middle-earth, he writes, "offers no security; instead there is a constant threat of physical violence [...] from trolls, goblins, giant spiders, a dragon and other perils" (211). But if we look solely at the Arcadian landscapes within Middle-earth, the "safe anchorages" (like Badger's sett in *The Wind in the Willows*), these are collectively signified by the presence of *good plain food*: Bilbo's hobbit hole, Beorn's farm, the house of Tom Bombadil, the Prancing Pony, and Lothlórien.

Likewise, in Narnia, 'plain domestic cookery' signals safety (at least for the duration of the meal): the Beavers' house, Prince Caspian's forest, Shasta's and Jill's respective feasts with the Narnian dwarfs. A comparison of Lewis's and Tolkien's *good plain food* with the food of Grahame, Potter, and Milne, reveals a common storehouse of imagery: not of shop-bought, processed and tinned food, but of timeless Arcadian fare.

All five authors – Grahame, Potter, Milne, Lewis, and Tolkien – exhibit nostalgia for the *same* idealized childhood regardless of when precisely each author was born and raised. Theirs are imaginary countries where life is slower and innocent, and the good food is simple, local, natural, and abundant. As Hemmings writes, this was "not their actual childhood but an impossibly sanitized and Edenic time and space" (2007: 55). The River Bank, the world of Peter Rabbit, the Hundred Acre Wood, Narnia, and Middle-earth are not reflections of any particular, realistic time or place; that much is plain. But then, neither are the depictions of the food there realistic or indicative of a realistic time or place. The food – milk, bread and butter, mushrooms, bacon and eggs – is not specifically Georgian, or Victorian, or Edwardian, but is quintessentially and timelessly *English*. In their depictions of food, Lewis and Tolkien (as well as their predecessors) offer readers the *experience* of memory rather than the reality. They use Arcadian depictions of food to help erase childhood (and adult) trauma. Hemmings writes, "Being comforted by coziness, story-telling, and a belly filled by cheery meals may appeal to some children, but it is certainly a carefree state that appeals to an adult writer or reader embroiled in and seeking escape from the toil and struggle of (post)modern industrialized life" (2007: 67). Within these mythic settings, memories of parental loss, industrialization, and violence may be held at bay – at least for a little while – by nostalgic fantasies of *good plain food*.

## About the Author

Kris Swank is a librarian and lecturer at Pima Community College and Signum University. She holds an MA in Literature and Languages with a concentration in Tolkien Studies from Signum University, and is currently pursuing a PhD in English Literature at the University of Glasgow. Kris has been published in *Tolkien Studies, Mythlore,* the *Journal of Tolkien Research*, and a dozen edited collections. Her essay, 'The Child's Voyage and the *Immram* Tradition in Lewis, Tolkien, and Pullman,' appeared in *Mythlore* 38.1 (2019).

## Bibliography

Austin, Linda M. 2003. 'Children of Childhood: Nostalgia and the Romantic Legacy.' *Studies in Romanticism* 42.1, 75-98.

Boym, Svetlana. 2002. *The Future of Nostalgia*. New York: Basic Books.

Burns, Marjorie. 2005. 'Eating, Devouring, Sacrifice and Ultimate Just Desserts (Why Elves Are Vegetarian and the Unrefined Are Not).' *Perilous Realms: Celtic and Norse in Tolkien's Middle-earth*. Toronto: University of Toronto Press, 156-71.

Canadian Legion of the British Empire Service League. *Souvenir Song Book*. Ninth Provincial Convention, Winnipeg, Man[itoba]. 25-7 May 1939. Wartime Canada, 2020. <https://wartimecanada.ca/document/first-world-war/music/sing-along-ex-soldiers>. Accessed 4 July 2023.

Carpenter, Humphrey. 1985. *Secret Gardens: A Study of the Golden Age of Children's Literature*. London: George Allen and Unwin.

2000. *J.R.R. Tolkien: A Biography*. Boston, MA: Houghton Mifflin.

Clarkson, Leslie and Margaret Crawford. 2001. *Feast and Famine: Food and Nutrition in Ireland 1500-1920*. Oxford: Oxford University Press.

Dennison, Matthew. 2017. *Over the Hills and Far Away: The Life of Beatrix Potter*. New York: Pegasus.

Dickerson, Matthew T. and David O'Hara. 2009. *Narnia and the Fields of Arbol: The Environmental Vision of C.S. Lewis*. Lexington, KT: University Press of Kentucky.

Dickson Wright, Clarissa. 2011. *A History of English Food*. Kindle ed. [London]: Random House UK.

'Dig for Victory.' *The Imperial War Museum*. 2020. <https://www.iwm.org.uk/collections/item/object/19342>. Accessed 4 July 2023.

Duane, Diane. 2010. 'Eating in Narnia: Or, Don't Bother Bringing the Sandwiches.' *Through the Wardrobe: Your Favorite Authors on C.S. Lewis's Chronicles of Narnia*. Ed. Herbie Brennan. Dallas, TX: Smart Pop/BenBella Books, 89-107.

'Food that Fuelled the Front.' *The Imperial War Museum*. 2020. <https://www.iwm.org.uk/history/the-food-that-fuelled-the-front>. Accessed 18 August 2020.

Grahame, Kenneth. 2020. *The Wind in the Willows*. London: Egmont.

Hemmings, Robert. 2007. 'A Taste of Nostalgia: Children's Books from the Golden Age – Carroll, Grahame, and Milne.' *Children's Literature* 35, 54-79.

Hofer, Johannes. 1934. *Medical Dissertation on Nostalgia by Johannes Hofer*. Transl. Carolyn Kiser Anspach. *Bulletin of the Institute of the History of Medicine* 2, 376-91.

Honegger, Thomas. 2013. '"Raw Forest" Versus "Cooked City": Lévi-Strauss in Middle-earth.' *Tolkien: The Forest and the City*. Eds. Helen Conrad-O'Briain and Gerard Hynes. Dublin: Four Courts Press, 76-86.

Jacobs, Alan. 2006. *The Narnian: The Life and Imagination of C.S. Lewis*. New York: HarperOne.

Kaščáková, Janka. 2010. '"It Snowed Food and Rained Drink" in *The Lord of the Rings*.' *Middle-earth and Beyond: Essays on the World of J.R.R. Tolkien*. Eds. Janka Kaščáková and Kathleen Dubs. Newcastle upon Tyne: Cambridge Scholars, 91-104.

Langford, Jonathan. 1996. 'Sitting Down to the Sacramental Feast: Food and Cultural Diversity in *The Lord of the Rings*.' *Foods of the Gods: Eating and the Eaten in Fantasy and Science Fiction*. Eds. Gary Westfahl, George Edgar Slusser, Eric S. Rabkin. Athens, GA: University of Georgia Press, 117-41.

Lewis, Clive Staples. 2004. *The Collected Letters of C.S. Lewis, Volume I: Family Letters 1905-1931*. Ed. Walter Hooper. San Francisco, CA: HarperSanFrancisco.

2006. *The Collected Letters of C.S. Lewis, Volume III: Narnia, Cambridge, and Joy 1950-1963*. Ed. Walter Hooper. San Francisco, CA: HarperSanFrancisco.

2014. *The Horse and His Boy*. London: HarperCollins.

2014. *The Last Battle*. London: HarperCollins.

2017. *Letters of C.S. Lewis*. Eds. W.H. Lewis and Walter Hooper. New York: HarperOne.

2014. *The Lion, the Witch and the Wardrobe*. London: HarperCollins.

2014. *The Magician's Nephew*. London: HarperCollins.

2017. *Of Other Worlds: Essays and Stories*. San Francisco, CA: HarperOne.

2013. *Out of the Silent Planet.* C.S. Lewis. *The Space Trilogy.* London: HarperCollins, 1-146.

2013. *Perelandra.* C.S. Lewis. *The Space Trilogy.* London: HarperCollins, 147-341.

2014. *Prince Caspian.* London: HarperCollins.

2014. *The Silver Chair.* London: HarperCollins.

2016. *Surprised by Joy.* London: William Collins.

2014. *The Voyage of the Dawn Treader.* London: HarperCollins.

Martindale, Wayne, and Kathryn Welch. 2005. 'Food for the Soul: Eating in Narnia.' *Narnia Beckons.* Eds. Ted Baehr and James Baehr. Nashville, TN: Broadman & Holman, 103-11.

Milne, Alan Alexander. 2016. *Winnie-the-Pooh.* London: Egmont.

Murphy, Maureen. 'Review of Feast and Famine: Food and Nutrition in Ireland 1500-1920.' *Reviews in History,* 295a, February 2010. <https://reviews.history.ac.uk/review/295a>. Accessed 18 August 2020.

Navarette, Susan J. 1996. 'The Fine Reality of Hunger Satisfied: Food and Desire in C.S. Lewis's *Perelandra.*' *Foods of the Gods: Eating and the Eaten in Fantasy and Science Fiction.* Eds. Gary Westfahl, George Edgar Slusser and Eric S. Rabkin. Athens, GA: University of Georgia Press, 97-114.

Oddy, Derek J. 2003. *From Plain Fare to Fusion Food: British Diet from the 1890s to the 1990s.* Rochester, NY: Boydell Press.

Oseland, Chris-Rachael. 2014. *An Unexpected Cookbook: The Unofficial Book of Hobbit Cookery.* Austin, TX: Kitchen Overlord.

Patterson, Nancy-Lou. 1998. 'Miraculous Bread… Miraculous Wine: Eucharistic Motifs in the Fantasies of C.S. Lewis.' *Mythlore* 22.2, 28-46.

Potter, Beatrix. 2007. *Beatrix Potter Treasury.* London: Warne.

Resnick, Henry. 1967. 'An Interview with Tolkien [March 2, 1966].' *Niekas* 18, 37-42.

Spacks, Patricia Meyer. 1959. 'Ethical Patterns in *The Lord of the Rings.*' *Critique* 3, 30-42.

Spirito, Guglielmo and Emanuele Rimoli. 2011. 'Simple Pleasures in Tolkien's Poetry: Eating and Drinking and the Depth of Things.' *Hither Shore* 8, 242-60.

Starobinski, Jean. 1966. 'The Idea of Nostalgia.' Transl. William S. Kemp. *Diogenes* 54, 81-103.

Tolkien, John Ronald Reuel. 2018. *The Hobbit*. Facsimile Gift Edition. London: HarperCollins.

2007. *The Hobbit, or There and Back Again*. London: HarperCollins.

1981. *The Letters of J.R.R. Tolkien*. Ed. Humphrey Carpenter with the assistance of Christopher Tolkien. Boston, MA: Houghton Mifflin.

2005. *The Lord of the Rings. Part 1. The Fellowship of the Ring*. London: HarperCollins.

2005. *The Lord of the Rings. Part 2. The Two Towers*. London: HarperCollins.

2005. *The Lord of the Rings. Part 3. The Return of the King*. London: HarperCollins.

2002. *The Treason of Isengard*. The History of Middle-earth 7. Ed. Christopher Tolkien. London: HarperCollins.

Tolkien, John and Priscilla Tolkien. 1992. *The Tolkien Family Album*. Boston, MA: Houghton Mifflin.

# Abbreviations

## Tolkien

| | | |
|---|---|---|
| *BLT 2* | - | *The Book of Lost Tales Vol. II* |
| *BMC* | - | *Beowulf: The Monsters and the Critics* |
| *FA* | - | *The Fall of Arthur* |
| *FR* | - | *The Fellowship of the Ring* |
| *Hobbit* | - | *The Hobbit* |
| *Lays* | - | *The Lays of Beleriand* |
| *Letters* | - | *The Letters of J.R.R. Tolkien* |
| *LR* | - | *The Lost Road and Other Writings* |
| *MR* | - | *Morgoth's Ring* |
| *Myth* | - | 'Mythopoeia' |
| *NME* | - | *The Nature of Middle-earth* |
| *PME* | - | *The Peoples of Middle-earth* |
| *RK* | - | *The Return of the King* |
| *RS* | - | *The Return of the Shadow* |
| *Sil* | - | *The Silmarillion* |
| *SWM* | - | *Smith of Wootton Major* |
| *TI* | - | *The Treason of Isengard* |
| *TL* | - | *Tree and Leaf* |
| *TOFS* | - | *Tolkien on Fairy-Stories* |
| *TT* | - | *The Two Towers* |
| *UT* | - | *The Unfinished Tales* |
| *WJ* | - | *The War of the Jewels* |

## Lewis

| | | |
|---|---|---|
| *AL* | - | *The Allegory of Love* |
| *AM* | - | *The Abolition of Man* |
| *CL I* | - | *The Collected Letters of C.S. Lewis Vol. I* |
| *CL II* | - | *The Collected Letters of C.S. Lewis Vol. II* |
| *CL III* | - | *The Collected Letters of C.S. Lewis Vol. III* |
| *DI* | - | *The Discarded Image* |

| | | |
|---|---|---|
| *EC* | - | *An Experiment in Criticism* |
| *GD* | - | *God in the Dock* |
| *HHB* | - | *The Horse and His Boy* |
| *LB* | - | *The Last Battle* |
| *LM* | - | *Letters to Malcolm* |
| *LWW* | - | *The Lion, the Witch and the Wardrobe* |
| *MC* | - | *Mere Christianity* |
| *MN* | - | *The Magician's Nephew* |
| *OSP* | - | *Out of the Silent Planet* |
| *PC* | - | *Prince Caspian* |
| *PP* | - | *The Problem of Pain* |
| *RP* | - | *Reflections on the Psalms* |
| *SC* | - | *The Silver Chair* |
| *SJ* | - | *Surprised by Joy* |
| *SL* | - | *Screwtape Letters* |
| *SLE* | - | *Selected Literary Essays* |
| *SMRL* | - | *Studies in Medieval and Renaissance Literature* |
| *SPT* | - | *Screwtape Proposes a Toast* |
| *THS* | - | *That Hideous Strength* |
| *VDT* | - | *The Voyage of the Dawn Treader* |

## Other books

| | | |
|---|---|---|
| *BT* | - | *The Birth of Tragedy: Out of the Spirit of Music* (Friedrich Nietzsche) |
| *CCC* | - | *Catechism of the Catholic Church* |
| *CCT* | - | *The Catechism of the Council of Trent* |

## Bible

| | | |
|---|---|---|
| Acts | - | Acts of the Apostles |
| Col | - | Colossians |
| 1 Cor | - | 1 Corinthians |
| 2 Cor | - | 2 Corinthians |
| Ex | - | Exodus |
| Eph | - | Ephesians |
| Gal | - | Galatians |
| Gen | - | Genesis |
| Heb | - | Hebrews |
| Job | - | Job |

| | | |
|---|---|---|
| John | - | John |
| Judg | - | Judges |
| 1 Kings | - | 1 Kings |
| Lev | - | Leviticus |
| 2 Macc | - | 2 Maccabees |
| Matt | - | Matthew |
| 1 Pet | - | 1 Peter |
| Phil | - | Philipians |
| Rev | - | Revelation |
| Rom | - | Romans |
| Tob | - | Tobit |
| Wis | - | Wisdom |

# Index

## D



## E

## M

## N



## O

## T

## U



## V



## W



## Y

# Walking Tree Publishers

## Zurich and Jena

Walking Tree Publishers was founded in 1997 as a forum for publication of material related to Tolkien and Middle-earth studies.

www.walking-tree.org

## Cormarë Series

The *Cormarë Series* collects papers and studies dedicated exclusively to the exploration of Tolkien's work. It comprises monographs, thematic collections of essays, conference volumes, and reprints of important yet no longer (easily) accessible papers by leading scholars in the field. Manuscripts and project proposals are evaluated by members of an independent board of advisors who support the series editors in their endeavour to provide the readers with qualitatively superior yet accessible studies on Tolkien and his work.

*News from the Shire and Beyond. Studies on Tolkien*
Peter Buchs & Thomas Honegger (eds.), Zurich and Berne 2004, Reprint, First edition 1997 (Cormarë Series 1), ISBN 978-3-9521424-5-5

*Root and Branch. Approaches Towards Understanding Tolkien*
Thomas Honegger (ed.), Zurich and Berne 2005, Reprint, First edition 1999 (Cormarë Series 2), ISBN 978-3-905703-01-6

Richard Sturch, *Four Christian Fantasists. A Study of the Fantastic Writings of George MacDonald, Charles Williams, C.S. Lewis and J.R.R. Tolkien*
Zurich and Berne 2007, Reprint, First edition 2001 (Cormarë Series 3), ISBN 978-3-905703-04-7

*Tolkien in Translation*
Thomas Honegger (ed.), Zurich and Jena 2011, Reprint, First edition 2003 (Cormarë Series 4), ISBN 978-3-905703-15-3

Mark T. Hooker, *Tolkien Through Russian Eyes*
Zurich and Berne 2003 (Cormarë Series 5), ISBN 978-3-9521424-7-9

*Translating Tolkien: Text and Film*
Thomas Honegger (ed.), Zurich and Jena 2011, Reprint, First edition 2004 (Cormarë Series 6), ISBN 978-3-905703-16-0

Christopher Garbowski, *Recovery and Transcendence for the Contemporary Mythmaker. The Spiritual Dimension in the Works of J.R.R. Tolkien*
Zurich and Berne 2004, Reprint, First Edition by Marie Curie Sklodowska, University Press, Lublin 2000, (Cormarë Series 7), ISBN 978-3-9521424-8-6

*Reconsidering Tolkien*
Thomas Honegger (ed.), Zurich and Berne 2005 (Cormarë Series 8), ISBN 978-3-905703-00-9

*Tolkien and Modernity 1*
Frank Weinreich & Thomas Honegger (eds.), Zurich and Berne 2006 (Cormarë Series 9), ISBN 978-3-905703-02-3

*Tolkien and Modernity 2*
Thomas Honegger & Frank Weinreich (eds.), Zurich and Berne 2006 (Cormarë Series 10), ISBN 978-3-905703-03-0

Tom Shippey, *Roots and Branches. Selected Papers on Tolkien by Tom Shippey*
Zurich and Berne 2007 (Cormarë Series 11), ISBN 978-3-905703-05-4

Ross Smith, *Inside Language. Linguistic and Aesthetic Theory in Tolkien*
Zurich and Jena 2011, Reprint, First edition 2007 (Cormarë Series 12), ISBN 978-3-905703-20-7

*How We Became Middle-earth. A Collection of Essays on The Lord of the Rings*
Adam Lam & Nataliya Oryshchuk (eds.), Zurich and Berne 2007 (Cormarë Series 13), ISBN 978-3-905703-07-8

*Myth and Magic. Art According to the Inklings*
Eduardo Segura & Thomas Honegger (eds.), Zurich and Berne 2007 (Cormarë Series 14), ISBN 978-3-905703-08-5

*The Silmarillion – Thirty Years On*
Allan Turner (ed.), Zurich and Berne 2007 (Cormarë Series 15), ISBN 978-3-905703-10-8

Martin Simonson, *The Lord of the Rings and the Western Narrative Tradition*
Zurich and Jena 2008 (Cormarë Series 16), ISBN 978-3-905703-09-2

*Tolkien's Shorter Works. Proceedings of the 4th Seminar of the Deutsche Tolkien Gesellschaft & Walking Tree Publishers Decennial Conference*
Margaret Hiley & Frank Weinreich (eds.), Zurich and Jena 2008 (Cormarë Series 17), ISBN 978-3-905703-11-5

*Tolkien's The Lord of the Rings: Sources of Inspiration*
Stratford Caldecott & Thomas Honegger (eds.), Zurich and Jena 2008 (Cormarë Series 18), ISBN 978-3-905703-12-2

J.S. Ryan, *Tolkien's View: Windows into his World*
Zurich and Jena 2009 (Cormarë Series 19), ISBN 978-3-905703-13-9

*Music in Middle-earth*
Heidi Steimel & Friedhelm Schneidewind (eds.), Zurich and Jena 2010 (Cormarë Series 20), ISBN 978-3-905703-14-6

Liam Campbell, *The Ecological Augury in the Works of JRR Tolkien*
Zurich and Jena 2011 (Cormarë Series 21), ISBN 978-3-905703-18-4

Margaret Hiley, *The Loss and the Silence. Aspects of Modernism in the Works of C.S. Lewis, J.R.R. Tolkien and Charles Williams*
Zurich and Jena 2011 (Cormarë Series 22), ISBN 978-3-905703-19-1

Rainer Nagel, *Hobbit Place-names. A Linguistic Excursion through the Shire*
Zurich and Jena 2012 (Cormarë Series 23), ISBN 978-3-905703-22-1

Christopher MacLachlan, *Tolkien and Wagner: The Ring and Der Ring*
Zurich and Jena 2012 (Cormarë Series 24), ISBN 978-3-905703-21-4

Renée Vink, *Wagner and Tolkien: Mythmakers*
Zurich and Jena 2012 (Cormarë Series 25), ISBN 978-3-905703-25-2

*The Broken Scythe. Death and Immortality in the Works of J.R.R. Tolkien*
Roberto Arduini & Claudio Antonio Testi (eds.), Zurich and Jena 2012 (Cormarë Series 26), ISBN 978-3-905703-26-9

*Sub-creating Middle-earth: Constructions of Authorship and the Works of J.R.R. Tolkien*
Judith Klinger (ed.), Zurich and Jena 2012 (Cormarë Series 27), ISBN 978-3-905703-27-6

*Tolkien's Poetry*
Julian Eilmann & Allan Turner (eds.), Zurich and Jena 2013 (Cormarë Series 28), ISBN 978-3-905703-28-3

*O, What a Tangled Web. Tolkien and Medieval Literature. A View from Poland*
Barbara Kowalik (ed.), Zurich and Jena 2013 (Cormarë Series 29), ISBN 978-3-905703-29-0

J.S. Ryan, *In the Nameless Wood*
Zurich and Jena 2013 (Cormarë Series 30), ISBN 978-3-905703-30-6

*From Peterborough to Faëry; The Poetics and Mechanics of Secondary Worlds*
Thomas Honegger & Dirk Vanderbeke (eds.), Zurich and Jena 2014 (Cormarë Series 31), ISBN 978-3-905703-31-3

*Tolkien and Philosophy*
Roberto Arduini & Claudio R. Testi (eds.), Zurich and Jena 2014 (Cormarë Series 32), ISBN 978-3-905703-32-0

Patrick Curry, *Deep Roots in a Time of Frost. Essays on Tolkien*
Zurich and Jena 2014 (Cormarë Series 33), ISBN 978-3-905703-33-7

*Representations of Nature in Middle-earth*
Martin Simonson (ed.), Zurich and Jena 2015, (Cormarë Series 34), ISBN 978-3-905703-34-4

*Laughter in Middle-earth*
Thomas Honegger & Maureen F. Mann (eds.), Zurich and Jena 2016 (Cormarë Series 35), ISBN 978-3-905703-35-1

Julian Eilmann, *J.R.R. Tolkien – Romanticist and Poet*
Zurich and Jena 2017 (Cormarë Series 36), ISBN 978-3-905703-36-8

*Binding Them All. Interdisciplinary Perspectives on J.R.R. Tolkien and His Works*
Monika Kirner-Ludwig, Stephan Köser, Sebastian Streitberger (eds.), Zurich and Jena 2017 (Cormarë Series 37), ISBN 978-3-905703-37-5

Claudio Testi, *Pagan Saints in Middle-earth*
Zurich and Jena 2017 (Cormarë Series 38), ISBN 978-3-905703-38-2

*Music in Tolkien's Work and Beyond*
Julian Eilmann & Friedhelm Schneidewind (eds.), Zurich and Jena 2019 (Cormarë Series 39), ISBN 978-3-905703-39-9

*Sub-creating Arda: World-building in J.R.R. Tolkien's Works, its Precursors, and Legacies*
Dimitra Fimi & Thomas Honegger (eds.), Zurich and Jena 2019 (Cormarë Series 40), ISBN 978-3-905703-40-5

*"Something Has Gone Crack": New Perspectives on J.R.R. Tolkien and the Great War*
Janet Brennan Croft and Annika Röttinger (eds.), Zurich and Jena 2019 (Cormarë Series 41), ISBN 978-3-905703-41-2

*Tolkien and the Classics*
Roberto Arduini, Giampaolo Canzonieri & Claudio A. Testi (eds.), Zurich and Jena 2019 (Cormarë Series 42), ISBN 978-3-905703-42-9

José María Miranda Boto, *Law, Government, and Society in J.R.R. Tolkien's Works*
Zurich and Jena 2022 (Cormarë Series 43), ISBN 978-3-905703-43-6

*Middle-earth, or There and Back Again*
Łukasz Neubauer (ed.), Zurich and Jena 2020 (Cormarë Series 44), ISBN 978-3-905703-44-3

*Tolkien and the Classical World*
Hamish Williams (ed.), Zurich and Jena 2021 (Cormarë Series 45), ISBN 978-3-905703-45-0

Nancy Bunting and Seamus Hamill-Keays, *The Gallant Edith Bratt. J.R.R. Tolkien's Inspiration.* Zurich and Jena 2021 (Cormarë Series 46), ISBN 978-3-905703-46-7

*Nólë Hyarmenillo: An Anthology of Iberian Scholarship on Tolkien*
Nuno Simões Rodrigues, Martin Simonson, and Angélica Varandas (eds.), Zurich and Jena 2022 (Cormarë Series 47), ISBN 978-3-905703-47-4

*The Songs of the Spheres: Lewis, Tolkien and the Overlapping Realms of their Imaginations*
Łukasz Neubauer and Guglielmo Spirito (eds.), Zurich and Jena 2024 (Cormarë Series 48), ISBN 978-3-905703-48-1

Richard Z. Gallant, *Germanic Heroes, Courage, and Fate: Northern Narratives of J.R.R. Tolkien's Legendarium.* Zurich and Jena 2024 (Cormarë Series 49), ISBN 978-3-905703-49-8

Thomas Honegger, *Tweaking Things a Little. Essays on the Epic Fantasy of J.R.R. Tolkien and G.R.R. Martin.* Zurich and Jena 2023 (Cormarë Series 50), ISBN 978-3-905703-50-4

*The Romantic Spirit in the Works of J.R.R. Tolkien*
Will Sherwood and Julian Eilmann (eds.), Zurich and Jena 2024 (Cormarë Series 51), ISBN 978-3-905703-51-1

## Beowulf and the Dragon

The original Old English text of the 'Dragon Episode' of Beowulf is set in an authentic font and bound in hardback as a high quality art book. Illustrated by Anke Eissmann and accompanied by John Porter's translation. Introduction by Tom Shippey. Limited first edition of 500 copies. 84 pages. Selected pages can be previewed on: www.walking-tree.org/beowulf

*Beowulf and the Dragon*
Zurich and Jena 2009 , ISBN 978-3-905703-17-7

## Tales of Yore Series

The *Tales of Yore Series* provides a platform for qualitatively superior fiction that will appeal to readers familiar with Tolkien's world:

### The Monster Specialist

Sir Severus le Brewse, among the least known of King Arthur's Round Table knights, is preferred by nature, disposition, and training to fight against monsters rather than other knights. After youthful adventures of errantry with dragons, trolls, vampires, and assorted beasts, Severus joins the brilliant sorceress Lilava to face the Chimaera in The Greatest Monster Battle of All Time to free her folk from an age-old curse. But their adventures don't end there; together they meet elves and magicians, friends and foes; they join in the fight to save Camelot and even walk the Grey Paths of the Dead. With a mix of Malory, a touch of Tolkien, and a hint of humor, The Monster Specialist chronicles a tale of courage, tenacity, honor, and love.

*The Monster Specialist* is illustrated by Anke Eissmann.

Edward S. Louis, *The Monster Specialist*
Zurich and Jena 2014 (Tales of Yore Series No. 3), ISBN 978-3-905703-23-8

### Tales of Yore Series (earlier books, presently unavailable)

Kay Woollard, *The Terror of Tatty Walk. A Frightener*
CD and Booklet, Zurich and Berne 2000 (Tales of Yore Series No. 1), ISBN 978-3-9521424-2-4

Kay Woollard, *Wilmot's Very Strange Stone or What came of building "snobbits"*
CD and booklet, Zurich and Berne 2001 (Tales of Yore Series No. 2), ISBN 978-3-9521424-4-8

## Information for authors

Authors interested in contributing to our publications can learn more about the services we offer on the "services for authors" section of our web pages.

www.walking-tree.org/authors

Manuscripts and project proposals can be submitted to the board of editors:

Walking Tree Publishers
e-mail: info@walking-tree.org